AT&T

UNIX System Laboratories, Inc.

A Subsidiary of AT&T

UNIX® SYSTEM V/386 RELEASE 4

User's Reference Manual

Printed in USA

ACKNOWLEDGEMENT

USL gratefully acknowledges the X/Open Company Limited for permission to reproduce portions of its copyrighted *X/Open Portability Guide, Issue 3*.

IMPORTANT NOTE TO USERS

While every effort has been made to ensure the accuracy of all information in this document, USL assumes no liability to any party for any loss or damage caused by errors or omissions or by statements of any kind in this document, its updates, supplements, or special editions, whether such errors are omissions or statements resulting from negligence, accident, or any other cause. USL further assumes no liability arising out of the application or use of any product or system described herein; nor any liability for incidental or consequential damages arising from the use of this document. USL disclaims all warranties regarding the information contained herein, whether expressed, implied or statutory, *including implied warranties of merchantability or fitness for a particular purpose.* USL makes no representation that the interconnection of products in the manner described herein will not infringe on existing or future patent rights, nor do the descriptions contained herein imply the granting or license to make, use or sell equipment constructed in accordance with this description. USL reserves the right to make changes without further notice to any products herein to improve reliability, function, or design.

TRADEMARKS

IBM System/370 is a registered trademark of International Business Machines.
PDP-11/45 and VAX-11/750 are registered trademarks of Digital Equipment Corporation.
UNIX is a registered trademark of UNIX System Laboratories, Inc. in the USA and other countries.

10 9 8 7 6 5

ISBN 0-13-931510-1

UNIX
PRESS
A Prentice Hall Title

PRENTICE HALL

ORDERING INFORMATION

UNIX® SYSTEM V, RELEASE 4 DOCUMENTATION

To order single copies of UNIX® SYSTEM V, Release 4 documentation, please call (201) 767-5937.

ATTENTION DOCUMENTATION MANAGERS AND TRAINING DIRECTORS:
For bulk purchases in excess of 30 copies please write to:
Corporate Sales
Prentice Hall
Englewood Cliffs, N.J. 07632
Or call: (201) 592-2498

ATTENTION GOVERNMENT CUSTOMERS: For GSA and other pricing information please call (201) 767-5994.

Prentice-Hall International (UK) Limited, *London*
Prentice-Hall of Australia Pty. Limited, *Sydney*
Prentice-Hall Canada Inc., *Toronto*
Prentice-Hall Hispanoamericana, S.A., *Mexico*
Prentice-Hall of India Private Limited, *New Delhi*
Prentice-Hall of Japan, Inc., *Tokyo*
Simon & Schuster Asia Pte. Ltd., *Singapore*
Editora Prentice-Hall do Brasil, Ltda., *Rio de Janeiro*

AT&T UNIX® System V Release 4

General Use and System Administration

*UNIX® System V/386 Release 4 PC-Interface Administrator's Guide
*UNIX® System V/386 Release 4 Network User's and Administrator's Guide
*UNIX® System V/386 Release 4 Product Overview and Master Index
*UNIX® System V/386 Release 4 System Administrator's Reference Manual
*UNIX® System V/386 Release 4 User's Reference Manual
*UNIX® System V/386 Release 4 MULTIBUS® Reference Manual
*UNIX® System V/386 Release 4 MULTIBUS® Installation and Configuration Guide
*UNIX® System V/386 Release 4 Mouse Driver Administrator's Guide
*UNIX® System V/386 Release 4 Transport Application Interface Guide
UNIX® System V Release 4 User's Guide
UNIX® System V Release 4 System Administrator's Guide

General Programmer's Series

*UNIX® System V/386 Release 4 Programmer's Reference Manual
*UNIX® System V/386 Release 4 Programmer's Guide: SCSI Driver Interface
UNIX® System V Release 4 Programmer's Guide: ANSI C and Programming Support Tools
UNIX® System V Release 4 Programmer's Guide: Character User Interface (FMLI and ETI)
UNIX® System V Release 4 Programmer's Guide: Networking Interfaces
UNIX® System V Release 4 Programmer's Guide: POSIX Conformance
UNIX® System V Release 4 Programmer's Guide: Support Services and Application Packaging Tools

System Programmer's Series

*UNIX® System V/386 Release 4 Device Driver Interface/Driver-Kernel Interface (DDI/DKI) Reference Manual
*UNIX® System V/386 Release 4 Integrated Software Development Guide
UNIX® System V Release 4 Programmer's Guide: STREAMS

Migration Series

UNIX® System V Release 4 ANSI C Transition Guide
UNIX® System V Release 4 BSD/XENIX® Compatibility Guide
*UNIX® System V/386 Release 4 Migration Guide

Graphics Series

UNIX® System V Release 4 OPEN LOOK™ Graphical User Interface Programmer's Reference Manual
UNIX® System V Release 4 OPEN LOOK™ Graphical User Interface User's Guide
UNIX® System V Release 4 Programmer's Guide: XWIN™ Graphical Windowing System Xlib—C Language Interface
UNIX® System V Release 4 Programmer's Guide: OPEN LOOK™ Graphical User Interface
UNIX® System V Release 4 Programmer's Guide: X11/NeWS® Graphical Windowing System NeWS
UNIX® System V Release 4 Programmer's Guide: X11/NeWS® Graphical Windowing System Server Guide
UNIX® System V Release 4 Programmer's Guide: X11/NeWS® Graphical Windowing System tNt Technical Reference Manual
UNIX® System V Release 4 Programmer's Guide: X11/NeWS® Graphical Windowing System XVIEW™
UNIX® System V Release 4 Programmer's Guide: XWIN™ Graphical Windowing System Addenda: Technical Papers
UNIX® System V Release 4 Programmer's Guide: XWIN™ Graphical Windowing System The X Toolkit

*386 specific titles
Available from Prentice Hall

INTRODUCTION

INTRODUCTION

Introduction

This *User's Reference Manual* describes the commands that constitute the basic software running on a UNIX System V/386 system.

Several closely-related documents contain other valuable information:

- The *User's Guide* presents an overview of the UNIX system and tutorials on how to use text editors, automate repetitive jobs, and send information to others.
- The *Programmer's Guide* presents an overview of the UNIX system programming environment and tutorials on various programming tools.
- The *Programmer's Reference Manual* describes the commands, system calls, subroutines, libraries, file formats, and miscellaneous information used by programmers.
- The *System Administrator's Guide* provides procedures for and explanations of administrative tasks.
- The *System Administrator's Reference Manual* describes commands, file formats, and miscellaneous information used by system administrators.

Although the commands are each part of a specific Utilities Package, they appear in alphabetical order in a single section of this document called "Commands."

Section (1): Commands

The entries in Section (1) describe programs intended to be invoked directly by the user or by command language procedures, as opposed to subroutines, which are called by the user's programs. Commands generally reside in the directories `/usr/bin` and `/usr/sbin`. In addition, some commands reside in `/sbin`. These directories are searched automatically by the command interpreter called the *shell*. Also, UNIX systems often have a directory called `/usr/lbin`, containing local commands.

Throughout this manual, numbers following a command are intended for easy cross-reference. A command followed by a (1), (1C), or (1G) usually means that it is described in this manual. (Section (1) commands appropriate for use by programmers are located in the *Programmer's Reference Manual*.) A command with a (1M), (7), or (8) following it means that the command is in the corresponding section of the *System Administrator's Reference Manual*. A command with a (2) or (3) following it means that the command is in the corresponding section of the *Programmer's Reference Manual.* A command with a (4) or (5) following it usually means that the command is in the corresponding section of the *Programmer's Reference Manual* or the *System Administrator's Reference Manual.* However, manual pages used only for specialized applications are co-located with their appropriate Guides. See the Master Permuted Index in the *Product Overview and Master Index.*

Each entry in the Commands section appears under a single name shown at the upper corners of its page(s). Entries are alphabetized, with the exception of the `intro`(1) entry, which is first. Some entries may describe several commands. In such cases, the entry appears only once, alphabetized under its "primary" name, the name that appears at the upper corners of the page. The "secondary" commands are listed directly below their associated primary command. To learn which manual page describes a secondary command, locate its name in the middle column of the "Permuted Index" and follow across that line to the name of the manual page listed in the right column.

All entries are presented using the following format (though some of these headings might not appear in every entry):

- NAME gives the primary name [and secondary name(s), as the case may be] and briefly states its purpose.
- SYNOPSIS summarizes the usage of the program being described. A few explanatory conventions are used, particularly in the SYNOPSIS:
  - `Constant Width` strings are literals and are to be typed just as they appear.
  - *Italic* strings usually represent substitutable argument and command names found elsewhere in the manual.
  - Square brackets `[ ]` around an argument indicate that the argument is optional. When an argument is given as *name* or *file*, it always refers to a file name.
  - Ellipses `. . .` are used to show that the previous argument may be repeated.

- □ A final convention is used by the commands themselves. An argument beginning with a minus (–), plus (+), or an equal sign (=) is often taken to be a flag argument, even if it appears in a position where a file name could appear. Therefore, it is unwise to have files whose names begin with –, +, or =.

- **DESCRIPTION** discusses how to use these commands.
- **EXAMPLES** gives examples of usage, where appropriate.
- **FILES** contains the file names that are referenced by the program.
- **EXIT CODES** discusses values set when the command terminates. The value set is available in the shell environment variable "?" (see sh(1)).
- **NOTES** gives information that may be helpful under the particular circumstances described.
- **SEE ALSO** offers pointers to related information.
- **DIAGNOSTICS** discusses the error messages that may be produced. Messages that are intended to be self-explanatory are not listed.

Preceding Section 1 are a "Table of Contents" (listing both primary and secondary command entries) and a "Permuted Index." Each line of the "Table of Contents" contains the name of a manual page (with secondary entries, if they exist) and an abstract of that page. Each line of the "Permuted Index" represents a permutation (or sorting) of a line from the "Table of Contents" into three columns. Each line is arranged so that a keyword or phrase begins the middle column. Use the "Permuted Index" by searching this middle column for a topic or command. When you have found the entry you want, the right column of that line lists the name of the manual page on which information corresponding to that keyword may be found. The left column contains the remainder of the permutation that began in the middle column.

How to Get Started

This discussion provides the basic information you need to get started on the UNIX system: how to log in and log out, how to communicate through your terminal, and how to run a program. (See the *User's Guide* for a more complete introduction to the system.)

Logging In

You must connect to the UNIX system from a full-duplex ASCII terminal. You must also have a valid login ID, which may be obtained (together with how to access your UNIX system) from the administrator of your system. Common terminal speeds are 30, 120, 240, 480, 960, 1920, and 3840 characters per second (300, 1200, 2400, 4800, 9600, 19200, and 38400 baud). Some UNIX systems have different ways of accessing each available terminal speed, while other systems offer several speeds through a common access method. In the latter case, there is one "preferred" speed; if you access it from a terminal set to a different speed, you will be greeted by a string of meaningless characters. Keep hitting the BREAK, INTERRUPT, or ATTENTION key until the `login:` prompt appears.

Most terminals have a speed switch that should be set to the appropriate speed and a half-/full-duplex switch that should be set to full-duplex. When a connection has been established, the system types `login:`. You respond by typing your login ID followed by the RETURN key. If you have a password, the system asks for it but will not print, or "echo," it on the terminal. After you have logged in, the RETURN, NEW-LINE, and LINE-FEED keys all have equivalent meanings.

Make sure you type your login name in lowercase letters. Typing uppercase letters causes the UNIX system to assume that your terminal can generate only uppercase letters, and it will treat all letters as uppercase for the remainder of your login session. The shell will print a `$` on your screen when you have logged in successfully.

When you log in, a message-of-the-day may greet you before you receive your prompt. For more information, consult `login`(1), which discusses the login sequence in more detail, and `stty`(1), which tells you how to describe your terminal to the system. `profile`(4) (in the *System Administrator's Reference Manual*) explains how to accomplish this last task automatically every time you log in.

Logging Out

There are two ways to log out:

- If you've dialed in, you can simply hang up the phone.
- You can log out by typing an end-of-file indication (ASCII EOT character, usually typed as CTRL-d) to the shell. The shell will terminate, and the `login:` message will appear again.

How to Communicate Through Your Terminal

When you type to the UNIX system, your individual characters are being gathered and temporarily saved. Although they are echoed back to you, these characters will not be given to a program until you type a RETURN (or NEW-LINE) as described above in "Logging In."

UNIX system terminal input/output is full duplex. It has full read-ahead, which means that you can type at any time, even while a program is typing at you. Of course, if you type during output, your input characters will have output characters interspersed among them. In any case, whatever you type will be saved and interpreted in the correct sequence. There is a limit to the amount of read-ahead, but it is not likely to be exceeded.

The character `@` cancels all the characters typed before it on a line, effectively deleting the line. (`@` is called the "line kill" character.) The character `#` erases the last character typed. Successive uses of `#` will erase characters back to, but not beyond, the beginning of the line; `@` and `#` can be typed as themselves by preceding them with \ (thus, to erase a \, you need two `#`s). These default erase and line kill characters can be changed; see `stty`(1).

CTRL-s (also known as the ASCII DC3 character) is typed by pressing the CONTROL key and the alphabetic `s` simultaneously; it is used to stop output temporarily. It is useful with CRT terminals to prevent output from disappearing before it can be read. Output is resumed when a CTRL-q (also known as DC1) is typed. Thus, if you had typed `cat` *yourfile* and the contents of *yourfile* were passing by on the screen more rapidly than you could read it, you would type CTRL-s to freeze the output. Typing CTRL-q would allow the output to resume. The CTRL-s and CTRL-q characters are not passed to any other program when used in this manner.

The ASCII DEL (also called "rubout") character is not passed to programs but instead generates an interrupt signal, just like the BREAK, INTERRUPT, or ATTENTION signal. This signal generally causes whatever program you are running to terminate. It is typically used to stop a long printout that you do not want. Programs, however, can arrange either to ignore this signal altogether or to be notified and take a specific action when it happens (instead of being terminated). The editor `ed(1)`, for example, catches interrupts and stops what *it* is doing, instead of terminating, so an interrupt can be used to halt an editor printout without losing the file being edited.

Besides adapting to the speed of the terminal, the UNIX system tries to be intelligent as to whether you have a terminal with the NEW-LINE function, or whether it must be simulated with a CARRIAGE-RETURN and LINE-FEED pair. In the latter case, all *input* CARRIAGE-RETURN characters are changed to LINE-FEED characters (the standard line delimiter), and a CARRIAGE-RETURN and LINE-FEED pair is echoed to the terminal. If you get into the wrong mode, the `stty(1)` command will rescue you.

Tab characters are used freely in UNIX system source programs. If your terminal does not have the tab function, you can arrange to have tab characters changed into spaces during output, and echoed as spaces during input. Again, the `stty(1)` command will set or reset this mode. The system assumes that tabs are set every eight character positions. The `tabs(1)` command will set tab stops on your terminal, if that is possible.

How to Run a Program

When you have successfully logged into the UNIX system, a program called the shell is communicating with your terminal. The shell reads each line you type, splits the line into a command name and its arguments, and executes the command. A command is simply an executable program. Normally, the shell looks first in your current directory (see "The Current Directory" below) for the named program and, if none is there, then in system directories, such as `/usr/bin` and `/usr/usr/bin`. There is nothing special about system-provided commands except that they are kept in directories where the shell can find them. You can also keep commands in your own directories and instruct the shell to find them there. See the manual entry for `sh(1)`, under the sub-heading "Parameter Substitution," for the discussion of the PATH shell environmental variable.

The command name is the first word on an input line to the shell; the command and its arguments are separated from one another by space or tab characters.

When a program terminates, the shell will ordinarily regain control and give you back your prompt to indicate that it is ready for another command. The shell has many other capabilities, which are described in detail in sh(1).

The Current Directory

The UNIX system has a file system arranged in a hierarchy of directories. When you received your login ID, the system administrator also created a directory for you (ordinarily with the same name as your login ID, and known as your login or home directory). When you log in, that directory becomes your current or working directory, and any file name you type is, by default, assumed to be in that directory. Because you are the owner of this directory, you have full permissions to read, write, alter, or remove its contents. Permissions to enter or modify other directories and files will have been granted or denied to you by their respective owners or by the system administrator. To change the current directory, use cd(1).

Pathnames

To refer to files or directories not in the current directory, you must use a pathname. Full pathnames begin with /, which is the name of the root directory of the whole file system. After the slash comes the name of each directory containing the next subdirectory (followed by a /), until finally the file or directory name is reached (for example, `/usr/ae/filex` refers to file `filex` in directory ae, while ae is itself a subdirectory of `usr`, and `usr` is a subdirectory of the root directory). Use pwd(1) to print the full pathname of the directory you are working in. See `intro`(2) in the *Programmer's Reference Manual* for a formal definition of *pathname*.

If your current directory contains subdirectories, the pathnames of their respective files begin with the name of the corresponding subdirectory (without a prefixed /). A pathname may be used anywhere a file name is required.

Important commands that affect files are cp(1), mv, and rm(1), which respectively copy, move (that is, rename), and remove files. To find out the status of files or directories, use ls(1). Use mkdir(1) for making directories and rmdir (see rm(1)) for removing them.

Text Entry and Display

Almost all text is entered through an editor. Common examples of UNIX system editors are ed(1) and vi(1). The commands most often used to print text on a terminal are cat(1), pr(1), and pg(1). The cat command displays the contents of ASCII text files on the terminal, with no processing at all. The pr command paginates the text, supplies headings, and has a facility for multi-column output. The pg command displays text in successive portions no larger than your terminal screen.

Writing a Program

Once you have entered the text of your program into a file with an editor, you are ready to give the file to the appropriate language processor. The processor will accept only files observing the correct naming conventions: all C programs must end with the suffix .c, and Fortran programs must end with .f. The output of the language processor will be left in a file named a.out in the current directory, unless you have invoked an option to save it in another file. (Use mv to rename a.out.) If the program is written in assembly language, you will probably need to load library subroutines with it (see ld(1) in the *Programmer's Reference Manual*).

When you have completed this process without provoking any diagnostics, you may run the program by giving its name to the shell in response to the $ prompt. Your programs can receive arguments from the command line just as system programs do; see exec(2) in the *Programmer's Reference Manual*. For more information on writing and running programs, see the *Programmer's Guide*.

Communicating with Others

Certain commands provide inter-user communication. Even if you do not plan to use them, it's helpful to learn something about them because someone else may try to contact you. `mail`(1) or `mailx`(1) will leave a message whose presence will be announced to another user when he or she next logs in and at periodic intervals during the session. To communicate with another user currently logged in, use `write`(1). The corresponding entries in this manual also suggest how to respond to these two commands if you are their target.

See the tutorials in Chapters 11 and 12 of the *User's Guide* for more information on communicating with others.

TABLE OF CONTENTS

Table of Contents

1. Commands

PERMUTED INDEX

PERMUTED INDEX

Permuted Index

NAME

`intro` – introduction to commands and application programs

DESCRIPTION

This section describes, in alphabetical order, commands available for the AT&T 386 Computer. Certain distinctions of purpose are made in the headings.

The following Utility packages are delivered with the computer:

AT&T Windowing Utilities
Basic Networking Utilities
Cartridge Tape Controller Utilities
Directory and File Management Utilities
Editing Utilities
Essential Utilities
Framed Access Command Environment Utilities
Inter-process Communications Utilities
Job Accounting Utilities
Line Printer Spooling Utilities
Security Administration Utilities
Spell Utilities
System Performance Analysis Utilities
Terminal Information Utilities
Transmission Control Protocol
User Environment Utilities

The following Utility Packages are available for purchase:

Networking Support Utilities
Remote File Sharing Utilities

Manual Page Command Syntax

Unless otherwise noted, commands described in the **SYNOPSIS** section of a manual page accept options and other arguments according to the following syntax and should be interpreted as explained below.

name [–*option*...] [*cmdarg*...]
where:

[ ]	Surround an *option* or *cmdarg* that is not required.
...	Indicates multiple occurrences of the *option* or *cmdarg*.
name	The name of an executable file.
option	(Always preceded by a "–".) *noargletter*... or, *argletter optarg*[, ...]
noargletter	A single letter representing an option without an option-argument. Note that more than one *noargletter* option can be grouped after one "–" (Rule 5, below).
argletter	A single letter representing an option requiring an option-argument.

optarg An option-argument (character string) satisfying a preceding *argletter*. Note that groups of *optargs* following an *argletter* must be separated by commas, or separated by white space and quoted (Rule 8, below).

cmdarg Path name (or other command argument) *not* beginning with "–", or "–" by itself indicating the standard input.

Command Syntax Standard: Rules

These command syntax rules are not followed by all current commands, but all new commands will obey them. `getopts`(1) should be used by all shell procedures to parse positional parameters and to check for legal options. It supports Rules 3-10 below. The enforcement of the other rules must be done by the command itself.

1. Command names (*name* above) must be between two and nine characters long.
2. Command names must include only lower-case letters and digits.
3. Option names (*option* above) must be one character long.
4. All options must be preceded by "–".
5. Options with no arguments may be grouped after a single "–".
6. The first option-argument (*optarg* above) following an option must be preceded by white space.
7. Option-arguments cannot be optional.
8. Groups of option-arguments following an option must either be separated by commas or separated by white space and quoted (e.g., `-o xxx,z,yy` or `-o "xxx z yy"`).
9. All options must precede operands (*cmdarg* above) on the command line.
10. "––" may be used to indicate the end of the options.
11. The order of the options relative to one another should not matter.
12. The relative order of the operands (*cmdarg* above) may affect their significance in ways determined by the command with which they appear.
13. "–" preceded and followed by white space should only be used to mean standard input.

SEE ALSO

`getopts`(1).
`exit`(2), `wait`(2), `getopt`(3C) in the *Programmer's Reference Manual*.
How to Get Started, at the front of this document.

DIAGNOSTICS

Upon termination, each command returns two bytes of status, one supplied by the system and giving the cause for termination, and (in the case of "normal" termination) one supplied by the program [see `wait`(2) and `exit`(2)]. The former byte is 0 for normal termination; the latter is customarily 0 for successful execution and non-zero to indicate troubles such as erroneous parameters, or bad or inaccessible data. It is called variously "exit code", "exit status", or "return code", and is described only where special conventions are involved.

WARNINGS

Some commands produce unexpected results when processing files containing null characters. These commands often treat text input lines as strings and therefore become confused upon encountering a null character (the string terminator) within a line.

NAME

acctcom − search and print process accounting file(s)

SYNOPSIS

acctcom [*options*] [*file* . . .]

DESCRIPTION

acctcom reads *file*, the standard input, or /var/adm/pacct, in the form described by acct(4) and writes selected records to the standard output. Each record represents the execution of one process. The output shows the COMMAND NAME, USER, TTYNAME, START TIME, END TIME, REAL (SEC), CPU (SEC), MEAN SIZE (K), and optionally, F (the fork/exec flag: 1 for fork without exec), STAT (the system exit status), HOG FACTOR, KCORE MIN, CPU FACTOR, CHARS TRNSFD, and BLOCKS READ (total blocks read and written).

A # is prepended to the command name if the command was executed with superuser privileges. If a process is not associated with a known terminal, a ? is printed in the TTYNAME field.

If no *files* are specified, and if the standard input is associated with a terminal or /dev/null (as is the case when using & in the shell), /var/adm/pacct is read; otherwise, the standard input is read.

If any *file* arguments are given, they are read in their respective order. Each file is normally read forward, i.e., in chronological order by process completion time. The file /var/adm/pacct is usually the current file to be examined; a busy system may need several such files of which all but the current file are found in /var/adm/pacct*incr*.

The *options* are:

- −a Show some average statistics about the processes selected. The statistics will be printed after the output records.
- −b Read backwards, showing latest commands first. This option has no effect when the standard input is read.
- −f Print the fork/exec flag and system exit status columns in the output. The numeric output for this option will be in octal.
- −h Instead of mean memory size, show the fraction of total available CPU time consumed by the process during its execution. This "hog factor" is computed as (total CPU time)/(elapsed time).
- −i Print columns containing the I/O counts in the output.
- −k Instead of memory size, show total kcore-minutes.
- −m Show mean core size (the default).
- −r Show CPU factor (user-time/(system-time + user-time)).
- −t Show separate system and user CPU times.
- −v Exclude column headings from the output.
- −l *line* Show only processes belonging to terminal /dev/term/*line*.
- −u *user* Show only processes belonging to *user* that may be specified by: a user ID, a login name that is then converted to a user ID, a #, which designates only those processes executed with superuser privileges, or ?, which designates only those processes associated with unknown user IDs.

-g *group*	Show only processes belonging to *group*. The *group* may be designated by either the group ID or group name.
-s *time*	Select processes existing at or after *time*, given in the format *hr* [: *min* [: *sec*]].
-e *time*	Select processes existing at or before *time*.
-S *time*	Select processes starting at or after *time*.
-E *time*	Select processes ending at or before *time*. Using the same *time* for both -S and -E shows the processes that existed at *time*.
-n *pattern*	Show only commands matching *pattern* that may be a regular expression as in regcmp(3G), except + means one or more occurrences.
-q	Do not print any output records, just print the average statistics as with the -a option.
-o *ofile*	Copy selected process records in the input data format to *ofile*; suppress printing to standard output.
-H *factor*	Show only processes that exceed *factor*, where factor is the "hog factor" as explained in option -h above.
-O *sec*	Show only processes with CPU system time exceeding *sec* seconds.
-C *sec*	Show only processes with total CPU time (system-time + user-time) exceeding *sec* seconds.
-I *chars*	Show only processes transferring more characters than the cutoff number given by *chars*.

FILES

/etc/passwd
/var/adm/pacct*incr*
/etc/group

SEE ALSO

ps(1), su(1).
acct(2), regcmp(3G) in the *Programmer's Reference Manual.*
acct(1M), acctcms(1M), acctcon(1M), acctmerg(1M), acctprc(1M), acctsh(1M), fwtmp(1M), runacct(1M), acct(4), utmp(4) in the *System Administrator's Reference Manual.*

NOTES

acctcom reports only on processes that have terminated; use ps(1) for active processes.

If *time* exceeds the present time, then *time* is interpreted as occurring on the previous day.

NAME

ar − maintain portable archive or library

SYNOPSIS

ar [**-V**] − *key* [*arg*] [*posname*] *afile* [*name*. . .]

DESCRIPTION

The ar command maintains groups of files combined into a single archive file. Its main use is to create and update library files. However, it can be used for any similar purpose. The magic string and the file headers used by ar consist of printable ASCII characters. If an archive is composed of printable files, the entire archive is printable.

When ar creates an archive, it creates headers in a format that is portable across all machines. The portable archive format and structure are described in detail in ar(4). The archive symbol table [described in ar(4)] is used by the link editor ld to effect multiple passes over libraries of object files in an efficient manner. An archive symbol table is only created and maintained by ar when there is at least one object file in the archive. The archive symbol table is in a specially named file that is always the first file in the archive. This file is never mentioned or accessible to the user. Whenever the ar command is used to create or update the contents of such an archive, the symbol table is rebuilt. The s option described below will force the symbol table to be rebuilt.

The -V option causes ar to print its version number on standard error.

Unlike command options, the *key* is a required part of the ar command line. The *key* is formed with one of the following letters: drqtpmx. Arguments to the *key*, alternatively, are made with one of more of the following set: vuaibcls. *posname* is an archive member name used as a reference point in positioning other files in the archive. *afile* is the archive file. The *name*s are constituent files in the archive file. The meanings of the *key* characters are as follows:

d Delete the named files from the archive file.

r Replace the named files in the archive file. If the optional character u is used with r, then only those files with dates of modification later than the archive files are replaced. If an optional positioning character from the set abi is used, then the *posname* argument must be present and specifies that new files are to be placed after (a) or before (b or i) *posname*. Otherwise new files are placed at the end.

q Quickly append the named files to the end of the archive file. Optional positioning characters are invalid. The command does not check whether the added members are already in the archive. This option is useful to avoid quadratic behavior when creating a large archive piece-by-piece.

t Print a table of contents of the archive file. If no names are given, all files in the archive are listed. If names are given, only those files are listed.

p Print the named files in the archive.

m Move the named files to the end of the archive. If a positioning character is present, then the *posname* argument must be present and, as in r, specifies where the files are to be moved.

x Extract the named files. If no names are given, all files in the archive are extracted. In neither case does x alter the archive file.

The meanings of the other key arguments are as follows:

v Give a verbose file-by-file description of the making of a new archive file from the old archive and the constituent files. When used with t, give a long listing of all information about the files. When used with x, print the filename preceding each extraction.

c Suppress the message that is produced by default when *afile* is created.

l This option is obsolete. It is recognized, but ignored, and will be removed in the next release.

s Force the regeneration of the archive symbol table even if ar(1) is not invoked with a command which will modify the archive contents. This command is useful to restore the archive symbol table after the strip(1) command has been used on the archive.

SEE ALSO

ld(1), lorder(1), strip(1), a.out(4), ar(4).

NOTES

If the same file is mentioned twice in an argument list, it may be put in the archive twice.

Since the archiver no longer uses temporary files, the -l option is obsolete and will be removed in the next release.

By convention, archives are suffixed with the characters .a.

NAME

at, batch – execute commands at a later time

SYNOPSIS

at [-f *script*] [-m] *time* [*date*] [+ *increment*]

at -l [*job* ...]

at -r *job* ...

batch

DESCRIPTION

at and batch read commands from standard input to be executed at a later time. at allows you to specify when the commands should be executed, while jobs queued with batch will execute when system load level permits. at may be used with the following options:

-f *script* Reads commands to be executed from the named *script* file.

-l [*job*] Reports all jobs scheduled for the invoking user, or just the *jobs* specified.

-m Sends mail to the user after the job has been completed, indicating that the job is finished, even if the job produces no output. Mail is sent only if the job has not already generated a mail message.

-r *job* Removes specified *jobs* previously scheduled using at.

Standard output and standard error output are mailed to the user unless they are redirected elsewhere. The shell environment variables, current directory, umask, and ulimit are retained when the commands are executed. Open file descriptors, traps, and priority are lost.

Users are permitted to use at if their name appears in the file /usr/sbin/cron.d/at.allow. If that file does not exist, the file /usr/sbin/cron.d/at.deny is checked to determine if the user should be denied access to *at*. If neither file exists, only root is allowed to submit a job. If only at.deny exists and is empty, global usage is permitted. The allow/deny files consist of one user name per line. These files can only be modified by the privileged user.

If the DATEMSK environment variable is set, it points to a template file that at will use to determine the valid *time* and *date* values instead of the values described below. For more information about using DATEMSK, see the last paragraph of the DESCRIPTION section.

time may be specified as follows, where *h* is hours and *m* is minutes: *h*, *hh*, *hhmm*, *h*:*m*, *h*:*mm*, *hh*:*m*, *hh*:*mm*. A 24-hour clock is assumed, unless am or pm is appended to *time*. If zulu is appended to *time*, it means Greenwich Mean Time (GMT). *time* can also take on the values: noon, midnight, and now. at now responds with the error message too late; use now with the *increment* argument, such as: at now + 1 minute.

An optional *date* may be specified as either a month name followed by a day number (and possibly a year number preceded by a comma) or a day of the week. (Both the month name and the day of the week may be spelled out or abbreviated to three characters.) Two special "days", today and tomorrow are recognized. If no *date* is given, **today** is assumed if the given hour is greater than the current hour and **tomorrow** is assumed if it is less. If the given month is less than the current month (and no year is given), next year is assumed.

The optional *increment* is simply a number suffixed by one of the following: **minutes, hours, days, weeks, months,** or **years.** (The singular form is also accepted.) The modifier **next** may precede the *increment;* it means "+ 1."

Thus valid commands include:

```
at 0815am Jan 24
at 8:15am Jan 24
at now + 1 day
at now next day
at 5 pm Friday
```

at and **batch** write the job number and schedule time to standard error.

at -r removes jobs previously scheduled by **at** or **batch.** The job number is the number returned to you previously by the **at** or **batch** command. You can also get job numbers by typing **at -l.** You can only remove your own jobs unless you are the privileged user.

If the environment variable **DATEMSK** is set, **at** will use its value as the full path name of a template file containing format strings. The strings consist of field descriptors and text characters and are used to provide a richer set of allowable date formats in different languages by appropriate settings of the environment variable **LANG** or **LC_TIME** (see *environ*(5)). (See *getdate*(3C) for the allowable list of field descriptors; this list is a subset of the descriptors allowed by **calendar**(1) that are listed on the *date*(1) manual page.) The formats described above for the *time* and *date* arguments, the special names noon, **midnight, now, next, today, tomorrow,** and the *increment* argument are not recognized when **DATEMSK** is set.

EXAMPLES

The **at** and **batch** commands read from standard input the commands to be executed at a later time. **sh**(1) provides different ways of specifying standard input. Within your commands, it may be useful to redirect standard output.

This sequence can be used at a terminal:

```
batch
sort filename > outfile
<control-D> (hold down 'control' and depress 'd')
```

This sequence, which shows redirecting standard error to a pipe, is useful in a shell procedure (the sequence of output redirection specifications is significant):

```
batch <<!
sort filename 2>&1 > outfile | mail loginid
!
```

To have a job reschedule itself, invoke **at** from within the shell procedure, by including code similar to the following within the shell file:

```
echo "sh shellfile" | at 1900 thursday next week
```

The following example shows the possible contents of a template file `AT.TEMPL` in `/var/tmp`.

```
%I %p, the %est of %B of the year %Y run the following job
%I %p, the %end of %B of the year %Y run the following job
%I %p, the %erd of %B of the year %Y run the following job
%I %p, the %eth of %B of the year %Y run the following job
%d/%m/%y
%H:%M:%S
%I:%M%p
```

The following are examples of valid invocations if the environment variable DATEMSK is set to `/var/tmp/AT.TEMPL`.

```
at 2 PM, the 3rd of July of the year 2000 run the following job
at 3/4/99
at 10:30:30
at 2:30PM
```

FILES

`/usr/sbin/cron.d`	main cron directory
`/usr/sbin/cron.d/at.allow`	list of allowed users
`/usr/sbin/cron.d/at.deny`	list of denied users
`/usr/sbin/cron.d/queuedefs`	scheduling information
`/var/spool/cron/atjobs`	spool area

SEE ALSO

`atq`(1), `atrm`(1), `calendar`(1), `crontab`(1), `date`(1), `kill`(1), `mail`(1), `nice`(1), `ps`(1), `sh`(1), `sort`(1).

`cron`(1M), `environ`(5), in the *System Administrator's Reference Manual*.

`getdate`(3C) in the *Programmer's Reference Manual*.

DIAGNOSTICS

Complains about various syntax errors and times out of range.

NAME

`atq` – display the jobs queued to run at specified times

SYNOPSIS

`atq` [`-c`] [`-n`] [*username*...]

DESCRIPTION

`atq` displays the current user's queue of jobs submitted with `at` to be run at a later date. If invoked by the privileged user, `atq` will display all jobs in the queue.

If no options are given, the jobs are displayed in chronological order of execution.

When a privileged user invokes `atq` without specifying *username*, the entire queue is displayed; when a *username* is specified, only those jobs belonging to the named user are displayed.

The `atq` command can be used with the following options:

`-c` Display the queued jobs in the order they were created (that is, the time that the `at` command was given).

`-n` Display only the total number of jobs currently in the queue.

FILES

`/var/spool/cron` spool area

SEE ALSO

`at`(1), `atrm`(1).

`cron`(1M) in the *System Administrator's Reference Manual.*

NAME

atrm – remove jobs spooled by at or batch

SYNOPSIS

atrm [-afi] *arg* ...

DESCRIPTION

atrm removes delayed-execution jobs that were created with the at(1) command, but not yet executed. The list of these jobs and associated job numbers can be displayed by using atq(1).

arg a user name or job-number. atrm removes each job-number you specify, and/or all jobs belonging to the user you specify, provided that you own the indicated jobs.

Jobs belonging to other users can only be removed by the privileged user.

The atrm command can be used with the following options:

-a All. Remove all unexecuted jobs that were created by the current user. If invoked by the privileged user, the entire queue will be flushed.

-f Force. All information regarding the removal of the specified jobs is suppressed.

-i Interactive. atrm asks if a job should be removed. If you respond with a y, the job will be removed.

FILES

/var/spool/cron spool area

SEE ALSO

at(1), atq(1).

cron(1M) in the *System Administrator's Reference Manual.*

NAME

awk – pattern scanning and processing language

SYNOPSIS

awk [-Fc] [prog] [parameters] [files]

DESCRIPTION

awk scans each input *file* for lines that match any of a set of patterns specified in *prog*. With each pattern in *prog* there can be an associated action that will be performed when a line of a *file* matches the pattern. The set of patterns may appear literally as *prog*, or in a file specified as **-f** *file*. The *prog* string should be enclosed in single quotes (') to protect it from the shell.

Parameters, in the form x=... y=... etc., may be passed to *awk.*

Files are read in order; if there are no files, the standard input is read. The file name – means the standard input. Each line is matched against the pattern portion of every pattern-action statement; the associated action is performed for each matched pattern.

An input line is made up of fields separated by white space. (This default can be changed by using FS; see below). The fields are denoted **$1**, **$2**, ...; **$0** refers to the entire line.

A pattern-action statement has the form:

```
pattern { action }
```

A missing action means print the line; a missing pattern always matches. An action is a sequence of statements. A statement can be one of the following:

```
if ( conditional ) statement [ else statement ]
while ( conditional ) statement
for ( expression ; conditional ; expression ) statement
break
continue
{ [ statement ] ... }
variable = expression
print [ expression-list ] [ >expression ]
printf format [ , expression-list ] [ >expression ]
next   # skip remaining patterns on this input line
exit   # skip the rest of the input
```

Statements are terminated by semicolons, new-lines, or right braces. An empty expression-list stands for the whole line. Expressions take on string or numeric values as appropriate, and are built using the operators +, –, *, /, %, and concatenation (indicated by a blank). The **C** operators ++, ––, +=, –=, *=, /=, and %= are also available in expressions. Variables may be scalars, array elements (denoted x[i]) or fields. Variables are initialized to the null string. Array subscripts may be any string, not necessarily numeric; this allows for a form of associative memory. String constants are quoted (").

The *print* statement prints its arguments on the standard output (or on a file if >*expr* is present), separated by the current output field separator, and terminated by the output record separator. The `printf` statement formats its expression list according to the format [see *printf*(3S) in the *Programmer's Reference Manual*].

The built-in function *length* returns the length of its argument taken as a string, or of the whole line if no argument. There are also built-in functions `exp`, `log`, `sqrt`, and *int*. The last truncates its argument to an integer; *substr(s, m, n)* returns the *n*-character substring of *s* that begins at position *m*. The function `sprintf`(fmt , expr , *expr*, ...) formats the expressions according to the `printf`(3S) format given by *fmt* and returns the resulting string.

Patterns are arbitrary Boolean combinations (`!`, `||`, `&&`, and parentheses) of regular expressions and relational expressions. Regular expressions must be surrounded by slashes and are as in **egrep**(1). Isolated regular expressions in a pattern apply to the entire line. Regular expressions may also occur in relational expressions. A pattern may consist of two patterns separated by a comma; in this case, the action is performed for all lines between an occurrence of the first pattern and the next occurrence of the second.

A relational expression is one of the following:

expression matchop regular-expression
expression relop expression

where a relop is any of the six relational operators in C, and a matchop is either ~ (for *contains*) or `!~` (for *does not contain*). A conditional is an arithmetic expression, a relational expression, or a Boolean combination of these.

The special patterns BEGIN and END may be used to capture control before the first input line is read and after the last. BEGIN must be the first pattern, END the last.

A single character *c* may be used to separate the fields by starting the program with:

BEGIN { FS = *c* }

or by using the `-F`*c* option.

Other variable names with special meanings include NF, the number of fields in the current record; NR, the ordinal number of the current record; FILENAME, the name of the current input file; OFS, the output field separator (default blank); ORS, the output record separator (default new-line); and OFMT, the output format for numbers (default `%.6g`).

EXAMPLES

Print lines longer than 72 characters:

```
length > 72
```

Print first two fields in opposite order:

```
{ print $2, $1 }
```

Add up first column, print sum and average:

```
        { s += $1 }
END     { print "sum is", s, " average is", s/NR }
```

Print fields in reverse order:

```
{ for (i = NF; i > 0; --i) print $i }
```

Print all lines between start/stop pairs:

```
/start/, /stop/
```

Print all lines whose first field is different from previous one:

```
$1 != prev { print; prev = $1 }
```

Print file, filling in page numbers starting at 5:

```
/Page/ { $2 = n++; }
       { print }
```

command line: awk -f program n=5 input

SEE ALSO

grep(1), nawk(1), sed(1).
lex(1), printf(3S) in the *Programmer's Reference Manual.*

NOTES

Input white space is not preserved on output if fields are involved.
There are no explicit conversions between numbers and strings. To force an expression to be treated as a number add 0 to it; to force it to be treated as a string concatenate the null string ("") to it.

NAME

banner – make posters

SYNOPSIS

banner *strings*

DESCRIPTION

banner prints its arguments (each up to 10 characters long) in large letters on the standard output.

SEE ALSO

echo(1).

NAME

basename, **dirname** – deliver portions of path names

SYNOPSIS

basename *string* [*suffix*]
dirname *string*

DESCRIPTION

basename deletes any prefix ending in / and the *suffix* (if present in *string*) from *string*, and prints the result on the standard output. It is normally used inside substitution marks (` `) within shell procedures. The *suffix* is a pattern as defined on the ed(1) manual page.

dirname delivers all but the last level of the path name in *string*.

EXAMPLES

The following example, invoked with the argument /home/sms/personal/mail sets the environment variable NAME to the file named mail and the environment variable MYMAILPATH to the string /home/sms/personal.

```
NAME=`basename $HOME/personal/mail`
MYMAILPATH=`dirname $HOME/personal/mail`
```

This shell procedure, invoked with the argument /usr/src/bin/cat.c, compiles the named file and moves the output to cat in the current directory:

```
cc $1
mv a.out `basename $1 .c`
```

SEE ALSO

ed(1), sh(1).

NAME

bc – arbitrary-precision arithmetic language

SYNOPSIS

bc [-c] [-l] [*file*...]

DESCRIPTION

bc is an interactive processor for a language that resembles C but provides unlimited precision arithmetic. It takes input from any files given, then reads the standard input. bc is actually a preprocessor for the desk calculator program dc, which it invokes automatically unless the -c option is present. In this case the dc input is sent to the standard output instead. The options are as follows:

-c Compile only. The output is sent to the standard output.

-l Argument stands for the name of an arbitrary precision math library.

The syntax for bc programs is as follows: *L* means letter **a-z**, *E* means expression, *S* means statement.

Comments
    are enclosed in /* and */.

Names
    simple variables: *L*
    array elements: *L* [*E*]
    the words ibase, obase,and scale

Other operands
    arbitrarily long numbers with optional sign and decimal point
    (*E*)
    sqrt (*E*)
    length (*E*)   number of significant decimal digits
    scale (*E*)   number of digits right of decimal point
    L (*E* , ... , *E*)

Operators
    + - * / % ^
    (% is remainder; ^ is power)
    ++ -- (prefix and postfix; apply to names)
    == <= >= != < >
    = =+ =- =* =/ =% =^

Statements
    E
    { *S* ; ... ; *S* }
    if (*E*) *S*
    while (*E*) *S*
    for (*E* ; *E* ; *E*) *S*
    null statement
    break
    quit

Function definitions

```
define L ( L ,..., L ) {
        auto L ,..., L
        S ; ... S
        return ( E )
}
```

Functions in `-l` math library

`s(x)`	sine
`c(x)`	cosine
`e(x)`	exponential
`l(x)`	log
`a(x)`	arctangent
`j(n,x)`	Bessel function

All function arguments are passed by value.

The value of a statement that is an expression is printed unless the main operator is an assignment. Either semicolons or new-lines may separate statements. Assignment to `scale` influences the number of digits to be retained on arithmetic operations in the manner of dc. Assignments to `ibase` or `obase` set the input and output number radix respectively.

The same letter may be used as an array, a function, and a simple variable simultaneously. All variables are global to the program. `auto` variables are pushed down during function calls. When using arrays as function arguments or defining them as automatic variables, empty square brackets must follow the array name.

EXAMPLE

```
scale = 20
define e(x){
        auto a, b, c, i, s
        a = 1
        b = 1
        s = 1
        for(i=1; 1==1; i++){
                a = a*x
                b = b*i
                c = a/b
                if(c == 0) return(s)
                s = s+c
        }
}
```

defines a function to compute an approximate value of the exponential function and

```
for(i=1; i<=10; i++) e(i)
```

prints approximate values of the exponential function of the first ten integers.

FILES

`/usr/lib/lib.b`	mathematical library
`/usr/bin/dc`	desk calculator proper

SEE ALSO

dc(1).

NOTES

The `bc` command does not recognize the logical operators `&&` and `||`.

The `for` statement must have all three expressions (*E*'s).

The `quit` statement is interpreted when read, not when executed.

NAME

`bdiff` – big `diff`

SYNOPSIS

`bdiff` *file1 file2* [*n*] [-s]

DESCRIPTION

`bdiff` is used in a manner analogous to `diff` to find which lines in *file1* and *file2* must be changed to bring the files into agreement. Its purpose is to allow processing of files too large for `diff`. If *file1* (*file2*) is –, the standard input is read.

Valid options to `bdiff` are:

n The number of line segments. The value of *n* is 3500 by default. If the optional third argument is given and it is numeric, it is used as the value for *n*. This is useful in those cases in which 3500-line segments are too large for `diff`, causing it to fail.

`-s` Specifies that no diagnostics are to be printed by `bdiff` (silent option). Note, however, that this does not suppress possible diagnostic messages from `diff`, which `bdiff` calls.

`bdiff` ignores lines common to the beginning of both files, splits the remainder of each file into *n*-line segments, and invokes `diff` on corresponding segments. If both optional arguments are specified, they must appear in the order indicated above.

The output of `bdiff` is exactly that of `diff`, with line numbers adjusted to account for the segmenting of the files (that is, to make it look as if the files had been processed whole). Note that because of the segmenting of the files, `bdiff` does not necessarily find a smallest sufficient set of file differences.

FILES

`/tmp/bd`*?????*

SEE ALSO

`diff`(1), `help`(1)

DIAGNOSTICS

Use `help` for explanations.

NAME

bfs – big file scanner

SYNOPSIS

bfs [–] *file*

DESCRIPTION

The bfs command is similar to ed except that it is read-only and processes much larger files. Files can be up to 1024K bytes and 32K lines, with up to 512 characters, including new-line, per line (255 for 16-bit machines). bfs is usually more efficient than ed for scanning a file, since the file is not copied to a buffer. It is most useful for identifying sections of a large file where the csplit command can be used to divide it into more manageable pieces for editing.

Normally, the size of the file being scanned is printed, as is the size of any file written with the w command. The optional – suppresses printing of sizes. Input is prompted with * if P and a carriage return are typed, as in ed. Prompting can be turned off again by inputting another P and carriage return. Messages are given in response to errors if prompting is turned on.

All address expressions described under ed are supported. In addition, regular expressions may be surrounded with two symbols besides / and ?: > indicates downward search without wrap-around, and < indicates upward search without wrap-around. There is a slight difference in mark names: only the letters a through z may be used, and all 26 marks are remembered.

The e, g, v, k, p, q, w, =, ! and null commands operate as described under ed. Commands such as ---, +++-, +++=, -12, and +4p are accepted. Note that 1,10p and 1,10 both print the first ten lines. The f command only prints the name of the file being scanned; there is no remembered file name. The w command is independent of output diversion, truncation, or crunching (see the xo, xt, and xc commands, below). The following additional commands are available:

xf *file*
: Further commands are taken from the named *file*. When an end-of-file is reached, an interrupt signal is received or an error occurs, reading resumes with the file containing the xf. The xf commands may be nested to a depth of 10.

xn
: List the marks currently in use (marks are set by the k command).

xo [*file*]
: Further output from the p and null commands is diverted to the named *file*, which, if necessary, is created mode 666 (readable and writable by everyone), unless your umask setting dictates otherwise; see umask(1). If *file* is missing, output is diverted to the standard output. Note that each diversion causes truncation or creation of the file.

: *label*
: This positions a *label* in a command file. The *label* is terminated by new-line, and blanks between the : and the start of the *label* are ignored. This command may also be used to insert comments into a command file, since labels need not be referenced.

(. , .)xb/*regular expression*/*label*

A jump (either upward or downward) is made to *label* if the command succeeds. It fails under any of the following conditions:

1. Either address is not between 1 and $.
2. The second address is less than the first.
3. The regular expression does not match at least one line in the specified range, including the first and last lines.

On success, . is set to the line matched and a jump is made to *label*. This command is the only one that does not issue an error message on bad addresses, so it may be used to test whether addresses are bad before other commands are executed. Note that the command

```
xb/^/ label
```

is an unconditional jump.

The xb command is allowed only if it is read from someplace other than a terminal. If it is read from a pipe only a downward jump is possible.

xt *number*

Output from the p and null commands is truncated to at most *number* characters. The initial number is 255.

xv[*digit*] [*spaces*] [*value*]

The variable name is the specified *digit* following the xv. The commands xv5100 or xv5 100 both assign the value 100 to the variable 5. The command xv61,100p assigns the value 1,100p to the variable 6. To reference a variable, put a % in front of the variable name. For example, using the above assignments for variables 5 and 6:

```
1,%5p
1,%5
%6
```

all print the first 100 lines.

```
g/%5/p
```

globally searches for the characters 100 and prints each line containing a match. To escape the special meaning of %, a \ must precede it.

```
g/".*\%[cds]/p
```

could be used to match and list lines containing a printf of characters, decimal integers, or strings.

Another feature of the xv command is that the first line of output from a UNIX system command can be stored into a variable. The only requirement is that the first character of *value* be an !. For example:

```
.w junk
xv5!cat junk
!rm junk
!echo "%5"
xv6!expr %6 + 1
```

puts the current line into variable 5, prints it, and increments the variable 6 by one. To escape the special meaning of ! as the first character of *value*, precede it with a \.

```
xv7\!date
```

stores the value !date into variable 7.

xbz *label*

xbn *label*

These two commands test the last saved *return code* from the execution of a UNIX system command (!*command*) or nonzero value, respectively, to the specified label. The two examples below both search for the next five lines containing the string size.

```
xv55
: 1
/size/
xv5!expr %5 - 1
!if 0%5 != 0 exit 2
xbn 1
xv45
: 1
/size/
xv4!expr %4 - 1
!if 0%4 = 0 exit 2
xbz 1
```

xc [*switch*]

If *switch* is 1, output from the p and null commands is crunched; if *switch* is 0 it is not. Without an argument, xc reverses *switch*. Initially *switch* is set for no crunching. Crunched output has strings of tabs and blanks reduced to one blank and blank lines suppressed.

SEE ALSO

csplit(1), ed(1), umask(1).

DIAGNOSTICS

? for errors in commands, if prompting is turned off. Self-explanatory error messages when prompting is on.

NAME

`cal` – print calendar

SYNOPSIS

`cal` [[*month*] *year*]

DESCRIPTION

`cal` prints a calendar for the specified year. If a month is also specified, a calendar just for that month is printed. If neither is specified, a calendar for the present month is printed. The *month* is a number between 1 and 12. The *year* can be between 1 and 9999. The calendar produced is that for England and the United States.

NOTES

An unusual calendar is printed for September 1752. That is the month 11 days were skipped to make up for lack of leap year adjustments. To see this calendar, type: `cal 9 1752`

The command `cal 83` refers to the year 83, not 1983.

The year is always considered to start in January even though this is historically naive.

NAME

calendar – reminder service

SYNOPSIS

calendar [–]

DESCRIPTION

calendar consults the file calendar in the current directory and prints out lines that contain today's or tomorrow's date anywhere in the line. Most reasonable month-day dates such as Aug. 24, august 24, 8/24, etc., are recognized, but not 24 August or 24/8. On weekends "tomorrow" extends through Monday. calendar can be invoked regularly by using the crontab(1) or at(1) commands.

When an argument is present, calendar does its job for every user who has a file calendar in his or her login directory and sends them any positive results by mail(1). Normally this is done daily by facilities in the UNIX operating system (see cron(1M)).

If the environment variable DATEMSK is set, calendar will use its value as the full path name of a template file containing format strings. The strings consist of field descriptors and text characters and are used to provide a richer set of allowable date formats in different languages by appropriate settings of the environment variable LANG or LC_TIME (see environ(5)). (See date(1) for the allowable list of field descriptors.)

EXAMPLES

The following example shows the possible contents of a template:

```
%B %eth of the year %Y
```

%B represents the full month name, %e the day of month and %Y the year (4 digits).

If DATEMSK is set to this template, the following calendar file would be valid:

```
March 7th of the year 1989 < Reminder>
```

FILES

/usr/lib/calprog program used to figure out today's and tomorrow's dates
/etc/passwd
/tmp/cal*

SEE ALSO

at(1), date(1), crontab(1), mail(1).
cron(1M), environ(5) in the *System Administrator's Reference Manual* .

NOTES

Appropriate lines beginning with white space will not be printed.
Your calendar must be public information for you to get reminder service.
calendar's extended idea of "tomorrow" does not account for holidays.

NAME

cat – concatenate and print files

SYNOPSIS

cat [–u] [–s] [–v [–t] [–e]] *file*...

DESCRIPTION

cat reads each *file* in sequence and writes it on the standard output. Thus:

```
cat file
```

prints **file** on your terminal, and:

```
cat file1 file2 >file3
```

concatenates **file1** and **file2**, and writes the results in **file3**.

If no input file is given, or if the argument – is encountered, cat reads from the standard input file.

The following options apply to cat:

–u The output is not buffered. (The default is buffered output.)

–s cat is silent about non-existent files.

–v Causes non-printing characters (with the exception of tabs, new-lines and form-feeds) to be printed visibly. ASCII control characters (octal 000 – 037) are printed as ^*n*, where *n* is the corresponding ASCII character in the range octal 100 – 137 (@, A, B, C, . . ., X, Y, Z, [, \,], ^, and _); the DEL character (octal 0177) is printed ^?. Other non-printable characters are printed as M–*x*, where *x* is the ASCII character specified by the low-order seven bits.

When used with the –v option, the following options may be used:

–t Causes tabs to be printed as ^I's and formfeeds to be printed as ^L's.

–e Causes a $ character to be printed at the end of each line (prior to the new-line).

The –t and –e options are ignored if the –v option is not specified.

SEE ALSO

cp(1), pg(1), pr(1).

NOTES

Redirecting the output of cat onto one of the files being read will cause the loss of the data originally in the file being read. For example,

```
cat file1 file2 >file1
```

causes the original data in **file1** to be lost.

NAME

cd – change working directory

SYNOPSIS

cd [*directory*]

DESCRIPTION

If *directory* is not specified, the value of shell parameter $HOME is used as the new working directory. If *directory* specifies a complete path starting with /, ., or . ., *directory* becomes the new working directory. If neither case applies, cd tries to find the designated directory relative to one of the paths specified by the $CDPATH shell variable. $CDPATH has the same syntax as, and similar semantics to, the $PATH shell variable. cd must have execute (search) permission in *directory*.

Because a new process is created to execute each command, cd would be ineffective if it were written as a normal command; therefore, it is recognized by and is internal to the shell.

SEE ALSO

pwd(1), sh(1).
chdir(2) in the *Programmer's Reference Manual.*

NAME

chgrp – change the group ownership of a file

SYNOPSIS

chgrp [–R] [–h] *group file* ...

DESCRIPTION

chgrp changes the group ID of the *files* given as arguments to *group*. The group may be either a decimal group ID or a group name found in the group ID file, /etc/group.

You must be the owner of the file, or be the super-user to use this command.

The operating system has a configuration option {_POSIX_CHOWN_RESTRICTED}, to restrict ownership changes. When this option is in effect, the owner of the file may change the group of the file only to a group to which the owner belongs. Only the super-user can arbitrarily change owner IDs whether this option is in effect or not.

chgrp has one option:

–R Recursive. chgrp descends through the directory, and any subdirectories, setting the specified group ID as it proceeds. When symbolic links are encountered, they are traversed.

–h If the file is a symbolic link, change the group of the symbolic link. Without this option, the group of the file referenced by the symbolic link is changed.

FILES

/etc/group

SEE ALSO

chmod(1), chown(1), id(1M)
chown(2) in the *Programmer's Reference Manual.*
group(4), passwd(4) in the *System Administrator's Reference Manual.*

NOTES

In a Remote File Sharing environment, you may not have the permissions that the output of the ls –l command leads you to believe. For more information see the *Network User's and Administrator's Guide.*

NAME

chmod – change file mode

SYNOPSIS

chmod [-R] *mode file* ...
chmod [ugoa]{ + | – | = }[rwxlstugo] *file* ...

DESCRIPTION

chmod changes or assigns the mode of a file. The mode of a file specifies its permissions and other attributes. The mode may be absolute or symbolic.

An absolute *mode* is specified using octal numbers:

chmod *nnnn file* ...

where *n* is a number from 0 to 7. An absolute mode is constructed from the OR of any of the following modes:

4000	Set user ID on execution.
20#0	Set group ID on execution if # is 7, 5, 3, or 1. Enable mandatory locking if # is 6, 4, 2, or 0. This bit is ignored if the file is a directory; it may be set or cleared only using the symbolic mode.
1000	Turn on sticky bit [(see chmod(2)].
0400	Allow read by owner.
0200	Allow write by owner.
0100	Allow execute (search in directory) by owner.
0070	Allow read, write, and execute (search) by group.
0007	Allow read, write, and execute (search) by others.

A symbolic *mode* is specified in the following format:

chmod [*who*] *operator* [*permission(s)*] *file* ...

who is zero or more of the characters u, g, o, and a specifying whose permissions are to be changed or assigned:

u	user's permissions
g	group's permissions
o	others' permissions
a	all permissions (user, group, and other)

If *who* is omitted, it defaults to a.

operator is one of +, –, or =, signifying how permissions are to be changed:

+	Add permissions.
–	Take away permissions.
=	Assign permissions absolutely.

Unlike other symbolic operations, = has an absolute effect in that it resets all other bits. Omitting *permission*(s) is useful only with = to take away all permissions.

permission(s) is any compatible combination of the following letters:

`r`	read permission
`w`	write permission
`x`	execute permission
`s`	user or group set-ID
`t`	sticky bit
`l`	mandatory locking
`u, g, o`	indicate that *permission* is to be taken from the current user, group or other mode respectively.

Permissions to a file may vary depending on your user identification number (UID) or group identification number (GID). Permissions are described in three sequences each having three characters:

User	Group	Other
`rwx`	`rwx`	`rwx`

This example (user, group, and others all have permission to read, write, and execute a given file) demonstrates two categories for granting permissions: the access class and the permissions themselves.

Multiple symbolic modes separated by commas may be given, though no spaces may intervene between these modes. Operations are performed in the order given. Multiple symbolic letters following a single operator cause the corresponding operations to be performed simultaneously.

The letter `s` is only meaningful with `u` or `g`, and `t` only works with `u`.

Mandatory file and record locking (`l`) refers to a file's ability to have its reading or writing permissions locked while a program is accessing that file. It is not possible to permit group execution and enable a file to be locked on execution at the same time. In addition, it is not possible to turn on the set-group-ID bit and enable a file to be locked on execution at the same time. The following examples, therefore, are invalid and elicit error messages:

`chmod g+x,+l` *file*
`chmod g+s,+l` *file*

Only the owner of a file or directory (or the super-user) may change that file's or directory's mode. Only the super-user may set the sticky bit on a non-directory file. If you are not super-user, `chmod` will mask the sticky-bit but will not return an error. In order to turn on a file's set-group-ID bit, your own group ID must correspond to the file's and group execution must be set.

The `-R` option recursively descends through directory arguments, setting the mode for each file as described above.

EXAMPLES

Deny execute permission to everyone:

`chmod a-x` *file*

Allow read permission to everyone:

```
chmod 444 file
```

Make a file readable and writable by the group and others:

```
chmod go+rw file
chmod 066 file
```

Cause a file to be locked during access:

```
chmod +l file
```

Allow everyone to read, write, and execute the file and turn on the set group-ID.

```
chmod =rwx,g+s file
chmod 2777 file
```

Absolute changes don't work for the set-group-ID bit of a directory. You must use `g+s` or `g-s`.

SEE ALSO

`ls`(1).
chmod(2) in the *Programmer's Reference Manual*

NOTES

chmod permits you to produce useless modes so long as they are not illegal (e.g., making a text file executable). chmod does not check the file type to see if mandatory locking is available.

NAME

chown – change file owner

SYNOPSIS

chown [–R] [–h] *owner file* ...

DESCRIPTION

chown changes the owner of the *files* to *owner*. The *owner* may be either a decimal user ID or a login name found in /etc/passwd file.

If chown is invoked by other than the super-user, the set-user-ID bit of the file mode, 04000, is cleared.

Only the owner of a file (or the super-user) may change the owner of that file.

Valid options to chown are:

–R Recursive. chown descends through the directory, and any subdirectories, setting the ownership ID as it proceeds. When symbolic links are encountered, they are traversed.

–h If the file is a symbolic link, change the owner of the symbolic link. Without this option, the owner of the file referenced by the symbolic link is changed.

The operating system has a configuration option {_POSIX_CHOWN_RESTRICTED}, to restrict ownership changes. When this option is in effect the owner of the file is prevented from changing the owner ID of the file. Only the super-user can arbitrarily change owner IDs whether this option is in effect or not.

FILES

/etc/passwd

SEE ALSO

chgrp(1), chmod(1)

chown(2) in the *Programmer's Reference Manual*

passwd(4) in the *System Administrator's Reference Manual.*

NOTES

chgrp does not check group ID if it is in decimal form.

In a Remote File Sharing environment, you may not have the permissions that the output of the ls –l command leads you to believe. For more information see the "Mapping Remote Users" section of the Remote File Sharing chapter of the *Getting Started*.

NAME

clear – clear the terminal screen

SYNOPSIS

clear

DESCRIPTION

clear clears your screen if this is possible. It looks in the environment for the terminal type and then in the terminfo database to figure out how to clear the screen.

SEE ALSO

tput(1)

NAME

cmp – compare two files

SYNOPSIS

cmp [-l] [-s] *file1 file2*

DESCRIPTION

The two files are compared. (If *file1* is –, the standard input is used.) Under default options, cmp makes no comment if the files are the same; if they differ, it announces the byte and line number at which the difference occurred. If one file is an initial subsequence of the other, that fact is noted.

Options:

-l Print the byte number (decimal) and the differing bytes (octal) for each difference.

-s Print nothing for differing files; return codes only.

SEE ALSO

comm(1), diff(1).

DIAGNOSTICS

Exit code 0 is returned for identical files, 1 for different files, and 2 for an inaccessible or missing argument.

NAME

col − filter reverse line-feeds

SYNOPSIS

col [−b] [−f] [−x] [−p]

DESCRIPTION

col reads from the standard input and writes onto the standard output. It performs the line overlays implied by reverse line feeds (ASCII code ESC-7), and by forward and reverse half-line-feeds (ESC-9 and ESC-8). col is particularly useful for filtering multicolumn output made with the .rt command of nroff and output resulting from use of the tbl(1) preprocessor.

If the −b option is given, col assumes that the output device in use is not capable of backspacing. In this case, if two or more characters are to appear in the same place, only the last one read will be output.

Although col accepts half-line motions in its input, it normally does not emit them on output. Instead, text that would appear between lines is moved to the next lower full-line boundary. This treatment can be suppressed by the −f (fine) option; in this case, the output from col may contain forward half-line-feeds (ESC-9), but will still never contain either kind of reverse line motion.

Unless the −x option is given, col will convert white space to tabs on output wherever possible to shorten printing time.

The ASCII control characters SO (\017) and SI (\016) are assumed by col to start and end text in an alternate character set. The character set to which each input character belongs is remembered, and on output SI and SO characters are generated as appropriate to ensure that each character is printed in the correct character set.

On input, the only control characters accepted are space, backspace, tab, return, new-line, SI, SO, VT (\013), and ESC followed by 7, 8, or 9. The VT character is an alternate form of full reverse line-feed, included for compatibility with some earlier programs of this type. All other non-printing characters are ignored.

Normally, col will ignore any escape sequences unknown to it that are found in its input; the −p option may be used to cause col to output these sequences as regular characters, subject to overprinting from reverse line motions. The use of this option is highly discouraged unless the user is fully aware of the textual position of the escape sequences.

SEE ALSO

ascii(5)

nroff(1), tbl(1) in the *DOCUMENTER'S WORKBENCH Software Technical Discussion and Reference Manual* .

NOTES

The input format accepted by col matches the output produced by nroff with either the −T37 or −Tlp options. Use −T37 (and the −f option of col) if the ultimate disposition of the output of col will be a device that can interpret half-line motions, and −Tlp otherwise.

`col` cannot back up more than 128 lines or handle more than 800 characters per line.

Local vertical motions that would result in backing up over the first line of the document are ignored. As a result, the first line must not have any superscripts.

NAME

comm − select or reject lines common to two sorted files

SYNOPSIS

comm [− [123]] *file1 file2*

DESCRIPTION

comm reads *file1* and *file2*, which should be ordered in ASCII collating sequence [see sort(1)], and produces a three-column output: lines only in *file1*; lines only in *file2*; and lines in both files. The file name − means the standard input.

Flags 1, 2, or 3 suppress printing of the corresponding column. Thus comm −12 prints only the lines common to the two files; comm −23 prints only lines in the first file but not in the second; comm −123 prints nothing.

SEE ALSO

cmp(1), diff(1), sort(1), uniq(1).

NAME

compress, uncompress, zcat – compress, expand or display expanded files

SYNOPSIS

compress [-cfv] [-b *bits*] [*filename*...]
uncompress [-cv] [*filename*...]
zcat [*filename*...]

DESCRIPTION

compress reduces the size of the named files using adaptive Lempel-Ziv coding. Whenever possible, each file is replaced by one with a .Z, extension. The ownership modes, access time and modification time will stay the same. If no files are specified, the standard input is compressed to the standard output.

The amount of compression obtained depends on the size of the input, the number of *bits* per code, and the distribution of common substrings. Typically, text such as source code or English is reduced by 50–60%. Compression is generally much better than that achieved by Huffman coding [as used in pack(1)], and takes less time to compute. The *bits* parameter specified during compression is encoded within the compressed file, along with a magic number to ensure that neither decompression of random data nor recompression of compressed data is subsequently allowed.

Compressed files can be restored to their original form using uncompress.

zcat produces uncompressed output on the standard output, but leaves the compressed .Z file intact.

OPTIONS

-c Write to the standard output; no files are changed. The nondestructive behavior of zcat is identical to that of 'uncompress -c'.

-f Force compression, even if the file does not actually shrink, or the corresponding .Z file already exists. Except when running in the background (under /usr/bin/sh), if -f is not given, prompt to verify whether an existing .Z file should be overwritten.

-v Verbose. Display the percentage reduction for each file compressed.

-b *bits*
Set the upper limit (in bits) for common substring codes. *bits* must be between 9 and 16 (16 is the default). Lowering the number of bits will result in larger, less compressed files.

FILES

/usr/bin/sh

SEE ALSO

pack(1)

A Technique for High Performance Data Compression, Terry A. Welch, *IEEE Computer*, vol. 17, no. 6 (June 1984), pp. 8-19.

DIAGNOSTICS

Exit status is normally 0. If the last file was not compressed because it became larger, the status is 2. If an error occurs, exit status is 1.

`Usage: compress [-fvc] [-b maxbits]` [*filename* ...]
: Invalid options were specified on the command line.

`Missing maxbits`
: Maxbits must follow **-b**.

filename: `not in compressed format`
: The file specified to `uncompress` has not been compressed.

filename: `compressed with` *xx*`bits, can only handle` *yy*`bits`
: *filename* was compressed by a program that could deal with more *bits* than the compress code on this machine. Recompress the file with smaller *bits*.

filename: `already has .Z suffix -- no change`
: The file is assumed to be already compressed. Rename the file and try again.

filename: `already exists; do you wish to overwrite (y or n)?`
: Respond **y** if you want the output file to be replaced; **n** if not.

`uncompress: corrupt input`
: A `SIGSEGV` violation was detected, which usually means that the input file is corrupted.

`Compression:` *xx.xx*`%`
: Percentage of the input saved by compression. (Relevant only for -v.)

`-- not a regular file: unchanged`
: When the input file is not a regular file, (such as a directory), it is left unaltered.

`-- has` *xx* `other links: unchanged`
: The input file has links; it is left unchanged. See `ln`(1) for more information.

`-- file unchanged`
: No savings are achieved by compression. The input remains uncompressed.

NOTES

Although compressed files are compatible between machines with large memory, -b12 should be used for file transfer to architectures with a small process data space (64KB or less).

`compress` should be more flexible about the existence of the `.Z` suffix.

NAME

cp – copy files

SYNOPSIS

cp [-i] [-p] [-r] *file1* [*file2* ...] *target*

DESCRIPTION

The cp command copies *filen* to *target*. *filen* and *target* may not have the same name. (Care must be taken when using sh(1) metacharacters.) If *target* is not a directory, only one file may be specified before it; if it is a directory, more than one file may be specified. If *target* does not exist, cp creates a file named *target*. If *target* exists and is not a directory, its contents are overwritten. If *target* is a directory, the file(s) are copied to that directory.

The following options are recognized:

-i cp will prompt for confirmation whenever the copy would overwrite an existing *target*. A y answer means that the copy should proceed. Any other answer prevents cp from overwriting *target*.

-p cp will duplicate not only the contents of *filen*, but also preserves the modification time and permission modes.

-r If *filen* is a directory, cp will copy the directory and all its files, including any subdirectories and their files; *target* must be a directory.

If *filen* is a directory, *target* must be a directory in the same physical file system. *target* and *filen* do not have to share the same parent directory.

If *filen* is a file and *target* is a link to another file with links, the other links remain and *target* becomes a new file.

If *target* does not exist, cp creates a new file named *target* which has the same mode as *filen* except that the sticky bit is not set unless the user is a privileged user; the owner and group of *target* are those of the user.

If *target* is a file, its contents are overwritten, but the mode, owner, and group associated with it are not changed. The last modification time of *target* and the last access time of *filen* are set to the time the copy was made.

If *target* is a directory, then for each file named, a new file with the same mode is created in the target directory; the owner and the group are those of the user making the copy.

NOTES

A -- permits the user to mark the end of any command line options explicitly, thus allowing cp to recognize filename arguments that begin with a –. If a -- and a – both appear on the same command line, the second will be interpreted as a filename.

SEE ALSO

chmod(1), cpio(1), ln(1), mv(1), rm(1).

NAME

`cpio` – copy file archives in and out

SYNOPSIS

`cpio -i[bBcdfkmrsStuvV6]` [`-C` *bufsize*] [`-E` *file*] [`-H` *hdr*] [`-I` *file* [`-M` *message*]] [`-R` *ID*]] [*pattern* ...]

`cpio -o[aABcLvV]` [`-C` *bufsize*] [`-H` *hdr*] [`-O` *file* [`-M` *message*]]

`cpio -p[adlLmuvV]` [`-R` *ID*]] *directory*

DESCRIPTION

The `-i`, `-o`, and `-p` options select the action to be performed. The following list describes each of the actions (which are mutually exclusive).

`cpio -i` (copy in) extracts files from the standard input, which is assumed to be the product of a previous `cpio -o`. Only files with names that match *patterns* are selected. *patterns* are regular expressions given in the filename-generating notation of `sh`(1). In *patterns*, meta-characters `?`, `*`, and `[...]` match the slash (/) character, and backslash (\) is an escape character. A `!` meta-character means *not*. (For example, the `!abc*` pattern would exclude all files that begin with `abc`.) Multiple *patterns* may be specified and if no *patterns* are specified, the default for *patterns* is `*` (i.e., select all files). Each pattern must be enclosed in double quotes; otherwise, the name of a file in the current directory might be used. Extracted files are conditionally created and copied into the current directory tree based on the options described below. The permissions of the files will be those of the previous `cpio -o`. Owner and group permissions will be the same as the current user unless the current user is super-user. If this is true, owner and group permissions will be the same as those resulting from the previous `cpio -o`. NOTE: If `cpio -i` tries to create a file that already exists and the existing file is the same age or younger (**newer**), `cpio` will output a warning message and not replace the file. (The –u option can be used to overwrite, unconditionally, the existing file.)

`cpio -o` (copy out) reads the standard input to obtain a list of path names and copies those files onto the standard output together with path name and status information. Output is padded to a 512-byte boundary by default or to the user specified block size (with the `-B` or `-C` options) or to some device-dependent block size where necessary (as with the CTC tape).

`cpio -p` (pass) reads the standard input to obtain a list of path names of files that are conditionally created and copied into the destination *directory* tree based on the options described below.

The meanings of the available options are

`-a` Reset access times of input files after they have been copied. Access times are not reset for linked files when `cpio -pla` is specified (mutually exclusive with `-m`).

`-A` Append files to an archive. The `-A` option requires the `-O` option. Valid only with archives that are files, or that are on floppy diskettes or hard disk partitions.

−b R- of the bytes within each word. (Use only with the −i

be blocked 5,120 bytes to the record. The default
es when this and the −C options are not used. (−B
e *pass* option; −B is meaningful only with data
aracter special device, e.g. /dev/rmt/0m.)

formation in ASCII character form for portability.
r the −H option) when the origin and the desti-
ent types (mutually exclusive with −H and −6).
nded device numbers.)

d *bufsize* bytes to the record, where *bufsize* is
The default buffer size is 512 bytes when
d. For floppy disks, *bufsize* must be a mul-
(−C does not apply to the −p (pass) option
ith data directed to or from a character

−d ded.

−E *file* ins a list of filenames to be extracted
e).

−f C *ns*. (See the paragraph on cpio −i
for

−H *hdr* Rea format. Always use this option
or the and the destination machines are dif-
ferent t ive with −c and −6). Valid values for *hdr* are:

crc or C	II header with expanded device numbers and an additional per-file checksum
ustar or USTAR	IEEE/P1003 Data Interchange Standard header and format
tar or TAR	tar header and format
odc	ASCII header with small device numbers

−I *file* Read the contents of *file* as an input archive. If *file* is a character special device, and the current medium has been completely read, replace the medium and press RETURN to continue to the next medium. This option is used only with the −i option.

−k Attempt to skip corrupted file headers and I/O errors that may be encountered. If you want to copy files from a medium that is corrupted or out of sequence, this option lets you read only those files with good headers. (For cpio archives that contain other cpio archives, if an error is encountered cpio may terminate prematurely. cpio will find the next good header, which may be one for a smaller archive, and terminate when the smaller archive's trailer is encountered.) Used only with the −i option.

`-l` Whenever possible, link files rather than copying them. (Usable only with the `-p` option.)

`-L` Follow symbolic links. The default is not to follow symbolic links.

`-m` Retain previous file modification time. This option is ineffective on directories that are being copied (mutually exclusive with `-a`).

`-M` *message*
Define a *message* to use when switching media. When you use the `-O` or `-I` options and specify a character special device, you can use this option to define the message that is printed when you reach the end of the medium. One `%d` can be placed in *message* to print the sequence number of the next medium needed to continue.

`-O` *file* Direct the output of `cpio` to *file*. If *file* is a character special device and the current medium is full, replace the medium and type a carriage return to continue to the next medium. Use only with the `-o` option.

`-r` Interactively rename files. If the user types a carriage return alone, the file is skipped. If the user types a "." the original pathname will be retained. (Not available with `cpio -p`.)

`-R` *ID* Reassign ownership and group information for each file to *user ID* (*ID* must be a valid login ID from `/etc/passwd`). This option is valid only for the super-user.

`-s` Swap bytes within each half word.

`-S` Swap halfwords within each word.

`-t` Print a table of contents of the input. No files are created (mutually exclusive with `-V`).

`-u` Copy unconditionally (normally, an older file will not replace a newer file with the same name).

`-v` Verbose: causes a list of file names to be printed. When used with the `-t` option, the table of contents looks like the output of an `ls -l` command [see `ls`(1)].

`-V` Special Verbose: print a dot for each file read or written. Useful to assure the user that `cpio` is working without printing out all file names.

`-6` Process a UNIX System Sixth Edition archive format file. Use only with the `-i` option (mutually exclusive with `-c` and `-H`)).

NOTE: `cpio` assumes four-byte words.

If, when writing to a character device (`-o`) or reading from a character device (`-i`), `cpio` reaches the end of a medium (such as the end of a diskette), and the `-O` and `-I` options aren't used, `cpio` will print the following message:

```
If you want to go on, type device/file name when ready.
```

To continue, you must replace the medium and type the character special device name (`/dev/rdsk/f0` for example) and press RETURN. You may want to continue by directing `cpio` to use a different device. For example, if you have two floppy drives you may want to switch between them so `cpio` can proceed while you are changing the floppies. (Simply pressing RETURN causes the cpio process to exit.)

EXAMPLES

The following examples show three uses of cpio.

When standard input is directed through a pipe to cpio -o, it groups the files so they can be directed (>) to a single file (../newfile). The -c option insures that the file will be portable to other machines (as would the -H option). Instead of ls(1), you could use find(1), echo(1), cat(1), and so on, to pipe a list of names to cpio. You could direct the output to a device instead of a file.

```
ls | cpio -oc > ../newfile
```

cpio -i uses the output file of cpio -o (directed through a pipe with cat in the example below), extracts those files that match the patterns (memo/a1, memo/b*), creates directories below the current directory as needed (-d option), and places the files in the appropriate directories. The -c option is used if the input file was created with a portable header. If no patterns were given, all files from newfile would be placed in the directory.

```
cat newfile | cpio -icd "memo/a1" "memo/b*"
```

cpio -p takes the file names piped to it and copies or links (-l option) those files to another directory (newdir in the example below). The -d option says to create directories as needed. The -m option says retain the modification time. (It is important to use the -depth option of find(1) to generate path names for cpio. This eliminates problems cpio could have trying to create files under read-only directories.) The destination directory, newdir, must exist.

```
find . -depth -print | cpio -pdlmv newdir
```

Note that when you use cpio in conjunction with find, if you use the -L option with cpio then you must use the -follow option with find and vice versa. Otherwise there will be undesirable results.

SEE ALSO

ar(1), cat(1), echo(1), find(1), ls(1), tar(1).
archives(4) in the *System Administrator's Reference Manual.*

NOTES

An archive created with the -c option on a System V Release 4.0 system cannot be read on System V Release 3.2 systems, or earlier. Use the -H odc option, which is equivalent to the header created by the -c option in earlier System V Releases, if the cpio image will be read by a pre-System V Release 4.0 version of cpio.

System V Releases prior to Release 4.0 do not understand symbolic links. The result of copying in a symbolic link on an older release will be a regular file that contains the pathname of the referenced file.

Path names are restricted to 256 characters for the binary (the default) and -H odc header formats. Otherwise, path names are restricted to 1024 characters.

Only the super-user can copy special files.

Blocks are reported in 512-byte quantities.

If a file has 000 permissions, contains more than 0 characters of data, and the user is not root, the file will not be saved or restored.

NAME

crontab – user crontab file

SYNOPSIS

crontab [*file*]
crontab -e [*username*]
crontab -r [*username*]
crontab -l [*username*]

DESCRIPTION

crontab copies the specified file, or standard input if no file is specified, into a directory that holds all users' crontabs. The -e option edits a copy of the current user's crontab file, or creates an empty file to edit if crontab does not exist. When editing is complete, the file is installed as the user's crontab file. If a *username* is given, the specified user's crontab file is edited, rather than the current user's crontab file; this may only be done by a privileged user. The -e option invokes the editor specified by the VISUAL environment variable, and if that is null, it looks at the EDITOR environment variable, and if that is null, it invokes ed [see ed(1)]. The -r option removes a user's crontab from the crontab directory. crontab -l will list the crontab file for the invoking user. Only a privileged user can specify a *username* following the -r or -l options to remove or list the crontab file of the specified user.

Users are permitted to use crontab if their names appear in the file /etc/cron.d/cron.allow. If that file does not exist, the file /etc/cron.d/cron.deny is checked to determine if the user should be denied access to crontab. If neither file exists, only root is allowed to submit a job. If cron.allow does not exist and cron.deny exists but is empty, global usage is permitted. The allow/deny files consist of one user name per line.

A crontab file consists of lines of six fields each. The fields are separated by spaces or tabs. The first five are integer patterns that specify the following:

minute (0–59),
hour (0–23),
day of the month (1–31),
month of the year (1–12),
day of the week (0–6 with 0=Sunday).

Each of these patterns may be either an asterisk (meaning all legal values) or a list of elements separated by commas. An element is either a number or two numbers separated by a minus sign (meaning an inclusive range). Note that the specification of days may be made by two fields (day of the month and day of the week). If both are specified as a list of elements, both are adhered to. For example, `0 0 1,15 * 1` would run a command on the first and fifteenth of each month, as well as on every Monday. To specify days by only one field, the other field should be set to * (for example, `0 0 * * 1` would run a command only on Mondays).

The sixth field of a line in a crontab file is a string that is executed by the shell at the specified times. A percent character in this field (unless escaped by \) is translated to a new-line character. Only the first line (up to a % or end of line) of the command field is executed by the shell. The other lines are made available to the command as standard input.

Any line beginning with a # is a comment and will be ignored.

The shell is invoked from your `$HOME` directory with an `arg0` of `sh`. Users who desire to have their `.profile` executed must explicitly do so in the crontab file. `cron` supplies a default environment for every shell, defining `HOME`, `LOGNAME`, `SHELL(=/bin/sh)`, and `PATH(=:/bin:/usr/bin:/usr/lbin)`.

If you do not redirect the standard output and standard error of your commands, any generated output or errors will be mailed to you.

FILES

`/usr/sbin/cron.d`	main cron directory
`/var/spool/cron/crontabs`	spool area
`/var/cron/log`	accounting information
`/etc/cron.d/cron.allow`	list of allowed users
`/etc/cron.d/cron.deny`	list of denied users

NOTES

If you inadvertently enter the `crontab` command with no argument(s), do not attempt to get out with a CONTROL-D. This will cause all entries in your `crontab` file to be removed. Instead, exit with a DEL.

If a privileged user modifies another user's `crontab` file, resulting behavior may be unpredictable. Instead, the privileged user should first `su`(1M) to the other user's login before making any changes to the `crontab` file.

SEE ALSO

`atq`(1), `atrm`(1), `ed`(1), `sh`(1), `su`(1).

`cron`(1M) in the *System Administrator's Reference Manual.*

NAME

crypt – encode/decode

SYNOPSIS

crypt [*password*]
crypt [-k]

DESCRIPTION

crypt reads from the standard input and writes on the standard output. The *password* is a key that selects a particular transformation. If no argument is given, crypt demands a key from the terminal and turns off printing while the key is being typed in. If the -k option is used, crypt will use the key assigned to the environment variable CRYPTKEY. crypt encrypts and decrypts with the same key:

```
crypt key <clear >cypher
crypt key <cypher | pr
```

Files encrypted by crypt are compatible with those treated by the editors ed(1), edit(1), ex(1), and vi(1) in encryption mode.

The security of encrypted files depends on three factors: the fundamental method must be hard to solve; direct search of the key space must be infeasible; "sneak paths" by which keys or clear text can become visible must be minimized.

crypt implements a one-rotor machine designed along the lines of the German Enigma, but with a 256-element rotor. Methods of attack on such machines are known, but not widely; moreover the amount of work required is likely to be large.

The transformation of a key into the internal settings of the machine is deliberately designed to be expensive, i.e., to take a substantial fraction of a second to compute. However, if keys are restricted to (say) three lower-case letters, then encrypted files can be read by expending only a substantial fraction of five minutes of machine time.

If the key is an argument to the crypt command, it is potentially visible to users executing ps(1) or a derivative. The choice of keys and key security are the most vulnerable aspect of crypt.

FILES

/dev/tty for typed key

SEE ALSO

ed(1), edit(1), ex(1), makekey(1), nroff(1), pg(1), ps(1), stty(1), vi(1).

NOTES

This command is provided with the Security Administration Utilities, which is only available in the United States. If two or more files encrypted with the same key are concatenated and an attempt is made to decrypt the result, only the contents of the first of the original files will be decrypted correctly.

If output is piped to nroff and the encryption key is not given on the command line then do not pipe crypt through pg(1) or any other program that changes the tty settings. Doing so may cause crypt to leave terminal modes in a strange state [see stty(1)].

NAME

`csh` – shell command interpreter with a C-like syntax

SYNOPSIS

`csh` [`-bcefinstvVxX`] [*argument*...]

DESCRIPTION

`csh`, the C shell, is a command interpreter with a syntax reminiscent of the C language. It provides a number of convenient features for interactive use that are not available with the standard (Bourne) shell, including filename completion, command aliasing, history substitution, job control, and a number of built-in commands. As with the standard shell, the C shell provides variable, command and filename substitution.

Initialization and Termination

When first started, the C shell normally performs commands from the `.cshrc` file in your home directory, provided that it is readable and you either own it or your real group ID matches its group ID. If the shell is invoked with a name that starts with '–', as when started by `login`(1), the shell runs as a `login` shell. In this case, after executing commands from the `.cshrc` file, the shell executes commands from the `.login` file in your home directory; the same permission checks as those for `.cshrc` are applied to this file. Typically, the `.login` file contains commands to specify the terminal type and environment.

As a login shell terminates, it performs commands from the `.logout` file in your home directory; the same permission checks as those for `.cshrc` are applied to this file.

Interactive Operation

After startup processing is complete, an interactive C shell begins reading commands from the terminal, prompting with *hostname*`%` (or *hostname*`#` for the privileged user). The shell then repeatedly performs the following actions: a line of command input is read and broken into *words*. This sequence of words is placed on the history list and then parsed, as described under USAGE, below. Finally, the shell executes each command in the current line.

Noninteractive Operation

When running noninteractively, the shell does not prompt for input from the terminal. A noninteractive C shell can execute a command supplied as an *argument* on its command line, or interpret commands from a script.

The following options are available:

`-b` Force a break from option processing. Subsequent command-line arguments are not interpreted as C shell options. This allows the passing of options to a script without confusion. The shell does not run a set-user-ID script unless this option is present.

`-c` Read commands from the first filename *argument* (which must be present). Remaining arguments are placed in `argv`, the argument-list variable.

`-e` Exit if a command terminates abnormally or yields a nonzero exit status.

- `-f` Fast start. Read neither the `.cshrc` file, nor the `.login` file (if a login shell) upon startup.
- `-i` Forced interactive. Prompt for command-line input, even if the standard input does not appear to be a terminal (character-special device).
- `-n` Parse (interpret), but do not execute commands. This option can be used to check C shell scripts for syntax errors.
- `-s` Take commands from the standard input.
- `-t` Read and execute a single command line. A '\' (backslash) can be used to escape each newline for continuation of the command line onto subsequent input lines.
- `-v` Verbose. Set the `verbose` predefined variable; command input is echoed after history substitution (but before other substitutions) and before execution.
- `-V` Set `verbose` before reading `.cshrc`.
- `-x` Echo. Set the `echo` variable; echo commands after all substitutions and just before execution.
- `-X` Set `echo` before reading `.cshrc`.

Except with the options `-c`, `-i`, `-s` or `-t`, the first nonoption *argument* is taken to be the name of a command or script. It is passed as argument zero, and subsequent arguments are added to the argument list for that command or script.

USAGE

Filename Completion

When enabled by setting the variable `filec`, an interactive C shell can complete a partially typed filename or user name. When an unambiguous partial filename is followed by an ESC character on the terminal input line, the shell fills in the remaining characters of a matching filename from the working directory.

If a partial filename is followed by the EOF character (usually typed as CTRL-d), the shell lists all filenames that match. It then prompts once again, supplying the incomplete command line typed in so far.

When the last (partial) word begins with a tilde (~), the shell attempts completion with a user name, rather than a file in the working directory.

The terminal bell signals errors or multiple matches; this can be inhibited by setting the variable `nobeep`. You can exclude files with certain suffixes by listing those suffixes in the variable `fignore`. If, however, the only possible completion includes a suffix in the list, it is not ignored. `fignore` does not affect the listing of filenames by the EOF character.

Lexical Structure

The shell splits input lines into words at space and tab characters, except as noted below. The characters `&`, `|`, `;`, `<`, `>`, `(`, and `)` form separate words; if paired, the pairs form single words. These shell metacharacters can be made part of other words, and their special meaning can be suppressed by preceding them with a '\' (backslash). A newline preceded by a \ is equivalent to a space character.

In addition, a string enclosed in matched pairs of single-quotes (´), double-quotes ("), or backquotes (` ), forms a partial word; metacharacters in such a string, including any space or tab characters, do not form separate words. Within pairs of backquote ( `) or double-quote (") characters, a newline preceded by a '\' (backslash) gives a true newline character. Additional functions of each type of quote are described, below, under **Variable Substitution**, **Command Substitution**, and **Filename Substitution**.

When the shell's input is not a terminal, the character # introduces a comment that continues to the end of the input line. Its special meaning is suppressed when preceded by a \ or enclosed in matching quotes.

Command Line Parsing

A *simple command* is composed of a sequence of words. The first word (that is not part of an I/O redirection) specifies the command to be executed. A simple command, or a set of simple commands separated by | or |& characters, forms a *pipeline*. With |, the standard output of the preceding command is redirected to the standard input of the command that follows. With |&, both the standard error and the standard output are redirected through the pipeline.

Pipelines can be separated by semicolons (;), in which case they are executed sequentially. Pipelines that are separated by && or || form conditional sequences in which the execution of pipelines on the right depends upon the success or failure, respectively, of the pipeline on the left.

A pipeline or sequence can be enclosed within parentheses '( )' to form a simple command that can be a component in a pipeline or sequence.

A sequence of pipelines can be executed asynchronously, or in the background by appending an '&'; rather than waiting for the sequence to finish before issuing a prompt, the shell displays the job number (see Job Control, below) and associated process IDs, and prompts immediately.

History Substitution

History substitution allows you to use words from previous command lines in the command line you are typing. This simplifies spelling corrections and the repetition of complicated commands or arguments. Command lines are saved in the history list, the size of which is controlled by the **history** variable. The most recent command is retained in any case. A history substitution begins with a ! (although you can change this with the **histchars** variable) and may occur anywhere on the command line; history substitutions do not nest. The ! can be escaped with \ to suppress its special meaning.

Input lines containing history substitutions are echoed on the terminal after being expanded, but before any other substitutions take place or the command gets executed.

Event Designators

An event designator is a reference to a command-line entry in the history list.

! Start a history substitution, except when followed by a space character, tab, newline, = or (.

`!!`	Refer to the previous command. By itself, this substitution repeats the previous command.
`!`*n*	Refer to command-line *n*.
`!-`*n*	Refer to the current command-line minus *n*.
`!str`	Refer to the most recent command starting with `str`.
`!?`*str*[`?`]	Refer to the most recent command containing `str`.
`!{...}`	Insulate a history reference from adjacent characters (if necessary).

Word Designators

A ':' (colon) separates the event specification from the word designator. It can be omitted if the word designator begins with a `^`, `$`, `*`, `-` or `%`. If the word is to be selected from the previous command, the second `!` character can be omitted from the event specification. For instance, `!!:1` and `!:1` both refer to the first word of the previous command, while `!!$` and `!$` both refer to the last word in the previous command. Word designators include:

`#`	The entire command line typed so far.
`0`	The first input word (command).
n	The *n*'th argument.
`^`	The first argument, that is, `1`.
`$`	The last argument.
`%`	The word matched by (the most recent) `?`*s* search.
x–*y*	A range of words; –*y* abbreviates `0`–*y*.
`*`	All the arguments, or a null value if there is just one word in the event.
x`*`	Abbreviates *x*–`$`.
x–	Like *x*`*` but omitting word `$`.

Modifiers

After the optional word designator, you can add a sequence of one or more of the following modifiers, each preceded by a `:`.

`h`	Remove a trailing pathname component, leaving the head.
`r`	Remove a trailing suffix of the form '`.`*xxx*', leaving the basename.
`e`	Remove all but the suffix.
`s/`*l*`/`*r*[`/`]	Substitute *r* for *l*.
`t`	Remove all leading pathname components, leaving the tail.
`&`	Repeat the previous substitution.
`g`	Apply the change to the first occurrence of a match in each word, by prefixing the above (for example, `g&`).
`p`	Print the new command but do not execute it.
`q`	Quote the substituted words, escaping further substitutions.
`x`	Like `q`, but break into words at each space character, tab or newline.

Unless preceded by a `g`, the modification is applied only to the first string that matches *l*; an error results if no string matches.

The left-hand side of substitutions are not regular expressions, but character strings. Any character can be used as the delimiter in place of /. A backslash quotes the delimiter character. The character &, in the right hand side, is replaced by the text from the left-hand-side. The & can be quoted with a backslash. A null *l* uses the previous string either from a *l* or from a contextual scan string *s* from !?*s*. You can omit the rightmost delimiter if a newline immediately follows *r*; the rightmost ? in a context scan can similarly be omitted.

Without an event specification, a history reference refers either to the previous command, or to a previous history reference on the command line (if any).

Quick Substitution

^*l*^*r*[^]

This is equivalent to the history substitution: !:s^*l*^*r*[^].

Aliases

The C shell maintains a list of aliases that you can create, display, and modify using the **alias** and **unalias** commands. The shell checks the first word in each command to see if it matches the name of an existing alias. If it does, the command is reprocessed with the alias definition replacing its name; the history substitution mechanism is made available as though that command were the previous input line. This allows history substitutions, escaped with a backslash in the definition, to be replaced with actual command-line arguments when the alias is used. If no history substitution is called for, the arguments remain unchanged.

Aliases can be nested. That is, an alias definition can contain the name of another alias. Nested aliases are expanded before any history substitutions is applied. This is useful in pipelines such as

```
alias lm ´ls -l \!* | more´
```

which when called, pipes the output of ls(1V) through more(1).

Except for the first word, the name of the alias may not appear in its definition, nor in any alias referred to by its definition. Such loops are detected, and cause an error message.

I/O Redirection

The following metacharacters indicate that the subsequent word is the name of a file to which the command's standard input, standard output, or standard error is redirected; this word is variable, command, and filename expanded separately from the rest of the command.

<	Redirect the standard input.
<<*word*	Read the standard input, up to a line that is identical with *word*, and place the resulting lines in a temporary file. Unless *word* is escaped or quoted, variable and command substitutions are performed on these lines. Then, invoke the pipeline with the temporary file as its standard input. *word* is not subjected to variable, filename, or command substitution, and each line is compared to it before any substitutions are performed by the shell.

`> >! >& >&!`
: Redirect the standard output to a file. If the file does not exist, it is created. If it does exist, it is overwritten; its previous contents are lost.

  When set, the variable **noclobber** prevents destruction of existing files. It also prevents redirection to terminals and `/dev/null`, unless one of the `!` forms is used. The `&` forms redirect both standard output and the the standard error (diagnostic output) to the file.

`>> >>& >>! >>&!`
: Append the standard output. Like >, but places output at the end of the file rather than overwriting it. If **noclobber** is set, it is an error for the file not to exist, unless one of the `!` forms is used. The `&` forms append both the standard error and standard output to the file.

Variable Substitution

The C shell maintains a set of *variables*, each of which is composed of a *name* and a *value*. A variable name consists of up to 20 letters and digits, and starts with a letter (the underscore is considered a letter). A variable's value is a space-separated list of zero or more words.

To refer to a variable's value, precede its name with a '$'. Certain references (described below) can be used to select specific words from the value, or to display other information about the variable. Braces can be used to insulate the reference from other characters in an input-line word.

Variable substitution takes place after the input line is analyzed, aliases are resolved, and I/O redirections are applied. Exceptions to this are variable references in I/O redirections (substituted at the time the redirection is made), and backquoted strings (see Command Substitution).

Variable substitution can be suppressed by preceding the `$` with a \, except within double-quotes where it always occurs. Variable substitution is suppressed inside of single-quotes. A `$` is escaped if followed by a space character, tab or newline.

Variables can be created, displayed, or destroyed using the **set** and **unset** commands. Some variables are maintained or used by the shell. For instance, the **argv** variable contains an image of the shell's argument list. Of the variables used by the shell, a number are toggles; the shell does not care what their value is, only whether they are set or not.

Numerical values can be operated on as numbers (as with the `@` built-in). With numeric operations, an empty value is considered to be zero; the second and subsequent words of multiword values are ignored. For instance, when the **verbose** variable is set to any value (including an empty value), command input is echoed on the terminal.

Command and filename substitution is subsequently applied to the words that result from the variable substitution, except when suppressed by double-quotes, when **noglob** is set (suppressing filename substitution), or when the reference is quoted with the `:q` modifier. Within double-quotes, a reference is expanded to form (a portion of) a quoted string; multiword values are expanded to a string with embedded space characters. When the `:q` modifier is applied to the reference, it is expanded to a list of space-separated words, each of which is quoted to prevent subsequent command or filename substitutions.

Except as noted below, it is an error to refer to a variable that is not set.

`$`*var*
`${`*var*`}` These are replaced by words from the value of *var*, each separated by a space character. If *var* is an environment variable, its value is returned (but ':' modifiers and the other forms given below are not available).

`$`*var*`[`*index*`]`
`${`*var*`[`*index*`]}` These select only the indicated words from the value of *var*. Variable substitution is applied to *index*, which may consist of (or result in) a either single number, two numbers separated by a '–', or an asterisk. Words are indexed starting from 1; a '*' selects all words. If the first number of a range is omitted (as with `$argv[-2]`), it defaults to 1. If the last number of a range is omitted (as with `$argv[1-]`), it defaults to `$#`*var* (the word count). It is not an error for a range to be empty if the second argument is omitted (or within range).

`$#`*name*
`${#`*name*`}` These give the number of words in the variable.

`$0` This substitutes the name of the file from which command input is being read. An error occurs if the name is not known.

`$`*n*
`${`*n*`}` Equivalent to `$argv[`*n*`]`.

`$*` Equivalent to `$argv[*]`.

The modifiers `:e`, `:h`, `:q`, `:r`, `:t` and `:x` can be applied (see `History Substitution`), as can `:gh`, `:gt` and `:gr`. If `{ }` (braces) are used, then the modifiers must appear within the braces. The current implementation allows only one such modifier per expansion.

The following references may not be modified with `:` modifiers.

`$?`*var*
`${?`*var*`}`
Substitutes the string 1 if *var* is set or 0 if it is not set.

`$?0` Substitutes 1 if the current input filename is known, or 0 if it is not.

`$$` Substitute the process number of the (parent) shell.

`$<` Substitutes a line from the standard input, with no further interpretation thereafter. It can be used to read from the keyboard in a C shell script.

Command and Filename Substitutions

Command and filename substitutions are applied selectively to the arguments of built-in commands. Portions of expressions that are not evaluated are not expanded. For non-built-in commands, filename expansion of the command name is done separately from that of the argument list; expansion occurs in a subshell, after I/O redirection is performed.

Command Substitution

A command enclosed by backquotes (` ... `) is performed by a subshell. Its standard output is broken into separate words at each space character, tab and newline; null words are discarded. This text replaces the backquoted string on the current command line. Within double-quotes, only newline characters force new words; space and tab characters are preserved. However, a final newline is ignored. It is therefore possible for a command substitution to yield a partial word.

Filename Substitution

Unquoted words containing any of the characters *, ?, [or {, or that begin with ~, are expanded (also known as *globbing*) to an alphabetically sorted list of filenames, as follows:

*	Match any (zero or more) characters.
?	Match any single character.
[...]	Match any single character in the enclosed list(s) or range(s). A list is a string of characters. A range is two characters separated by a minus-sign (–), and includes all the characters in between in the ASCII collating sequence [see `ascii`(7)].
{ *str*, *str*, ... }	Expand to each string (or filename-matching pattern) in the comma-separated list. Unlike the pattern-matching expressions above, the expansion of this construct is not sorted. For instance, `{b,a}` expands to 'b' 'a', (not 'a' 'b'). As special cases, the characters { and }, along with the string { }, are passed undisturbed.
~[	*user*] Your home directory, as indicated by the value of the variable **home**, or that of *user*, as indicated by the password entry for *user*.

Only the patterns *, ? and [...] imply pattern matching; an error results if no filename matches a pattern that contains them. The '.' (dot character), when it is the first character in a filename or pathname component, must be matched explicitly. The / (slash) must also be matched explicitly.

Expressions and Operators

A number of C shell built-in commands accept expressions, in which the operators are similar to those of C and have the same precedence. These expressions typically appear in the `@`, `exit`, `if`, `set` and `while` commands, and are often used to regulate the flow of control for executing commands. Components of an expression are separated by white space.

Null or missing values are considered 0. The result of all expressions are strings, which may represent decimal numbers.

The following C shell operators are grouped in order of precedence:

(...)	grouping
~	one's complement
!	logical negation
* / %	multiplication, division, remainder (These are right associative, which can lead to unexpected results. Group combinations explicitly with parentheses.)
+ -	addition, subtraction (also right associative)
<< >>	bitwise shift left, bitwise shift right
< > <= >=	less than, greater than, less than or equal to, greater than or equal to
== != =~ !~	equal to, not equal to, filename-substitution pattern match (described below), filename-substitution pattern mismatch
&	bitwise AND
^	bitwise XOR (exclusive or)
|	bitwise inclusive OR
&&	logical AND
||	logical OR

The operators: ==, !=, =~, and !~ compare their arguments as strings; other operators use numbers. The operators =~ and !~ each check whether or not a string to the left matches a filename substitution pattern on the right. This reduces the need for **switch** statements when pattern-matching between strings is all that is required.

Also available are file inquiries:

- −r *filename* Return true, or 1 if the user has read access. Otherwise it returns false, or 0.
- −w *filename* True if the user has write access.
- −x *filename* True if the user has execute permission (or search permission on a directory).
- −e *filename* True if *file* exists.
- −o *filename* True if the user owns *file*.
- −z *filename* True if *file* is of zero length (empty).
- −f *filename* True if *file* is a plain file.
- −d *filename* True if *file* is a directory.

If *file* does not exist or is inaccessible, then all inquiries return false.

An inquiry as to the success of a command is also available:

{ *command* } If *command* runs successfully, the expression evaluates to true, 1. Otherwise it evaluates to false 0. (Note that, conversely, *command* itself typically returns 0 when it runs successfully, or some other value if it encounters a problem. If you want to get at the status directly, use the value of the **status** variable rather than this expression).

Control Flow

The shell contains a number of commands to regulate the flow of control in scripts, and within limits, from the terminal. These commands operate by forcing the shell either to reread input (to *loop*), or to skip input under certain conditions (to *branch*).

Each occurrence of a **foreach**, **switch**, **while**, **if**...**then** and **else** built-in must appear as the first word on its own input line.

If the shell's input is not seekable and a loop is being read, that input is buffered. The shell performs seeks within the internal buffer to accomplish the rereading implied by the loop. (To the extent that this allows, backward goto commands will succeed on nonseekable inputs.)

Command Execution

If the command is a C shell built-in, the shell executes it directly. Otherwise, the shell searches for a file by that name with execute access. If the command-name contains a /, the shell takes it as a pathname, and searches for it. If the command-name does not contain a /, the shell attempts to resolve it to a pathname, searching each directory in the path variable for the command. To speed the search, the shell uses its hash table (see the **rehash** built-in) to eliminate directories that have no applicable files. This hashing can be disabled with the -c or -t, options, or the unhash built-in.

As a special case, if there is no / in the name of the script and there is an alias for the word **shell**, the expansion of the **shell** alias is prepended (without modification), to the command line. The system attempts to execute the first word of this special (late-occurring) alias, which should be a full pathname. Remaining words of the alias's definition, along with the text of the input line, are treated as arguments.

When a pathname is found that has proper execute permissions, the shell forks a new process and passes it, along with its arguments to the kernel (using the execve(2) system call). The kernel then attempts to overlay the new process with the desired program. If the file is an executable binary (in a.out(4) format) the kernel succeeds, and begins executing the new process. If the file is a text file, and the first line begins with #!, the next word is taken to be the pathname of a shell (or command) to interpret that script. Subsequent words on the first line are taken as options for that shell. The kernel invokes (overlays) the indicated shell, using the name of the script as an argument.

If neither of the above conditions holds, the kernel cannot overlay the file (the execve(2) call fails); the C shell then attempts to execute the file by spawning a new shell, as follows:

- If the first character of the file is a #, a C shell is invoked.
- Otherwise, a standard (Bourne) shell is invoked.

Signal Handling

The shell normally ignores QUIT signals. Background jobs are immune to signals generated from the keyboard, including hangups (HUP). Other signals have the values that the C shell inherited from its environment. The shell's handling of interrupt and terminate signals within scripts can be controlled by the onintr built-in. Login shells catch the TERM signal; otherwise this signal is passed on to child processes. In no case are interrupts allowed when a login shell is reading the `.logout` file.

Job Control

The shell associates a numbered *job* with each command sequence, to keep track of those commands that are running in the background or have been stopped with TSTP signals (typically CTRL-z). When a command, or command sequence (semicolon separated list), is started in the background using the `&` metacharacter, the shell displays a line with the job number in brackets, and a list of associated process numbers:

```
[1] 1234
```

To see the current list of jobs, use the `jobs` built-in command. The job most recently stopped (or put into the background if none are stopped) is referred to as the *current* job, and is indicated with a '+'. The previous job is indicated with a '–'; when the current job is terminated or moved to the foreground, this job takes its place (becomes the new current job).

To manipulate jobs, refer to the `bg`, `fg`, `kill`, `stop` and `%` built-ins.

A reference to a job begins with a '`%`'. By itself, the percent-sign refers to the current job.

`%` `%+` `%%`	The current job.
`%-`	The previous job.
`%`*j*	Refer to job *j* as in: '`kill -9 %`*j*'. *j* can be a job number, or a string that uniquely specifies the command-line by which it was started; '`fg %vi`' might bring a stopped `vi` job to the foreground, for instance.
`%?`*string*	Specify the job for which the command-line uniquely contains *string*.

A job running in the background stops when it attempts to read from the terminal. Background jobs can normally produce output, but this can be suppressed using the '`stty tostop`' command.

Status Reporting

While running interactively, the shell tracks the status of each job and reports whenever a finishes or becomes blocked. It normally displays a message to this effect as it issues a prompt, so as to avoid disturbing the appearance of your input. When set, the `notify` variable indicates that the shell is to report status changes immediately. By default, the `notify` command marks the current process; after starting a background job, type `notify` to mark it.

Built-In Commands

Built-in commands are executed within the C shell. If a built-in command occurs as any component of a pipeline except the last, it is executed in a subshell.

`:`	Null command. This command is interpreted, but performs no action.

alias [*name* [*def*]]
Assign *def* to the alias *name*. *def* is a list of words that may contain escaped history-substitution metasyntax. *name* is not allowed to be **alias** or **unalias**. If *def* is omitted, the alias *name* is displayed along with its current definition. If both *name* and *def* are omitted, all aliases are displayed.

bg [%*job*] ...
Run the current or specified jobs in the background.

break Resume execution after the **end** of the nearest enclosing **foreach** or **while** loop. The remaining commands on the current line are executed. This allows multilevel breaks to be written as a list of **break** commands, all on one line.

breaksw Break from a **switch**, resuming after the **endsw**.

case *label*:
A label in a **switch** statement.

cd [*dir*]
chdir [*dir*]
Change the shell's working directory to directory *dir*. If no argument is given, change to the home directory of the user. If *dir* is a relative pathname not found in the current directory, check for it in those directories listed in the **cdpath** variable. If *dir* is the name of a shell variable whose value starts with a /, change to the directory named by that value.

continue Continue execution of the nearest enclosing **while** or **foreach**.

default: Labels the default case in a **switch** statement. The default should come after all **case** labels. Any remaining commands on the command line are first executed.

dirs [-l]
Print the directory stack, most recent to the left; the first directory shown is the current directory. With the **-l** argument, produce an unabbreviated printout; use of the ~ notation is suppressed.

echo [-n] *list*
The words in *list* are written to the shell's standard output, separated by space characters. The output is terminated with a newline unless the -n option is used.

eval *argument* ...
Reads the arguments as input to the shell, and executes the resulting command(s). This is usually used to execute commands generated as the result of command or variable substitution, since parsing occurs before these substitutions. See **tset**(1) for an example of how to use **eval**.

exec *command*
Execute *command* in place of the current shell, which terminates.

exit [(*expr*)]
The shell exits, either with the value of the STATUS variable, or with the value of the specified by the expression **expr**.

fg % [*job*]
Bring the current or specified *job* into the foreground.

foreach *var* (*wordlist*)
...
end The variable *var* is successively set to each member of *wordlist*. The sequence of commands between this command and the matching **end** is executed for each new value of *var*. (Both **foreach** and **end** must appear alone on separate lines.)

The built-in command **continue** may be used to continue the loop prematurely and the built-in command **break** to terminate it prematurely. When this command is read from the terminal, the loop is read up once prompting with ? before any statements in the loop are executed.

glob *wordlist*
Perform filename expansion on *wordlist*. Like **echo**, but no \ escapes are recognized. Words are delimited by NULL characters in the output.

goto *label* The specified *label* is filename and command expanded to yield a label. The shell rewinds its input as much as possible and searches for a line of the form *label*: possibly preceded by space or tab characters. Execution continues after the indicated line. It is an error to jump to a label that occurs between a **while** or **for** built-in, and its corresponding **end**.

hashstat Print a statistics line indicating how effective the internal hash table has been at locating commands (and avoiding **execs**). An **exec** is attempted for each component of the *path* where the hash function indicates a possible hit, and in each component that does not begin with a '/'.

history [-**hr**] [*n*]
Display the history list; if *n* is given, display only the *n* most recent events.

-**r** Reverse the order of printout to be most recent first rather than oldest first.

-**h** Display the history list without leading numbers. This is used to produce files suitable for sourcing using the -**h** option to *source*.

if (*expr*) *command*
If the specified expression evaluates to true, the single *command* with arguments is executed. Variable substitution on *command* happens early, at the same time it does for the rest of the *if* command. *command* must be a simple command, not a pipeline, a command list, or a parenthesized command list. Note: I/O redirection occurs even if **expr** is false, when *command* is *not* executed (this is a bug).

`if` (*expr*) `then`
`...`
`else if` (*expr2*) `then`
`...`
`else`
`...`
`endif`

If **expr**"" is true, commands up to the first **else** are executed. Otherwise, if *expr2* is true, the commands between the **else if** and the second **else** are executed. Otherwise, commands between the **else** and the **endif** are executed. Any number of **else if** pairs are allowed, but only one **else**. Only one **endif** is needed, but it is required. The words **else** and **endif** must be the first nonwhite characters on a line. The **if** must appear alone on its input line or after an **else**.)

`jobs`[`-l`]
List the active jobs under job control.

`-l` List process IDs, in addition to the normal information.

kill [*-sig*] [*pid*] [*%job*] ...
kill -l Send the TERM (terminate) signal, by default, or the signal specified, to the specified process ID, the *job* indicated, or the current *job*. Signals are either given by number or by name. There is no default. Typing **kill** does not send a signal to the current job. If the signal being sent is TERM (terminate) or HUP (hangup), then the job or process is sent a CONT (continue) signal as well.

`-l` List the signal names that can be sent.

`limit` [`-h`] [*resource* [*max-use*]]
Limit the consumption by the current process or any process it spawns, each not to exceed *max-use* on the specified *resource*. If *max-use* is omitted, print the current limit; if *resource* is omitted, display all limits.

`-h` Use hard limits instead of the current limits. Hard limits impose a ceiling on the values of the current limits. Only the privileged user may raise the hard limits.

resource is one of:

`cputime`	Maximum CPU seconds per process.
`filesize`	Largest single file allowed.
`datasize`	Maximum data size (including stack) for the process.
`stacksize`	Maximum stack size for the process.
`coredumpsize`	Maximum size of a core dump (file).

max-use is a number, with an optional scaling factor, as follows:

*n*h	Hours (for `cputime`).
*n*k	*n* kilobytes. This is the default for all but `cputime`.
*n*m	*n* megabytes or minutes (for `cputime`).
mm:*ss*	Minutes and seconds (for `cputime`).

`login` [*username* |`-p`]
Terminate a login shell and invoke `login`(1). The `.logout` file is not processed. If *username* is omitted, `login` prompts for the name of a user.

`-p` Preserve the current environment (variables).

`logout` Terminate a login shell.

`nice` [+*n* |-*n*] [*command*]
Increment the process priority value for the shell or for *command* by *n*. The higher the priority value, the lower the priority of a process, and the slower it runs. When given, *command* is always run in a subshell, and the restrictions placed on commands in simple `if` commands apply. If *command* is omitted, `nice` increments the value for the current shell. If no increment is specified, `nice` sets the process priority value to 4. The range of process priority values is from −20 to 20. Values of *n* outside this range set the value to the lower, or to the higher boundary, respectively.

+*n* Increment the process priority value by *n*.
−*n* Decrement by *n*. This argument can be used only by the privileged user.

`nohup` [*command*]
Run *command* with HUPs ignored. With no arguments, ignore HUPs throughout the remainder of a script. When given, *command* is always run in a subshell, and the restrictions placed on commands in simple `if` commands apply. All processes detached with `&` are effectively nohup'd.

`notify` [`%`*job*] ...
Notify the user asynchronously when the status of the current, or of specified jobs, changes.

`onintr` [− | *label*]
Control the action of the shell on interrupts. With no arguments, `onintr` restores the default action of the shell on interrupts. (The shell terminates shell scripts and returns to the terminal command input level). With the − argument, the shell ignores all interrupts. With a *label* argument, the shell executes a `goto` *label* when an interrupt is received or a child process terminates because it was interrupted.

`popd` [+*n*] Pop the directory stack, and `cd` to the new top directory. The elements of the directory stack are numbered from 0 starting at the top.

+*n* Discard the *n*'th entry in the stack.

`pushd` [+*n* | *dir*]
Push a directory onto the directory stack. With no arguments, exchange the top two elements.

+n Rotate the *n*'th entry to the top of the stack and `cd` to it.
dir Push the current working directory onto the stack and change to *dir*.

`rehash` Recompute the internal hash table of the contents of directories listed in the *path* variable to account for new commands added.

`repeat` *count command*
Repeat *command count* times. *command* is subject to the same restrictions as with the one-line `if` statement.

`set` [*var* [= *value*]]
`set` *var*[*n*] = *word*
With no arguments, `set` displays the values of all shell variables. Multiword values are displayed as a parenthesized list. With the *var* argument alone, `set` assigns an empty (null) value to the variable *var*. With arguments of the form *var* = *value* `set` assigns *value* to *var*, where *value* is one of:

word A single word (or quoted string).
(*wordlist*) A space-separated list of words enclosed in parentheses.

Values are command and filename expanded before being assigned. The form `set` *var*[*n*] = *word* replaces the *n*'th word in a multiword value with *word*.

`setenv` [*VAR* [*word*]]
With no arguments, `setenv` displays all environment variables. With the *VAR* argument sets the environment variable *VAR* to have an empty (null) value. (By convention, environment variables are normally given upper-case names.) With both *VAR* and *word* arguments `setenv` sets the environment variable `NAME` to the value *word*, which must be either a single word or a quoted string. The most commonly used environment variables, `USER`, `TERM`, and `PATH`, are automatically imported to and exported from the `csh` variables `user`, `term`, and `path`; there is no need to use `setenv` for these. In addition, the shell sets the `PWD` environment variable from the `csh` variable `cwd` whenever the latter changes.

`shift` [*variable*]
The components of `argv`, or *variable*, if supplied, are shifted to the left, discarding the first component. It is an error for the variable not to be set, or to have a null value.

`source` [`-h`] *name*

Reads commands from *name*. **source** commands may be nested, but if they are nested too deeply the shell may run out of file descriptors. An error in a sourced file at any level terminates all nested **source** commands.

`-h` Place commands from the the file *name* on the history list without executing them.

`stop` [`%`*job*] ...

Stop the current or specified background job.

`suspend` Stop the shell in its tracks, much as if it had been sent a stop signal with `^Z`. This is most often used to stop shells started by **su**.

```
switch (string)
case label:
...
breaksw
...
default:
...
breaksw
endsw
```

Each *label* is successively matched, against the specified *string*, which is first command and filename expanded. The file metacharacters `*`, `?` and `[...]` may be used in the case labels, which are variable expanded. If none of the labels match before a default label is found, execution begins after the default label. Each `case` statement and the `default` statement must appear at the beginning of a line. The command **breaksw** continues execution after the **endsw**. Otherwise control falls through subsequent `case` and `default` statements as with C. If no label matches and there is no default, execution continues after the **endsw**.

`time` [*command*]

With no argument, print a summary of time used by this C shell and its children. With an optional *command*, execute *command* and print a summary of the time it uses.

`umask` [*value*]

Display the file creation mask. With *value* set the file creation mask. *value* is given in octal, and is XORed with the permissions of 666 for files and 777 for directories to arrive at the permissions for new files. Common values include 002, giving complete access to the group, and read (and directory search) access to others, or 022, giving read (and directory search) but not write permission to the group and others.

`unalias` *pattern*

Discard aliases that match (filename substitution) *pattern*. All aliases are removed by `unalias *`.

unhash Disable the internal hash table.

unlimit [-h] [*resource*]

Remove a limitation on *resource*. If no *resource* is specified, then all *resource* limitations are removed. See the description of the limit command for the list of *resource* names.

-h Remove corresponding hard limits. Only the privileged user may do this.

unset *pattern*

Remove variables whose names match (filename substitution) *pattern*. All variables are removed by 'unset *'; this has noticeably distasteful side-effects.

unsetenv *variable*

Remove *variable* from the environment. Pattern matching, as with unset is not performed.

wait Wait for background jobs to finish (or for an interrupt) before prompting.

while (*expr*)

...

end While expr is true (evaluates to non-zero), repeat commands between the while and the matching end statement. break and continue may be used to terminate or continue the loop prematurely. The while and end must appear alone on their input lines. If the shell's input is a terminal, it prompts for commands with a question-mark until the end command is entered and then performs the commands in the loop.

%[*job*] [&]

Bring the current or indicated *job* to the foreground. With the ampersand, continue running *job* in the background.

@ [*var* =expr]
@ [*var*[*n*] =expr]

With no arguments, display the values for all shell variables. With arguments, the variable *var*, or the *n*'th word in the value of *var*, to the value that expr evaluates to. (If [*n*] is supplied, both *var* and its *n*'th component must already exist.)

If the expression contains the characters >, <, & or |, then at least this part of expr must be placed within parentheses.

The operators *=, +=, etc., are available as in C. The space separating the name from the assignment operator is optional. Spaces are, however, mandatory in separating components of expr that would otherwise be single words.

Special postfix operators, ++ and -- increment or decrement *name*, respectively.

Environment Variables and Predefined Shell Variables

Unlike the standard shell, the C shell maintains a distinction between environment variables, which are automatically exported to processes it invokes, and shell variables, which are not. Both types of variables are treated similarly under variable substitution. The shell sets the variables **argv**, **cwd**, **home**, **path**, **prompt**, **shell**, and **status** upon initialization. The shell copies the environment variable `USER` into the shell variable **user**, `TERM` into **term**, and `HOME` into **home**, and copies each back into the respective environment variable whenever the shell variables are reset. `PATH` and **path** are similarly handled. You need only set **path** once in the `.cshrc` or `.login` file. The environment variable `PWD` is set from **cwd** whenever the latter changes. The following shell variables have predefined meanings:

`argv` Argument list. Contains the list of command line arguments supplied to the current invocation of the shell. This variable determines the value of the positional parameters **$1**, **$2**, and so on.

`cdpath` Contains a list of directories to be searched by the **cd**, **chdir**, and **popd** commands, if the directory argument each accepts is not a subdirectory of the current directory.

`cwd` The full pathname of the current directory.

`echo` Echo commands (after substitutions), just before execution.

`fignore` A list of filename suffixes to ignore when attempting filename completion. Typically the single word '`.o`'.

`filec` Enable filename completion, in which case the CTRL-d character CTRL-d) and the ESC character have special significance when typed in at the end of a terminal input line:

EOT Print a list of all filenames that start with the preceding string.

ESC Replace the preceding string with the longest unambiguous extension.

`hardpaths` If set, pathnames in the directory stack are resolved to contain no symbolic-link components.

`histchars` A two-character string. The first character replaces ! as the history-substitution character. The second replaces the carat (^) for quick substitutions.

`history` The number of lines saved in the history list. A very large number may use up all of the C shell's memory. If not set, the C shell saves only the most recent command.

`home` The user's home directory. The filename expansion of ~ refers to the value of this variable.

`ignoreeof` If set, the shell ignores EOF from terminals. This protects against accidentally killing a C shell by typing a CTRL-d.

`mail` — A list of files where the C shell checks for mail. If the first word of the value is a number, it specifies a mail checking interval in seconds (default 5 minutes).

`nobeep` — Suppress the bell during command completion when asking the C shell to extend an ambiguous filename.

`noclobber` — Restrict output redirection so that existing files are not destroyed by accident. > redirections can only be made to new files. >> redirections can only be made to existing files.

`noglob` — Inhibit filename substitution. This is most useful in shell scripts once filenames (if any) are obtained and no further expansion is desired.

`nonomatch` — Returns the filename substitution pattern, rather than an error, if the pattern is not matched. Malformed patterns still result in errors.

`notify` — If set, the shell notifies you immediately as jobs are completed, rather than waiting until just before issuing a prompt.

`path` — The list of directories in which to search for commands. `path` is initialized from the environment variable `PATH`, which the C shell updates whenever `path` changes. A null word specifies the current directory. The default is typically: `(. /usr/ucb /usr/bin)`. If `path` becomes unset only full pathnames will execute. An interactive C shell will normally hash the contents of the directories listed after reading `.cshrc`, and whenever `path` is reset. If new commands are added, use the `rehash` command to update the table.

`prompt` — The string an interactive C shell prompts with. Noninteractive shells leave the `prompt` variable unset. Aliases and other commands in the `.cshrc` file that are only useful interactively, can be placed after the following test: '`if ($?prompt == 0) exit`', to reduce startup time for noninteractive shells. A `!` in the `prompt` string is replaced by the current event number. The default prompt is *hostname*`%` for mere mortals, or *hostname*`#` for the privileged user.

`savehist` — The number of lines from the history list that are saved in `~/.history` when the user logs out. Large values for `savehist` slow down the C shell during startup.

`shell` — The file in which the C shell resides. This is used in forking shells to interpret files that have execute bits set, but that are not executable by the system.

`status` — The status returned by the most recent command. If that command terminated abnormally, 0200 is added to the status. Built-in commands that fail return exit status 1, all other built-in commands set status to 0.

`time` Control automatic timing of commands. Can be supplied with one or two values. The first is the reporting threshold in CPU seconds. The second is a string of tags and text indicating which resources to report on. A tag is a percent sign (`%`) followed by a single *upper-case* letter (unrecognized tags print as text):

`%D`	Average amount of unshared data space used in Kilobytes.
`%E`	Elapsed (wallclock) time for the command.
`%F`	Page faults.
`%I`	Number of block input operations.
`%K`	Average amount of unshared stack space used in Kilobytes.
`%M`	Maximum real memory used during execution of the process.
`%O`	Number of block output operations.
`%P`	Total CPU time — U (user) plus S (system) — as a percentage of E (elapsed) time.
`%S`	Number of seconds of CPU time consumed by the kernel on behalf of the user's process.
`%U`	Number of seconds of CPU time devoted to the user's process.
`%W`	Number of swaps.
`%X`	Average amount of shared memory used in Kilobytes.

The default summary display outputs from the `%U`, `%S`, `%E`, `%P`, `%X`, `%D`, `%I`, `%O`, `%F` and `%W` tags, in that order.

`verbose` Display each command after history substitution takes place.

FILES

`~/.cshrc`	Read at beginning of execution by each shell.
`~/.login`	Read by login shells after `.cshrc` at login.
`~/.logout`	Read by login shells at logout.
`~/.history`	Saved history for use at next login.
`/usr/bin/sh`	Standard shell, for shell scripts not starting with a '`#`'.
`/tmp/sh*`	Temporary file for '<<'.
`/etc/passwd`	Source of home directories for '~*name*'.

SEE ALSO

`login`(1), `sh`(1)
`access`(2), `exec`(2), `fork`(2), `pipe`(2) in the *Programmer's Reference Manual*.
`a.out`(4), `environ`(4), `termio`(4), `ascii`(5) in the *System Administrator's Reference Manual*.

DIAGNOSTICS

`You have stopped jobs.`
You attempted to exit the C shell with stopped jobs under job control. An immediate second attempt to exit will succeed, terminating the stopped jobs.

NOTES

Words can be no longer than 1024 characters. The system limits argument lists to 1,048,576 characters. However, the maximum number of arguments to a command for which filename expansion applies is 1706. Command substitutions may expand to no more characters than are allowed in the argument list. To detect looping, the shell restricts the number of **alias** substitutions on a single line to 20.

When a command is restarted from a stop, the shell prints the directory it started in if this is different from the current directory; this can be misleading (that is, wrong) as the job may have changed directories internally.

Shell built-in functions are not stoppable/restartable. Command sequences of the form *a* ; *b* ; *c* are also not handled gracefully when stopping is attempted. If you suspend *b*, the shell never executes *c*. This is especially noticeable if the expansion results from an alias. It can be avoided by placing the sequence in parentheses to force it into a subshell.

Control over terminal output after processes are started is primitive; use the Sun Window system if you need better output control.

Multiline shell procedures should be provided, as they are with the standard (Bourne) shell.

Commands within loops, prompted for by `?`, are not placed in the *history* list.

Control structures should be parsed rather than being recognized as built-in commands. This would allow control commands to be placed anywhere, to be combined with `|`, and to be used with `&` and `;` metasyntax.

It should be possible to use the `:` modifiers on the output of command substitutions. There are two problems with `:` modifier usage on variable substitutions: not all of the modifiers are available, and only one modifier per substitution is allowed.

The `g` (global) flag in history substitutions applies only to the first match in each word, rather than all matches in all words. The the standard text editors consistently do the latter when given the `g` flag in a substitution command.

Quoting conventions are confusing. Overriding the escape character to force variable substitutions within double quotes is counterintuitive and inconsistent with the Bourne shell.

Symbolic links can fool the shell. Setting the **hardpaths** variable alleviates this.

'`set path`' should remove duplicate pathnames from the pathname list. These often occur because a shell script or a `.cshrc` file does something like '`set path=(/usr/local /usr/hosts $path)`' to ensure that the named directories are in the pathname list.

The only way to direct the standard output and standard error separately is by invoking a subshell, as follows:

```
example% (command > outfile) >& errorfile
```

Although robust enough for general use, adventures into the esoteric periphery of the C shell may reveal unexpected quirks.

NAME

csplit – context split

SYNOPSIS

csplit [**-s**] [**-k**] [**-f** *prefix*] *file arg1* [... *argn*]

DESCRIPTION

csplit reads *file* and separates it into n+1 sections, defined by the arguments *arg1*...*argn*. By default the sections are placed in xx00...xx*n* (*n* may not be greater than 99). These sections get the following pieces of *file*:

00: From the start of *file* up to (but not including) the line referenced by *arg1*.

01: From the line referenced by *arg1* up to the line referenced by *arg2*.

⋮

n: From the line referenced by *argn* to the end of *file*.

If the *file* argument is a –, then standard input is used.

The options to **csplit** are:

-s **csplit** normally prints the character counts for each file created. If the **-s** option is present, **csplit** suppresses the printing of all character counts.

-k **csplit** normally removes created files if an error occurs. If the **-k** option is present, **csplit** leaves previously created files intact.

-f *prefix* If the **-f** option is used, the created files are named *prefix*00...*prefixn*. The default is xx00...xx*n*.

The arguments (*arg1*...*argn*) to **csplit** can be a combination of the following:

/rexp/ A file is to be created for the section from the current line up to (but not including) the line containing the regular expression *rexp*. The current line becomes the line containing *rexp*. This argument may be followed by an optional + or – some number of lines (e.g., /Page/-5). See **ed**(1) for a description of how to specify a regular expression.

%rexp% This argument is the same as */rexp/*, except that no file is created for the section.

lnno A file is to be created from the current line up to (but not including) *lnno*. The current line becomes *lnno*.

{*num*} Repeat argument. This argument may follow any of the above arguments. If it follows a *rexp* type argument, that argument is applied *num* more times. If it follows *lnno*, the file will be split every *lnno* lines (*num* times) from that point.

Enclose all *rexp* type arguments that contain blanks or other characters meaningful to the shell in the appropriate quotes. Regular expressions may not contain embedded new-lines. **csplit** does not affect the original file; it is the user's responsibility to remove it if it is no longer wanted.

EXAMPLES

```
csplit -f cobol file '/procedure division/' /par5./ /par16./
```

This example creates four files, cobol00...cobol03. After editing the "split" files, they can be recombined as follows:

```
cat cobol0[0-3] > file
```

Note that this example overwrites the original file.

```
csplit -k file 100 {99}
```

This example splits the file at every 100 lines, up to 10,000 lines. The **-k** option causes the created files to be retained if there are less than 10,000 lines; however, an error message would still be printed.

```
csplit -k prog.c '%main(%' '/^}/+1' {20}
```

If `prog.c` follows the normal C coding convention (the last line of a routine consists only of a } in the first character position), this example creates a file for each separate C routine (up to 21) in `prog.c`.

SEE ALSO

ed(1), sh(1).

DIAGNOSTICS

Self-explanatory except for:

arg - out of range

which means that the given argument did not reference a line between the current position and the end of the file.

NAME

ct − spawn login to a remote terminal

SYNOPSIS

ct [options] telno ...

DESCRIPTION

ct dials the telephone number of a modem that is attached to a terminal and spawns a login process to that terminal. *Telno* is a telephone number, with equal signs for secondary dial tones and minus signs for delays at appropriate places. (The set of legal characters for *telno* is 0 through 9, -, =, *, and #. The maximum length *telno* is 31 characters). If more than one telephone number is specified, ct will try each in succession until one answers; this is useful for specifying alternate dialing paths.

ct will try each line listed in the file /etc/uucp/Devices until it finds an available line with appropriate attributes, or runs out of entries. ct uses the following options:

−h — Normally, ct will hang up the current line so that it can be used to answer the incoming call. The −h option will prevent this action. The −h option will also wait for the termination of the specified ct process before returning control to the user's terminal.

−s*speed* — The data rate may be set with the −s option. *speed* is expressed in baud rates. The default baud rate is 1200.

−v — If the −v (verbose) option is used, ct will send a running narrative to the standard error output stream.

−w*n* — If there are no free lines ct will ask if it should wait for one, and if so, for how many minutes it should wait before it gives up. ct will continue to try to open the dialers at one-minute intervals until the specified limit is exceeded. This dialogue may be overridden by specifying the −w*n* option. *n* is the maximum number of minutes that ct is to wait for a line.

−x*n* — This option is used for debugging; it produces a detailed output of the program execution on stderr. *n* is a single number between 0 and 9. As *n* increases to 9, more detailed debugging information is given.

After the user on the destination terminal logs out, there are two things that could occur depending on what type of port monitor is monitoring the port. In the case of no port monitor, ct prompts: Reconnect? If the response begins with the letter n, the line will be dropped; otherwise, *ttymon* will be started again and the login: prompt will be printed. In the second case, where a port monitor is monitoring the port, the port monitor reissues the login: prompt.

The user should log out properly before disconnecting.

FILES

/etc/uucp/Devices
/var/adm/ctlog

SEE ALSO

cu(1C), login(1), uucp(1C).
ttymon(1M) in the *System Administrator's Reference Manual*.

NOTES

The ct program will not work with a DATAKIT Multiplex interface.

For a shared port, one used for both dial-in and dial-out, the *ttymon* program running on the line must have the -r and -b options specified (see *ttymon*(1M)).

NAME

ctags – create a tags file for use with vi

SYNOPSIS

ctags [-aBFtuvwx] [-f *tagsfile*] *filename*...

DESCRIPTION

ctags makes a tags file for ex(1) from the specified C, Pascal, FORTRAN, YACC, and LEX sources. A tags file gives the locations of specified objects (in this case functions and typedefs) in a group of files. Each line of the tags file contains the object name, the file in which it is defined, and an address specification for the object definition. Functions are searched with a pattern, typedefs with a line number. Specifiers are given in separate fields on the line, separated by SPACE or TAB characters. Using the tags file, ex can quickly find these objects definitions.

Normally ctags places the tag descriptions in a file called tags; this may be overridden with the -f option.

Files with names ending in .c or .h are assumed to be C source files and are searched for C routine and macro definitions. Files with names ending in .y are assumed to be YACC source files. Files with names ending in .l are assumed to be LEX files. Others are first examined to see if they contain any Pascal or FORTRAN routine definitions; if not, they are processed again looking for C definitions.

The tag main is treated specially in C programs. The tag formed is created by prepending M to *filename*, with a trailing .c removed, if any, and leading pathname components also removed. This makes use of ctags practical in directories with more than one program.

The following options are available:

- -a Append output to an existing tags file.
- -B Use backward searching patterns (?...?).
- -F Use forward searching patterns (/.../) (default).
- -t Create tags for typedefs.
- -u Update the specified files in tags, that is, all references to them are deleted, and the new values are appended to the file. Beware: this option is implemented in a way which is rather slow; it is usually faster to simply rebuild the tags file.
- -v Produce on the standard output an index listing the function name, file name, and page number (assuming 64 line pages). Since the output will be sorted into lexicographic order, it may be desired to run the output through sort -f.
- -w Suppress warning diagnostics.
- -x Produce a list of object names, the line number and file name on which each is defined, as well as the text of that line and prints this on the standard output. This is a simple index which can be printed out as an offline readable function index.

FILES

`tags` output tags file

USAGE

The `-v` option is mainly used with `vgrind` which will be part of the optional BSD Compatibility Package.

SEE ALSO

`ex(1)`, `vgrind(1)`, `vi(1)`

NOTES

Recognition of `functions`, `subroutines` and `procedures` for FORTRAN and Pascal is done is a very simpleminded way. No attempt is made to deal with block structure; if you have two Pascal procedures in different blocks with the same name you lose.

The method of deciding whether to look for C or Pascal and FORTRAN functions is a hack.

`ctags` does not know about `#ifdefs`.

`ctags` should know about Pascal types. Relies on the input being well formed to detect typedefs. Use of `-tx` shows only the last line of typedefs.

NAME

cu – call another UNIX system

SYNOPSIS

cu [options] [destination]

DESCRIPTION

cu calls up another UNIX system, a terminal, or possibly a non-UNIX system. It manages an interactive conversation with possible transfers of files. It is convenient to think of cu as operating in two phases. The first phase is the connection phase in which the connection is established. cu then enters the conversation phase. The –d option is the only one that applies to both phases.

–d Causes diagnostic traces to be printed.

Connection Phase

cu uses the same mechanism that uucp does to establish a connection. This means that it will use the uucp control files **/etc/uucp/Devices** and **/etc/uucp/Systems**. This gives cu the ability to choose from several different media to establish the connection. The possible media include telephone lines, direct connections, and local area networks (LAN). The **Devices** file contains a list of media that are available on your system. The **Systems** file contains information for connecting to remote systems, but it is not generally readable.

The *destination* parameter from the command line is used to tell cu what system you wish to connect to. *destination* can be blank, a telephone number, a system name, or a LAN specific address. A telephone number is a string consisting of the tone dial characters (the digits 0 through 9, *, and #) plus the special characters = and –. The equal sign designates a secondary dial tone and the minus sign creates a 4 second delay. A system name is the name of any computer that uucp can call; the uuname command prints a list of these names. The documentation for your LAN will show the form of the LAN specific address.

If cu's default behavior is invoked (not using the –c or –l options), cu will use *destination* to determine which medium to use. If *destination* is a telephone number, cu will assume that you wish to use a telephone line and it will select an automatic call unit (ACU). If the *destination* is not a telephone number, then cu will assume that it is a system name. cu will follow the uucp calling mechanism and use the **Systems** and **Devices** files to obtain the best available connection. Since cu will choose a speed that is appropriate for the medium that it selects, you may not use the **–s** option when *destination* is a system name.

The –c and –l options modify this default behavior. –c is most often used to select a LAN by specifying a Type field from the Devices file. Here, *destination* is assumed to be a system name. If the connection attempt to system name fails, a connection will be attempted using *destination* as a LAN specific address. The –l option is used to specify a device associated with a direct connection. If the connection is truly a direct connection to the remote machine, then there is no need to specify a *destination*. This is the only case where a blank *destination* is allowed. On the other hand, there may be cases in which the specified device connects to a dialer, so it is valid to specify a telephone number as a *destination*. The –c and –l options should not be specified on the same command line.

cu accepts many options. The -c, -l, and -s options play a part in selecting the medium; the remaining options are used in configuring the line.

-s*speed* Specifies the transmission speed (300, 1200, 2400, 4800, 9600). The default value is "Any" speed which will depend on the order of the lines in the /etc/uucp/Devices file. Most modems are either 300, 1200, or 2400 baud. Directly connected lines may be set to a speed higher than 2400 baud.

-c*type* The first field in the Devices file is the "Type" field. The -c option forces cu to only use entries in the "Type" field that match the user specified *type*. The specified *type* is usually the name of a local area network.

-lline Specifies a device name to use as the communication line. This can be used to override the search that would otherwise take place for the first available line having the right speed. When the -l option is used without the -s option, the speed of a line is taken from the Devices file record in which line matches the second field (the Line field). When the -l and -s options are both used together, cu will search the Devices file to check if the requested speed for the requested line is available. If so, the connection will be made at the requested speed, otherwise, an error message will be printed and the call will not be made. In the general case where a specified device is a directly connected asynchronous line (e.g., /dev/term/*ab*), a telephone number (*telno*) is not required. The specified device need not be in the /dev directory. If the specified device is associated with an auto dialer, a telephone number must be provided. If *destination* is used with this option, it must be a telephone number.

-b*n* Forces *n* to be the number of bits processed on the line. *n* is either 7 or 8. This allows connection between systems with different character sizes. By default, the character size of the line is set to the same as the current local terminal.

-e Set an EVEN data parity. This option designates that EVEN parity is to be generated for data sent to the remote system.

-h Set communication mode to half-duplex. This option emulates the local echo(1) command in order to support calls to other computer systems that expect terminals to be set to half-duplex mode.

-n Request user prompt for telephone number. For added security, this option will prompt the user to provide the telephone number to be dialed, rather than taking it from the command line.

-o Set an ODD data parity. This option designates that ODD parity is to be generated for data sent to the remote system.

-t Used to dial a terminal which has been set to auto answer. Appropriate mapping of carriage-return to carriage-return-line-feed pairs is set.

Conversation Phase

After making the connection, **cu** runs as two processes: the *transmit* process reads data from the standard input and, except for lines beginning with ~, passes it to the remote system; the *receive* process accepts data from the remote system and, except for lines beginning with ~, passes it to the standard output. Normally, an automatic DC3/DC1 protocol is used to control input from the remote so the buffer is not overrun. Lines beginning with ~ have special meanings.

The *transmit* process interprets the following user initiated commands:

`~.`	terminate the conversation.
`~!`	escape to an interactive shell on the local system.
`~!`*cmd*...	run *cmd* on the local system (via `sh -c`).
`~$`*cmd*...	run *cmd* locally and send its output to the remote system.
`~%cd`	change the directory on the local system. Note: `~!cd` will cause the command to be run by a sub-shell, probably not what was intended.
`~%take` *from* [*to*]	copy file *from* (on the remote system) to file *to* on the local system. If *to* is omitted, the *from* argument is used in both places.
`~%put` *from* [*to*]	copy file *from* (on local system) to file *to* on remote system. If *to* is omitted, the *from* argument is used in both places.
`~~ line`	send the line `~ line` to the remote system.
`~%break`	transmit a **BREAK** to the remote system (which can also be specified as `~%b`).
`~%debug`	toggles the `-d` debugging option on or off (which can also be specified as `~%d`).
`~t`	prints the values of the termio structure variables for the user's terminal (useful for debugging).
`~l`	prints the values of the termio structure variables for the remote communication line (useful for debugging).
`~%ifc`	toggles between DC3/DC1 input control protocol and no input control. This is useful when the remote system does not respond properly to the DC3 and DC1 characters. (can also be specified as `~%nostop`).
`~%ofc`	toggles the output flow control setting. When enabled, outgoing data may be flow controlled by the remote host (can also be specified as `~%noostop`).
`~%divert`	allow/disallow unsolicited diversions. That is, diversions not specified by `~%take`.
`~%old`	allow/disallow old style syntax for received diversions.

The *receive* process normally copies data from the remote system to the standard output of the local system. It may also direct the output to local files.

The use of ~%put requires stty(1) and cat(1) on the remote side. It also requires that the current erase and kill characters on the remote system be identical to these current control characters on the local system. Backslashes are inserted at appropriate places.

The use of ~%take requires the existence of echo(1) and cat(1) on the remote system. Also, tabs mode (See *stty(1))* should be set on the remote system if tabs are to be copied without expansion to spaces.

When cu is used on system X to connect to system Y and subsequently used on system Y to connect to system Z, commands on system Y can be executed by using ~~. Executing a tilde command reminds the user of the local system uname. For example, uname can be executed on Z, X, and Y as follows:

```
uname
Z
~[X]!uname
X
~~[Y]!uname
Y
```

In general, ~ causes the command to be executed on the original machine. ~~ causes the command to be executed on the next machine in the chain.

EXAMPLES

To dial a system whose telephone number is 9 1 201 555 1234 using 1200 baud (where dialtone is expected after the 9):

```
cu -s1200 9=12015551234
```

If the speed is not specified, "Any" is the default value.

To login to a system that is on a Datakit VCS local area network, but which has not been defined by your administrator (i.e. is not entered in the /etc/uucp/Systems file(s)):

```
cu -c DK address
```

DK is the name of the Datakit local area network, and *address* is the Datakit address which is of the form, /area/exchange/machine.

To login to a system connected by a direct line:

```
cu -l /dev/term/XX
```

or

```
cu -l term/XX
```

To dial a system with a specific line and speed:

```
cu -s1200 -l term/XX
```

To dial a system using a specific line associated with an auto dialer:

```
cu -l culXX 9=12015551234
```

To use a system name:

```
cu systemname
```

FILES

/etc/uucp/Sysfiles
/etc/uucp/Systems
/etc/uucp/Devices
/var/spool/locks/*

SEE ALSO

`cat`(1), `ct`(1C), `echo`(1), `stty`(1), `uucp`(1C), `uname`(1), `uuname`(1).
System Administrator's Guide.

DIAGNOSTICS

Exit code is zero for normal exit, otherwise, one.

NOTES

The `cu` command does not do any integrity checking on data it transfers. Data fields with special `cu` characters may not be transmitted properly. Depending on the interconnection hardware, it may be necessary to use a `~.` to terminate the conversion, even if `stty 0` has been used. Non-printing characters are not dependably transmitted using either the `~%put` or `~%take` commands. `cu`, between an IMBR1 and a PENRIL modem, will not return a login prompt immediately upon connection. A carriage return will return the prompt.

`~%put` and `~%take` cannot be used over multiple links. Files must be moved one link at a time.

There is an artificial slowing of transmission by `cu` during the `~%put` operation so that loss of data is unlikely. Files transferred using `~%take` or `~%put` must contain a trailing newline, otherwise, the operation will hang. Entering a CTRL-d command usually clears the hang condition.

NAME

cut – cut out selected fields of each line of a file

SYNOPSIS

```
cut -clist [file ...]
cut -flist [-dchar] [-s] [file ...]
```

DESCRIPTION

Use `cut` to cut out columns from a table or fields from each line of a file; in data base parlance, it implements the projection of a relation. The fields as specified by *list* can be fixed length, i.e., character positions as on a punched card (-c option) or the length can vary from line to line and be marked with a field delimiter character like *tab* (`-f` option). `cut` can be used as a filter; if no files are given, the standard input is used. In addition, a file name of "–" explicitly refers to standard input.

The meanings of the options are:

list A comma-separated list of integer field numbers (in increasing order), with optional – to indicate ranges [e.g., `1,4,7`; `1-3,8`; `-5,10` (short for `1-5,10`); or `3-` (short for third through last field)].

-c*list* The *list* following `-c` (no space) specifies character positions (e.g., `-c1-72` would pass the first 72 characters of each line).

-f*list* The *list* following `-f` is a list of fields assumed to be separated in the file by a delimiter character (see `-d`); e.g., `-f1,7` copies the first and seventh field only. Lines with no field delimiters will be passed through intact (useful for table subheadings), unless `-s` is specified.

-d*char* The character following `-d` is the field delimiter (`-f` option only). Default is *tab*. Space or other characters with special meaning to the shell must be quoted.

`-s` Suppresses lines with no delimiter characters in case of `-f` option. Unless specified, lines with no delimiters will be passed through untouched.

Either the `-c` or `-f` option must be specified.

Use `grep`(1) to make horizontal "cuts" (by context) through a file, or `paste`(1) to put files together column-wise (i.e., horizontally). To reorder columns in a table, use `cut` and `paste`.

EXAMPLES

`cut -d: -f1,5 /etc/passwd` mapping of user IDs to names

``name=`who am i | cut -f1 -d" "` `` to set `name` to current login name.

DIAGNOSTICS

I `"ERROR: line too long"`
A line can have no more than 1023 characters or fields, or there is no new-line character.

`"ERROR: bad list for c/f option"`
Missing `-c` or `-f` option or incorrectly specified *list*. No error occurs if a line has fewer fields than the *list* calls for.

"ERROR: no fields"
The *list* is empty.

"ERROR: no delimeter"
Missing *char* on -d option.

"ERROR: cannot handle multiple adjacent backspaces"
Adjacent backspaces cannot be processed correctly.

"WARNING: cannot open <filename>"
Either *filename* cannot be read or does not exist. If multiple filenames are present, prcessing continues.

SEE ALSO

grep(1), paste(1).

NAME

date − print and set the date

SYNOPSIS

date [−u] [+*format*]
date [−a [−] *sss.fff*] [−u] [[*mmdd*] *HHMM* | *mmddHHMM* [*cc*] *yy*]

DESCRIPTION

If no argument is given, or if the argument begins with +, the current date and time are printed. Otherwise, the current date is set (only by super-user).

−a [−] *sss.fff*
Slowly adjust the time by *sss.fff* seconds (*fff* represents fractions of a second). This adjustment can be positive or negative. The system's clock will be sped up or slowed down until it has drifted by the number of seconds specified.

−u Display (or set) the date in Greenwich Mean Time (GMT—universal time), bypassing the normal conversion to (or from) local time.

mm is the month number

dd is the day number in the month

HH is the hour number (24 hour system)

MM is the minute number

cc is the century minus one

yy is the last 2 digits of the year number

The month, day, year, and century may be omitted; the current values are C|pplied as defaults. For example:

```
date 10080045
```

sets the date to Oct 8, 12:45 AM. The current year is the default because no year is supplied. The system operates in GMT. date takes care of the conversion to and from local standard and daylight time. Only the super-user may change the date. After successfully setting the date and time, date displays the new date according to the default format. The date command uses TZ to determine the correct time zone information (see environ(5)).

+*format* If the argument begins with +, the output of date is under the control of the user. Each Field Descriptor, described below, is preceded by % and is replaced in the output by its corresponding value. A single % is encoded by %%. All other characters are copied to the output without change. The string is always terminated with a new-line character. If the argument contains embedded blanks it must be quoted (see the EXAMPLE section).

Specifications of native language translations of month and weekday names are supported. The month and weekday names used for a language are based on the locale specified by the environment variables LC_TIME and LANG (see environ(5)).

The month and weekday names used for a language are taken from a file whose format is specified in `strftime`(4). This file also defines country-specific date and time formats such as `%c`, which specifies the default date format. The following form is the default for `%c`:

`%a %b %e %T %Z %Y`
e.g., Fri Dec 23 10:10:42 EST 1988

Field Descriptors (must be preceded by a `%`):

- `a` abbreviated weekday name
- `A` full weekday name
- `b` abbreviated month name
- `B` full month name
- `c` country-specific date and time format
- `d` day of month – 01 to 31
- `D` date as `%m/%d/%y`
- `e` day of month – 1 to 31 (single digits are preceded by a blank)
- `h` abbreviated month name (alias for `%b`)
- `H` hour – 00 to 23
- `I` hour – 01 to 12
- `j` day of year – 001 to 366
- `m` month of year – 01 to 12
- `M` minute – 00 to 59
- `n` insert a new-line character
- `p` string containing ante-meridiem or post-meridiem indicator (by default, AM or PM)
- `r` time as `%I:%M:%S %p`
- `R` time as `%H:%M`
- `S` second – 00 to 61, allows for leap seconds
- `t` insert a tab character
- `T` time as `%H:%M:%S`
- `U` week number of year (Sunday as the first day of the week) – 00 to 53
- `w` day of week – Sunday = 0
- `W` week number of year (Monday as the first day of the week) – 00 to 53
- `x` Country-specific date format
- `X` Country-specific time format
- `y` year within century – 00 to 99
- `Y` year as *ccyy* (4 digits)
- `Z` timezone name

EXAMPLE

The command

```
date '+DATE: %m/%d/%y%nTIME: %H:%M:%S'
```

generates as output:

```
DATE: 08/01/76
TIME: 14:45:05
```

DIAGNOSTICS

`No permission`	You are not the super-user and you try to change the date.
`bad conversion`	The date set is syntactically incorrect.

NOTES

Should you need to change the date while the system is running multi-user, use the **datetime** command of **sysadm**(1M).

If you attempt to set the current date to one of the dates that the standard and alternate time zones change (for example, the date that daylight time is starting or ending), and you attempt to set the time to a time in the interval between the end of standard time and the beginning of the alternate time (or the end of the alternate time and the beginning of standard time), the results are unpredictable.

SEE ALSO

sysadm(1M), **strftime**(4), **environ**(5) in the *System Administrator's Reference Manual.*

NAME

dc – desk calculator

SYNOPSIS

dc [*file*]

DESCRIPTION

dc is an arbitrary precision arithmetic package. Ordinarily it operates on decimal integers, but one may specify an input base, output base, and a number of fractional digits to be maintained. [bc is a preprocessor for dc that provides infix notation and a C-like syntax that implements functions. bc also provides reasonable control structures for programs. See bc(1).] The overall structure of dc is a stacking (reverse Polish) calculator. If an argument is given, input is taken from that file until its end, then from the standard input. The following constructions are recognized:

number
: The value of the number is pushed on the stack. A number is an unbroken string of the digits 0–9. It may be preceded by an underscore (_) to input a negative number. Numbers may contain decimal points.

+ – / * % ^
: The top two values on the stack are added (+), subtracted (–), multiplied (*), divided (/), remaindered (%), or exponentiated (^). The two entries are popped off the stack; the result is pushed on the stack in their place. Any fractional part of an exponent is ignored.

s*x* The top of the stack is popped and stored into a register named *x*, where *x* may be any character. If the s is capitalized, *x* is treated as a stack and the value is pushed on it.

l*x* The value in register *x* is pushed on the stack. The register *x* is not altered. All registers start with zero value. If the l is capitalized, register *x* is treated as a stack and its top value is popped onto the main stack.

d The top value on the stack is duplicated.

p The top value on the stack is printed. The top value remains unchanged.

P Interprets the top of the stack as an ASCII string, removes it, and prints it.

f All values on the stack are printed.

q Exits the program. If executing a string, the recursion level is popped by two.

Q Exits the program. The top value on the stack is popped and the string execution level is popped by that value.

x Treats the top element of the stack as a character string and executes it as a string of dc commands.

X Replaces the number on the top of the stack with its scale factor.

[...]
: Puts the bracketed ASCII string onto the top of the stack.

<*x* >*x* =*x*
: The top two elements of the stack are popped and compared. Register *x* is evaluated if they obey the stated relation.

`v` Replaces the top element on the stack by its square root. Any existing fractional part of the argument is taken into account, but otherwise the scale factor is ignored.

`!` Interprets the rest of the line as a UNIX system command.

`c` All values on the stack are popped.

`i` The top value on the stack is popped and used as the number radix for further input.

`I` Pushes the input base on the top of the stack.

`o` The top value on the stack is popped and used as the number radix for further output.

`O` Pushes the output base on the top of the stack.

`k` The top of the stack is popped, and that value is used as a non-negative scale factor: the appropriate number of places are printed on output, and maintained during multiplication, division, and exponentiation. The interaction of scale factor, input base, and output base will be reasonable if all are changed together.

`z` The stack level is pushed onto the stack.

`Z` Replaces the number on the top of the stack with its length.

`?` A line of input is taken from the input source (usually the terminal) and executed.

`; :` are used by bc(1) for array operations.

EXAMPLE

This example prints the first ten values of n!:

```
[la1+dsa*pla10>y]sy
0sa1
lyx
```

SEE ALSO

bc(1).

DIAGNOSTICS

`x is unimplemented`: *x* is an octal number.

`stack empty`: not enough elements on the stack to do what was asked.

`Out of space`: the free list is exhausted (too many digits).

`Out of headers`: too many numbers being kept around.

`Out of pushdown`: too many items on the stack.

`Nesting Depth`: too many levels of nested execution.

NAME

dd – convert and copy a file

SYNOPSIS

dd [option=value] ...

DESCRIPTION

dd copies the specified input file to the specified output with possible conversions. The standard input and output are used by default. The input and output block sizes may be specified to take advantage of raw physical I/O.

option	**values**
`if=`*file*	input file name; standard input is default
`of=`*file*	output file name; standard output is default
`ibs=`*n*	input block size *n* bytes (default 512)
`obs=`*n*	output block size *n* bytes (default 512)
`bs=`*n*	set both input and output block size, superseding *ibs* and *obs*; also, if no conversion is specified, preserve the input block size instead of packing short blocks into the output buffer (this is particularly efficient since no in-core copy need be done)
`cbs=`*n*	conversion buffer size (logical record length)
`files=`*n*	copy and concatenate *n* input files before terminating (makes sense only where input is a magnetic tape or similar device)
`skip=`*n*	skip *n* input blocks before starting copy (appropriate for magnetic tape, where *iseek* is undefined)
`iseek=`*n*	seek *n* blocks from beginning of input file before copying (appropriate for disk files, where *skip* can be incredibly slow)
`oseek=`*n*	seek *n* blocks from beginning of output file before copying
`seek=`*n*	identical to *oseek*, retained for backward compatibility
`count=`*n*	copy only *n* input blocks
`conv=ascii`	convert EBCDIC to ASCII
`ebcdic`	convert ASCII to EBCDIC
`ibm`	slightly different map of ASCII to EBCDIC
`block`	convert new-line terminated ASCII records to fixed length
`unblock`	convert fixed length ASCII records to new-line terminated records
`lcase`	map alphabetics to lower case
`ucase`	map alphabetics to upper case
`swab`	swap every pair of bytes
`noerror`	do not stop processing on an error (limit of 5 consecutive errors)
`sync`	pad every input block to *ibs*
`. . . , . . .`	several comma-separated conversions

Where sizes are specified, a number of bytes is expected. A number may end with `k`, `b`, or `w` to specify multiplication by 1024, 512, or 2, respectively; a pair of numbers may be separated by `x` to indicate multiplication.

cbs is used only if `ascii`, *unblock*, *ebcdic*, *ibm*, or *block* conversion is specified. In the first two cases, *cbs* characters are copied into the conversion buffer, any specified character mapping is done, trailing blanks are trimmed and a new-line is added before sending the line to the output. In the latter three cases, characters are read into the conversion buffer and blanks are added to make up an output record of size *cbs*. If *cbs* is unspecified or zero, the `ascii`, *ebcdic*, and *ibm* options convert the character set without changing the block structure of the input file; the *unblock* and *block* options become a simple file copy.

After completion, **dd** reports the number of whole and partial input and output blocks.

EXAMPLE

This command will read an EBCDIC tape blocked ten 80-byte EBCDIC card images per tape block into the ASCII file *x*:

```
dd  if=/dev/rmt/0h  of=x  ibs=800  obs=8k  cbs=80  conv=ascii,lcase
```

Note the use of raw magnetic tape. **dd** is especially suited to I/O on the raw physical devices because it allows reading and writing in arbitrary block sizes.

SEE ALSO

cp(1)

NOTES

Do not use **dd** to copy files between filesystems having different block sizes.

Using a blocked device to copy a file will result in extra nulls being added to the file to pad the final block to the block boundary.

DIAGNOSTICS

f+p records in(out) numbers of full and partial blocks read(written)

NAME

deroff – remove nroff/troff, tbl, and eqn constructs

SYNOPSIS

deroff [-m *x*] [-w] [*files*]

DESCRIPTION

deroff reads each of the *files* in sequence and removes all troff(1) requests, macro calls, backslash constructs, eqn(1) constructs (between .EQ and .EN lines, and between delimiters), and tbl(1) descriptions, perhaps replacing them with white space (blanks and blank lines), and writes the remainder of the file on the standard output.

Note: troff(1), nroff(1), and eqn(1) are not part of this UNIX system release.

deroff follows chains of included files (.so and .nx troff commands); if a file has already been included, a .so naming that file is ignored and a .nx naming that file terminates execution. If no input file is given, deroff reads the standard input.

The -m option may be followed by an m, s, or l. The -mm option causes the macros to be interpreted so that only running text is output (i.e., no text from macro lines.) The -ml option forces the -mm option and also causes deletion of lists associated with the mm macros.

If the -w option is given, the output is a word list, one "word" per line, with all other characters deleted. Otherwise, the output follows the original, with the deletions mentioned above. In text, a "word" is any string that *contains* at least two letters and is composed of letters, digits, ampersands (&), and apostrophes ('); in a macro call, however, a "word" is a string that *begins* with at least two letters and contains a total of at least three letters. Delimiters are any characters other than letters, digits, apostrophes, and ampersands. Trailing apostrophes and ampersands are removed from "words."

SEE ALSO

eqn(1), nroff(1), tbl(1), troff(1) in the *DOCUMENTER'S WORKBENCH Software Technical Discussion and Reference Manual.*

NOTES

deroff is not a complete troff interpreter, so it can be confused by subtle constructs. Most such errors result in too much rather than too little output.

The -ml option does not handle nested lists correctly.

NAME

df (generic) – report number of free disk blocks and files

SYNOPSIS

df [-F *FSType*] [-begklntV] [*current_options*] [-o *specific_options*] [*directory* | *special* | *resource*...]

DESCRIPTION

df prints the allocation portions of the generic superblock for mounted or unmounted file systems, directories or mounted resources. *directory* represents a valid directory name. If *directory* is specified df reports on the device that contains the *directory*. *special* represents a special device (e.g., /dev/dsk/0s1). *resource* is an RFS/NFS resource name. If arguments to df are pathnames, df produces a report on the file system containing the named file.

current_options are options supported by the s5-specific module of df. Other FSTypes do not necessarily support these options. *specific_options* indicate suboptions specified in a comma-separated list of suboptions and/or keyword-attribute pairs for interpretation by the *FSType*-specific module of the command.

The generic options are:

-F Specify the *FSType* on which to operate. This is only needed if the file system is unmounted. The *FSType* should be specified here or are determined from /etc/vfstab by matching the *mount_point*, *special*, or *resource* with an entry in the table.

-b Print only the number of kilobytes free.

-e Print only the number of files free.

-g Print the entire statvfs structure. Used only for mounted file systems. Can not be used with *current_options* or with the -o option. This option will override the -b, -e, -k, -n, and -t options.

-k Print allocation in kilobytes. This option should be invoked by itself because its output format is different from that of the other options.

-l Report on local file systems only. Used only for mounted file systems. Can not be used with *current_options* or with the -o option.

-n Print only the *FSType* name. Invoked with no arguments this option prints a list of mounted file system types. Used only for mounted file systems. Can not be used with *current_options* or with the -o option.

-t Print full listings with totals. This option will override the -b, -e, and -n options.

-V Echo the complete command line, but do not execute the command. The command line is generated by using the options and arguments provided by the user and adding to them information derived from /etc/mnttab or /etc/vfstab. This option should be used to verify and validate the command line.

-o Specify FSType-specific options.

`-v` Reports percent of blocks used as well as the number of blocks used and free.

If no arguments or options are specified, the free space on all local and remotely mounted file systems is printed.

NOTES

The `-F` option is intended for use with unmounted file systems.

This command may not be supported for all FSTypes.

FILES

`/dev/dsk/*`	
`/etc/mnttab`	mount table
`/etc/vfstab`	list of default parameters for each file system

SEE ALSO

`mount`(1M), `mnttab`(4), `vfstab`(4).
`statvfs`(2) in the *Programmer's Reference Manual*.
Manual pages for the FSType-specific modules of **df**.

NAME

`diff` – differential file comparator

SYNOPSIS

`diff` [`-bitw`] [`-c` | `-e` | `-f` | `-h` | `-n`] *filename1 filename2*
`diff` [`-bitw`] [`-C` *number*] *filename1 filename2*
`diff` [`-bitw`] [`-D` *string*] *filename1 filename2*
`diff` [`-bitw`] [`-c` | `-e` | `-f` | `-h` | `-n`] [`-l`] [`-r`] [`-s`] [`-S` *name*] *directory1 directory2*

DESCRIPTION

`diff` tells what lines must be changed in two files to bring them into agreement. If *filename1* (*filename2*) is –, the standard input is used. If *filename1* (*filename2*) is a directory, then a file in that directory with the name *filename2* (*filename1*) is used. The normal output contains lines of these forms:

n1 a *n3,n4*
n1,n2 d *n3*
n1,n2 c *n3,n4*

These lines resemble `ed` commands to convert *filename1* into *filename2*. The numbers after the letters pertain to *filename2*. In fact, by exchanging `a` for `d` and reading backward one may ascertain equally how to convert *filename2* into *filename1*. As in `ed`, identical pairs, where *n1* = *n2* or *n3* = *n4*, are abbreviated as a single number.

Following each of these lines come all the lines that are affected in the first file flagged by <, then all the lines that are affected in the second file flagged by >.

`-b` Ignores trailing blanks (spaces and tabs) and treats other strings of blanks as equivalent.

`-i` Ignores the case of letters; for example, 'A' will compare equal to 'a'.

`-t` Expands TAB characters in output lines. Normal or `-c` output adds character(s) to the front of each line that may adversely affect the indentation of the original source lines and make the output lines difficult to interpret. This option will preserve the original source's indentation.

`-w` Ignores all blanks (SPACE and TAB characters) and treats all other strings of blanks as equivalent; for example, '`if ( a == b )`' will compare equal to '`if(a==b)`'.

The following options are mutually exclusive:

`-c` Produces a listing of differences with three lines of context. With this option output format is modified slightly: output begins with identification of the files involved and their creation dates, then each change is separated by a line with a dozen *'s. The lines removed from *filename1* are marked with '—'; those added to *filename2* are marked '+'. Lines that are changed from one file to the other are marked in both files with '!'.

–C *number*
: Produces a listing of differences identical to that produced by –c with *number* lines of context.

–e
: Produces a script of *a*, *c*, and *d* commands for the editor ed, which will recreate *filename2* from *filename1*. In connection with –e, the following shell program may help maintain multiple versions of a file. Only an ancestral file ($1) and a chain of version-to-version ed scripts ($2,$3,...) made by diff need be on hand. A "latest version" appears on the standard output.

```
(shift; cat $*; echo '1,$p') | ed - $1
```

Except in rare circumstances, diff finds a smallest sufficient set of file differences.

–f
: Produces a similar script, not useful with ed, in the opposite order.

–h
: Does a fast, half-hearted job. It works only when changed stretches are short and well separated, but does work on files of unlimited length. Options –e and –f are unavailable with –h.

–n
: Produces a script similar to –e, but in the opposite order and with a count of changed lines on each insert or delete command.

–D *string*
: Creates a merged version of *filename1* and *filename2* with C preprocessor controls included so that a compilation of the result without defining *string* is equivalent to compiling *filename1*, while defining *string* will yield *filename2*.

The following options are used for comparing directories:

–l
: Produce output in long format. Before the diff, each text file is piped through pr(1) to paginate it. Other differences are remembered and summarized after all text file differences are reported.

–r
: Applies diff recursively to common subdirectories encountered.

–s
: Reports files that are the identical; these would not otherwise be mentioned.

–S *name*
: Starts a directory diff in the middle, beginning with the file *name*.

FILES

/tmp/d?????
/usr/lib/diffh for –h
/usr/bin/pr

SEE ALSO

bdiff(1), cmp(1), comm(1), ed(1), pr(1).

DIAGNOSTICS

Exit status is 0 for no differences, 1 for some differences, 2 for trouble.

NOTES

Editing scripts produced under the `-e` or `-f` option are naive about creating lines consisting of a single period (.).

`Missing newline at end of file X`
indicates that the last line of file X did not have a new-line. If the lines are different, they will be flagged and output; although the output will seem to indicate they are the same.

NAME

`diff3` – 3-way differential file comparison

SYNOPSIS

`diff3` [`-exEX3`] *file1 file2 file3*

DESCRIPTION

`diff3` compares three versions of a file, and publishes disagreeing ranges of text flagged with these codes:

====	all three files differ
====1	*file1* is different
====2	*file2* is different
====3	*file3* is different

The type of change suffered in converting a given range of a given file to some other is indicated in one of these ways:

f : *n1* a	Text is to be appended after line number *n1* in file *f*, where *f* = 1, 2, or 3.
f : *n1* , *n2* c	Text is to be changed in the range line *n1* to line *n2*. If *n1* = *n2*, the range may be abbreviated to *n1*.

The original contents of the range follows immediately after a c indication. When the contents of two files are identical, the contents of the lower-numbered file is suppressed.

`-e` Produce a script for the editor ed(1) that will incorporate into *file1* all changes between *file2* and *file3*, i.e., the changes that normally would be flagged ==== and ====3.

`-x` Produce a script to incorporate only changes flagged ====.

`-3` Produce a script to incorporate only changes flagged ====3.

`-E` Produce a script that will incorporate all changes between *file2* and *file3*, but treat overlapping changes (that is, changes that would be flagged with ==== in the normal listing) differently. The overlapping lines from both files will be inserted by the edit script, bracketed by <<<<<< and >>>>>> lines.

`-X` Produce a script that will incorporate only changes flagged ====, but treat these changes in the manner of the `-E` option.

The following command will apply the resulting script to *file1*.

(cat script; echo '1,$p') | ed – *file1*

FILES

`/tmp/d3*`
`/usr/lib/diff3prog`

SEE ALSO

`diff`(1).

NOTES

Text lines that consist of a single . will defeat **−e**.
Files longer than 64K bytes will not work.

NAME

`dircmp` – directory comparison

SYNOPSIS

`dircmp` [`-d`] [`-s`] [`-w`*n*] *dir1 dir2*

DESCRIPTION

`dircmp` examines *dir1* and *dir2* and generates various tabulated information about the contents of the directories. Listings of files that are unique to each directory are generated for all the options. If no option is entered, a list is output indicating whether the file names common to both directories have the same contents.

`-d` Compare the contents of files with the same name in both directories and output a list telling what must be changed in the two files to bring them into agreement. The list format is described in `diff`(1).

`-s` Suppress messages about identical files.

`-w`*n* Change the width of the output line to *n* characters. The default width is 72.

SEE ALSO

`cmp`(1), `diff`(1).

NAME

dos: doscat, doscp, dosdir, dosformat, dosmkdir, dosls, dosrm, dosrmdir – access and manipulate DOS files

SYNOPSIS

doscat [-r | -m] *file* ...

doscp [-r | -m] *file1 file2*

doscp [-r | -m] *file ... directory*

dosdir *directory*

dosformat [-fqv] *drive*

dosls *directory* ...

dosmkdir *directory* ...

dosrm *file* ...

dosrmdir *directory* ...

DESCRIPTION

The dos commands allow access to files and directories on a DOS hard disk partition or diskette. The DOS partition must be bootable, although not active.

Below is a description of the dos commands:

doscat — Copies one or more DOS files to the standard output. If -r is given, the files are copied without newline conversions. If -m is given, the files are copied with newline conversions.

doscp — Copies files from/to a DOS diskette or a DOS hard disk partition to/from a UNIX file system. If *file1* and *file2* are given, *file1* is copied to *file2*. If a *directory* is given, one or more *files* are copied to that directory. If -r is given, the files are copied without new line conversions. If -m is given, the files are copied with newline conversions.

dosdir — Lists DOS files in the standard DOS style directory format. (See the DOS DIR command.)

dosformat — Creates a DOS 2.0 formatted diskette. It cannot be used to format a hard disk partition. The drive may be specified in either DOS drive convention, using the default file /etc/default/msdos, or using the UNIX special file name. The -f option suppresses the interactive feature. The -q (quiet) option is used to suppress information normally displayed during dosformat, but it does not suppress the interactive feature. The -v option prompts the user for a volume label after the diskette has been formatted. The maximum size of the volume label is 11 characters.

dosls — Lists DOS directories and files in a UNIX system style format [see ls(1)].

`dosrm`	Removes DOS files.
`dosmkdir`	Creates DOS directories.
`dosrmdir`	Deletes DOS directories.

The *file* and *directory* arguments for DOS files and directories have the form:

device:*name*

where *device* is a UNIX system path name for the special device file containing the DOS disk, and *name* is a path name to a file or directory on the DOS disk. The two components are separated by a colon (:). For example, the argument:

`/dev/rdsk/f0t:/src/file.c`

specifies the DOS file `file.asm` in the directory `/src` on diskette `/dev/rdsk/fd0t`. Note that slashes (and not backslashes) are used as file name separators for DOS path names. Arguments without a *device*: are assumed to be UNIX files.

For convenience, the user-configurable default file `/etc/default/msdos` can define DOS drive names to be used in place of the special device file path names. It may contain the following lines:

```
A=/dev/rdsk/f0t
C=/dev/rdsk/f1t
D=/dev/rdsk/0s5
```

The drive letter "`A`" may be used in place of special device file path name `/dev/rdsk/f0t` when referencing DOS files (see "Examples" below). The drive letter "`B`" or "`D`" refer to the DOS partition on the first or second hard disk.

The commands operate on the following types of disks:

DOS partitions on a hard disk
5-1/4 inch DOS
3-1/2 inch DOS
8, 9, 15, or 18 sectors per track
40 tracks per side
1 or 2 sides
DOS versions 1.0, 2.0, or 3.0

In the case of `doscp`, certain name conversions can be performed when copying a UNIX system file. File names with a base name longer than eight characters are truncated. Filename extensions (the part of the name following the separating period) longer than three characters are truncated. For example, the file 123456789.12345 becomes 12345678.123. A message informs the user that the name has been changed and the altered name is displayed. File names containing illegal DOS characters are stripped when writing to the DOS format. A message informs the user that characters have been removed and displays the name as written.

All DOS text files use a carriage-return/linefeed combination, CR-LF, to indicate a newline. UNIX system text files use a single newline LF character. When the `doscat` and `doscp` commands transfer DOS text files to UNIX system text files, they automatically strip the CR. When text files are transferred to DOS, the commands insert a CR before each LF character.

Under some circumstances, the automatic newline conversions do not occur. The -m option may be used to ensure the newline conversion. The -r option can be used to override the automatic conversion and force the command to perform a true byte copy regardless of file type.

EXAMPLES

```
doscat /dev/rdsk/f0t:tmp/output.1
doscat /tmp/f1 /tmp/f2/A:prog/output.1

dosdir /dev/rdsk/f0t:/prog
dosdir /D:/prog

doscp /mine/file.out/dev/rdsk/f0t:/mine/file.2
doscp /tmp/f1 /tmp/f2 D:

dosformat /dev/rdsk/f0d8dt

dosls /dev/rdsk:/src
dosls B:

dosmkdir /dev/fd0:/usr/docs

dosrm /dev/rdsk:/docs/memo.txt
dosrm /A:/docs/memo1.txt

dosrmdir /dev/rdsk:/usr/docs
```

FILES

/etc/default/msdos	Default information
/dev/rdsk/f0t	Floppy disk devices
/dev/rdsk/0s5	Hard disk devices

SEE ALSO

assign(C), dtype(C).
See your MS-DOS Documentation.

NOTES

Problems may occur when you type

doscp -m a:*DOS_file UNIX_file*

or

doscp -m *UNIX_file* a:*DOS _file*.

The space for the carriage returns added to each line is not allocated and the final part of the file is not written out to the DOS file system. Reading the file back with:

doscp -m a:*DOS_file UNIX_file*

results in an error message of `Sector not found`.

This will be fixed in the next release of the command.

Workaround: Use the following procedure:

doscp -m *UNIX_file UNIX_tmp_file*
doscp *UNIX_tmp_file* a:*DOS_file*

The file can be read without error with the normal command/procedure:

`doscp -m a:`*DOS_file UNIX_file*

It is not possible to refer to DOS directories with wild card specifications. The programs mentioned above cooperate among themselves so no two programs will access the same DOS disk. If a process attempts to access a device almost in use, it displays the error message, "`Device Busy`", and exits with and exit code of 1.

The device argument to dosformat must be specific. For example, use `/dev/rdsk/f0d9dt` not `/dev/rdsk/f0t` or `t:`.

NAME

du – summarize disk usage

SYNOPSIS

du [-sar] [*name* ...]

DESCRIPTION

The du command reports the number of blocks contained in all files and (recursively) directories within each directory and file specified. The block count includes the indirect blocks of the file. If no *names* are given, the current directory is used.

The optional arguments are as follows:

-s causes only the grand total (for each of the specified *names*) to be given.

-a causes an output line to be generated for each file.

If neither -s or -a is specified, an output line is generated for each directory only.

-r will cause du to generate messages about directories that cannot be be read, files that cannot be opened, etc., rather than being silent (the default).

A file with two or more links is only counted once.

NOTES

If the -a option is not used, non-directories given as arguments are not listed.

If there are links between files in different directories where the directories are on separate branches of the file system hierarchy, du will count the excess files more than once.

Files with holes in them will get an incorrect block count.

SEE ALSO

The "File System Administration" chapter in the *System Administrator's Guide*.

NAME

echo − echo arguments

SYNOPSIS

echo [*arg*] ...
echo [−n] [*arg*]

DESCRIPTION

echo writes its arguments separated by blanks and terminated by a new-line on the standard output.

The `/usr/bin/sh` version understands the following C-like escape conventions; beware of conflicts with the shell's use of \:

`\b`	backspace
`\c`	print line without new-line
`\f`	form-feed
`\n`	new-line
`\r`	carriage return
`\t`	tab
`\v`	vertical tab
`\\`	backslash
`\0`*n*	where *n* is the 8-bit character whose ASCII code is the 1-, 2- or 3-digit octal number representing that character.

The following option is available to `/usr/bin/sh` users only if `/usr/ucb` precedes `/usr/bin` in the user's PATH. It is available to `/usr/csh` users, regardless of PATH:

−n Do not add the newline to the output.

echo is useful for producing diagnostics in command files, for sending known data into a pipe, and for displaying the contents of environment variables.

SEE ALSO

sh(1).

NOTES

The −n option is a transition aid for BSD applications, and may not be supported in future releases.

When representing an 8-bit character by using the escape convention `\0`*n*, the *n* must **always** be preceded by the digit zero (0).

For example, typing: echo `'WARNING:\07'` will print the phrase `WARNING:` and sound the "bell" on your terminal. The use of single (or double) quotes (or two backslashes) is required to protect the "\" that precedes the "07".

Following the `\0`, up to three digits are used in constructing the octal output character. If, following the `\0`*n*, you want to echo additional digits that are not part of the octal representation, you must use the full 3-digit *n*. For example, if you want to echo "ESC 7" you must use the three digits "033" rather than just the two digits "33" after the `\0`.

2 digits	Incorrect:	`echo "\0337"   | od -xc`	
	produces:	`df0a`	(hex)
		`337`	(ascii)
3 digits	Correct:	`echo "\00337" | od -xc`	
	produces:	`1b37 0a00`	(hex)
		`033 7`	(ascii)

For the octal equivalents of each character, see ascii(5), in the *System Administrator's Reference Manual.*

NAME

ed, red – text editor

SYNOPSIS

ed [–s] [–p *string*] [–x] [–C] [*file*]

red [–s] [–p *string*] [–x] [–C] [*file*]

DESCRIPTION

ed is the standard text editor. If the *file* argument is given, ed simulates an e command (see below) on the named file; that is to say, the file is read into ed's buffer so that it can be edited.

–s Suppresses the printing of character counts by e, r, and w commands, of diagnostics from e and q commands, and of the ! prompt after a !*shell command*.

–p Allows the user to specify a prompt string.

–x Encryption option; when used, ed simulates an X command and prompts the user for a key. This key is used to encrypt and decrypt text using the algorithm of crypt(1). The X command makes an educated guess to determine whether text read in is encrypted or not. The temporary buffer file is encrypted also, using a transformed version of the key typed in for the –x option. See crypt(1). Also, see the NOTES section at the end of this manual page.

–C Encryption option; the same as the –x option, except that ed simulates a C command. The C command is like the X command, except that all text read in is assumed to have been encrypted.

ed operates on a copy of the file it is editing; changes made to the copy have no effect on the file until a w (write) command is given. The copy of the text being edited resides in a temporary file called the *buffer*. There is only one buffer.

red is a restricted version of ed. It will only allow editing of files in the current directory. It prohibits executing shell commands via !*shell command*. Attempts to bypass these restrictions result in an error message (*restricted shell*).

Both ed and red support the fspec(4) formatting capability. After including a format specification as the first line of *file* and invoking ed with your terminal in stty –tabs or stty tab3 mode [see stty(1)], the specified tab stops will automatically be used when scanning *file*. For example, if the first line of a file contained:

```
<:t5,10,15 s72:>
```

tab stops would be set at columns 5, 10, and 15, and a maximum line length of 72 would be imposed. NOTE: when you are entering text into the file, this format is not in effect; instead, because of being in stty –tabs or stty tab3 mode, tabs are expanded to every eighth column.

Commands to ed have a simple and regular structure: zero, one, or two *addresses* followed by a single-character *command*, possibly followed by parameters to that command. These addresses specify one or more lines in the buffer. Every command that requires addresses has default addresses, so that the addresses can very often be omitted.

In general, only one command may appear on a line. Certain commands allow the input of text. This text is placed in the appropriate place in the buffer. While ed is accepting text, it is said to be in *input mode*. In this mode, *no* commands are recognized; all input is merely collected. Leave input mode by typing a period (.) at the beginning of a line, followed immediately by a carriage return.

ed supports a limited form of *regular expression* notation; regular expressions are used in addresses to specify lines and in some commands (e.g., **s**) to specify portions of a line that are to be substituted. A regular expression (RE) specifies a set of character strings. A member of this set of strings is said to be *matched* by the RE. The REs allowed by ed are constructed as follows:

The following *one-character RE*s match a *single* character:

1.1 An ordinary character (*not* one of those discussed in 1.2 below) is a one-character RE that matches itself.

1.2 A backslash (\) followed by any special character is a one-character RE that matches the special character itself. The special characters are:

   a. ., *, [, and \ (period, asterisk, left square bracket, and backslash, respectively), which are always special, *except* when they appear within square brackets ([ ] ; see 1.4 below).

   b. ^ (caret or circumflex), which is special at the *beginning* of an *entire* RE (see 4.1 and 4.3 below), or when it immediately follows the left of a pair of square brackets ([ ]) (see 1.4 below).

   c. $ (dollar sign), which is special at the end of an *entire* RE (see 4.2 below).

   d. The character used to bound (i.e., delimit) an entire RE, which is special for that RE (for example, see how slash (/) is used in the g command, below.)

1.3 A period (.) is a one-character RE that matches any character except new-line.

1.4 A non-empty string of characters enclosed in square brackets ([ ]) is a one-character RE that matches *any one* character in that string. If, however, the first character of the string is a circumflex (^), the one-character RE matches any character *except* new-line and the remaining characters in the string. The ^ has this special meaning *only* if it occurs first in the string. The minus (–) may be used to indicate a range of consecutive characters; for example, [0-9] is equivalent to [0123456789]. The - loses this special meaning if it occurs first (after an initial ^, if any) or last in the string. The right square bracket (]) does not terminate such a string when it is the first character within it (after an initial ^, if any); e.g., [ ]a-f] matches either a right square bracket (]) or one of the ASCII letters a through f inclusive. The four characters listed in 1.2.a above stand for themselves within such a string of characters.

The following rules may be used to construct *RE*s from one-character REs:

2.1 A one-character RE is a RE that matches whatever the one-character RE matches.

2.2 A one-character RE followed by an asterisk (*) is a RE that matches *zero* or more occurrences of the one-character RE. If there is any choice, the longest leftmost string that permits a match is chosen.

2.3 A one-character RE followed by \{*m*\}, \{*m*,\}, or \{*m*,*n*\} is a RE that matches a *range* of occurrences of the one-character RE. The values of *m* and *n* must be non-negative integers less than 256; \{*m*\} matches *exactly* *m* occurrences; \{*m*,\} matches *at least* *m* occurrences; \{*m*,*n*\} matches *any number* of occurrences *between* *m* and *n* inclusive. Whenever a choice exists, the RE matches as many occurrences as possible.

2.4 The concatenation of REs is a RE that matches the concatenation of the strings matched by each component of the RE.

2.5 A RE enclosed between the character sequences \(and \) is a RE that matches whatever the unadorned RE matches.

2.6 The expression *n* matches the same string of characters as was matched by an expression enclosed between \(and \) *earlier* in the same RE. Here *n* is a digit; the sub-expression specified is that beginning with the *n*-th occurrence of \(counting from the left. For example, the expression ^\(.*\)\1$ matches a line consisting of two repeated appearances of the same string.

A RE may be constrained to match words.

3.1 \< constrains a RE to match the beginning of a string or to follow a character that is not a digit, underscore, or letter. The first character matching the RE must be a digit, underscore, or letter.

3.2 \> constrains a RE to match the end of a string or to precede a character that is not a digit, underscore, or letter.

An *entire RE* may be constrained to match only an initial segment or final segment of a line (or both).

4.1 A circumflex (^) at the beginning of an entire RE constrains that RE to match an *initial* segment of a line.

4.2 A dollar sign ($) at the end of an entire RE constrains that RE to match a *final* segment of a line.

4.3 The construction ^*entire RE*$ constrains the entire RE to match the entire line.

The null RE (e.g., //) is equivalent to the last RE encountered. See also the last paragraph before FILES below.

To understand addressing in ed it is necessary to know that at any time there is a *current line*. Generally speaking, the current line is the last line affected by a command; the exact effect on the current line is discussed under the description of each command. *Addresses* are constructed as follows:

1. The character . addresses the current line.
2. The character $ addresses the last line of the buffer.
3. A decimal number *n* addresses the *n*-th line of the buffer.
4. '*x* addresses the line marked with the mark name character *x*, which must be an ASCII lower-case letter (a–z). Lines are marked with the **k** command described below.
5. A RE enclosed by slashes (/) addresses the first line found by searching *forward* from the line *following* the current line toward the end of the buffer and stopping at the first line containing a string matching the RE. If necessary, the search wraps around to the beginning of the buffer and continues up to and including the current line, so that the entire buffer is searched. See also the last paragraph before FILES below.
6. A RE enclosed in question marks (?) addresses the first line found by searching *backward* from the line *preceding* the current line toward the beginning of the buffer and stopping at the first line containing a string matching the RE. If necessary, the search wraps around to the end of the buffer and continues up to and including the current line. See also the last paragraph before FILES below.
7. An address followed by a plus sign (+) or a minus sign (–) followed by a decimal number specifies that address plus (respectively minus) the indicated number of lines. A shorthand for .+5 is .5.
8. If an address begins with + or –, the addition or subtraction is taken with respect to the current line; e.g, –5 is understood to mean .–5.
9. If an address ends with + or –, then 1 is added to or subtracted from the address, respectively. As a consequence of this rule and of Rule 8, immediately above, the address – refers to the line preceding the current line. (To maintain compatibility with earlier versions of the editor, the character ^ in addresses is entirely equivalent to –.) Moreover, trailing + and – characters have a cumulative effect, so –– refers to the current line less 2.
10. For convenience, a comma (,) stands for the address pair 1,$, while a semicolon (;) stands for the pair .,$.

Commands may require zero, one, or two addresses. Commands that require no addresses regard the presence of an address as an error. Commands that accept one or two addresses assume default addresses when an insufficient number of addresses is given; if more addresses are given than such a command requires, the last one(s) are used.

Typically, addresses are separated from each other by a comma (,). They may also be separated by a semicolon (;). In the latter case, the first address is calculated, the current line (.) is set to that value, and then the second address is calculated. This feature can be used to determine the starting line for forward and backward searches (see Rules 5 and 6, above). The second address of any two-address sequence must correspond to a line in the buffer that follows the line corresponding to the first address.

In the following list of **ed** commands, the parentheses shown prior to the command are *not* part of the address; rather they show the default address(es) for the command.

It is generally illegal for more than one command to appear on a line. However, any command (except **e**, **f**, **r**, or **w**) may be suffixed by **l**, **n**, or **p** in which case the current line is either listed, numbered or printed, respectively, as discussed below under the **l**, **n**, and **p** commands.

(.)a
<text>
.

The append command accepts zero or more lines of text and appends it after the addressed line in the buffer. The current line (.) is left at the last inserted line, or, if there were none, at the addressed line. Address 0 is legal for this command: it causes the "appended" text to be placed at the beginning of the buffer. The maximum number of characters that may be entered from a terminal is 256 per line (including the new-line character).

(.)c
<text>
.

The change command deletes the addressed lines from the buffer, then accepts zero or more lines of text that replaces these lines in the buffer. The current line (.) is left at the last line input, or, if there were none, at the first line that was not deleted.

C

Same as the **X** command, described later, except that **ed** assumes all text read in for the **e** and **r** commands is encrypted unless a null key is typed in.

(.,.)d

The delete command deletes the addressed lines from the buffer. The line after the last line deleted becomes the current line; if the lines deleted were originally at the end of the buffer, the new last line becomes the current line.

e *file*

The edit command deletes the entire contents of the buffer and then reads the contents of *file* into the buffer. The current line (.) is set to the last line of the buffer. If *file* is not given, the currently remembered file name, if any, is used (see the **f** command). The number of characters read in is printed; *file* is remembered for possible use as a default file name in subsequent **e**, **r**, and **w** commands. If *file* is replaced by **!**, the rest of the line is taken to be a shell [sh(1)] command whose output is to be read in. Such a shell command is *not* remembered as the current file name. See also DIAGNOSTICS below.

E *file*

The Edit command is like e, except that the editor does not check to see if any changes have been made to the buffer since the last w command.

f *file*

If *file* is given, the file-name command changes the currently remembered file name to *file*; otherwise, it prints the currently remembered file name.

(1,$)g/*RE*/*command list*

In the global command, the first step is to mark every line that matches the given RE. Then, for every such line, the given *command list* is executed with the current line (.) initially set to that line. A single command or the first of a list of commands appears on the same line as the global command. All lines of a multi-line list except the last line must be ended with a \; a, i, and c commands and associated input are permitted. The . terminating input mode may be omitted if it would be the last line of the *command list*. An empty *command list* is equivalent to the p command. The g, G, v, and V commands are *not* permitted in the *command list*. See also the NOTES and the last paragraph before FILES below.

(1,$)G/*RE*/

In the interactive Global command, the first step is to mark every line that matches the given RE. Then, for every such line, that line is printed, the current line (.) is changed to that line, and any *one* command (other than one of the a, c, i, g, G, v, and V commands) may be input and is executed. After the execution of that command, the next marked line is printed, and so on; a new-line acts as a null command; an & causes the re-execution of the most recent command executed within the current invocation of G. Note that the commands input as part of the execution of the G command may address and affect *any* lines in the buffer. The G command can be terminated by an interrupt signal (ASCII DEL or BREAK).

h

The help command gives a short error message that explains the reason for the most recent ? diagnostic.

H

The Help command causes ed to enter a mode in which error messages are printed for all subsequent ? diagnostics. It will also explain the previous ? if there was one. The H command alternately turns this mode on and off; it is initially off.

(.)i
<text>
.

The insert command accepts zero or more lines of text and inserts it before the addressed line in the buffer. The current line (.) is left at the last inserted line, or, if there were none, at the addressed line. This command differs from the a command only in the placement of the input text. Address 0 is not legal for this command. The maximum number of characters that may be entered from a terminal is 256 per line (including the new-line character).

(.,.+1)j
The join command joins contiguous lines by removing the appropriate new-line characters. If exactly one address is given, this command does nothing.

(.)k*x*
The mark command marks the addressed line with name *x*, which must be an ASCII lower-case letter (a–z). The address '*x* then addresses this line; the current line (.) is unchanged.

(.,.)l
The list command prints the addressed lines in an unambiguous way: a few non-printing characters (e.g., *tab, backspace*) are represented by visually mnemonic overstrikes. All other non-printing characters are printed in octal, and long lines are folded. An l command may be appended to any command other than e, f, r, or w.

(.,.)m*a*
The move command repositions the addressed line(s) after the line addressed by *a*. Address 0 is legal for *a* and causes the addressed line(s) to be moved to the beginning of the file. It is an error if address *a* falls within the range of moved lines; the current line (.) is left at the last line moved.

(.,.)n
The number command prints the addressed lines, preceding each line by its line number and a tab character; the current line (.) is left at the last line printed. The n command may be appended to any command other than e, f, r, or w.

(.,.)p
The print command prints the addressed lines; the current line (.) is left at the last line printed. The p command may be appended to any command other than e, f, r, or w. For example, dp deletes the current line and prints the new current line.

P
The editor will prompt with a * for all subsequent commands. The P command alternately turns this mode on and off; it is initially off.

q
The quit command causes ed to exit. No automatic write of a file is done; however, see DIAGNOSTICS , below.

Q
The editor exits without checking if changes have been made in the buffer since the last w command.

($)r *file*
The read command reads the contents of *file* into the buffer. If *file* is not given, the currently remembered file name, if any, is used (see the e and f commands). The currently remembered file name is *not* changed unless *file* is the very first file name mentioned since ed was invoked. Address 0 is legal for r and causes the file to be read in at the beginning of the buffer. If the read is successful, the number of characters read in is

printed; the current line (.) is set to the last line read in. If *file* is replaced by !, the rest of the line is taken to be a shell [see sh(1)] command whose output is to be read in. For example, $r !ls appends current directory to the end of the file being edited. Such a shell command is *not* remembered as the current file name.

(. , .)s/*RE*/*replacement*/ or
(. , .)s/*RE*/*replacement*/g or
(. , .)s/*RE*/*replacement*/*n* n = 1-512

The substitute command searches each addressed line for an occurrence of the specified RE. In each line in which a match is found, all (non-overlapped) matched strings are replaced by the *replacement* if the global replacement indicator g appears after the command. If the global indicator does not appear, only the first occurrence of the matched string is replaced. If a number *n*, appears after the command, only the *n*-th occurrence of the matched string on each addressed line is replaced. It is an error if the substitution fails on *all* addressed lines. Any character other than space or new-line may be used instead of / to delimit the RE and the *replacement*; the current line (.) is left at the last line on which a substitution occurred. See also the last paragraph before FILES below.

An ampersand (&) appearing in the *replacement* is replaced by the string matching the RE on the current line. The special meaning of & in this context may be suppressed by preceding it by \. As a more general feature, the characters *n*, where *n* is a digit, are replaced by the text matched by the *n*-th regular subexpression of the specified RE enclosed between \(and \). When nested parenthesized subexpressions are present, *n* is determined by counting occurrences of \(starting from the left. When the character % is the only character in the *replacement*, the *replacement* used in the most recent substitute command is used as the *replacement* in the current substitute command. The % loses its special meaning when it is in a replacement string of more than one character or is preceded by a \.

A line may be split by substituting a new-line character into it. The new-line in the *replacement* must be escaped by preceding it by \. Such substitution cannot be done as part of a g or v command list.

(. , .)t*a*

This command acts just like the m command, except that a *copy* of the addressed lines is placed after address a (which may be 0); the current line (.) is left at the last line copied.

u

The undo command nullifies the effect of the most recent command that modified anything in the buffer, namely the most recent a, c, d, g, i, j, m, r, s, t, v, G, or V command.

(1 , $)v/*RE*/*command list*

This command is the same as the global command g, except that the lines marked during the first step are those that do *not* match the RE.

(1,$)V/*RE*/
This command is the same as the interactive global command G, except that the lines that are marked during the first step are those that do *not* match the RE.

(1,$)w *file*
The write command writes the addressed lines into *file*. If *file* does not exist, it is created with mode 666 (readable and writable by everyone), unless your file creation mask dictates otherwise; see the description of the **umask** special command on **sh**(1). The currently remembered file name is *not* changed unless *file* is the very first file name mentioned since **ed** was invoked. If no file name is given, the currently remembered file name, if any, is used (see the **e** and **f** commands); the current line (.) is unchanged. If the command is successful, the number of characters written is printed. If *file* is replaced by !, the rest of the line is taken to be a shell [see **sh**(1)] command whose standard input is the addressed lines. Such a shell command is *not* remembered as the current file name.

(1,$)W *file*
This command is the same as the write command above, except that it appends the addressed lines to the end of *file* if it exists. If *file* does not exist, it is created as described above for the *w* command.

X
A key is prompted for, and it is used in subsequent **e**, **r**, and **w** commands to decrypt and encrypt text using the **crypt**(1) algorithm. An educated guess is made to determine whether text read in for the **e** and **r** commands is encrypted. A null key turns off encryption. Subsequent **e**, **r**, and **w** commands will use this key to encrypt or decrypt the text [see **crypt**(1)]. An explicitly empty key turns off encryption. Also, see the **-x** option of **ed**.

($)=
The line number of the addressed line is typed; the current line (.) is unchanged by this command.

!*shell command*
The remainder of the line after the ! is sent to the UNIX system shell [see **sh**(1)] to be interpreted as a command. Within the text of that command, the unescaped character % is replaced with the remembered file name; if a ! appears as the first character of the shell command, it is replaced with the text of the previous shell command. Thus, !! will repeat the last shell command. If any expansion is performed, the expanded line is echoed; the current line (.) is unchanged.

(.+1)<new-line>
An address alone on a line causes the addressed line to be printed. A new-line alone is equivalent to .+1p; it is useful for stepping forward through the buffer.

If an interrupt signal (ASCII DEL or BREAK) is sent, **ed** prints a **?** and returns to *its* command level.

Some size limitations: 512 characters in a line, 256 characters in a global command list, and 64 characters in the pathname of a file (counting slashes). The limit on the number of lines depends on the amount of user memory: each line takes 1 word.

When reading a file, **ed** discards ASCII NUL characters.

If a file is not terminated by a new-line character, **ed** adds one and puts out a message explaining what it did.

If the closing delimiter of a RE or of a replacement string (e.g., /) would be the last character before a new-line, that delimiter may be omitted, in which case the addressed line is printed. The following pairs of commands are equivalent:

```
s/s1/s2         s/s1/s2/p
g/s1            g/s1/p
?s1             ?s1?
```

FILES

$TMPDIR	if this environmental variable is not null, its value is used in place of /var/tmp as the directory name for the temporary work file.
/var/tmp	if /var/tmp exists, it is used as the directory name for the temporary work file.
/tmp	if the environmental variable TMPDIR does not exist or is null, and if /var/tmp does not exist, then /tmp is used as the directory name for the temporary work file.
ed.hup	work is saved here if the terminal is hung up.

SEE ALSO

edit(1), **ex**(1), **grep**(1), **sed**(1), **sh**(1), **stty**(1), **umask**(1), **vi**(1).
fspec(4), **regexp**(5) in the *System Administrator's Reference Manual*.

DIAGNOSTICS

?	for command errors.
?*file*	for an inaccessible file. (use the **help** and **Help** commands for detailed explanations).

If changes have been made in the buffer since the last **w** command that wrote the entire buffer, **ed** warns the user if an attempt is made to destroy **ed**'s buffer via the **e** or **q** commands. It prints **?** and allows one to continue editing. A second **e** or **q** command at this point will take effect. The **-s** command-line option inhibits this feature.

NOTES

The **-** option, although it continues to be supported, has been replaced in the documentation by the **-s** option that follows the Command Syntax Standard [see **intro**(1)].

The encryption options and commands are provided with the Security Administration Utilities package, which is available only in the United States.

A ! command cannot be subject to a **g** or a **v** command.

The ! command and the ! escape from the **e**, **r**, and **w** commands cannot be used if the editor is invoked from a restricted shell [see **sh**(1)].

The sequence \n in a RE does not match a new-line character.

If the editor input is coming from a command file (e.g., **ed** *file* < *ed_cmd_file*), the editor exits at the first failure.

NAME

edit – text editor (variant of ex for casual users)

SYNOPSIS

edit [-r] [-x] [-C] *name*...

DESCRIPTION

edit is a variant of the text editor **ex** recommended for new or casual users who wish to use a command-oriented editor. It operates precisely as **ex** with the following options automatically set:

novice	ON
report	ON
showmode	ON
magic	OFF

These options can be turned on or off via the **set** command in **ex**(1).

-r Recover file after an editor or system crash.

-x Encryption option; when used the file will be encrypted as it is being written and will require an encryption key to be read. **edit** makes an educated guess to determine if a file is encrypted or not. See **crypt**(1). Also, see the NOTES section at the end of this manual page.

-C Encryption option; the same as -x except that **edit** assumes files are encrypted.

The following brief introduction should help you get started with **edit**. If you are using a CRT terminal you may want to learn about the display editor **vi**.

To edit the contents of an existing file you begin with the command **edit** *name* to the shell. **edit** makes a copy of the file that you can then edit, and tells you how many lines and characters are in the file. To create a new file, you also begin with the command **edit** with a filename: **edit** *name*; the editor will tell you it is a **[New File]**.

The **edit** command prompt is the colon (:), which you should see after starting the editor. If you are editing an existing file, then you will have some lines in **edit**'s buffer (its name for the copy of the file you are editing). When you start editing, **edit** makes the last line of the file the current line. Most commands to **edit** use the current line if you do not tell them which line to use. Thus if you say **print** (which can be abbreviated **p**) and type carriage return (as you should after all **edit** commands), the current line will be printed. If you **delete** (**d**) the current line, **edit** will print the new current line, which is usually the next line in the file. If you **delete** the last line, then the new last line becomes the current one.

If you start with an empty file or wish to add some new lines, then the **append** (**a**) command can be used. After you execute this command (typing a carriage return after the word **append**), **edit** will read lines from your terminal until you type a line consisting of just a dot (.); it places these lines after the current line. The last line you type then becomes the current line. The **insert** (**i**) command is like **append**, but places the lines you type before, rather than after, the current line.

edit numbers the lines in the buffer, with the first line having number 1. If you execute the command **1**, then **edit** will type the first line of the buffer. If you then execute the command **d**, **edit** will delete the first line, line 2 will become line 1, and **edit** will print the current line (the new line 1) so you can see where you are. In general, the current line will always be the last line affected by a command.

You can make a change to some text within the current line by using the **substitute** (**s**) command: **s**/*old* /*new*/ where *old* is the string of characters you want to replace and *new* is the string of characters you want to replace *old* with.

The **file** (**f**) command will tell you how many lines there are in the buffer you are editing and will say **[Modified]** if you have changed the buffer. After modifying a file, you can save the contents of the file by executing a **write** (**w**) command. You can leave the editor by issuing a **quit** (**q**) command. If you run **edit** on a file, but do not change it, it is not necessary (but does no harm) to **write** the file back. If you try to **quit** from **edit** after modifying the buffer without writing it out, you will receive the message **No write since last change (:quit! overrides)**, and **edit** will wait for another command. If you do not want to write the buffer out, issue the **quit** command followed by an exclamation point (**q!**). The buffer is then irretrievably discarded and you return to the shell.

By using the **d** and **a** commands and giving line numbers to see lines in the file, you can make any changes you want. You should learn at least a few more things, however, if you will use **edit** more than a few times.

The **change** (**c**) command changes the current line to a sequence of lines you supply (as in **append**, you type lines up to a line consisting of only a dot (**.**). You can tell **change** to change more than one line by giving the line numbers of the lines you want to change, i.e., **3,5c**. You can print lines this way too: **1,23p** prints the first 23 lines of the file.

The **undo** (**u**) command reverses the effect of the last command you executed that changed the buffer. Thus if you execute a **substitute** command that does not do what you want, type **u** and the old contents of the line will be restored. You can also **undo** an **undo** command. **edit** will give you a warning message when a command affects more than one line of the buffer. Note that commands such as **write** and **quit** cannot be undone.

To look at the next line in the buffer, type carriage return. To look at a number of lines, type **^D** (while holding down the control key, press **d**) rather than carriage return. This will show you a half-screen of lines on a CRT or 12 lines on a hardcopy terminal. You can look at nearby text by executing the **z** command. The current line will appear in the middle of the text displayed, and the last line displayed will become the current line; you can get back to the line where you were before you executed the **z** command by typing **´´**. The **z** command has other options: **z−** prints a screen of text (or 24 lines) ending where you are; **z+** prints the next screenful. If you want less than a screenful of lines, type **z.11** to display five lines before and five lines after the current line. (Typing **z.***n*, when *n* is an odd number, displays a total of *n* lines, centered about the current line; when *n* is an even number, it displays *n*−1 lines, so that the lines displayed are centered around the current line.) You can give counts after other commands; for example, you can delete 5 lines starting with the current line with the command `d5` .

To find things in the file, you can use line numbers if you happen to know them; since the line numbers change when you insert and delete lines this is somewhat unreliable. You can search backwards and forwards in the file for strings by giving commands of the form /*text*/ to search forward for *text* or ?*text*? to search backward for *text* . If a search reaches the end of the file without finding *text*, it wraps around and continues to search back to the line where you are. A useful feature here is a search of the form /^*text*/ which searches for *text* at the beginning of a line. Similarly /*text*$/ searches for *text* at the end of a line. You can leave off the trailing / or ? in these commands.

The current line has the symbolic name dot (`.`); this is most useful in a range of lines as in `.,$p` which prints the current line plus the rest of the lines in the file. To move to the last line in the file, you can refer to it by its symbolic name $. Thus the command `$d` deletes the last line in the file, no matter what the current line is. Arithmetic with line references is also possible. Thus the line `$-5` is the fifth before the last and `.+20` is 20 lines after the current line.

You can find out the current line by typing `.=`. This is useful if you wish to move or copy a section of text within a file or between files. Find the first and last line numbers you wish to copy or move. To move lines 10 through 20, type `10,20d a` to delete these lines from the file and place them in a buffer named `a`. `edit` has 26 such buffers named `a` through `z`. To put the contents of buffer `a` after the current line, type `put a`. If you want to move or copy these lines to another file, execute an `edit` (`e`) command after copying the lines; following the `e` command with the name of the other file you wish to edit, i.e., `edit chapter2`. To copy lines without deleting them, use `yank` (`y`) in place of `d`. If the text you wish to move or copy is all within one file, it is not necessary to use named buffers. For example, to move lines 10 through 20 to the end of the file, type `10,20m $`.

SEE ALSO

ed(1), ex(1), vi(1).

NOTES

The encryption options are provided with the Security Administration Utilities package, which is available only in the United States.

NAME

egrep – search a file for a pattern using full regular expressions

SYNOPSIS

egrep [*options*] **full regular expression** [*file* ...]

DESCRIPTION

egrep (*expression grep*) searches files for a pattern of characters and prints all lines that contain that pattern. **egrep** uses full regular expressions (expressions that have string values that use the full set of alphanumeric and special characters) to match the patterns. It uses a fast deterministic algorithm that sometimes needs exponential space.

egrep accepts full regular expressions as in **ed**(1), except for `\(` and `\)`, with the addition of:

1. A full regular expression followed by `+` that matches one or more occurrences of the full regular expression.
2. A full regular expression followed by `?` that matches 0 or 1 occurrences of the full regular expression.
3. Full regular expressions separated by | or by a new-line that match strings that are matched by any of the expressions.
4. A full regular expression that may be enclosed in parentheses `()` for grouping.

Be careful using the characters `$`, `*`, `[`, `^`, |, `(`, `)`, and \ in *full regular expression*, because they are also meaningful to the shell. It is safest to enclose the entire *full regular expression* in single quotes `'...'`.

The order of precedence of operators is `[]`, then `*?+`, then concatenation, then | and new-line.

If no files are specified, **egrep** assumes standard input. Normally, each line found is copied to the standard output. The file name is printed before each line found if there is more than one input file.

Command line options are:

- **-b** Precede each line by the block number on which it was found. This can be useful in locating block numbers by context (first block is 0).
- **-c** Print only a count of the lines that contain the pattern.
- **-i** Ignore upper/lower case distinction during comparisons.
- **-h** Suppress printing of filenames when searching multiple files.
- **-l** Print the names of files with matching lines once, separated by new-lines. Does not repeat the names of files when the pattern is found more than once.
- **-n** Precede each line by its line number in the file (first line is 1).
- **-v** Print all lines except those that contain the pattern.
- **-e** *special_expression*
  Search for a *special expression* (*full regular expression* that begins with a –).
- **-f** *file*
  Take the list of *full regular expressions* from *file*.

SEE ALSO

ed(1), fgrep(1), grep(1), sed(1), sh(1).

DIAGNOSTICS

Exit status is 0 if any matches are found, 1 if none, 2 for syntax errors or inaccessible files (even if matches were found).

NOTES

Ideally there should be only one grep command, but there is not a single algorithm that spans a wide enough range of space-time tradeoffs. Lines are limited to BUFSIZ characters; longer lines are truncated. BUFSIZ is defined in /usr/include/stdio.h.

NAME

enable, disable – enable/disable LP printers

SYNOPSIS

enable *printers*
disable [*options*] *printers*

DESCRIPTION

The **enable** command activates the named *printers*, enabling them to print requests submitted by the **lp** command. If the printer is remote, the command will only enable the transfer of requests to the remote system; the **enable** command must be run again, on the remote system, to activate the printer. (Run **lpstat -p** to get the status of printers.)

The **disable** command deactivates the named *printers*, disabling them from printing requests submitted by **lp**. By default, any requests that are currently printing on the designated printers will be reprinted in their entirety either on the same printer or on another member of the same class of printers. If the printer is remote, this command will only stop the transmission of jobs to the remote system. The **disable** command must be run on the remote system to disable the printer. (Run **lpstat -p** to get the status of printers.) Options for use with **disable** are:

-c Cancel any requests that are currently printing on any of the designated printers. This option cannot be used with the **-W** option. If the printer is remote, the **-c** option will be silently ignored.

-r *reason* Assign a *reason* for the disabling of the printers. This *reason* applies to all *printers* specified. This *reason* is reported by **lpstat -p**. *reason* must be enclosed in quotes if it contains blanks. The default reason is **unknown reason** for existing printers, and **new printer** for printers just added to the system but not yet enabled.

-W Wait until the request currently being printed is finished before disabling the specified printer. This option cannot be used with the **-c** option. If the printer is remote, the **-W** option will be silently ignored.

FILES

/var/spool/lp/*

SEE ALSO

lp(1), lpstat(1).

NAME

env – set environment for command execution

SYNOPSIS

env [–] [name=value] ... [command args]

DESCRIPTION

env obtains the current *environment*, modifies it according to its arguments, then executes the command with the modified environment. Arguments of the form *name=value* are merged into the inherited environment before the command is executed. The – flag causes the inherited environment to be ignored completely, so that the command is executed with exactly the environment specified by the arguments.

If no command is specified, the resulting environment is printed, one name-value pair per line.

SEE ALSO

sh(1).
exec(2) in the *Programmer's Reference Manual.*
profile(4), **environ**(5) in the *System Administrator's Reference Manual.*

NAME

ex – text editor

SYNOPSIS

ex [**-s**] [**-v**] [**-t** *tag*] [**-r** *file*] [**-L**] [**-R**] [**-x**] [**-C**] [**-c** *command*] *file* ...

DESCRIPTION

ex is the root of a family of editors: **ex** and **vi**. **ex** is a superset of **ed**, with the most notable extension being a display editing facility. Display based editing is the focus of **vi**.

If you have a CRT terminal, you may wish to use a display based editor; in this case see **vi**(1), which is a command which focuses on the display-editing portion of **ex**.

For ed Users

If you have used **ed** you will find that, in addition to having all of the **ed** commands available, **ex** has a number of additional features useful on CRT terminals. Intelligent terminals and high speed terminals are very pleasant to use with **vi**. Generally, the **ex** editor uses far more of the capabilities of terminals than **ed** does, and uses the terminal capability data base [see **terminfo**(4)] and the type of the terminal you are using from the environmental variable TERM to determine how to drive your terminal efficiently. The editor makes use of features such as insert and delete character and line in its **visual** command (which can be abbreviated **vi**) and which is the central mode of editing when using the **vi** command.

ex contains a number of features for easily viewing the text of the file. The **z** command gives easy access to windows of text. Typing ^D (control-d) causes the editor to scroll a half-window of text and is more useful for quickly stepping through a file than just typing return. Of course, the screen-oriented **visual** mode gives constant access to editing context.

ex gives you help when you make mistakes. The **undo** (**u**) command allows you to reverse any single change which goes astray. **ex** gives you a lot of feedback, normally printing changed lines, and indicates when more than a few lines are affected by a command so that it is easy to detect when a command has affected more lines than it should have.

The editor also normally prevents overwriting existing files, unless you edited them, so that you do not accidentally overwrite a file other than the one you are editing. If the system (or editor) crashes, or you accidentally hang up the telephone, you can use the editor **recover** command (or **-r** *file* option) to retrieve your work. This will get you back to within a few lines of where you left off.

ex has several features for dealing with more than one file at a time. You can give it a list of files on the command line and use the **next** (**n**) command to deal with each in turn. The **next** command can also be given a list of file names, or a pattern as used by the shell to specify a new set of files to be dealt with. In general, file names in the editor may be formed with full shell metasyntax. The metacharacter '%' is also available in forming file names and is replaced by the name of the current file.

The editor has a group of buffers whose names are the ASCII lower-case letters (a-z). You can place text in these named buffers where it is available to be inserted elsewhere in the file. The contents of these buffers remain available when you begin editing a new file using the `edit` (`e`) command.

There is a command `&` in **ex** which repeats the last `substitute` command. In addition, there is a confirmed substitute command. You give a range of substitutions to be done and the editor interactively asks whether each substitution is desired.

It is possible to ignore the case of letters in searches and substitutions. **ex** also allows regular expressions which match words to be constructed. This is convenient, for example, in searching for the word "edit" if your document also contains the word "editor."

ex has a set of options which you can set to tailor it to your liking. One option which is very useful is the `autoindent` option that allows the editor to supply leading white space to align text automatically. You can then use `^D` as a backtab and space or tab to move forward to align new code easily.

Miscellaneous useful features include an intelligent `join` (`j`) command that supplies white space between joined lines automatically, commands < and > which shift groups of lines, and the ability to filter portions of the buffer through commands such as `sort`.

Invocation Options

The following invocation options are interpreted by **ex** (previously documented options are discussed in the **NOTES** section at the end of this manual page):

`-s`	Suppress all interactive-user feedback. This is useful in processing editor scripts.
`-v`	Invoke `vi`.
`-t` *tag*	Edit the file containing the *tag* and position the editor at its definition.
`-r` *file*	Edit *file* after an editor or system crash. (Recovers the version of *file* that was in the buffer when the crash occurred.)
`-L`	List the names of all files saved as the result of an editor or system crash.
`-R`	`Readonly` mode; the `readonly` flag is set, preventing accidental overwriting of the file.
`-x`	Encryption option; when used, **ex** simulates an `X` command and prompts the user for a key. This key is used to encrypt and decrypt text using the algorithm of the `crypt` command. The `X` command makes an educated guess to determine whether text read in is encrypted or not. The temporary buffer file is encrypted also, using a transformed version of the key typed in for the `-x` option. See `crypt`(1). Also, see the **NOTES** section at the end of this manual page.

-C Encryption option; the same as the -x option, except that ex simulates a C command. The C command is like the X command, except that all text read in is assumed to have been encrypted.

-c *command* Begin editing by executing the specified editor *command* (usually a search or positioning command).

The *file* argument indicates one or more files to be edited.

ex States

Command Normal and initial state. Input prompted for by :. Your line kill character cancels a partial command.

Insert Entered by a, i, or c. Arbitrary text may be entered. Insert state normally is terminated by a line having only "." on it, or, abnormally, with an interrupt.

Visual Entered by typing vi; terminated by typing Q or ^\ (control-\).

ex Command Names and Abbreviations

abbrev	ab	map		set	se
append	a	mark	ma	shell	sh
args	ar	move	m	source	so
change	c	next	n	substitute	s
copy	co	number	nu	unabbrev	unab
delete	d	preserve	pre	undo	u
edit	e	print	p	unmap	unm
file	f	put	pu	version	ve
global	g	quit	q	visual	vi
insert	i	read	r	write	w
join	j	recover	rec	xit	x
list	l	rewind	rew	yank	ya

ex Commands

forced encryption	C	heuristic encryption	X
resubst	&	print next	CR
rshift	>	lshift	<
scroll	^D	window	z
shell escape	!		

ex Command Addresses

n	line *n*	*/pat*	next with *pat*
.	current	*?pat*	previous with *pat*
$	last	*x−n*	*n* before *x*
+	next	*x,y*	*x* through *y*
−	previous	*´x*	marked with *x*
+*n*	*n* forward	´´	previous context
%	1,$		

Initializing options

`EXINIT`	place `set`'s here in environment variable
`$HOME/.exrc`	editor initialization file
`./.exrc`	editor initialization file
`set` *x*	enable option *x*
`set no`*x*	disable option *x*
`set` *x*`=val`	give value *val* to option *x*
`set`	show changed options
`set all`	show all options
`set` *x*`?`	show value of option *x*

Most useful options and their abbreviations

autoindent	`ai`	supply indent
autowrite	`aw`	write before changing files
directory		pathname of directory for temporary work files
exrc	`ex`	allow `vi/ex` to read the `.exrc` in the current directory. This option is set in the `EXINIT` shell variable or in the `.exrc` file in the `$HOME` directory.
ignorecase	`ic`	ignore case of letters in scanning
list		print `^I` for tab, $ at end
magic		treat `.` `[` `*` special in patterns
modelines		first five lines and last five lines executed as `vi/ex` commands if they are of the form `ex:`*command*`:` or `vi:`*command*`:`
number	`nu`	number lines
paragraphs	`para`	macro names that start paragraphs
redraw		simulate smart terminal
report		informs you if the number of lines modified by the last command is greater than the value of the `report` variable
scroll		command mode lines
sections	`sect`	macro names that start sections
shiftwidth	`sw`	for < >, and input `^D`
showmatch	`sm`	to `)` and `}` as typed
showmode	`smd`	show insert mode in `vi`
slowopen	`slow`	stop updates during insert
term		specifies to `vi` the type of terminal being used (the default is the value of the environmental variable `TERM`)
window		visual mode lines
wrapmargin	`wm`	automatic line splitting
wrapscan	`ws`	search around end (or beginning) of buffer

Scanning pattern formation

^	beginning of line
$	end of line
.	any character
\<	beginning of word
\>	end of word
[str]	any character in *str*
[^str]	any character not in *str*
[*x*–*y*]	any character between *x* and *y*
*	any number of preceding characters

AUTHOR

vi and ex are based on software developed by The University of California, Berkeley California, Computer Science Division, Department of Electrical Engineering and Computer Science.

FILES

/usr/lib/exstrings	error messages
/usr/lib/exrecover	recover command
/usr/lib/expreserve	preserve command
/usr/share/lib/terminfo/*	describes capabilities of terminals
$HOME/.exrc	editor startup file
./.exrc	editor startup file
/tmp/Ex*nnnnn*	editor temporary
/tmp/Rx*nnnnn*	named buffer temporary
/var/preserve/login	preservation directory (where login is the user's login)

NOTES

Several options, although they continue to be supported, have been replaced in the documentation by options that follow the Command Syntax Standard [see intro(1)]. The – option has been replaced by -s, a -r option that is not followed with an option-argument has been replaced by -L, and +*command* has been replaced by -c *command*.

The encryption options and commands are provided with the Security Administration Utilities package, which is available only in the United States.

The z command prints the number of logical rather than physical lines. More than a screen full of output may result if long lines are present.

File input/output errors do not print a name if the command line -s option is used.

There is no easy way to do a single scan ignoring case.

The editor does not warn if text is placed in named buffers and not used before exiting the editor.

Null characters are discarded in input files and cannot appear in resultant files.

SEE ALSO

crypt(1), **ed**(1), **edit**(1), **grep**(1), **sed**(1), **sort**(1), **vi**(1).
curses(3X), in the *Programmer's Reference Manual.*
term(4), **terminfo**(4) in the *System Administrator's Reference Manual.*
User's Guide.
Editing Guide.
curses/terminfo chapter of the *Programmer's Guide*.

NAME

expr – evaluate arguments as an expression

SYNOPSIS

expr *arguments*

DESCRIPTION

The *arguments* are taken as an expression. After evaluation, the result is written on the standard output. Terms of the expression must be separated by blanks. Characters special to the shell must be escaped. Note that 0 is returned to indicate a zero value, rather than the null string. Strings containing blanks or other special characters should be quoted. Integer-valued arguments may be preceded by a unary minus sign. Internally, integers are treated as 32-bit, 2s complement numbers. The length of the expression is limited to 512 characters.

The operators and keywords are listed below. Characters that need to be escaped in the shell [see **sh**(1)] are preceded by \. The list is in order of increasing precedence, with equal precedence operators grouped within { } symbols.

expr \| *expr*
: returns the first *expr* if it is neither null nor 0, otherwise returns the second *expr*.

expr \& *expr*
: returns the first *expr* if neither *expr* is null or 0, otherwise returns 0.

expr { =, \>, \>=, \<, \<=, != } *expr*
: returns the result of an integer comparison if both arguments are integers, otherwise returns the result of a lexical comparison.

expr { +, – } *expr*
: addition or subtraction of integer-valued arguments.

expr { *, /, % } *expr*
: multiplication, division, or remainder of the integer-valued arguments.

expr : *expr*
: The matching operator : compares the first argument with the second argument, which must be a regular expression. Regular expression syntax is the same as that of **ed**(1), except that all patterns are "anchored" (i.e., begin with ^) and, therefore, ^ is not a special character, in that context. Normally, the matching operator returns the number of bytes matched (0 on failure). Alternatively, the \(. . . \) pattern symbols can be used to return a portion of the first argument.

EXAMPLES

Add 1 to the shell variable a:

```
a=`expr $a + 1`
```

The following example emulates **basename**(1)—it returns the last segment of the path name $a. For $a equal to either /usr/abc/file or just file, the example returns `file`. (Watch out for / alone as an argument: **expr** takes it as the division operator; see the NOTES below.)

```
expr $a : '.*/\(.*\)' \| $a
```

Here is a better version of the previous example. The addition of the // characters eliminates any ambiguity about the division operator and simplifies the whole expression.

```
expr //$a : '.*/\(.*\)'
```

Return the number of characters in **$VAR**:

```
expr $VAR : '.*'
```

SEE ALSO

ed(1), sh(1).

DIAGNOSTICS

As a side effect of expression evaluation, **expr** returns the following exit values:

- 0 if the expression is neither null nor 0
- 1 if the expression *is* null or 0
- 2 for invalid expressions.

`syntax error`	for operator/operand errors
`non-numeric argument`	if arithmetic is attempted on such a string

NOTES

After argument processing by the shell, **expr** cannot tell the difference between an operator and an operand except by the value. If **$a** is an =, the command:

```
expr $a = '='
```

looks like:

```
expr = = =
```

as the arguments are passed to **expr** (and they are all taken as the = operator). The following works:

```
expr X$a = X=
```

NAME

exstr – extract strings from source files

SYNOPSIS

exstr *file* ...
exstr -e *file* ...
exstr -r [-d] *file* ...

DESCRIPTION

The **exstr** utility is used to extract strings from C-language source files and replace them by calls to the message retrieval function (see **gettxt**(3C)). This utility will extract all character strings surrounded by double quotes, not just strings used as arguments to the **printf** command or the **printf** routine. In the first form, **exstr** finds all strings in the source files and writes them on the standard output. Each string is preceded by the source file name and a colon. The meanings of the options are:

-e Extract a list of strings from the named C-language source files, with positional information. This list is produced on standard output in the following format:

file:line:position:msgfile:msgnum:string

file	the name of a C-language source file
line	line number in the file
position	character position in the line
msgfile	null
msgnum	null
string	the extracted text string

Normally you would redirect this output into a file. Then you would edit this file to add the values you want to use for *msgfile* and *msgnum*:

msgfile	the file that contains the text strings that will replace *string*. A file with this name must be created and installed in the appropriate place by the **mkmsgs**(1) utility.
msgnum	the sequence number of the string in *msgfile*.

The next step is to use **exstr -r** to replace *string*s in *file*.

-r Replace strings in a C-language source file with function calls to the message retrieval function **gettxt**().

-d This option is used together with the **-r** option. If the message retrieval fails when **gettxt**() is invoked at run-time, then the extracted string is printed.

You would use the capability provided by **exstr** on an application program that needs to run in an international environment and have messages print in more than one language. **exstr** replaces text strings with function calls that point at strings in a message data base. The data base used depends on the run-time value of the **LC_MESSAGES** environment variable (see **environ**(5)).

The first step is to use `exstr -e` to extract a list of strings and save it in a file. Next, examine this list and determine which strings can be translated and subsequently retrieved by the message retrieval function. Then, modify this file by deleting lines that can't be translated and, for lines that can be translated, by adding the message file names and the message numbers as the fourth (*msgfile*) and fifth (*msgnum*) entries on a line. The message files named must have been created by `mkmsgs`(1) and exist in `/usr/lib/locale/`*locale*`/LC_MESSAGES`. (The directory *locale* corresponds to the language in which the text strings are written; see `setlocale`(3C)). The message numbers used must correspond to the sequence numbers of strings in the message files.

Now use this modified file as input to `exstr -r` to produce a new version of the original C-language source file in which the strings have been replaced by calls to the message retrieval function `gettxt`(). The *msgfile* and *msgnum* fields are used to construct the first argument to `gettxt`(). The second argument to `gettxt`() is printed if the message retrieval fails at run-time. This argument is the null string, unless the `-d` option is used.

This utility cannot replace strings in all instances. For example, a static initialized character string cannot be replaced by a function call. A second example is that a string could be in a form of an escape sequence which could not be translated. In order not to break existing code, the files created by invoking `exstr -e` must be examined and lines containing strings not replaceable by function calls must be deleted. In some cases the code may require modifications so that strings can be extracted and replaced by calls to the message retrieval function.

EXAMPLES

The following examples show uses of `exstr`.

Assume that the file `foo.c` contains two strings:

```
main()
{
        printf("This is an example\n");
        printf("Hello world!\n");
}
```

The `exstr` utility, invoked with the argument `foo.c` extracts strings from the named file and prints them on the standard output.

`exstr foo.c` produces the following output:

```
foo.c:This is an example\n
foo.c:Hello world!\n
```

`exstr -e foo.c > foo.stringsout` produces the following output in the file `foo.stringsout`:

```
foo.c:3:8:::This is an example\n
foo.c:4:8:::Hello world!\n
```

You must edit `foo.stringsout` to add the values you want to use for the *msgfile* and *msgnum* fields before these strings can be replaced by calls to the retrieval function. If `UX` is the name of the message file, and the numbers `1` and `2` represent the sequence number of the strings in the file, here is what `foo.stringsout` looks like after you add this information:

```
foo.c:3:8:UX:1:This is an example\n
foo.c:4:8:UX:2:Hello world!\n
```

The `exstr` utility can now be invoked with the `-r` option to replace the strings in the source file by calls to the message retrieval function `gettxt()`.

`exstr -r foo.c <foo.stringsout >intlfoo.c` produces the following output:

```
extern char *gettxt();
main()
{
        printf(gettxt("UX:1", ""));
        printf(gettxt("UX:2", ""));
}
```

`exstr -rd foo.c <foo.stringsout >intlfoo.c` uses the extracted strings as a second argument to `gettxt()`.

```
extern char *gettxt();
main()
{
        printf(gettxt("UX:1", "This is an example\n"));
        printf(gettxt("UX:2", "Hello world!\n"));
}
```

FILES

`/usr/lib/locale/`*locale*`/LC_MESSAGES/*`   files created by `mkmsgs`(1)

SEE ALSO

`gettxt`(1), `mkmsgs`(1), `printf`(1), `srchtxt`(1).
`gettxt`(3C), `printf`(3S), `setlocale`(3C) in the *Programmer's Reference Manual*.
`environ`(5) in the *System Administrator's Reference Manual*.

DIAGNOSTICS

The error messages produced by `exstr` are intended to be self-explanatory. They indicate errors in the command line or format errors encountered within the input file.

NAME

face – executable for the Framed Access Command Environment Interface

SYNOPSIS

face [-i *init_file*] [-c *command_file*] [-a *alias_file*] [*file...*]

DESCRIPTION

file is the full pathname of the file describing the object to be opened initially, and must follow the naming convention **Menu.***xxx* for a menu, **Form.***xxx* for a form, and **Text.***xxx* for a text file, where *xxx* is any string that conforms to the UNIX system file naming conventions. The FMLI descriptor **lifetime** will be ignored for all frames opened by argument to **face**. These frames have a lifetime of **immortal** by default. If *file* is not specified on the command line, the AT&T FACE Menu will be opened along with those objects specified by the **LOGINWIN** environment variables. These variables are found in the user's .environ file.

FILES

$HOME/pref/.environ

SEE ALSO

env(4)

DIAGNOSTICS

The **face** command will exit with a non-zero exit code if the user is not properly set up as a FACE user.

NAME

`factor` – obtain the prime factors of a number

SYNOPSIS

`factor` [*integer*]

DESCRIPTION

When you use `factor` without an argument, it waits for you to give it an integer. After you give it a positive integer less than or equal to 10^{14}, it factors the integer, prints its prime factors the proper number of times, and then waits for another integer. `factor` exits if it encounters a zero or any non-numeric character.

If you invoke `factor` with an argument, it factors the integer as described above, and then it exits.

The maximum time to factor an integer is proportional to $\sqrt{n}$. `factor` will take this time when n is prime or the square of a prime.

DIAGNOSTICS

`factor` prints the error message, `Ouch`, for input out of range or for garbage input.

NAME

fgrep – search a file for a character string

SYNOPSIS

fgrep [options] string [file ...]

DESCRIPTION

fgrep (fast **grep**) seaches files for a character string and prints all lines that contain that string. **fgrep** is different from *grep(1)* and *egrep(1)* because it searches for a string, instead of searching for a pattern that matches an expression. It uses a fast and compact algorithm.

The characters $, *, [, ^, |, (,), and \ are interpreted literally by **fgrep**, that is, **fgrep** does not recognize full regular expressions as does **egrep**. Since these characters have special meaning to the shell, it is safest to enclose the entire *string* in single quotes ' ... '.

If no files are specified, **fgrep** assumes standard input. Normally, each line found is copied to the standard output. The file name is printed before each line found if there is more than one input file.

Command line options are:

- **-b** Precede each line by the block number on which it was found. This can be useful in locating block numbers by context (first block is 0).
- **-c** Print only a count of the lines that contain the pattern.
- **-h** Suppress printing of filenames when searching multiple files.
- **-i** Ignore upper/lower case distinction during comparisons.
- **-l** Print the names of files with matching lines once, separated by new-lines. Does not repeat the names of files when the pattern is found more than once.
- **-n** Precede each line by its line number in the file (first line is 1).
- **-v** Print all lines except those that contain the pattern.
- **-x** Print only lines matched entirely.
- **-e** *special_string*
  Search for a *special string* (*string* begins with a –).
- **-f** *file*
  Take the list of *strings* from *file*.

SEE ALSO

ed(1), **egrep**(1), **grep**(1), **sed**(1), **sh**(1).

DIAGNOSTICS

Exit status is 0 if any matches are found, 1 if none, 2 for syntax errors or inaccessible files (even if matches were found).

NOTES

Ideally there should be only one **grep** command, but there is not a single algorithm that spans a wide enough range of space-time tradeoffs. Lines are limited to BUFSIZ characters; longer lines are truncated. BUFSIZ is defined in `/usr/include/stdio.h`.

NAME

`file` – determine file type

SYNOPSIS

`file` [-h] [-m *mfile*] [-f *ffile*] *arg* ...
`file` [-h] [-m *mfile*] -f *ffile*
`file` -c [-m *mfile*]

DESCRIPTION

`file` performs a series of tests on each file supplied by *arg* and, optionally, on each file supplied in *ffile* in an attempt to classify it. If *arg* appears to be a text file, `file` examines the first 512 bytes and tries to guess its programming language. If *arg* is an executable `a.out`, `file` prints the version stamp, provided it is greater than 0. If *arg* is a symbolic link, by default the link is followed and `file` tests the file that the symbolic link references.

-c Check the magic file for format errors. For reasons of efficiency, this validation is normally not carried out.

-f *ffile* *ffile* contains the names of the files to be examined.

-h Do not follow symbolic links.

-m *mfile* Use *mfile* as an alternate magic file, instead of `/etc/magic`.

`file` uses `/etc/magic` to identify files that have a magic number. A magic number is a numeric or string constant that indicates the file type. Commentary at the beginning of `/etc/magic` explains its format.

FILES

`/etc/magic`

SEE ALSO

`filehdr`(4) in the *System Administrator's Reference Manual.*

DIAGNOSTICS

If the -h option is specified and *arg* is a symbolic link, `file` prints the error message:

`symbolic link to` *arg*

NAME

`find` – find files

SYNOPSIS

`find` *path-name-list expression*

DESCRIPTION

`find` recursively descends the directory hierarchy for each path name in the *path-name-list* (that is, one or more path names) seeking files that match a boolean *expression* written in the primaries given below. In the descriptions, the argument *n* is used as a decimal integer where +*n* means more than *n*, –*n* means less than *n* and *n* means exactly *n*. Valid expressions are:

`-name` *pattern*	True if *pattern* matches the current file name. Normal shell file name generation characters (see `sh`(1)) may be used. A backslash (\) is used as an escape character within the pattern. The pattern should be escaped or quoted when `find` is invoked from the shell.
`-perm` [–]*onum*	True if the file permission flags exactly match the octal number *onum* (see `chmod`(1)). If *onum* is prefixed by a minus sign (–), only the bits that are set in *onum* are compared with the file permission flags, and the expression evaluates true if they match.
`-size` *n*[c]	True if the file is *n* blocks long (512 bytes per block). If *n* is followed by a `c`, the size is in characters.
`-atime` *n*	True if the file was accessed *n* days ago. The access time of directories in *path-name-list* is changed by `find` itself.
`-mtime` *n*	True if the file's data was modified *n* days ago.
`-ctime` *n*	True if the file's status was changed *n* days ago.
`-exec` *cmd*	True if the executed *cmd* returns a zero value as exit status. The end of *cmd* must be punctuated by an escaped semicolon. A command argument `{}` is replaced by the current path name.
`-ok` *cmd*	Like `-exec` except that the generated command line is printed with a question mark first, and is executed only if the user responds by typing `y`.
`-print`	Always true; causes the current path name to be printed.
`-newer` *file*	True if the current file has been modified more recently than the argument *file*.
`-depth`	Always true; causes descent of the directory hierarchy to be done so that all entries in a directory are acted on before the directory itself. This can be useful when `find` is used with `cpio`(1) to transfer files that are contained in directories without write permission.
`-mount`	Always true; restricts the search to the file system containing the directory specified.

`-local` True if the file physically resides on the local system.

`(` *expression* `)` True if the parenthesized expression is true (parentheses are special to the shell and must be escaped).

`-type` *c* True if the type of the file is *c*, where *c* is `b`, `c`, `d`, `l`, `p`, or `f` for block special file, character special file, directory, symbolic link, fifo (named pipe), or plain file, respectively.

`-follow` Always true; causes symbolic links to be followed. When following symbolic links, `find` keeps track of the directories visited so that it can detect infinite loops; for example, such a loop would occur if a symbolic link pointed to an ancestor. This expression should not be used with the `-type l` expression.

`-links` *n* True if the file has *n* links.

`-user` *uname* True if the file belongs to the user *uname*. If *uname* is numeric and does not appear as a login name in the `/etc/passwd` file, it is taken as a user ID.

`-nouser` True if the file belongs to a user not in the `/etc/passwd` file.

`-group` *gname* True if the file belongs to the group *gname*. If *gname* is numeric and does not appear in the `/etc/group` file, it is taken as a group ID.

`-nogroup` True if the file belongs to a group not in the `/etc/group` file.

`-fstype` *type* True if the filesystem to which the file belongs is of type *type*.

`-inum` *n* True if the file has inode number *n*.

`-prune` Always yields true. Do not examine any directories or files in the directory structure below the *pattern* just matched. See the examples, below.

The primaries may be combined using the following operators (in order of decreasing precedence):

1) The negation of a primary (`!` is the unary *not* operator).

2) Concatenation of primaries (the *and* operation is implied by the juxtaposition of two primaries).

3) Alternation of primaries (`-o` is the *or* operator).

Note that when you use `find` in conjunction with `cpio`, if you use the `-L` option with `cpio` then you must use the `-follow` expression with `find` and vice versa. Otherwise there will be undesirable results.

EXAMPLES

Remove all files in your home directory named `a.out` or `*.o` that have not been accessed for a week:

```
find $HOME \( -name a.out -o -name '*.o' \) -atime +7 -exec rm {} \;
```

Recursively print all file names in the current directory and below, but skipping SCCS directories:

```
find . -name SCCS -prune -o -print
```

Recursively print all file names in the current directory and below, skipping the contents of SCCS directories, but printing out the SCCS directory name:

```
find . -print -name SCCS -prune
```

FILES

/etc/passwd, /etc/group

SEE ALSO

`chmod`(1), `sh`(1), `test`(1).
`stat`(2), and `umask`(2) in the *Programmer's Reference Manual*.
`fs`(4) in the *System Administrator's Reference Manual*.

NOTE

When using `find` to determine files modified within a range of time, one must use the `?time` argument BEFORE the `-print` argument otherwise `find` will give all files.

The following option is obsolete and will not be supported in future releases.

`-cpio` *device* Always true; write the current file on *device* in `cpio`(1) format (5120-byte records).

NAME

`finger` – display information about local and remote users

SYNOPSIS

`finger [ -bfhilmpqsw ]` *username*...

`finger [-l]` *username@hostname*... (TC/IP)

DESCRIPTION

By default, the `finger` command displays information about each , logged-in user, including login name, full name, terminal name (prepended with a '*' if write-permission is denied), idle time, login time, and location if known.

Idle time is minutes if it is a single integer, hours and minutes if a ':' is present, or days and hours if a `d` is present.

When one or more *username* arguments are given, more detailed information is given for each *username* specified, whether they are logged in or not. *username* must be that of a local user, and may be a first or last name, or an account name. When `finger` is used to find users on a remote device, the user and the name of the remote device are specified in the form *username@hostname.* Information is presented in a multi-line format, and includes, in addition to the information mentioned above:

> the user's home directory and login shell
>
> time the user logged in if currently logged in, or the time the user last logged in if not, as well as the terminal or host from which the user logged in and, if a terminal.
>
> last time the user received mail, and the last time the user read their mail
>
> any plan contained in the file `.plan` in the user's home directory
>
> and any project on which the user is working described in the file `.project` (also in the user's home directory)

The following options are available:

`-b` Suppress printing the user's home directory and shell in a long format printout.

`-f` Suppress printing the header that is normally printed in a non-long format printout.

`-h` Suppress printing of the `.project` file in a long format printout.

`-i` Force "idle" output format, which is similar to short format except that only the login name, terminal, login time, and idle time are printed.

`-l` Force long output format.

`-m` Match arguments only on user name (not first or last name).

`-p` Suppress printing of the `.plan` file in a long format printout.

`-q` Force quick output format, which is similar to short format except that only the login name, terminal, and login time are printed.

`-s` Force short output format.

`-w` Suppress printing the full name in a short format printout.

Within the TCP/IP network, the `-l` option can be used remotely.

FILES

/var/adm/utmp	who is logged in
/etc/passwd	for users' names
/var/adm/lastlog	last login times
~/.plan	plans
~/.project	projects

SEE ALSO

passwd(1), who(1), whois(1)

NOTES

Only the first line of the `~/.project` file is printed.

NAME

fmli – invoke FMLI

SYNOPSIS

fmli [-a *alias_file*] [-c *command_file*] [-i *initialization_file*] *file* ...

DESCRIPTION

The fmli command invokes the Form and Menu Language Interpreter and opens the frame(s) specified by the *file* argument. The *file* argument is the pathname of the initial frame definition file(s), and must follow the naming convention Menu.*xxx*, Form.*xxx* or Text.*xxx* for a menu, form or text frame respectively, where *xxx* is any string that conforms to UNIX system file naming conventions. The FMLI descriptor lifetime will be ignored for all frames opened by argument to fmli. These frames have a lifetime of immortal by default.

The available options are as follows:

-a If -a is specified, *alias_file* is the name of a file which contains lines of the form *alias=pathname*. Thereafter, $*alias* can be used in definition files to simplify references to objects or devices with lengthy pathnames, or to define a search path (similar to $PATH in the UNIX system shell).

-c If -c is specified, *command_file* is the name of a file in which default FMLI commands can be disabled, and new application-specific commands can be defined. The contents of *command_file* are reflected in the FMLI Command Menu.

-i If -i is specified, *initialization_file* is the name of a file in which the following characteristics of the application as a whole can be specified:

- A transient introductory frame displaying product information
- A banner, its position, and other elements of the banner line
- Color attributes for all elements of the screen
- Screen Labeled Keys (SLKs) and their layout on the screen.

Environment Variables

LOADPFK

Leaving this environment variable unset tells FMLI, for certain terminals like the AT&T 5620 and 630, to download its equivalent character sequences for using function keys into the terminal's programmable function keys, wiping out any settings the user may already have set in the function keys. Setting LOADPFK=NO in the environment will prevent this downloading. See Appendix A of the *Programmer's Guide: Character User Interface (FMLI and ETI).*

COLUMNS

Can be used to override the width of the logical screen defined for the terminal set in TERM. For terminals with a 132-column mode, for example, invoking FMLI with the line

COLUMNS=132 fmli *frame-file*

will allow this wider screen width to be used.

`LINES`
Can be used to override the length of the logical screen defined for the terminal set in `TERM`.

EXAMPLES

To invoke `fmli`:

```
fmli Menu.start
```

where `Menu.start` is an example of *file* named according to the file name conventions for menu definition files explained above.

To invoke `fmli` and name an initialization file:

```
fmli -i init.myapp Menu.start
```

where `init.myapp` is an example of *initialization_file*.

DIAGNOSTICS

If *file* is not supplied to the `fmli` command, `fmli` returns the message:

```
Initial object must be specified.
```

If *file* does not exist or is not readable, `fmli` returns an error message and exits. The example command line above returns the following message and exits:

```
Can't open object "Menu.start"
```

If *file* exists, but does not start with one of the three correct object names (`Menu.`, `Form.`, or `Text.`) or if it is named correctly but does not contain the proper data, `fmli` starts to build the screen by putting out the screen labels for function keys, after which it flashes the message:

```
I do not recognize that kind of object
```

and then exits.

FILES

`/usr/bin/fmli`

SEE ALSO

`vsig`(1F).

NAME

`fmt` – simple text formatters

SYNOPSIS

`fmt` [`-cs`] [`-w` *width*] [*file*...]

DESCRIPTION

`fmt` is a simple text formatter that fills and joins lines to produce output lines of (up to) the number of characters specified in the `-w` *width* option. The default *width* is 72. `fmt` concatenates the *inputfiles* listed as arguments. If none are given, `fmt` formats text from the standard input.

Blank lines are preserved in the output, as is the spacing between words. `fmt` does not fill lines beginning with a "." (dot), for compatibility with `nroff`(1). Nor does it fill lines starting with "`From:`".

Indentation is preserved in the output, and input lines with differing indentation are not joined (unless `-c` is used).

`fmt` can also be used as an in-line text filter for `vi`(1); the `vi` command:

```
!}fmt
```

reformats the text between the cursor location and the end of the paragraph.

OPTIONS

`-c` Crown margin mode. Preserve the indentation of the first two lines within a paragraph, and align the left margin of each subsequent line with that of the second line. This is useful for tagged paragraphs.

`-s` Split lines only. Do not join short lines to form longer ones. This prevents sample lines of code, and other such formatted text, from being unduly combined.

`-w` *width* Fill output lines to up to *width* columns.

SEE ALSO

`nroff`(1), `vi`(1)

NOTES

The *-width* option is acceptable for BSD compatibility, but it may go away in future releases.

NAME

`fmtmsg` – display a message on `stderr` or system console

SYNOPSIS

`fmtmsg` [`-c` *class*] [`-u` *subclass*] [`-l` *label*] [`-s` *severity*] [`-t` *tag*] [`-a` *action*] *text*

DESCRIPTION

Based on a message's classification component, `fmtmsg` either writes a formatted message to `stderr` or writes a formatted message to the console.

A formatted message consists of up to five standard components as defined below. The classification and subclass components are not displayed as part of the standard message, but rather define the source of the message and direct the display of the formatted message. The valid options are:

`-c` *class* Describes the source of the message. Valid keywords are:

`hard`	The source of the condition is hardware.
`soft`	The source of the condition is software.
`firm`	The source of the condition is firmware.

`-u` *subclass* A list of keywords (separated by commas) that further defines the message and directs the display of the message. Valid keywords are:

`appl`	The condition originated in an application. This keyword should not be used in combination with either `util` or `opsys`.
`util`	The condition originated in a utility. This keyword should not be used in combination with either `appl` or `opsys`.
`opsys`	The message originated in the kernel. This keyword should not be used in combination with either `appl` or `util`.
`recov`	The application will recover from the condition. This keyword should not be used in combination with `nrecov`.
`nrecov`	The application will not recover from the condition. This keyword should not be used in combination with `recov`.
`print`	Print the message to the standard error stream `stderr`.
`console`	Write the message to the system console. `print`, `console`, or both may be used.

`-l` *label* Identifies the source of the message.

`-s` *severity* Indicates the seriousness of the error. The keywords and definitions of the standard levels of *severity* are:

`halt`	The application has encountered a severe fault and is halting.

`error`	The application has detected a fault.
`warn`	The application has detected a condition that is out of the ordinary and might be a problem.
`info`	The application is providing information about a condition that is not in error.

`-t` *tag* The string containing an identifier for the message.

`-a` *action* A text string describing the first step in the error recovery process. This string must be written so that the entire *action* argument is interpreted as a single argument. `fmtmsg` precedes each action string with the `TO FIX:` prefix.

text A text string describing the condition. Must be written so that the entire *text* argument is interpreted as a single argument.

The environment variables `MSGVERB` and `SEV_LEVEL` control the behavior of `fmtmsg`. `MSGVERB` is set by the administrator in the `/etc/profile` for the system. Users can override the value of `MSGVERB` set by the system by resetting `MSGVERB` in their own `.profile` files or by changing the value in their current shell session. `SEV_LEVEL` can be used in shell scripts.

`MSGVERB` tells `fmtmsg` which message components to select when writing messages to `stderr`. The value of `MSGVERB` is a colon separated list of optional keywords. `MSGVERB` can be set as follows:

MSGVERB=[*keyword*[:*keyword*[:...]]]
`export MSGVERB`

Valid *keywords* are: `label`, `severity`, `text`, `action`, and `tag`. If `MSGVERB` contains a keyword for a component and the component's value is not the component's null value, `fmtmsg` includes that component in the message when writing the message to `stderr`. If `MSGVERB` does not include a keyword for a message component, that component is not included in the display of the message. The keywords may appear in any order. If `MSGVERB` is not defined, if its value is the null string, if its value is not of the correct format, or if it contains keywords other than the valid ones listed above, `fmtmsg` selects all components.

`MSGVERB` affects only which message components are selected for display. All message components are included in console messages.

`SEV_LEVEL` defines severity levels and associates print strings with them for use by `fmtmsg`. The standard severity levels shown below cannot be modified. Additional severity levels can be defined, redefined, and removed.

0 (no severity is used)
1 HALT
2 ERROR
3 WARNING
4 INFO

SEV_LEVEL is set as follows:

```
SEV_LEVEL=[description[:description[:...]]]
export SEV_LEVEL
```

description is a comma-separated list containing three fields:

description=severity_keyword,level,printstring

severity_keyword is a character string used as the keyword with the **-s** *severity* option to **fmtmsg**.

level is a character string that evaluates to a positive integer (other than 0, 1, 2, 3, or 4, which are reserved for the standard severity levels). If the keyword *severity_keyword* is used, *level* is the severity value passed on to **fmtmsg**(3C).

printstring is the character string used by **fmtmsg** in the standard message format whenever the severity value *level* is used.

If SEV_LEVEL is not defined, or if its value is null, no severity levels other than the defaults are available. If a *description* in the colon separated list is not a comma separated list containing three fields, or if the second field of a comma separated list does not evaluate to a positive integer, that *description* in the colon separated list is ignored.

DIAGNOSTICS

The exit codes for **fmtmsg** are the following:

- 0 All the requested functions were executed successfully.
- 1 The command contains a syntax error, an invalid option, or an invalid argument to an option.
- 2 The function executed with partial success, however the message was not displayed on stderr.
- 4 The function executed with partial success, however the message was not displayed on the system console.
- 32 No requested functions were executed successfully.

EXAMPLES

Example 1: The following example of **fmtmsg** produces a complete message in the standard message format and displays it to the standard error stream:

```
fmtmsg -c soft -u recov,print,appl -l UX:cat -s error -t
UX:cat:001 -a "refer to manual" "invalid syntax"
```

produces:

```
UX:cat: ERROR: invalid syntax
TO FIX: refer to manual    UX:cat:138
```

Example 2: When the environment variable MSGVERB is set as follows:

```
MSGVERB=severity:text:action
```

and Example 1 is used, fmtmsg produces:

```
ERROR: invalid syntax
TO FIX: refer to manual
```

Example 3: When the environment variable SEV_LEVEL is set as follows:

```
SEV_LEVEL=note,5,NOTE
```

the following fmtmsg command:

```
fmtmsg -c soft -u print -l UX:cat -s note -a "refer to
manual" "invalid syntax"
```

produces:

```
UX:cat: NOTE: invalid syntax
TO FIX: refer to manual
```

and displays the message on stderr.

SEE ALSO

addsverity(3C), fmtmsg(3C) in the *Programmer's Reference Manual.*

NAME

`fold` – fold long lines

SYNOPSIS

`fold` [**-w** *width* | *-width*] [*filename* ...]

DESCRIPTION

Fold the contents of the specified *filename*s, or the standard input if no files are specified, breaking the lines to have maximum width *width*. The default for *width* is 80. *width* should be a multiple of 8 if tabs are present, or the tabs should be expanded.

SEE ALSO

`pr`(1)

NOTES

Folding may not work correctly if underlining is present.

The *-width* option is provided as a transition tool only. It will be removed in future releases.

NAME

ftp – file transfer program

SYNOPSIS

ftp [-dgintv] [*hostname*]

DESCRIPTION

The ftp command is the user interface to the ARPANET standard File Transfer Protocol (FTP). ftp transfers files to and from a remote network site.

The client host with which ftp is to communicate may be specified on the command line. If this is done, ftp immediately attempts to establish a connection to an FTP server on that host; otherwise, ftp enters its command interpreter and awaits instructions from the user. When ftp is awaiting commands from the user, it displays the prompt ftp>.

The following options may be specified at the command line, or to the command interpreter:

-d Enable debugging.

-g Disable filename globbing.

-i Turn off interactive prompting during multiple file transfers.

-n Do not attempt auto-login upon initial connection. If auto-login is not disabled, ftp checks the .netrc file in the user's home directory for an entry describing an account on the remote machine. If no entry exists, ftp will prompt for the login name of the account on the remote machine (the default is the login name on the local machine), and, if necessary, prompts for a password and an account with which to login.

-t Enable packet tracing (unimplemented).

-v Show all responses from the remote server, as well as report on data transfer statistics. This is turned on by default if ftp is running interactively with its input coming from the user's terminal.

The following commands can be specified to the command interpreter:

! [*command*]
Run *command* as a shell command on the local machine. If no *command* is given, invoke an interactive shell.

$ *macro-name* [*args*]
Execute the macro *macro-name* that was defined with the macdef command. Arguments are passed to the macro unglobbed.

account [*passwd*]
Supply a supplemental password required by a remote system for access to resources once a login has been successfully completed. If no argument is included, the user will be prompted for an account password in a non-echoing input mode.

`append` *local-file* [*remote-file*]
Append a local file to a file on the remote machine. If *remote-file* is not specified, the local file name is used, subject to alteration by any `ntrans` or `nmap` settings. File transfer uses the current settings for representation type, file structure, and transfer mode.

`ascii` Set the representation type to network ASCII. This is the default type.

`bell` Sound a bell after each file transfer command is completed.

`binary`
Set the representation type to image.

`bye` Terminate the FTP session with the remote server and exit `ftp`. An EOF will also terminate the session and exit.

`case` Toggle remote computer file name case mapping during `mget` commands. When `case` is on (default is off), remote computer file names with all letters in upper case are written in the local directory with the letters mapped to lower case.

`cd` *remote-directory*
Change the working directory on the remote machine to *remote-directory*.

`cdup` Change the remote machine working directory to the parent of the current remote machine working directory.

`close` Terminate the FTP session with the remote server, and return to the command interpreter. Any defined macros are erased.

`cr` Toggle RETURN stripping during network ASCII type file retrieval. Records are denoted by a RETURN/LINEFEED sequence during network ASCII type file transfer. When `cr` is on (the default), RETURN characters are stripped from this sequence to conform with the UNIX system single LINEFEED record delimiter. Records on non-UNIX-system remote hosts may contain single LINEFEED characters; when an network ASCII type transfer is made, these LINEFEED characters may be distinguished from a record delimiter only when `cr` is off.

`delete` *remote-file*
Delete the file *remote-file* on the remote machine.

`debug`
Toggle debugging mode. When debugging is on, `ftp` prints each command sent to the remote machine, preceded by the string -->.

`dir` [*remote-directory*] [*local-file*]
Print a listing of the directory contents in the directory, *remote-directory*, and, optionally, placing the output in *local-file*. If no directory is specified, the current working directory on the remote machine is used. If no local file is specified, or *local-file* is –, output is sent to the terminal.

`disconnect`
A synonym for `close`.

`form` [*format-name*]
Set the carriage control format subtype of the representation type to *format-name*. The only valid *format-name* is `non-print`, which corresponds to the default non-print subtype.

`get` *remote-file* [*local-file*]
Retrieve the *remote-file* and store it on the local machine. If the local file name is not specified, it is given the same name it has on the remote machine, subject to alteration by the current `case`, `ntrans`, and `nmap` settings. The current settings for representation type, file structure, and transfer mode are used while transferring the file.

`glob` Toggle filename expansion, or globbing, for `mdelete`, `mget` and `mput`. If globbing is turned off, filenames are taken literally.

Globbing for `mput` is done as in `sh`(1). For `mdelete` and `mget`, each remote file name is expanded separately on the remote machine, and the lists are not merged.

Expansion of a directory name is likely to be radically different from expansion of the name of an ordinary file: the exact result depends on the remote operating system and FTP server, and can be previewed by doing `mls` *remote-files* –.

`mget` and `mput` are not meant to transfer entire directory subtrees of files. You can do this by transferring a `tar`(1) archive of the subtree (using a representation type of image as set by the `binary` command).

`hash` Toggle hash-sign (#) printing for each data block transferred. The size of a data block is 8192 bytes.

`help` [*command*]
Print an informative message about the meaning of *command*. If no argument is given, `ftp` prints a list of the known commands.

`lcd` [*directory*]
Change the working directory on the local machine. If no *directory* is specified, the user's home directory is used.

`ls` [*remote-directory*] [*local-file*]
Print an abbreviated listing of the contents of a directory on the remote machine. If *remote-directory* is left unspecified, the current working directory is used. If no local file is specified, or if *local-file* is –, the output is sent to the terminal.

`macdef` *macro-name*
Define a macro. Subsequent lines are stored as the macro *macro-name*; a null line (consecutive NEWLINE characters in a file or RETURN characters from the terminal) terminates macro input mode. There is a limit of 16 macros and 4096 total characters in all defined macros. Macros remain defined until a `close` command is executed.

The macro processor interprets `$` and `\` as special characters. A `$` followed by a number (or numbers) is replaced by the corresponding argument on the macro invocation command line. A `$` followed by an `i` signals that macro processor that the executing macro is to be looped. On the first pass `$i` is replaced by the first argument on the macro invocation command line, on the second pass it is replaced by the second argument, and so on. A \ followed by any character is replaced by that character. Use the \ to prevent special treatment of the `$`.

`mdelete` [*remote-files*]
: Delete the *remote-files* on the remote machine.

`mdir` *remote-files local-file*
: Like `dir`, except multiple remote files may be specified. If interactive prompting is on, `ftp` will prompt the user to verify that the last argument is indeed the target local file for receiving `mdir` output.

`mget` *remote-files*
: Expand the *remote-files* on the remote machine and do a `get` for each file name thus produced. See `glob` for details on the filename expansion. Resulting file names will then be processed according to `case`, `ntrans`, and `nmap` settings. Files are transferred into the local working directory, which can be changed with `lcd` *directory*; new local directories can be created with `! mkdir` *directory*.

`mkdir` *directory-name*
: Make a directory on the remote machine.

`mls` *remote-files local-file*
: Like `ls`(1), except multiple remote files may be specified. If interactive prompting is on, `ftp` will prompt the user to verify that the last argument is indeed the target local file for receiving `mls` output.

`mode` [*mode-name*]
: Set the transfer mode to *mode-name*. The only valid *mode-name* is `stream`, which corresponds to the default stream mode. This implementation only supports `stream`, and requires that it be specified.

`mput` *local-files*
: Expand wild cards in the list of local files given as arguments and do a `put` for each file in the resulting list. See `glob` for details of filename expansion. Resulting file names will then be processed according to `ntrans` and `nmap` settings.

`nmap` [*inpattern outpattern*]
: Set or unset the filename mapping mechanism. If no arguments are specified, the filename mapping mechanism is unset. If arguments are specified, remote filenames are mapped during `mput` commands and `put` commands issued without a specified remote target filename. If arguments are specified, local filenames are mapped during `mget` commands and `get` commands issued without a specified local target filename.

  This command is useful when connecting to a non-UNIX-system remote host with different file naming conventions or practices. The mapping follows the pattern set by *inpattern* and *outpattern*. *inpattern* is a template for incoming filenames (which may have already been processed according to the `ntrans` and `case` settings). Variable templating is accomplished by including the sequences `$1`, `$2`, ..., `$9` in *inpattern*. Use \ to prevent this special treatment of the `$` character. All other characters are treated literally, and are used to determine the **nmap** *inpattern* variable values.

For example, given *inpattern* `$1.$2` and the remote file name `mydata.data`, `$1` would have the value `mydata`, and `$2` would have the value `data`.

The *outpattern* determines the resulting mapped filename. The sequences `$1`, `$2`, ..., `$9` are replaced by any value resulting from the *inpattern* template. The sequence `$0` is replaced by the original filename. Additionally, the sequence [*seq1* , *seq2*] is replaced by *seq1* if *seq1* is not a null string; otherwise it is replaced by *seq2*.

For example, the command `nmap $1.$2.$3 [$1,$2].[$2,file]` would yield the output filename `myfile.data` for input filenames `myfile.data` and `myfile.data.old`, `myfile.file` for the input filename `myfile`, and `myfile.myfile` for the input filename `myfile`. SPACE characters may be included in *outpattern*, as in the example `nmap $1 | sed "s/  *$//" > $1`. Use the \ character to prevent special treatment of the `$`, `[`, `]`, and `,` characters.

`ntrans` [*inchars* [*outchars*]]

Set or unset the filename character translation mechanism. If no arguments are specified, the filename character translation mechanism is unset. If arguments are specified, characters in remote filenames are translated during `mput` commands and `put` commands issued without a specified remote target filename, and characters in local filenames are translated during `mget` commands and `get` commands issued without a specified local target filename.

This command is useful when connecting to a non-UNIX-system remote host with different file naming conventions or practices. Characters in a filename matching a character in *inchars* are replaced with the corresponding character in *outchars*. If the character's position in *inchars* is longer than the length of *outchars*, the character is deleted from the file name.

`open` *host* [*port*]

Establish a connection to the specified *host* FTP server. An optional port number may be supplied, in which case, `ftp` will attempt to contact an FTP server at that port. If the *auto-login* option is on (default setting), `ftp` will also attempt to automatically log the user in to the FTP server.

`prompt`

Toggle interactive prompting. Interactive prompting occurs during multiple file transfers to allow the user to selectively retrieve or store files. By default, prompting is turned on. If prompting is turned off, any `mget` or `mput` will transfer all files, and any `mdelete` will delete all files.

`proxy` *ftp-command*

Execute an FTP command on a secondary control connection. This command allows simultaneous connection to two remote FTP servers for transferring files between the two servers. The first `proxy` command should be an `open`, to establish the secondary control connection. Enter the command `proxy ?` to see other FTP commands executable on the secondary connection.

The following commands behave differently when prefaced by `proxy`: `open` will not define new macros during the auto-login process, `close` will not erase existing macro definitions, `get` and `mget` transfer files from the host on the primary control connection to the host on the secondary control connection, and `put`, `mputd`, and `append` transfer files from the host on the secondary control connection to the host on the primary control connection.

Third party file transfers depend upon support of the `PASV` command by the server on the secondary control connection.

`put` *local-file* [*remote-file*]
: Store a local file on the remote machine. If *remote-file* is left unspecified, the local file name is used after processing according to any `ntrans` or `nmap` settings in naming the remote file. File transfer uses the current settings for representation type, file structure, and transfer mode.

`pwd` Print the name of the current working directory on the remote machine.

`quit` A synonym for `bye`.

`quote` *arg1 arg2 ...*
: Send the arguments specified, verbatim, to the remote FTP server. A single FTP reply code is expected in return. (The `remotehelp` command displays a list of valid arguments.)

`quote` should be used only by experienced users who are familiar with the FTP protocol.

`recv` *remote-file* [*local-file*]
: A synonym for `get`.

`remotehelp` [*command-name*]
: Request help from the remote FTP server. If a *command-name* is specified it is supplied to the server as well.

`rename` *from to*
: Rename the file *from* on the remote machine to have the name *to*.

`reset` Clear reply queue. This command re-synchronizes command/reply sequencing with the remote FTP server. Resynchronization may be necessary following a violation of the FTP protocol by the remote server.

`rmdir` *directory-name*
: Delete a directory on the remote machine.

`runique`
: Toggle storing of files on the local system with unique filenames. If a file already exists with a name equal to the target local filename for a `get` or `mget` command, a `.1` is appended to the name. If the resulting name matches another existing file, a `.2` is appended to the original name. If this process continues up to `.99`, an error message is printed, and the transfer does not take place. The generated unique filename will be

reported. `runique` will not affect local files generated from a shell command. The default value is off.

`send` *local-file* [*remote-file*]
A synonym for `put`.

`sendport`
Toggle the use of `PORT` commands. By default, `ftp` will attempt to use a `PORT` command when establishing a connection for each data transfer. The use of `PORT` commands can prevent delays when performing multiple file transfers. If the `PORT` command fails, `ftp` will use the default data port. When the use of `PORT` commands is disabled, no attempt will be made to use `PORT` commands for each data transfer. This is useful when connected to certain FTP implementations that ignore `PORT` commands but incorrectly indicate they have been accepted.

`status`
Show the current status of `ftp`.

`struct` [*struct-name*]
Set the file structure to *struct-name*. The only valid *struct-name* is `file`, which corresponds to the default file structure. The implementation only supports `file`, and requires that it be specified.

`sunique`
Toggle storing of files on remote machine under unique file names. The remote FTP server must support the `STOU` command for successful completion. The remote server will report the unique name. Default value is off.

`tenex` Set the representation type to that needed to talk to TENEX machines.

`trace` Toggle packet tracing (unimplemented).

`type` [*type-name*]
Set the representation type to *type-name*. The valid *type-name*s are `ascii` for network ASCII, `binary` or `image` for image, and `tenex` for local byte size with a byte size of 8 (used to talk to TENEX machines). If no type is specified, the current type is printed. The default type is network ASCII.

`user` *user-name* [*password*] [*account*]
Identify yourself to the remote FTP server. If the password is not specified and the server requires it, `ftp` will prompt the user for it (after disabling local echo). If an account field is not specified, and the FTP server requires it, the user will be prompted for it. If an account field is specified, an account command will be relayed to the remote server after the login sequence is completed if the remote server did not require it for logging in. Unless `ftp` is invoked with auto-login disabled, this process is done automatically on initial connection to the FTP server.

`verbose`
Toggle verbose mode. In verbose mode, all responses from the FTP server are displayed to the user. In addition, if verbose mode is on, when a file transfer completes, statistics regarding the efficiency of the transfer are

reported. By default, verbose mode is on if ftp's commands are coming from a terminal, and off otherwise.

? [*command*]
A synonym for help.

Command arguments which have embedded spaces may be quoted with quote (") marks.

If any command argument which is not indicated as being optional is not specified, ftp will prompt for that argument.

ABORTING A FILE TRANSFER

To abort a file transfer, use the terminal interrupt key. Sending transfers will be immediately halted. Receiving transfers will be halted by sending an FTP protocol ABOR command to the remote server, and discarding any further data received. The speed at which this is accomplished depends upon the remote server's support for ABOR processing. If the remote server does not support the ABOR command, an ftp> prompt will not appear until the remote server has completed sending the requested file.

The terminal interrupt key sequence will be ignored when ftp has completed any local processing and is awaiting a reply from the remote server. A long delay in this mode may result from the ABOR processing described above, or from unexpected behavior by the remote server, including violations of the ftp protocol. If the delay results from unexpected remote server behavior, the local ftp program must be killed by hand.

FILE NAMING CONVENTIONS

Local files specified as arguments to ftp commands are processed according to the following rules.

1) If the file name – is specified, the standard input (for reading) or standard output (for writing) is used.

2) If the first character of the file name is |, the remainder of the argument is interpreted as a shell command. ftp then forks a shell, using popen(3S) with the argument supplied, and reads (writes) from the standard output (standard input) of that shell. If the shell command includes SPACE characters, the argument must be quoted; for example "| ls -lt". A particularly useful example of this mechanism is: "dir | more".

3) Failing the above checks, if globbing is enabled, local file names are expanded according to the rules used in the sh(1); see the glob command. If the ftp command expects a single local file (for example, put), only the first filename generated by the globbing operation is used.

4) For mget commands and get commands with unspecified local file names, the local filename is the remote filename, which may be altered by a case, ntrans, or nmap setting. The resulting filename may then be altered if runique is on.

5) For mput commands and put commands with unspecified remote file names, the remote filename is the local filename, which may be altered by a ntrans or nmap setting. The resulting filename may then be altered by the remote server if sunique is on.

FILE TRANSFER PARAMETERS

The FTP specification specifies many parameters which may affect a file transfer.

The representation type may be one of network ASCII, EBCDIC, image, or local byte size with a specified byte size (for PDP-10's and PDP-20's mostly). The network ASCII and EBCDIC types have a further subtype which specifies whether vertical format control (NEWLINE characters, form feeds, etc.) are to be passed through (non-print), provided in TELNET format (TELNET format controls), or provided in ASA (FORTRAN) (carriage control (ASA)) format. **ftp** supports the network ASCII (subtype non-print only) and image types, plus local byte size with a byte size of 8 for communicating with TENEX machines.

The file structure may be one of **file** (no record structure), **record**, or **page**. **ftp** supports only the default value, which is **file**.

The transfer mode may be one of **stream**, **block**, or **compressed**. **ftp** supports only the default value, which is **stream**.

SEE ALSO

ls(1), rcp(1), tar(1), sh(1), ftpd(1M), popen(3S), netrc(4).

NOTES

Correct execution of many commands depends upon proper behavior by the remote server.

An error in the treatment of carriage returns in the 4.2 BSD code handling transfers with a representation type of network ASCII has been corrected. This correction may result in incorrect transfers of binary files to and from 4.2 BSD servers using a representation type of network ASCII. Avoid this problem by using the image type.

NAME

gcore − get core images of running processes

SYNOPSIS

gcore [−o *filename*] *process-id* ...

DESCRIPTION

gcore creates a core image of each specified process. Such an image may be used with debuggers such as **sdb**. The name of the core image file for the process whose process ID is *process-id* will be core.*process-id*.

The −o option substitutes *filename* in place of core as the first part of the name of the core image files.

FILES

core.*process-id*   core images

SEE ALSO

kill(1), csh(1)
sdb(1), ptrace(2) in the *Programmer's Reference Manual*.

NAME

gencat – generate a formatted message catalogue

SYNOPSIS

gencat [-m] *catfile msgfile* ...

DESCRIPTION

The gencat utility merges the message text source file(s) msgfile into a formatted message database *catfile*. The database *catfile* will be created if it does not already exist. If *catfile* does exist its messages will be included in the new *catfile*. If set and message numbers collide, the new message-text defined in *msgfile* will replace the old message text currently contained in *catfile*. The message text source file (or set of files) input to gencat can contain either set and message numbers or simply message numbers, in which case the set **NL_SETD** [see **nl_types**(5)] is assumed.

The format of a message text source file is defined as follows. Note that the fields of a message text source line are separated by a single ASCII space or tab character. Any other ASCII spaces or tabs are considered as being part of the subsequent field.

`$set n comment`

Where *n* specifies the set identifier of the following messages until the next `$set`, `$delset` or end-of-file appears. *n* must be a number in the range (1–{NL_SETMAX}). Set identifiers within a single source file need not be contiguous. Any string following the set identifier is treated as a comment. If no `$set` directive is specified in a message text source file, all messages will be located in the default message set NL_SETD.

`$delset n comment`

Deletes message set *n* from an existing message catalogue. Any string following the set number is treated as a comment.

(Note: if *n* is not a valid set it is ignored.)

`$ comment`

A line beginning with a dollar symbol $ followed by an ASCII space or tab character is treated as a comment.

`m message-text`

The *m* denotes the message identifier, which is a number in the range (1-{NL_MSGMAX}). The message-text is stored in the message catalogue with the set identifier specified by the last `$set` directive, and with message identifier *m*. If the message-text is empty, and an ASCII space or tab field separator is present, an empty string is stored in the message catalogue. If a message source line has a message number, but neither a field separator nor message-text , the existing message with that number (if any) is deleted from the catalogue. Message identifiers need not be contiguous. The length of message-text must be in the range (0–{NL_TEXTMAX}).

`$quote c`

This line specifies an optional quote character *c*, which can be used to surround message-text so that trailing spaces or null (empty) messages are visible in a message source line. By default, or if an empty `$quote` directive is supplied, no quoting of message-text will be recognized.

Empty lines in a message text source file are ignored.

Text strings can contain the special characters and escape sequences defined in the following table:

Description	Symbol	Sequence
newline	NL(LF)	\n
horizontal tab	HT	\t
vertical tab	VT	\v
backspace	BS	\b
carriage return	CR	\r
form feed	FF	\f
backslash	\	\\
bit pattern	ddd	\ddd

The escape sequence \ddd consists of backslash followed by 1, 2 or 3 octal digits, which are taken to specify the value of the desired character. If the character following a backslash is not one of those specified, the backslash is ignored.

Backslash followed by an ASCII newline character is also used to continue a string on the following line. Thus, the following two lines describe a single message string:

```
1 This line continues \
to the next line
```

which is equivalent to:

```
1 This line continues to the next line
```

NOTES

This version of gencat is built upon the mkmsgs utility. The gencat database comprises of two files *catfile*.m *which is an* mkmsgs format catalogue and the file *catfile* which contains the information required to translate an set and message number into a simple message number which can be used in a call to gettxt.

Using gettxt constrains the catalogues to be located in a subdirectory under /usr/lib/locale. This restriction is lifted by placing only a symbolic link to the catalogue in the directory /usr/lib/locale/Xopen/LC_MESSAGES when the catalogue is opened. It is this link that gettxt uses when attempting to access the catalogue. The link is removed when the catalogue is closed but occasionally as applications exit abnormally without closing catlogues redundant symbolic links will be left in the directory.

For compatibility with previous version of gencat released in a number of specialized internationalization products, the -m option is supplied. This option will cause gencat to build a single file *catfile* which is compatible with the format catalogues produced by the earlier versions. The retrieval routines detect the type of catalogue they are using and will act appropriately.

SEE ALSO

mkmsgs(1)
catopen(3C), catgets(3C), catclose(3C), gettxt(3C), nl_types(5) in the *Programmer's Reference Manual.*

NAME

getopt – parse command options

SYNOPSIS

set -- `getopt *optstring* $*`

DESCRIPTION

The getopts command supercedes getopt. For more information, see the NOTES below.

getopt is used to break up options in command lines for easy parsing by shell procedures and to check for legal options. *optstring* is a string of recognized option letters; see getopt(3C). If a letter is followed by a colon, the option is expected to have an argument which may or may not be separated from it by white space. The special option -- is used to delimit the end of the options. If it is used explicitly, getopt recognizes it; otherwise, getopt generates it; in either case, getopt places it at the end of the options. The positional parameters ($1 $2 ...) of the shell are reset so that each option is preceded by a – and is in its own positional parameter; each option argument is also parsed into its own positional parameter.

EXAMPLE

The following code fragment shows how one might process the arguments for a command that can take the options a or b, as well as the option o, which requires an argument:

```
set -- `getopt abo: $*`
if [ $? != 0 ]
then
        echo $USAGE
        exit 2
fi
for i in $*
do
        case $i in
        -a | -b)        FLAG=$i; shift;;
        -o)             OARG=$2; shift 2;;
        --)             shift; break;;
        esac
done
```

This code accepts any of the following as equivalent:

```
cmd -aoarg file file
cmd -a -o arg file file
cmd -oarg -a file file
cmd -a -oarg -- file file
```

SEE ALSO

getopts(1), sh(1).
getopt(3C) in the *Programmer's Reference Manual.*

DIAGNOSTICS

getopt prints an error message on the standard error when it encounters an option letter not included in *optstring*.

NOTES

getopt will not be supported in the next major release. For this release a conversion tool has been provided, getoptcvt. For more information about getopts and getoptcvt, see getopts(1).

Reset optind to 1 when rescanning the options.

getopt does not support the part of Rule 8 of the command syntax standard [see intro(1)] that permits groups of option-arguments following an option to be separated by white space and quoted. For example,

```
cmd -a -b -o "xxx z yy" file
```

is not handled correctly. To correct this deficiency, use the getopts command in place of getopt.

If an option that takes an option-argument is followed by a value that is the same as one of the options listed in *optstring* (referring to the earlier EXAMPLE section, but using the following command line: cmd -o -a file), getopt always treats -a as an option-argument to -o; it never recognizes -a as an option. For this case, the for loop in the example shifts past the *file* argument.

NAME

getopts, getoptcvt – parse command options

SYNOPSIS

getopts *optstring name* [*arg* ...]

/usr/lib/getoptcvt [-b] *file*

DESCRIPTION

getopts is used by shell procedures to parse positional parameters and to check for valid options. It supports all applicable rules of the command syntax standard (see Rules 3-10, intro(1)). It should be used in place of the getopt command. (See the NOTES section below.)

optstring must contain the option letters the command using getopts will recognize; if a letter is followed by a colon, the option is expected to have an argument, or group of arguments, which must be separated from it by white space.

Each time it is invoked, getopts places the next option in the shell variable *name* and the index of the next argument to be processed in the shell variable OPTIND. Whenever the shell or a shell procedure is invoked, OPTIND is initialized to 1.

When an option requires an option-argument, getopts places it in the shell variable OPTARG.

If an illegal option is encountered, ? will be placed in *name*.

When the end of options is encountered, getopts exits with a non-zero exit status. The special option -- may be used to delimit the end of the options.

By default, getopts parses the positional parameters. If extra arguments (*arg* ...) are given on the getopts command line, getopts parsees them instead.

/usr/lib/getoptcvt reads the shell script in *file*, converts it to use getopts instead of getopt, and writes the results on the standard output.

-b Make the converted script portable to earlier releases of the UNIX system. /usr/lib/getoptcvt modifies the shell script in *file* so that when the resulting shell script is executed, it determines at run time whether to invoke getopts or getopt.

So all new commands will adhere to the command syntax standard described in intro(1), they should use getopts or getopt to parse positional parameters and check for options that are valid for that command (see the NOTES section below).

EXAMPLE

The following fragment of a shell program shows how one might process the arguments for a command that can take the options a or b, as well as the option o, which requires an option-argument:

```
while getopts abo: c
do
        case $c in
        a | b)          FLAG=$c;;
        o)              OARG=$OPTARG;;
        \?)             echo $USAGE
                        exit 2;;
        esac
```

```
done
shift `expr $OPTIND - 1`
```

This code accepts any of the following as equivalent:

```
cmd -a -b -o "xxx z yy" file
cmd -a -b -o "xxx z yy" -- file
cmd -ab -o xxx,z,yy file
cmd -ab -o "xxx z yy" file
cmd -o xxx,z,yy -b -a file
```

SEE ALSO

intro(1), sh(1).
getopt(3C) in the *Programmer's Reference Manual*.

NOTES

Although the following command syntax rule [see intro(1)] relaxations are permitted under the current implementation, they should not be used because they may not be supported in future releases of the system. As in the EXAMPLE section above, a and b are options, and the option o requires an option-argument. The following example violates Rule 5: options with option-arguments must not be grouped with other options:

```
cmd -aboxxx file
```

The following example violates Rule 6: there must be white space after an option that takes an option-argument:

```
cmd -ab -oxxx file
```

Changing the value of the shell variable OPTIND or parsing different sets of arguments may lead to unexpected results.

DIAGNOSTICS

getopts prints an error message on the standard error when it encounters an option letter not included in *optstring*.

NAME

gettxt – retrieve a text string from a message data base

SYNOPSIS

gettxt *msgfile*:*msgnum* [*dflt_msg*]

DESCRIPTION

gettxt retrieves a text string from a message file in the directory /usr/lib/locale/*locale*/LC_MESSAGES. The directory name *locale* corresponds to the language in which the text strings are written; see setlocale(3C).

msgfile Name of the file in the directory /usr/lib/locale/*locale*/LC_MESSAGES to retrieve *msgnum* from. The name of *msgfile* can be up to 14 characters in length, but may not contain either \0 (null) or the ASCII code for / (slash) or : (colon).

msgnum Sequence number of the string to retrieve from *msgfile*. The strings in *msgfile* are numbered sequentially from *1* to *n*, where *n* is the number of strings in the file.

dflt_msg Default string to be displayed if gettxt fails to retrieve *msgnum* from *msgfile*. Nongraphic characters must be represented as alphabetic escape sequences.

The text string to be retrieved is in the file *msgfile*, created by the mkmsgs(1) utility and installed under the directory /usr/lib/locale/*locale*/LC_MESSAGES. You control which directory is searched by setting the environment variable LC_MESSAGES. If LC_MESSAGES is not set, the environment variable LANG will be used. If LANG is not set, the files containing the strings are under the directory /usr/lib/locale/C/LC_MESSAGES.

If gettxt fails to retrieve a message in the requested language, it will try to retrieve the same message from /usr/lib/locale/C/LC_MESSAGES/*msgfile*. If this also fails, and if *dflt_msg* is present and non-null, then it will display the value of *dflt_msg*; if *dflt_msg* is not present or is null, then it will display the string Message not found!!.

EXAMPLE

If the environment variables LANG or LC_MESSAGES have not been set to other than their default values,

```
gettxt UX:10 "hello world\n"
```

will try to retrieve the 10th message from /usr/lib/locale/C/UX/*msgfile*. If the retrieval fails, the message "hello world," followed by a new-line, will be displayed.

FILES

/usr/lib/locale/C/LC_MESSAGES/*	default message files created by mkmsgs(1)
/usr/lib/locale/*locale*/LC_MESSAGES/*	message files for different languages created by mkmsgs(1)

SEE ALSO

exstr(1), mkmsgs(1), srchtxt(1).
gettxt(3C), setlocale(3C) in the *Programmer's Reference Manual*.

NAME

`grep` – search a file for a pattern

SYNOPSIS

`grep` [*options*] `limited regular expression` [*file* ...]

DESCRIPTION

`grep` searches files for a pattern and prints all lines that contain that pattern. `grep` uses limited regular expressions (expressions that have string values that use a subset of the possible alphanumeric and special characters) like those used with `ed`(1) to match the patterns. It uses a compact non-deterministic algorithm.

Be careful using the characters `$`, `*`, `[`, `^`, |, `(`, `)`, and \ in the *limited regular expression* because they are also meaningful to the shell. It is safest to enclose the entire *limited regular expression* in single quotes `'...'`.

If no files are specified, `grep` assumes standard input. Normally, each line found is copied to standard output. The file name is printed before each line found if there is more than one input file.

Command line options are:

- `-b` Precede each line by the block number on which it was found. This can be useful in locating block numbers by context (first block is 0).
- `-c` Print only a count of the lines that contain the pattern.
- `-i` Ignore upper/lower case distinction during comparisons.
- `-h` Prevents the name of the file containing the matching line from being appended to that line. Used when searching multiple files.
- `-l` Print the names of files with matching lines once, separated by new-lines. Does not repeat the names of files when the pattern is found more than once.
- `-n` Precede each line by its line number in the file (first line is 1).
- `-s` Suppress error messages about nonexistent or unreadable files
- `-v` Print all lines except those that contain the pattern.

SEE ALSO

`ed`(1), `egrep`(1), `fgrep`(1), `sed`(1), `sh`(1).

DIAGNOSTICS

Exit status is 0 if any matches are found, 1 if none, 2 for syntax errors or inaccessible files (even if matches were found).

NOTES

Lines are limited to BUFSIZ characters; longer lines are truncated. BUFSIZ is defined in `/usr/include/stdio.h`.
If there is a line with embedded nulls, `grep` will only match up to the first null; if it matches, it will print the entire line.

NAME

groups – print group membership of user

SYNOPSIS

groups [*user*]

DESCRIPTION

The command **groups** prints on standard output the groups to which you or the optionally specified user belong. Each user belongs to a group specified in `/etc/passwd` and possibly to other groups as specified in `/etc/group`.

SEE ALSO

setgroups(2), group(4), passwd(4).

FILES

/etc/passwd
/etc/group

NAME

head – display first few lines of files

SYNOPSIS

head [*–n*] [*file*...]

DESCRIPTION

head copies the first *n* lines of each *file* to the standard output. If no *file* is given, **head** copies lines from the standard input. The default value of *n* is 10 lines.

When more than one file is specified, the start of each file will look like:

==>*file*<==

Thus, a common way to display a set of short files, identifying each one, is:

head -9999 *file1 file2* ...

SEE ALSO

cat(1), more(1), pg(1), tail(1)

NAME

iconv – code set conversion utility

SYNOPSIS

iconv -f *fromcode* -t *tocode* [*file*]

DESCRIPTION

iconv converts the characters or sequences of characters in *file* from one code set to another and writes the results to standard output. Should no conversion exist for a particular character then it is converted to the underscore '_' in the target codeset.

The required arguments *fromcode* and *tocode* identify the input and output code sets, respectively. If no *file* argument is specified on the command line, iconv reads the standard input.

iconv will always convert to or from the ISO 8859-1 Latin alphabet No.1, from or to an ISO 646 ASCII variant codeset for a particular language. The ISO 8859-1 codeset will support the majority of 8 bit codesets. The conversions attempted by iconv accommodate the most commonly used languages.

The following table lists the supported conversions.

Code Set Conversions Supported				
Code	Symbol	Target Code	Symbol	comment
ISO 646	646	ISO 8859-1	8859	US Ascii
ISO 646de	646de	ISO 8859-1	8859	German
ISO 646da	646da	ISO 8859-1	8859	Danish
ISO 646en	646en	ISO 8859-1	8859	English Ascii
ISO 646es	646es	ISO 8859-1	8859	Spanish
ISO 646fr	646fr	ISO 8859-1	8859	French
ISO 646it	646it	ISO 8859-1	8859	Italian
ISO 646sv	646sv	ISO 8859-1	8859	Swedish
ISO 8859-1	8859	ISO 646	646	7 bit Ascii
ISO 8859-1	8859	ISO 646de	646de	German
ISO 8859-1	8859	ISO 646da	646da	Danish
ISO 8859-1	8859	ISO 646en	646en	English Ascii
ISO 8859-1	8859	ISO 646es	646es	Spanish
ISO 8859-1	8859	ISO 646fr	646fr	French
ISO 8859-1	8859	ISO 646it	646it	Italian
ISO 8859-1	8859	ISO 646sv	646sv	Swedish

The conversions are performed according to the tables found on the iconv(5) manual page.

EXAMPLES

The following converts the contents of file mail1 from code set 8859 to 646fr and stores the results in file mail.local.

```
iconv -f 8859 -t 646fr mail1 > mail.local
```

FILES

/usr/lib/iconv/iconv_data	lists the conversions supported.
/usr/lib/iconv/*.t	conversion tables.

SEE ALSO

iconv(5) in the *System Administrator's Reference Manual.*

DIAGNOSTICS

iconv returns 0 upon successful completion, 1 otherwise.

NAME

id – print the user name and ID, and group name and ID

SYNOPSIS

id [-a]

DESCRIPTION

id displays the calling process's ID and name. It also displays the group ID and name. If the real effective IDs do not match, both are printed.

The -a option reports all the groups to which the invoking process belongs. ID, and your username. If your real and effective IDs do not match, both are printed.

The -a option reports all the groups to which the invoking user belongs.

SEE ALSO

getuid(2) in the *Programmer's Reference Manual.*

NAME

ipcrm – remove a message queue, semaphore set, or shared memory ID

SYNOPSIS

ipcrm [*options*]

DESCRIPTION

ipcrm removes one or more messages, semaphores, or shared memory identifiers. The identifiers are specified by the following *options*:

-q *msqid* Remove the message queue identifier *msqid* from the system and destroy the message queue and data structure associated with it.

-m *shmid* Remove the shared memory identifier *shmid* from the system. The shared memory segment and data structure associated with it are destroyed after the last detach.

-s *semid* Remove the semaphore identifier *semid* from the system and destroy the set of semaphores and data structure associated with it.

-Q *msgkey* Remove the message queue identifier, created with key *msgkey*, from the system and destroy the message queue and data structure associated with it.

-M *shmkey* Removes the shared memory identifier, created with key *shmkey*, from the system. The shared memory segment and data structure associated with it are destroyed after the last detach.

-S *semkey* Remove the semaphore identifier, created with key *semkey*, from the system and destroy the set of semaphores and data structure associated with it.

The details of the removes are described in msgctl(2), shmctl(2), and semctl(2). Use the ipcs command to find the identifiers and keys.

SEE ALSO

ipcs(1).
msgctl(2), msgget(2), msgop(2), semctl(2), semget(2), semop(2), shmctl(2), shmget(2), shmop(2) in the *Programmer's Reference Manual.*

NAME

ipcs – report inter-process communication facilities status

SYNOPSIS

ipcs [*options*]

DESCRIPTION

ipcs prints information about active inter-process communication facilities. Without *options*, information is printed in short format for message queues, shared memory, and semaphores that are currently active in the system. Otherwise, the information that is displayed is controlled by the following *options*:

–q Print information about active message queues.

–m Print information about active shared memory segments.

–s Print information about active semaphores.

If –q, –m, or –s are specified, information about only those indicated is printed. If none of these three are specified, information about all three is printed subject to these options:

–b Print information on biggest allowable size: maximum number of bytes in messages on queue for message queues, size of segments for shared memory, and number of semaphores in each set for semaphores. See below for meaning of columns in a listing.

–c Print creator's login name and group name. See below.

–o Print information on outstanding usage: number of messages on queue and total number of bytes in messages on queue for message queues and number of processes attached to shared memory segments.

–p Print process number information: process ID of last process to send a message, process ID of last process to receive a message on message queues, process ID of creating process, and process ID of last process to attach or detach on shared memory segments. See below.

–t Print time information: time of the last control operation that changed the access permissions for all facilities, time of last msgsnd and last msgrcv on message queues, time of last shmat and last shmdt on shared memory, time of last semop on semaphores. See below.

–a Use all print options. (This is a shorthand notation for –b, –c, –o, –p, and –t.)

–C *corefile*
Use the file *corefile* in place of /dev/kmem.

–N *namelist*
Use the file *namelist* in place of /stand/unix.

–X Print information about XENIX interprocess communication, in addition to the standard interprocess communication status. The XENIX process information describes a second set of semaphores and shared memory.

Note that the `-p` option does not print process number information for XENIX shared memory, and the `-t` option does not print time information about XENIX semaphores and shared memory.

The column headings and the meaning of the columns in an `ipcs` listing are given below; the letters in parentheses indicate the options that cause the corresponding heading to appear; "all" means that the heading always appears. Note that these options only determine what information is provided for each facility; they do not determine which facilities are listed.

`T` (all) Type of the facility:

- `q` message queue
- `m` shared memory segment
- `s` semaphore

`ID` (all) The identifier for the facility entry.

`KEY` (all) The key used as an argument to `msgget`, `semget`, or `shmget` to create the facility entry. (Note: The key of a shared memory segment is changed to `IPC_PRIVATE` when the segment has been removed until all processes attached to the segment detach it.)

`MODE` (all) The facility access modes and flags: The mode consists of 11 characters that are interpreted as follows. The first two characters are:

- `R` A process is waiting on a *msgrcv*.
- `S` A process is waiting on a *msgsnd*.
- `D` The associated shared memory segment has been removed. It will disappear when the last process attached to the segment detaches it.
- `C` The associated shared memory segment is to be cleared when the first attach is executed.
- `-` The corresponding special flag is not set.

The next nine characters are interpreted as three sets of three bits each. The first set refers to the owner's permissions; the next to permissions of others in the user-group of the facility entry; and the last to all others. Within each set, the first character indicates permission to read, the second character indicates permission to write or alter the facility entry, and the last character is currently unused.

The permissions are indicated as follows:

- `r` Read permission is granted.
- `w` Write permission is granted.
- `a` Alter permission is granted.
- `-` The indicated permission is not granted.

`OWNER` (all) The login name of the owner of the facility entry.

GROUP	(all)	The group name of the group of the owner of the facility entry.
CREATOR	(a,c)	The login name of the creator of the facility entry.
CGROUP	(a,c)	The group name of the group of the creator of the facility entry.
CBYTES	(a,o)	The number of bytes in messages currently outstanding on the associated message queue.
QNUM	(a,o)	The number of messages currently outstanding on the associated message queue.
QBYTES	(a,b)	The maximum number of bytes allowed in messages outstanding on the associated message queue.
LSPID	(a,p)	The process ID of the last process to send a message to the associated queue.
LRPID	(a,p)	The process ID of the last process to receive a message from the associated queue.
STIME	(a,t)	The time the last message was sent to the associated queue.
RTIME	(a,t)	The time the last message was received from the associated queue.
CTIME	(a,t)	The time when the associated entry was created or changed.
NATTCH	(a,o)	The number of processes attached to the associated shared memory segment.
SEGSZ	(a,b)	The size of the associated shared memory segment.
CPID	(a,p)	The process ID of the creator of the shared memory entry.
LPID	(a,p)	The process ID of the last process to attach or detach the shared memory segment.
ATIME	(a,t)	The time the last attach was completed to the associated shared memory segment.
DTIME	(a,t)	The time the last detach was completed on the associated shared memory segment.
NSEMS	(a,b)	The number of semaphores in the set associated with the semaphore entry.
OTIME	(a,t)	The time the last semaphore operation was completed on the set associated with the semaphore entry.

FILES

/stand/unix	system namelist
/dev/kmem	memory
/etc/passwd	user names
/etc/group	group names

NOTES

If the user specifies either the -C or -N flag, the real and effective *UID/GID* is set to the real *UID/GID* of the user invoking ipcs.

Things can change while `ipcs` is running; the information it gives is guaranteed to be accurate only when it was retrieved.

SEE ALSO

`msgop`(2), `semop`(2), `shmop`(2) in the *Programmer's Reference Manual.*

NAME

ismpx – return windowing terminal state

SYNOPSIS

ismpx [–s]

DESCRIPTION

The **ismpx** command reports whether its standard input is connected to a multiplexed xt channel; i.e., whether it's running under **layers** or not. It is useful for shell scripts that download programs to a windowing terminal.

ismpx prints **yes** and returns 0 if invoked under **layers**, and prints no and returns 1 otherwise.

–s Do not print anything; just return the proper exit status.

SEE ALSO

layers(1), jwin(1), xt(7).

EXAMPLE

```
if ismpx -s
then
        jwin
fi
```

NAME

`join` – relational database operator

SYNOPSIS

`join` [*options*] *file1 file2*

DESCRIPTION

`join` forms, on the standard output, a join of the two relations specified by the lines of *file1* and *file2*. If *file1* is –, the standard input is used.

file1 and *file2* must be sorted in increasing ASCII collating sequence on the fields on which they are to be joined, normally the first in each line [see `sort`(1)].

There is one line in the output for each pair of lines in *file1* and *file2* that have identical join fields. The output line normally consists of the common field, then the rest of the line from *file1*, then the rest of the line from *file2*.

The default input field separators are blank, tab, or new-line. In this case, multiple separators count as one field separator, and leading separators are ignored. The default output field separator is a blank.

Some of the options below use the argument *n*. This argument should be a `1` or a `2` referring to either *file1* or *file2*, respectively. The following options are recognized:

–a*n* In addition to the normal output, produce a line for each unpairable line in file *n*, where *n* is 1 or 2.

–e *s* Replace empty output fields with string *s*.

–j*n m* Join on the *m*th field of file *n*. If *n* is missing, use the *m*th field in each file. Fields are numbered starting with `1`.

–o *list* Each output line includes the fields specified in *list*, each element of which has the form *n*.*m*, where *n* is a file number and *m* is a field number. The common field is not printed unless specifically requested.

–t*c* Use character *c* as a separator (tab character). Every appearance of *c* in a line is significant. The character *c* is used as the field separator for both input and output.

EXAMPLE

The following command line will join the password file and the group file, matching on the numeric group ID, and outputting the login name, the group name and the login directory. It is assumed that the files have been sorted in ASCII collating sequence on the group ID fields.

```
join -j1 4 -j2 3 -o 1.1 2.1 1.6 -t: /etc/passwd /etc/group
```

SEE ALSO

`awk`(1), `comm`(1), `sort`(1), `uniq`(1).

NOTES

With default field separation, the collating sequence is that of `sort -b`; with `-t`, the sequence is that of a plain sort.

The conventions of the `join`, `sort`, `comm`, `uniq`, and **awk** commands are wildly incongruous.

Filenames that are numeric may cause conflict when the −o option is used just before listing filenames.

NAME

`jterm` – reset layer of windowing terminal

SYNOPSIS

`jterm`

DESCRIPTION

The `jterm` command is used to reset a layer of a windowing terminal after downloading a terminal program that changes the terminal attributes of the layer. It is functional only under `layers`. In practice, it is most commonly used to restart the default terminal emulator after using an alternate one provided with a terminal-specific application package. For example, on the AT&T 630 MTG terminal, after executing the `xproof` command in a layer, issuing the `jterm` command will restart the default terminal emulator in that layer.

EXIT STATUS

Returns `0` upon successful completion, `1` otherwise.

NOTES

The layer that is reset is the one attached to standard error — that is, the window you are in when you type the `jterm` command.

SEE ALSO

`layers`(1).

NAME

`jwin` – print size of layer

SYNOPSIS

`jwin`

DESCRIPTION

`jwin` is functional only under **`layers`**(1) and is used to determine the size of the window associated with the current process. It prints the width and the height of the window in bytes (number of characters across and number of lines, respectively). For bit-mapped terminals only, it also prints the width and height of the window in bits.

EXIT STATUS

Returns `0` on successful completion, `1` otherwise.

DIAGNOSTICS

If `layers`(1) has not been invoked, an error message is printed:

```
jwin: not mpx
```

NOTE

The window whose size is printed is the one attached to standard input; that is, the window you are in when you type the `jwin` command.

SEE ALSO

`layers`(1).

EXAMPLE

```
jwin
bytes:  86 25
bits:   780 406
```

NAME

`kill` – terminate a process by default

SYNOPSIS

```
kill [-signal] pid...
kill -signal -pgid...
kill -l
```

DESCRIPTION

`kill` sends a signal to the specified processes. The value of `signal` may be numeric or symbolic. [see *signal*(5)]. The symbolic signal name is the name as it appears in `/usr/include/sys/signal.h`, with the `SIG` prefix stripped off. Signal 15 (`SIGTERM`) is sent by default; this will normally kill processes that do not catch or ignore the signal.

pid and *pgid* are unsigned numeric strings that identify which process(es) should receive the signal. If *pid* is used, the process with process ID *pid* is selected. If *pgid* is used, all processes with process group ID *pgid* are selected.

The process number of each asynchronous process started with `&` is reported by the shell (unless more than one process is started in a pipeline, in which case the number of the last process in the pipeline is reported). Process numbers can also be found by using `ps`(1).

When invoked with the *-l* option, `kill` will print a list of symbolic signal names. The details of the kill are described in *kill*(2). For example, if process number 0 is specified, all processes in the process group are signaled.

The signalled process must belong to the current user unless the user is the super-user.

SEE ALSO

`ps`(1), `sh`(1).
`kill`(2), `signal`(2), `signal`(5) in the *Programmer's Reference Manual.*

NAME

ksh, rksh – KornShell, a standard/restricted command and programming language

SYNOPSIS

ksh [**±aefhikmnprstuvx**] [**±o** *option*] ... [**–c** *string*] [*arg* ...]
rksh [**±aefhikmnprstuvx**] [**±o** *option*] ... [**–c** *string*] [*arg* ...]

DESCRIPTION

Ksh is a command and programming language that executes commands read from a terminal or a file. *Rksh* is a restricted version of the command interpreter *ksh*; it is used to set up login names and execution environments whose capabilities are more controlled than those of the standard shell. See *Invocation* below for the meaning of arguments to the shell.

Definitions.

A *metacharacter* is one of the following characters:

; & ( ) | < > new-line space tab

A *blank* is a **tab** or a **space**. An *identifier* is a sequence of letters, digits, or underscores starting with a letter or underscore. Identifiers are used as names for *functions* and *variables*. A *word* is a sequence of *characters* separated by one or more non-quoted *metacharacters*.

A *command* is a sequence of characters in the syntax of the shell language. The shell reads each command and carries out the desired action either directly or by invoking separate utilities. A special command is a command that is carried out by the shell without creating a separate process. Except for documented side effects, most special commands can be implemented as separate utilities.

Commands.

A *simple-command* is a sequence of *blank* separated words which may be preceded by a variable assignment list (see *Environment* below). The first word specifies the name of the command to be executed. Except as specified below, the remaining words are passed as arguments to the invoked command. The command name is passed as argument 0 [see **exec**(2)]. The *value* of a simple-command is its exit status if it terminates normally, or (octal) 200+*status* if it terminates abnormally [see **signal**(2) for a list of status values].

A *pipeline* is a sequence of one or more *commands* separated by **|**. The standard output of each command but the last is connected by a **pipe**(2) to the standard input of the next command. Each command is run as a separate process; the shell waits for the last command to terminate. The exit status of a pipeline is the exit status of the last command.

A *list* is a sequence of one or more pipelines separated by **;**, **&**, **&&**, or **||**, and optionally terminated by **;**, **&**, or **|&**. Of these five symbols, **;**, **&**, and **|&** have equal precedence, which is lower than that of **&&** and **||**. The symbols **&&** and **||** also have equal precedence. A semicolon (**;**) causes sequential execution of the preceding pipeline; an ampersand (**&**) causes asynchronous execution of the preceding pipeline (i.e., the shell does *not* wait for that pipeline to finish). The symbol **|&** causes asynchronous execution of the preceding command or pipeline with a two-way pipe established to the parent shell. The standard input and output of the spawned command can be written to and read from by the parent

Shell using the **-p** option of the special commands **read** and **print** described later. The symbol && (||) causes the *list* following it to be executed only if the preceding pipeline returns a zero (non-zero) value. An arbitrary number of newlines may appear in a *list*, instead of a semicolon, to delimit a command.

A *command* is either a simple-command or one of the following. Unless otherwise stated, the value returned by a command is that of the last simple-command executed in the command.

for *identifier* [in *word* ...] ;do *list* ;done
: Each time a **for** command is executed, *identifier* is set to the next *word* taken from the **in** *word* list. If **in** *word* ... is omitted, then the **for** command executes the do *list* once for each positional parameter that is set (see *Parameter Substitution* below). Execution ends when there are no more words in the list.

select *identifier* [in *word* ...] ;do *list* ;done
: A **select** command prints on standard error (file descriptor 2), the set of *words*, each preceded by a number. If **in** *word* ... is omitted, then the positional parameters are used instead (see *Parameter Substitution* below). The **PS3** prompt is printed and a line is read from the standard input. If this line consists of the number of one of the listed *words*, then the value of the parameter *identifier* is set to the *word* corresponding to this number. If this line is empty the selection list is printed again. Otherwise the value of the parameter *identifier* is set to **null**. The contents of the line read from standard input is saved in the variable **REPLY**. The *list* is executed for each selection until a **break** or *end-of-file* is encountered.

case *word* in [[( ]*pattern* [| *pattern*] ...) *list* ;;] ... esac
: A **case** command executes the *list* associated with the first *pattern* that matches *word*. The form of the patterns is the same as that used for file-name generation (see *File Name Generation* below).

if *list* ;then *list* [elif *list* ;then *list*] ... [;else *list*] ;fi
: The *list* following **if** is executed and, if it returns a zero exit status, the *list* following the first **then** is executed. Otherwise, the *list* following **elif** is executed and, if its value is zero, the *list* following the next **then** is executed. Failing that, the **else** *list* is executed. If no **else** *list* or **then** *list* is executed, then the **if** command returns a zero exit status.

while *list* ;do *list* ;done
until *list* ;do *list* ;done
: A **while** command repeatedly executes the **while** *list* and, if the exit status of the last command in the list is zero, executes the do *list*; otherwise the loop terminates. If no commands in the do *list* are executed, then the **while** command returns a zero exit status; **until** may be used in place of **while** to negate the loop termination test.

(*list*)
: Execute *list* in a separate environment. Note, that if two adjacent open parentheses are needed for nesting, a space must be inserted to avoid arithmetic evaluation as described below.

{ *list* ; }
: *list* is simply executed. The { must be followed by a space. Note that unlike the metacharacters (and), { and } are *reserved words* and must be typed at the beginning of a line or after a ; in order to be recognized.

[[*expression*]]
: Evaluates *expression* and returns a zero exit status when *expression* is true. See *Conditional Expressions* below, for a description of *expression*.

`function` *identifier* { *list* ; }
identifier () { *list* ; }
: Define a function which is referenced by *identifier*. The body of the function is the *list* of commands between { and }. (see *Functions* below). The { must be followed by a space.

`time` *pipeline*
: The *pipeline* is executed and the elapsed time as well as the user and system time are printed on standard error.

The following reserved words are only recognized as the first word of a command and when not quoted:

```
if     then    else    elif    fi      case     esac     for     while
until  do      done    {       }       function select   time    [[  ]]
```

Comments.

A word beginning with # causes that word and all the following characters up to a new-line to be ignored.

Aliasing.

The first word of each command is replaced by the text of an `alias` if an `alias` for this word has been defined. An alias name consists of any number of characters excluding meta-characters, quoting characters, file expansion characters, parameter and command substitution characters and =. The replacement string can contain any valid Shell script including the metacharacters listed above. The first word of each command in the replaced text, other than any that are in the process of being replaced, will be tested for aliases. If the last character of the alias value is a *blank* then the word following the alias will also be checked for alias substitution. Aliases can be used to redefine special builtin commands but cannot be used to redefine the reserved words listed above. Aliases can be created, listed, and exported with the `alias` command and can be removed with the `unalias` command. Exported aliases remain in effect for scripts invoked by name, but must be reinitialized for separate invocations of the Shell (see *Invocation* below).

Aliasing is performed when scripts are read, not while they are executed. Therefore, for an alias to take effect the `alias` definition command has to be executed before the command which references the alias is read.

Aliases are frequently used as a short hand for full path names. An option to the aliasing facility allows the value of the alias to be automatically set to the full pathname of the corresponding command. These aliases are called *tracked* aliases. The value of a *tracked* alias is defined the first time the corresponding command is looked up and becomes undefined each time the `PATH` variable is reset. These aliases remain *tracked* so that the next subsequent reference will redefine the value. Several tracked aliases are compiled into the shell. The `-h` option of the `set` command makes each referenced command name into a tracked alias.

The following *exported aliases* are compiled into the shell but can be unset or redefined:

```
autoload='typeset -fu'
false='let 0'
functions='typeset -f'
hash='alias -t'
history='fc -l'
integer='typeset -i'
nohup='nohup '
r='fc -e -'
true=':'
type='whence -v'
```

Tilde Substitution.

After alias substitution is performed, each word is checked to see if it begins with an unquoted ~. If it does, then the word up to a / is checked to see if it matches a user name in the `/etc/passwd` file. If a match is found, the ~ and the matched login name is replaced by the login directory of the matched user. This is called a *tilde* substitution. If no match is found, the original text is left unchanged. A ~ by itself, or in front of a /, is replaced by `$HOME`. A ~ followed by a + or – is replaced by `$PWD` and `$OLDPWD` respectively.

In addition, *tilde* substitution is attempted when the value of a *variable assignment* begins with a ~.

Command Substitution.

The standard output from a command enclosed in parentheses preceded by a dollar sign (`$()`) or a pair of grave accents (`` ` ` ``) may be used as part or all of a word; trailing new-lines are removed. In the second (archaic) form, the string between the quotes is processed for special quoting characters before the command is executed (see *Quoting* below). The command substitution `$(cat file)` can be replaced by the equivalent but faster `$(<file)`. Command substitution of most special commands that do not perform input/output redirection are carried out without creating a separate process.

An arithmetic expression enclosed in double parentheses and preceded by a dollar sign [`$(())`] is replaced by the value of the arithmetic expression within the double parentheses.

Parameter Substitution.

A *parameter* is an *identifier*, one or more digits, or any of the characters `*`, `@`, `#`, `?`, `-`, `$`, and `!`. A *variable* (a parameter denoted by an identifier) has a *value* and zero or more *attributes*. *Variables* can be assigned `values` and *attributes* by using the `typeset` special command. The attributes supported by the Shell are described later with the `typeset` special command. Exported parameters pass values and attributes to the environment.

The shell supports a one-dimensional array facility. An element of an array variable is referenced by a *subscript*. A *subscript* is denoted by a `[`, followed by an *arithmetic expression* (see *Arithmetic Evaluation* below) followed by a `]`. To assign values to an array, use `set -A` *name value* .... The value of all subscripts must be in the range of 0 through 1023. Arrays need not be declared. Any reference to a variable with a valid subscript is legal and an array will be created if necessary. Referencing an array without a subscript is equivalent to referencing the element zero.

The *value* of a *variable* may also be assigned by writing:

name=*value* [*name*=*value*] ...

If the integer attribute, `-i`, is set for *name* the *value* is subject to arithmetic evaluation as described below.
Positional parameters, parameters denoted by a number, may be assigned values with the `set` special command. Parameter `$0` is set from argument zero when the shell is invoked.
The character `$` is used to introduce substitutable *parameters*.

`${`*parameter*`}`
: The shell reads all the characters from `${` to the matching `}` as part of the same word even if it contains braces or metacharacters. The value, if any, of the parameter is substituted. The braces are required when *parameter* is followed by a letter, digit, or underscore that is not to be interpreted as part of its name or when a variable is subscripted. If *parameter* is one or more digits then it is a positional parameter. A positional parameter of more than one digit must be enclosed in braces. If *parameter* is `*` or `@`, then all the positional parameters, starting with `$1`, are substituted (separated by a field separator character). If an array *identifier* with subscript `*` or `@` is used, then the value for each of the elements is substituted (separated by a field separator character).

`${#`*parameter*`}`
: If *parameter* is `*` or `@`, the number of positional parameters is substituted. Otherwise, the length of the value of the *parameter* is substituted.

`${#`*identifier*`[*]}`
: The number of elements in the array *identifier* is substituted.

`${`*parameter*`:-`*word*`}`
: If *parameter* is set and is non-null then substitute its value; otherwise substitute *word*.

`${`*parameter*`:=`*word*`}`
: If *parameter* is not set or is null then set it to *word*; the value of the parameter is then substituted. Positional parameters may not be assigned to in this way.

`${`*parameter*`:?`*word*`}`
: If *parameter* is set and is non-null then substitute its value; otherwise, print *word* and exit from the shell. If *word* is omitted then a standard message is printed.

`${`*parameter*`:+`*word*`}`
: If *parameter* is set and is non-null then substitute *word*; otherwise substitute nothing.

${*parameter*#*pattern*}
${*parameter*##*pattern*}
: If the Shell *pattern* matches the beginning of the value of *parameter*, then the value of this substitution is the value of the *parameter* with the matched portion deleted; otherwise the value of this *parameter* is substituted. In the first form the smallest matching pattern is deleted and in the second form the largest matching pattern is deleted.

${*parameter*%*pattern*}
${*parameter*%%*pattern*}
: If the Shell *pattern* matches the end of the value of *parameter*, then the value of this substitution is the value of the *parameter* with the matched part deleted; otherwise substitute the value of *parameter*. In the first form the smallest matching pattern is deleted and in the second form the largest matching pattern is deleted.

In the above, *word* is not evaluated unless it is to be used as the substituted string, so that, in the following example, **pwd** is executed only if **d** is not set or is null:

```
echo ${d:-$(pwd)}
```

If the colon (:) is omitted from the above expressions, then the shell only checks whether *parameter* is set or not.

The following parameters are automatically set by the shell:

- **#** The number of positional parameters in decimal.
- **-** Flags supplied to the shell on invocation or by the **set** command.
- **?** The decimal value returned by the last executed command.
- **$** The process number of this shell.
- **_** Initially, the value _ is an absolute pathname of the shell or script being executed as passed in the *environment*. Subsequently it is assigned the last argument of the previous command. This parameter is not set for commands which are asynchronous. This parameter is also used to hold the name of the matching **MAIL** file when checking for mail.
- **!** The process number of the last background command invoked.
- **ERRNO** The value of *errno* as set by the most recently failed system call. This value is system dependent and is intended for debugging purposes.
- **LINENO**
  The line number of the current line within the script or function being executed.
- **OLDPWD**
  The previous working directory set by the **cd** command.
- **OPTARG**
  The value of the last option argument processed by the **getopts** special command.
- **OPTIND**
  The index of the last option argument processed by the **getopts** special command.

PPID The process number of the parent of the shell.

PWD The present working directory set by the **cd** command.

RANDOM
: Each time this variable is referenced, a random integer, uniformly distributed between 0 and 32767, is generated. The sequence of random numbers can be initialized by assigning a numeric value to **RANDOM**.

REPLY This variable is set by the **select** statement and by the **read** special command when no arguments are supplied.

SECONDS
: Each time this variable is referenced, the number of seconds since shell invocation is returned. If this variable is assigned a value, then the value returned upon reference will be the value that was assigned plus the number of seconds since the assignment.

The following variables are used by the shell:

CDPATH
: The search path for the **cd** command.

COLUMNS
: If this variable is set, the value is used to define the width of the edit window for the shell edit modes and for printing **select** lists.

EDITOR
: If the value of this variable ends in **vi** and the **VISUAL** variable is not set, then the corresponding option (see *Special Command* **set** below) will be turned on.

ENV If this variable is set, then parameter substitution is performed on the value to generate the pathname of the script that will be executed when the *shell* is invoked (see *Invocation* below). This file is typically used for *alias* and *function* definitions.

FCEDIT
: The default editor name for the **fc** command.

FPATH The search path for function definitions. This path is searched when a function with the **-u** attribute is referenced and when a command is not found. If an executable file is found, then it is read and executed in the current environment.

IFS Internal field separators, normally **space**, **tab**, and **new-line** that is used to separate command words which result from command or parameter substitution and for separating words with the special command **read**. The first character of the **IFS** variable is used to separate arguments for the **"$*"** substitution (see *Quoting* below).

HISTFILE
: If this variable is set when the shell is invoked, then the value is the pathname of the file that will be used to store the command history (see *Command re-entry* below).

HISTSIZE
: If this variable is set when the shell is invoked, then the number of previously entered commands that are accessible by this shell will be greater than or equal to this number. The default is 128.

HOME The default argument (home directory) for the cd command.

LINES If this variable is set, the value is used to determine the column length for printing select lists. Select lists will print vertically until about two-thirds of LINES lines are filled.

MAIL If this variable is set to the name of a mail file *and* the MAILPATH variable is not set, then the shell informs the user of arrival of mail in the specified file.

MAILCHECK
: This variable specifies how often (in seconds) the shell will check for changes in the modification time of any of the files specified by the MAILPATH or MAIL variables. The default value is 600 seconds. When the time has elapsed the shell will check before issuing the next prompt.

MAILPATH
: A colon (:) separated list of file names. If this variable is set then the shell informs the user of any modifications to the specified files that have occurred within the last MAILCHECK seconds. Each file name can be followed by a ? and a message that will be printed. The message will undergo parameter substitution with the variable, $_ defined as the name of the file that has changed. The default message is *you have mail in $_*.

PATH The search path for commands (see *Execution* below). The user may not change PATH if executing under *rksh* (except in *.profile*).

PS1 The value of this variable is expanded for parameter substitution to define the primary prompt string which by default is "$ ". The character ! in the primary prompt string is replaced by the *command* number (see *Command Re-entry* below).

PS2 Secondary prompt string, by default "> ".

PS3 Selection prompt string used within a select loop, by default "#? ".

PS4 The value of this variable is expanded for parameter substitution and precedes each line of an execution trace. If omitted, the execution trace prompt is "+ ".

SHELL The pathname of the *shell* is kept in the environment. At invocation, if the basename of this variable matches the pattern *r*sh, then the shell becomes restricted.

TMOUT If set to a value greater than zero, the shell will terminate if a command is not entered within the prescribed number of seconds after issuing the PS1 prompt. (Note that the shell can be compiled with a maximum bound for this value which cannot be exceeded.)

VISUAL
: If the value of this variable ends in vi then the corresponding option (see *Special Command* set below) will be turned on.

The shell gives default values to PATH, PS1, PS2, MAILCHECK, TMOUT and IFS. HOME, MAIL and SHELL are set by login(1).

Blank Interpretation.

After parameter and command substitution, the results of substitutions are scanned for the field separator characters (those found in **IFS**) and split into distinct arguments where such characters are found. Explicit null arguments ("" or '') are retained. Implicit null arguments (those resulting from *parameters* that have no values) are removed.

File Name Generation.

Following substitution, each command *word* is scanned for the characters *, ?, and [unless the **-f** option has been **set**. If one of these characters appears then the word is regarded as a *pattern*. The word is replaced with lexicographically sorted file names that match the pattern. If no file name is found that matches the pattern, then the word is left unchanged. When a *pattern* is used for file name generation, the character . at the start of a file name or immediately following a /, as well as the character / itself, must be matched explicitly. In other instances of pattern matching the / and . are not treated specially.

- `*` Matches any string, including the null string.
- `?` Matches any single character.
- `[...]` Matches any one of the enclosed characters. A pair of characters separated by - matches any character lexically between the pair, inclusive. If the first character following the opening "[" is a "!" then any character not enclosed is matched. A - can be included in the character set by putting it as the first or last character.

A *pattern-list* is a list of one or more patterns separated from each other with a |. Composite patterns can be formed with one or more of the following:

?(*pattern-list*)
: Optionally matches any one of the given patterns.

*(*pattern-list*)
: Matches zero or more occurrences of the given patterns.

+(*pattern-list*)
: Matches one or more occurrences of the given patterns.

@(*pattern-list*)
: Matches exactly one of the given patterns.

!(*pattern-list*)
: Matches anything, except one of the given patterns.

Quoting.

Each of the *metacharacters* listed above (see *Definitions* above) has a special meaning to the shell and causes termination of a word unless quoted. A character may be *quoted* (i.e., made to stand for itself) by preceding it with a \. The pair \`newline` is removed. All characters enclosed between a pair of single quote marks (''), are quoted. A single quote cannot appear within single quotes. Inside double quote marks (""), parameter and command substitution occurs and \ quotes the characters \, `, ", and $. The meaning of `$*` and `$@` is identical when not quoted or when used as a variable assignment value or as a file name. However, when used as a command argument, "`$*`" is equivalent to "`$1`*d*`$2`*d*...", where *d* is the first character of the `IFS` variable, whereas "`$@`" is equivalent to "`$1`"*d*"`$2`"*d*... Inside grave quote marks (``) \ quotes the characters \, `, and $. If the grave quotes occur within double quotes then \ also quotes the character ".

The special meaning of reserved words or aliases can be removed by quoting any character of the reserved word. The recognition of function names or special command names listed below cannot be altered by quoting them.

Arithmetic Evaluation.

An ability to perform integer arithmetic is provided with the special command `let`. Evaluations are performed using *long* arithmetic. Constants are of the form [*base#*]*n* where *base* is a decimal number between two and thirty-six representing the arithmetic base and *n* is a number in that base. If *base#* is omitted then base 10 is used.

An arithmetic expression uses the same syntax, precedence, and associativity of expression of the C language. All the integral operators, other than ++, −−, ?:, and , are supported. Variables can be referenced by name within an arithmetic expression without using the parameter substitution syntax. When a variable is referenced, its value is evaluated as an arithmetic expression.

An internal integer representation of a *variable* can be specified with the `-i` option of the `typeset` special command. Arithmetic evaluation is performed on the value of each assignment to a variable with the `-i` attribute. If you do not specify an arithmetic base, the first assignment to the variable determines the arithmetic base. This base is used when parameter substitution occurs.

Since many of the arithmetic operators require quoting, an alternative form of the `let` command is provided. For any command which begins with a `((`, all the characters until a matching `))` are treated as a quoted expression. More precisely, `((...))` is equivalent to `let "..."`.

Prompting.

When used interactively, the shell prompts with the parameter expanded value of `PS1` before reading a command. If at any time a new-line is typed and further input is needed to complete a command, then the secondary prompt (i.e., the value of `PS2`) is issued.

Conditional Expressions.

A *conditional expression* is used with the `[[` compound command to test attributes of files and to compare strings. Word splitting and file name generation are not performed on the words between `[[` and `]]`. Each expression can be constructed from one or more of the following unary or binary expressions:

-a *file*	True, if *file* exists.
-b *file*	True, if *file* exists and is a block special file.
-c *file*	True, if *file* exists and is a character special file.
-d *file*	True, if *file* exists and is a directory.
-f *file*	True, if *file* exists and is an ordinary file.
-g *file*	True, if *file* exists and is has its setgid bit set.
-k *file*	True, if *file* exists and is has its sticky bit set.
-n *string*	True, if length of *string* is non-zero.
-o *option*	True, if option named *option* is on.
-p *file*	True, if *file* exists and is a fifo special file or a pipe.
-r *file*	True, if *file* exists and is readable by current process.

`-s` *file*	True, if *file* exists and has size greater than zero.
`-t` *fildes*	True, if file descriptor number *fildes* is open and associated with a terminal device.
`-u` *file*	True, if *file* exists and is has its setuid bit set.
`-w` *file*	True, if *file* exists and is writable by current process.
`-x` *file*	True, if *file* exists and is executable by current process. If *file* exists and is a directory, then the current process has permission to search in the directory.
`-z` *string*	True, if length of *string* is zero.
`-L` *file*	True, if *file* exists and is a symbolic link.
`-O` *file*	True, if *file* exists and is owned by the effective user id of this process.
`-G` *file*	True, if *file* exists and its group matches the effective group id of this process.
`-S` *file*	True, if *file* exists and is a socket.
file1 `-nt` *file2*	True, if *file1* exists and is newer than *file2*.
file1 `-ot` *file2*	True, if *file1* exists and is older than *file2*.
file1 `-ef` *file2*	True, if *file1* and *file2* exist and refer to the same file.
string = *pattern*	True, if *string* matches *pattern*.
string != *pattern*	True, if *string* does not match *pattern*.
string1 < *string2*	True, if *string1* comes before *string2* based on ASCII value of their characters.
string1 > *string2*	True, if *string1* comes after *string2* based on ASCII value of their characters.
exp1 `-eq` *exp2*	True, if *exp1* is equal to *exp2*.
exp1 `-ne` *exp2*	True, if *exp1* is not equal to *exp2*.
exp1 `-lt` *exp2*	True, if *exp1* is less than *exp2*.
exp1 `-gt` *exp2*	True, if *exp1* is greater than *exp2*.
exp1 `-le` *exp2*	True, if *exp1* is less than or equal to *exp2*.
exp1 `-ge` *exp2*	True, if *exp1* is greater than or equal to *exp2*.

In each of the above expressions, if *file* is of the form `/dev/fd/`*n*, where *n* is an integer, then the test applied to the open file whose descriptor number is *n*.

A compound expression can be constructed from these primitives by using any of the following, listed in decreasing order of precedence.

`(`*expression*`)`
: True, if *expression* is true. Used to group expressions.

`!` *expression*
: True if *expression* is false.

expression1 `&&` *expression2*
: True, if *expression1* and *expression2* are both true.

expression1 `||` *expression2*
: True, if either *expression1* or *expression2* is true.

Input/Output.

Before a command is executed, its input and output may be redirected using a special notation interpreted by the shell. The following may appear anywhere in a simple-command or may precede or follow a *command* and are *not* passed on to the invoked command. Command and parameter substitution occurs before *word* or *digit* is used except as noted below. File name generation occurs only if the pattern matches a single file and blank interpretation is not performed.

<*word* Use file *word* as standard input (file descriptor 0).

>*word* Use file *word* as standard output (file descriptor 1). If the file does not exist then it is created. If the file exists, is a regular file, and the `noclobber` option is on, this causes an error; otherwise, it is truncated to zero length.

>|*word* Sames as >, except that it overrides the `noclobber` option.

>>*word* Use file *word* as standard output. If the file exists then output is appended to it (by first seeking to the end-of-file); otherwise, the file is created.

<>*word* Open file *word* for reading and writing as standard input.

<<[−]*word* The shell input is read up to a line that is the same as *word*, or to an end-of-file. No parameter substitution, command substitution or file name generation is performed on *word*. The resulting document, called a *here-document*, becomes the standard input. If any character of *word* is quoted, then no interpretation is placed upon the characters of the document; otherwise, parameter and command substitution occurs, `\new-line` is ignored, and \ must be used to quote the characters \, `$`, `‘`, and the first character of *word*. If − is appended to <<, then all leading tabs are stripped from *word* and from the document.

<&*digit* The standard input is duplicated from file descriptor *digit* [see dup(2)]. Similarly for the standard output using >& *digit*.

<&− The standard input is closed. Similarly for the standard output using >&−.

<&p The input from the co-process is moved to standard input.

>&p The output to the co-process is moved to standard output.

If one of the above is preceded by a digit, then the file descriptor number referred to is that specified by the digit (instead of the default 0 or 1). For example:

... 2>&1

means file descriptor 2 is to be opened for writing as a duplicate of file descriptor 1.

The order in which redirections are specified is significant. The shell evaluates each redirection in terms of the (*file descriptor*, *file*) association at the time of evaluation. For example:

... 1>*fname* 2>&1

first associates file descriptor 1 with file *fname*. It then associates file descriptor 2 with the file associated with file descriptor 1 (i.e. *fname*). If the order of redirections were reversed, file descriptor 2 would be associated with the terminal (assuming file descriptor 1 had been) and then file descriptor 1 would be associated with file *fname*.

If a command is followed by `&` and job control is not active, then the default standard input for the command is the empty file `/dev/null`. Otherwise, the environment for the execution of a command contains the file descriptors of the invoking shell as modified by input/output specifications.

Environment.

The *environment* [see **environ**(5)] is a list of name-value pairs that is passed to an executed program in the same way as a normal argument list. The names must be *identifiers* and the values are character strings. The shell interacts with the environment in several ways. On invocation, the shell scans the environment and creates a variable for each name found, giving it the corresponding value and marking it *export* . Executed commands inherit the environment. If the user modifies the values of these variables or creates new ones, using the `export` or `typeset -x` commands they become part of the environment. The environment seen by any executed command is thus composed of any name-value pairs originally inherited by the shell, whose values may be modified by the current shell, plus any additions which must be noted in `export` or `typeset -x` commands.

The environment for any *simple-command* or function may be augmented by prefixing it with one or more variable assignments. A variable assignment argument is a word of the form *identifier=value*. Thus:

```
TERM=450 cmd args                    and
(export TERM; TERM=450; cmd args)
```

are equivalent (as far as the above execution of *cmd* is concerned except for commands listed with one or two daggers, †, in the Special Commands section).

If the `-k` flag is set, *all* variable assignment arguments are placed in the environment, even if they occur after the command name. The following first prints `a=b c` and then `c`:

```
echo a=b c
set -k
echo a=b c
```

This feature is intended for use with scripts written for early versions of the shell and its use in new scripts is strongly discouraged. It is likely to disappear someday.

Functions.

The `function` reserved word, described in the *Commands* section above, is used to define shell functions. Shell functions are read in and stored internally. Alias names are resolved when the function is read. Functions are executed like commands with the arguments passed as positional parameters (see *Execution* below).

Functions execute in the same process as the caller and share all files and present working directory with the caller. Traps caught by the caller are reset to their default action inside the function. A trap condition that is not caught or ignored by the function causes the function to terminate and the condition to be passed on to the caller. A trap on `EXIT` set inside a function is executed after the function completes in the environment of the caller. Ordinarily, variables are shared between the calling program and the function. However, the `typeset` special command used within a function defines local variables whose scope includes the current function and all functions it calls.

The special command `return` is used to return from function calls. Errors within functions return control to the caller.

Function identifiers can be listed with the `-f` or `+f` option of the **typeset** special command. The text of functions may also be listed with `-f`. Function can be undefined with the `-f` option of the `unset` special command.

Ordinarily, functions are unset when the shell executes a shell script. The `-xf` option of the **typeset** command allows a function to be exported to scripts that are executed without a separate invocation of the shell. Functions that need to be defined across separate invocations of the shell should be specified in the **ENV** file with the `-xf` option of **typeset**.

Jobs.

If the `monitor` option of the `set` command is turned on, an interactive shell associates a *job* with each pipeline. It keeps a table of current jobs, printed by the `jobs` command, and assigns them small integer numbers. When a job is started asynchronously with `&`, the shell prints a line which looks like:

[1] 1234

indicating that the job which was started asynchronously was job number 1 and had one (top-level) process, whose process id was 1234.

If you are running a job and wish to do something else you may hit the key `^Z` (ctrl-z) which sends a STOP signal to the current job. The shell will then normally indicate that the job has been 'Stopped', and print another prompt. You can then manipulate the state of this job, putting it in the background with the `bg` command, or run some other commands and then eventually bring the job back into the foreground with the foreground command `fg`. A `^Z` takes effect immediately and is like an interrupt in that pending output and unread input are discarded when it is typed.

A job being run in the background will stop if it tries to read from the terminal. Background jobs are normally allowed to produce output, but this can be disabled by giving the command "stty tostop". If you set this tty option, then background jobs will stop when they try to produce output like they do when they try to read input.

There are several ways to refer to jobs in the shell. A job can be referred to by the process id of any process of the job or by one of the following:

`%`*number*
: The job with the given number.

`%`*string*
: Any job whose command line begins with *string*.

`%?`*string*
: Any job whose command line contains *string*.

`%%` Current job.

`%+` Equivalent to `%%`.

`%-` Previous job.

This shell learns immediately whenever a process changes state. It normally informs you whenever a job becomes blocked so that no further progress is possible, but only just before it prints a prompt. This is done so that it does not otherwise disturb your work.

When the monitor mode is on, each background job that completes triggers any trap set for `CHLD`.

When you try to leave the shell while jobs are running or stopped, you will be warned that 'You have stopped(running) jobs.' You may use the `jobs` command to see what they are. If you do this or immediately try to exit again, the shell will not warn you a second time, and the stopped jobs will be terminated.

Signals.

The INT and QUIT signals for an invoked command are ignored if the command is followed by `&` and job `monitor` option is not active. Otherwise, signals have the values inherited by the shell from its parent (but see also the `trap` command below).

Execution.

Each time a command is executed, the above substitutions are carried out. If the command name matches one of the *Special Commands* listed below, it is executed within the current shell process. Next, the command name is checked to see if it matches one of the user defined functions. If it does, the positional parameters are saved and then reset to the arguments of the *function* call. When the *function* completes or issues a `return`, the positional parameter list is restored and any trap set on `EXIT` within the function is executed. The value of a *function* is the value of the last command executed. A function is also executed in the current shell process. If a command name is not a *special command* or a user defined *function*, a process is created and an attempt is made to execute the command via exec(2).

The shell variable `PATH` defines the search path for the directory containing the command. Alternative directory names are separated by a colon (`:`). The default path is `/usr/bin:` (specifying `/usr/bin` and the current directory in that order). The current directory can be specified by two or more adjacent colons, or by a colon at the beginning or end of the path list. If the command name contains a / then the search path is not used. Otherwise, each directory in the path is searched for an executable file. If the file has execute permission but is not a directory or an `a.out` file, it is assumed to be a file containing shell commands. A sub-shell is spawned to read it. All non-exported aliases, functions, and variables, are removed in this case. A parenthesized command is executed in a sub-shell without removing non-exported quantities.

Command Re-entry.

The text of the last `HISTSIZE` (default 128) commands entered from a terminal device is saved in a *history* file. The file `$HOME/.sh_history` is used if the file denoted by the `HISTFILE` variable is not set or is not writable. A shell can access the commands of all *interactive* shells which use the same named `HISTFILE`. The special command `fc` is used to list or edit a portion of this file. The portion of the file to be edited or listed can be selected by number or by giving the first character or characters of the command. A single command or range of commands can be specified. If you do not specify an editor program as an argument to `fc` then the value of the variable `FCEDIT` is used. If `FCEDIT` is not defined then `/usr/bin/ed` is used. The edited command(s) is printed and re-executed upon leaving the editor. The editor name – is used to skip the editing phase and to re-execute the command. In this case a substitution variable of the form *old=new* can be used to modify the command before execution. For example, if `r` is aliased to `'fc -e -'` then typing `'r bad=good c'` will re-execute the most recent command which starts with the letter c, replacing the first occurrence of the string bad with the string good.

In-line Editing Options

Normally, each command line entered from a terminal device is simply typed followed by a new-line ('RETURN' or 'LINE FEED'). If the `vi` option is active, the user can edit the command line. To be in this edit mode `set` the `vi` option. An editing option is automatically selected each time the `VISUAL` or `EDITOR` variable is assigned a value ending in either of these option names.

The editing features require that the user's terminal accept 'RETURN' as carriage return without line feed and that a space (' ') must overwrite the current character on the screen. ADM terminal users should set the "space - advance" switch to 'space'. Hewlett-Packard series 2621 terminal users should set the straps to 'bcGHxZ etX'.

The editing mode implements a concept where the user is looking through a window at the current line. The window width is the value of `COLUMNS` if it is defined, otherwise 80. If the line is longer than the window width minus two, a mark is displayed at the end of the window to notify the user. As the cursor moves and reaches the window boundaries the window will be centered about the cursor. The mark is a `>` (`<`, `*`) if the line extends on the right (left, both) side(s) of the window.

The search commands in each edit mode provide access to the history file. Only strings are matched, not patterns, although a leading `^` in the string restricts the match to begin at the first character in the line.

Vi Editing Mode

There are two typing modes. Initially, when you enter a command you are in the *input* mode. To edit, the user enters *control* mode by typing ESC (\033) and moves the cursor to the point needing correction and then inserts or deletes characters or words as needed. Most control commands accept an optional repeat *count* prior to the command.

When in `vi` mode on most systems, canonical processing is initially enabled and the command will be echoed again if the speed is 1200 baud or greater and it contains any control characters or less than one second has elapsed since the prompt was printed. The ESC character terminates canonical processing for the remainder of the command and the user can then modify the command line. This scheme has the advantages of canonical processing with the type-ahead echoing of raw mode.

If the option `viraw` is also set, the terminal will always have canonical processing disabled.

Input Edit Commands

By default the editor is in input mode.

erase (User defined erase character as defined by the stty command, usually `^H` or `#`.) Delete previous character.

^W	Delete the previous blank separated word.
^D	Terminate the shell.
^V	Escape next character. Editing characters, the user's erase or kill characters may be entered in a command line or in a search string if preceded by a ^V. The ^V removes the next character's editing features (if any).
\	Escape the next *erase* or kill character.

Motion Edit Commands

These commands will move the cursor.

[*count*]l	Cursor forward (right) one character.
[*count*]w	Cursor forward one alpha-numeric word.
[*count*]W	Cursor to the beginning of the next word that follows a blank.
[*count*]e	Cursor to end of word.
[*count*]E	Cursor to end of the current blank delimited word.
[*count*]h	Cursor backward (left) one character.
[*count*]b	Cursor backward one word.
[*count*]B	Cursor to preceding blank separated word.
[*count*]|	Cursor to column *count*.
[*count*]f*c*	Find the next character *c* in the current line.
[*count*]F*c*	Find the previous character *c* in the current line.
[*count*]t*c*	Equivalent to f followed by h.
[*count*]T*c*	Equivalent to F followed by l.
[*count*];	Repeats *count* times, the last single character find command, f, F, t, or T.
[*count*],	Reverses the last single character find command *count* times.
0	Cursor to start of line.
^	Cursor to first non-blank character in line.
$	Cursor to end of line.

Search Edit Commands

These commands access your command history.

[*count*]k	Fetch previous command. Each time k is entered the previous command back in time is accessed.
[*count*]-	Equivalent to k.
[*count*]j	Fetch next command. Each time j is entered the next command forward in time is accessed.
[*count*]+	Equivalent to j.
[*count*]G	The command number *count* is fetched. The default is the least recent history command.

/string Search backward through history for a previous command containing *string*. *String* is terminated by a "RETURN" or "NEW LINE". If string is preceded by a ^, the matched line must begin with *string*. If *string* is null the previous string will be used.

?string Same as / except that search will be in the forward direction.

n Search for next match of the last pattern to / or ? commands.

N Search for next match of the last pattern to / or ?, but in reverse direction. Search history for the *string* entered by the previous / command.

Text Modification Edit Commands

These commands will modify the line.

a Enter input mode and enter text after the current character.

A Append text to the end of the line. Equivalent to $a.

[*count*]c*motion*

c[*count*]*motion*
Delete current character through the character that *motion* would move the cursor to and enter input mode. If *motion* is c, the entire line will be deleted and input mode entered.

C Delete the current character through the end of line and enter input mode. Equivalent to c$.

S Equivalent to cc.

D Delete the current character through the end of line. Equivalent to d$.

[*count*]d*motion*

d[*count*]*motion*
Delete current character through the character that *motion* would move to. If *motion* is d, the entire line will be deleted.

i Enter input mode and insert text before the current character.

I Insert text before the beginning of the line. Equivalent to 0i.

[*count*]P Place the previous text modification before the cursor.

[*count*]p Place the previous text modification after the cursor.

R Enter input mode and replace characters on the screen with characters you type overlay fashion.

[*count*]r*c* Replace the *count* character(s) starting at the current cursor position with *c*, and advance the cursor.

[*count*]x Delete current character.

[*count*]X Delete preceding character.

[*count*]. Repeat the previous text modification command.

[*count*]~ Invert the case of the *count* character(s) starting at the current cursor position and advance the cursor.

[*count*]_ Causes the *count* word of the previous command to be appended and input mode entered. The last word is used if *count* is omitted.

* Causes an * to be appended to the current word and file name generation attempted. If no match is found, it rings the bell. Otherwise, the word is replaced by the matching pattern and input mode is entered.

\ Filename completion. Replaces the current word with the longest common prefix of all filenames matching the current word with an asterisk appended. If the match is unique, a / is appended if the file is a directory and a space is appended if the file is not a directory.

Other Edit Commands

Miscellaneous commands.

[*count*]y*motion*

y[*count*]*motion*

Yank current character through character that *motion* would move the cursor to and puts them into the delete buffer. The text and cursor are unchanged.

`Y` Yanks from current position to end of line. Equivalent to `y$`.

`u` Undo the last text modifying command.

`U` Undo all the text modifying commands performed on the line.

[*count*]v Returns the command `fc -e ${VISUAL:-${EDITOR:-vi}}` *count* in the input buffer. If *count* is omitted, then the current line is used.

`^L` Line feed and print current line. Has effect only in control mode.

`^J` (New line) Execute the current line, regardless of mode.

`^M` (Return) Execute the current line, regardless of mode.

`#` Sends the line after inserting a `#` in front of the line. Useful for causing the current line to be inserted in the history without being executed.

= List the file names that match the current word if an asterisk were appended it.

@*letter* Your alias list is searched for an alias by the name _*letter* and if an alias of this name is defined, its value will be inserted on the input queue for processing.

Special Commands.

The following simple-commands are executed in the shell process. Input/Output redirection is permitted. Unless otherwise indicated, the output is written on file descriptor 1 and the exit status, when there is no syntax error, is zero. Commands that are preceded by one or two † are treated specially in the following ways:

1. Variable assignment lists preceding the command remain in effect when the command completes.
2. I/O redirections are processed after variable assignments.
3. Errors cause a script that contains them to abort.
4. Words, following a command preceded by †† that are in the format of a variable assignment, are expanded with the same rules as a variable assignment. This means that tilde substitution is performed after the = sign and word splitting and file name generation are not performed.

† : [*arg* ...]
: The command only expands parameters.

† . *file* [*arg* . . .]
: Read the complete *file* then execute the commands. The commands are executed in the current Shell environment. The search path specified by `PATH` is used to find the directory containing *file*. If any arguments *arg* are given, they become the positional parameters. Otherwise the positional parameters are unchanged. The exit status is the exit status of the last command executed.

†† `alias` [`-tx`] [*name*[*=value*]] ...
: *Alias* with no arguments prints the list of aliases in the form *name=value* on standard output. An *alias* is defined for each name whose *value* is given. A trailing space in *value* causes the next word to be checked for alias substitution. The `-t` flag is used to set and list tracked aliases. The value of a tracked alias is the full pathname corresponding to the given *name*. The value becomes undefined when the value of `PATH` is reset but the aliases remain tracked. Without the `-t` flag, for each *name* in the argument list for which no *value* is given, the name and value of the alias is printed. The `-x` flag is used to set or print exported aliases. An exported alias is defined for scripts invoked by name. The exit status is non-zero if a *name* is given, but no value, for which no alias has been defined.

bg [*job*...]
: This command is only on systems that support job control. Puts each specified *job* into the background. The current job is put in the background if *job* is not specified. See *Jobs* for a description of the format of *job*.

† `break` [*n*]
: Exit from the enclosing `for`, `while`, `until` or `select` loop, if any. If *n* is specified then break *n* levels.

† `continue` [*n*]
: Resume the next iteration of the enclosing `for`, `while`, `until` or `select` loop. If *n* is specified then resume at the *n*-th enclosing loop.

cd [*arg*]
cd *old new*

This command can be in either of two forms. In the first form it changes the current directory to *arg*. If *arg* is – the directory is changed to the previous directory. The shell variable HOME is the default *arg*. The variable PWD is set to the current directory. The shell variable CDPATH defines the search path for the directory containing *arg*. Alternative directory names are separated by a colon (:). The default path is <null> (specifying the current directory). Note that the current directory is specified by a null path name, which can appear immediately after the equal sign or between the colon delimiters anywhere else in the path list. If *arg* begins with a / then the search path is not used. Otherwise, each directory in the path is searched for *arg*.

The second form of cd substitutes the string *new* for the string *old* in the current directory name, PWD and tries to change to this new directory.

The cd command may not be executed by *rksh*.

echo [*arg* ...]

See echo(1) for usage and description.

† eval [*arg* ...]

The arguments are read as input to the shell and the resulting command(s) executed.

† exec [*arg* ...]

If *arg* is given, the command specified by the arguments is executed in place of this shell without creating a new process. Input/output arguments may appear and affect the current process. If no arguments are given the effect of this command is to modify file descriptors as prescribed by the input/output redirection list. In this case, any file descriptor numbers greater than 2 that are opened with this mechanism are closed when invoking another program.

† exit [*n*]

Causes the shell to exit with the exit status specified by *n*. If *n* is omitted then the exit status is that of the last command executed. An end-of-file will also cause the shell to exit except for a shell which has the *ignoreeof* option (see set below) turned on.

†† export [*name*[=*value*]] ...

The given *names* are marked for automatic export to the *environment* of subsequently-executed commands.

fc [-e *ename*] [-nlr] [*first* [*last*]]
fc -e - [*old=new*] [*command*]

In the first form, a range of commands from *first* to *last* is selected from the last HISTSIZE commands that were typed at the terminal. The arguments *first* and *last* may be specified as a number or as a string. A string is used to locate the most recent command starting with the given string. A negative number is used as an offset to the current command number. If the flag -l, is selected, the commands are listed on standard output. Otherwise, the editor program *ename* is invoked on a file containing these keyboard commands. If *ename* is not supplied, then the value of the variable FCEDIT (default /usr/bin/ed) is used as the editor. When editing is complete, the edited command(s) is executed. If *last* is not specified then it will be set to *first*. If *first* is not specified the default is the previous command for editing and −16 for listing. The flag -r reverses the order of the commands and the flag -n suppresses command numbers when listing. In the second form the *command* is re-executed after the substitution *old*=*new* is performed.

fg [*job*...]
: This command is only on systems that support job control. Each *job* specified is brought to the foreground. Otherwise, the current job is brought into the foreground. See *Jobs* for a description of the format of *job*.

getopts *optstring name* [*arg* ...]
: Checks *arg* for legal options. If *arg* is omitted, the positional parameters are used. An option argument begins with a + or a −. An option not beginning with + or − or the argument −− ends the options. *optstring* contains the letters that getopts recognizes. If a letter is followed by a :, that option is expected to have an argument. The options can be separated from the argument by blanks.

getopts places the next option letter it finds inside variable *name* each time it is invoked with a + prepended when *arg* begins with a +. The index of the next *arg* is stored in OPTIND. The option argument, if any, gets stored in OPTARG.

A leading : in *optstring* causes getopts to store the letter of an invalid option in OPTARG, and to set *name* to ? for an unknown option and to : when a required option is missing. Otherwise, getopts prints an error message. The exit status is non-zero when there are no more options.

jobs [-lnp] [*job* ...]
: Lists information about each given job; or all active jobs if *job* is omitted. The -l flag lists process ids in addition to the normal information. The -n flag only displays jobs that have stopped or exited since last notified. The -p flag causes only the process group to be listed. See *Jobs* for a description of the format of *job*.

kill [*−sig*] *job* ...
kill -l
: Sends either the TERM (terminate) signal or the specified signal to the specified jobs or processes. Signals are either given by number or by names (as given in /usr/include/signal.h, stripped of the prefix "SIG"). If the signal being sent is TERM (terminate) or HUP (hangup), then the job or process will be sent a CONT (continue) signal if it is stopped. The argument *job* can the process id of a process that is not a member of one of the active jobs. See *Jobs* for a description of the format of *job*. In the second form, kill -l, the signal numbers and names are listed.

`let` *arg* ...
: Each *arg* is a separate *arithmetic expression* to be evaluated. See *Arithmetic Evaluation* above, for a description of arithmetic expression evaluation.

  The exit status is 0 if the value of the last expression is non-zero, and 1 otherwise.

† `newgrp` [*arg* ...]
: Equivalent to `exec /usr/bin/newgrp` *arg* ....

`print` [`-Rnprsu`[*n*]] [*arg* ...]
: The shell output mechanism. With no flags or with flag - or -- the arguments are printed on standard output as described by echo(1). In raw mode, `-R` or `-r`, the escape conventions of **echo** are ignored. The `-R` option will print all subsequent arguments and options other than -n. The `-p` option causes the arguments to be written onto the pipe of the process spawned with `|&` instead of standard output. The `-s` option causes the arguments to be written onto the history file instead of standard output. The -u flag can be used to specify a one digit file descriptor unit number n on which the output will be placed. The default is 1. If the flag -n is used, no `new-line` is added to the output.

`pwd` Equivalent to `print -r - $PWD`

`read` [`-prsu`[*n*]] [*name?prompt*] [*name* ...]
: The shell input mechanism. One line is read and is broken up into fields using the characters in `IFS` as separators. In raw mode, `-r`, a \ at the end of a line does not signify line continuation. The first field is assigned to the first *name*, the second field to the second *name*, etc., with leftover fields assigned to the last *name*. The -p option causes the input line to be taken from the input pipe of a process spawned by the shell using `|&`. If the `-s` flag is present, the input will be saved as a command in the history file. The flag -u can be used to specify a one digit file descriptor unit to read from. The file descriptor can be opened with the **exec** special command. The default value of *n* is 0. If *name* is omitted then `REPLY` is used as the default *name*. The exit status is 0 unless an end-of-file is encountered. An end-of-file with the -p option causes cleanup for this process so that another can be spawned. If the first argument contains a `?`, the remainder of this word is used as a *prompt* on standard error when the shell is interactive. The exit status is 0 unless an end-of-file is encountered.

†† `readonly` [*name*[*=value*]] ...
: The given *names* are marked readonly and these names cannot be changed by subsequent assignment.

† `return` [*n*]
: Causes a shell *function* to return to the invoking script with the return status specified by *n*. If *n* is omitted then the return status is that of the last command executed. If `return` is invoked while not in a *function* or a . script, then it is the same as an `exit`.

set [±aefhkmnpstuvx] [±o *option*]... [±A *name*] [*arg* ...]

The flags for this command have meaning as follows:

- -A Array assignment. Unset the variable *name* and assign values sequentially from the list *arg*. If +A is used, the variable *name* is not unset first.
- -a All subsequent variables that are defined are automatically exported.
- -e If a command has a non-zero exit status, execute the ERR trap, if set, and exit. This mode is disabled while reading profiles.
- -f Disables file name generation.
- -h Each command becomes a tracked alias when first encountered.
- -k All variable assignment arguments are placed in the environment for a command, not just those that precede the command name.
- -m Background jobs will run in a separate process group and a line will print upon completion. The exit status of background jobs is reported in a completion message. On systems with job control, this flag is turned on automatically for interactive shells.
- -n Read commands and check them for syntax errors, but do not execute them. Ignored for interactive shells.
- -o The following argument can be one of the following option names:

allexport	Same as -a.
errexit	Same as -e.
bgnice	All background jobs are run at a lower priority. This is the default mode.
ignoreeof	The shell will not exit on end-of-file. The command exit must be used.
keyword	Same as -k.
markdirs	All directory names resulting from file name generation have a trailing / appended.
monitor	Same as -m.
noclobber	Prevents redirection > from truncating existing files. Require >| to truncate a file when turned on.
noexec	Same as -n.
noglob	Same as -f.
nolog	Do not save function definitions in history file.
nounset	Same as -u.
privileged	Same as -p.
verbose	Same as -v.
trackall	Same as -h.
vi	Puts you in insert mode of a vi style in-line editor until you hit escape character 033. This puts you in move mode. A return sends the line.
viraw	Each character is processed as it is typed in vi mode.
xtrace	Same as -x.

If no option name is supplied then the current option settings are printed.

- **-p** Disables processing of the **$HOME/.profile** file and uses the file **/etc/suid_profile** instead of the **ENV** file. This mode is on whenever the effective uid (gid) is not equal to the real uid (gid). Turning this off causes the effective uid and gid to be set to the real uid and gid.
- **-s** Sort the positional parameters lexicographically.
- **-t** Exit after reading and executing one command.
- **-u** Treat unset parameters as an error when substituting.
- **-v** Print shell input lines as they are read.
- **-x** Print commands and their arguments as they are executed.
- **-** Turns off **-x** and **-v** flags and stops examining arguments for flags.
- **--** Do not change any of the flags; useful in setting **$1** to a value beginning with -. If no arguments follow this flag then the positional parameters are unset.

Using + rather than - causes these flags to be turned off. These flags can also be used upon invocation of the shell. The current set of flags may be found in **$-**. Unless **-A** is specified, the remaining arguments are positional parameters and are assigned, in order, to **$1 $2** .... If no arguments are given then the names and values of all variables are printed on the standard output.

† **shift** [*n*]
The positional parameters from **$***n***+1** ... are renamed **$1** ... , default *n* is 1. The parameter *n* can be any arithmetic expression that evaluates to a non-negative number less than or equal to **$#**.

† **times** Print the accumulated user and system times for the shell and for processes run from the shell.

† **trap** [*arg*] [*sig*] ...
arg is a command to be read and executed when the shell receives signal(s) *sig*. (Note that *arg* is scanned once when the trap is set and once when the trap is taken.) Each *sig* can be given as a number or as the name of the signal. Trap commands are executed in order of signal number. Any attempt to set a trap on a signal that was ignored on entry to the current shell is ineffective. If *arg* is omitted or is -, then all trap(s) *sig* are reset to their original values. If *arg* is the null string then this signal is ignored by the shell and by the commands it invokes. If *sig* is **ERR** then *arg* will be executed whenever a command has a non-zero exit status. *sig* is **DEBUG** then *arg* will be executed after each command. If *sig* is 0 or **EXIT** and the **trap** statement is executed inside the body of a function, then the command *arg* is executed after the function completes. If *sig* is 0 or **EXIT** for a **trap** set outside any function then the command *arg* is executed on exit from the shell. The **trap** command with no arguments prints a list of commands associated with each signal number.

†† **typeset** [**±HLRZfilrtux**[*n*]] [*name*[**=***value*]] ...
Sets attributes and values for shell variables. When invoked inside

a function, a new instance of the variable *name* is created. The parameter value and type are restored when the function completes. The following list of attributes may be specified:

- `-H` This flag provides UNIX to host-name file mapping on non-UNIX machines.
- `-L` Left justify and remove leading blanks from *value*. If *n* is non-zero it defines the width of the field, otherwise it is determined by the width of the value of first assignment. When the variable is assigned to, it is filled on the right with blanks or truncated, if necessary, to fit into the field. Leading zeros are removed if the `-Z` flag is also set. The `-R` flag is turned off.
- `-R` Right justify and fill with leading blanks. If *n* is non-zero it defines the width of the field, otherwise it is determined by the width of the value of first assignment. The field is left filled with blanks or truncated from the end if the variable is reassigned. The `L` flag is turned off.
- `-Z` Right justify and fill with leading zeros if the first non-blank character is a digit and the `-L` flag has not been set. If *n* is non-zero it defines the width of the field, otherwise it is determined by the width of the value of first assignment.
- `-f` The names refer to function names rather than variable names. No assignments can be made and the only other valid flags are `-t`, `-u` and `-x`. The flag `-t` turns on execution tracing for this function. The flag `-u` causes this function to be marked undefined. The **FPATH** variable will be searched to find the function definition when the function is referenced. The flag `-x` allows the function definition to remain in effect across shell procedures invoked by name.
- `-i` Variable is an integer. This makes arithmetic faster. If *n* is non-zero it defines the output arithmetic base, otherwise the first assignment determines the output base.
- `-l` All upper-case characters converted to lower-case. The upper-case flag, `-u` is turned off.
- `-r` The given *names* are marked readonly and these names cannot be changed by subsequent assignment.
- `-t` Tags the variables. Tags are user definable and have no special meaning to the shell.
- `-u` All lower-case characters are converted to upper-case characters. The lower-case flag, `-l` is turned off.
- `-x` The given *names* are marked for automatic export to the *environment* of subsequently-executed commands.

Using + rather than − causes these flags to be turned off. If no *name* arguments are given but flags are specified, a list of *names* (and optionally the `values`) of the *variables* which have these flags set is printed. (Using + rather than − keeps the values from being printed.) If no *names* and flags are given, the *names* and *attributes* of all *variables* are printed.

`ulimit [ -[HS][a | cdfnstv] ]`

`ulimit [ -[HS][c | d | f | n | s | t | v] ]` *limit*

`ulimit` prints or sets hard or soft resource limits. These limits are described in `getrlimit(2)`.

If *limit* is not present, `ulimit` prints the specified limits. Any number of limits may be printed at one time. The `-a` option prints all limits.

If *limit* is present, `ulimit` sets the specified limit to *limit*. The string `unlimited` requests the largest valid limit. Limits may be set for only one resource at a time. Any user may set a soft limit to any value below the hard limit. Any user may lower a hard limit. Only a super-user may raise a hard limit; see **su**(1).

The `-H` option specifies a hard limit. The `-S` option specifies a soft limit. If neither option is specified, `ulimit` will set both limits and print the soft limit.

The following options specify the resource whose limits are to be printed or set. If no option is specified, the file size limit is printed or set.

- `-c` maximum core file size (in 512-byte blocks)
- `-d` maximum size of data segment or heap (in kbytes)
- `-f` maximum file size (in 512-byte blocks)
- `-n` maximum file descriptor plus 1
- `-s` maximum size of stack segment (in kbytes)
- `-t` maximum CPU time (in seconds)
- `-v` maximum size of virtual memory (in kbytes)

If no option is given, `-f` is assumed.

`umask [` *mask* `]`

The user file-creation mask is set to *mask* [see **umask**(2)]. *mask* can either be an octal number or a symbolic value as described in **chmod**(1). If a symbolic value is given, the new umask value is the complement of the result of applying *mask* to the complement of the previous umask value. If *mask* is omitted, the current value of the mask is printed.

`unalias` *name ...*

The variables given by the list of *names* are removed from the *alias* list.

`unset [ -f ]` *name ...*

The variables given by the list of *names* are unassigned, i. e., their values and attributes are erased. Read-only variables cannot be unset. If the flag, `-f`, is set, then the names refer to *function* names. Unsetting `ERRNO`, `LINENO`, `MAILCHECK`, `OPTARG`, `OPTIND`, `RANDOM`, `SECONDS`, `TMOUT`, and `_` causes removes their special meaning even if they are subsequently assigned to.

† wait [*job*]

Wait for the specified *job* and report its termination status. If *job* is not given then all currently active child processes are waited for. The exit status from this command is that of the process waited for. See *Jobs* for a description of the format of *job*.

whence [-pv] *name* ...

For each *name*, indicate how it would be interpreted if used as a command name.

-v produces a more verbose report.

-p does a path search for *name* even if name is an alias, a function, or a reserved word.

Invocation.

If the shell is invoked by exec(2), and the first character of argument zero ($0) is -, then the shell is assumed to be a login shell and commands are read from /etc/profile and then from either .profile in the current directory or $HOME/.profile, if either file exists. Next, commands are read from the file named by performing parameter substitution on the value of the environment variable ENV if the file exists. If the -s flag is not present and *arg* is, then a path search is performed on the first *arg* to determine the name of the script to execute. The script *arg* must have read permission and any setuid and setgid settings will be ignored. Commands are then read as described below; the following flags are interpreted by the shell when it is invoked:

-c *string* If the -c flag is present then commands are read from *string*.

-s If the -s flag is present or if no arguments remain then commands are read from the standard input. Shell output, except for the output of the *Special commands* listed above, is written to file descriptor 2.

-i If the -i flag is present or if the shell input and output are attached to a terminal (as told by ioctl(2)) then this shell is *interactive*. In this case TERM is ignored (so that kill 0 does not kill an interactive shell) and INTR is caught and ignored (so that wait is interruptible). In all cases, QUIT is ignored by the shell.

-r If the -r flag is present the shell is a restricted shell.

The remaining flags and arguments are described under the set command above.

Rksh Only.

Rksh is used to set up login names and execution environments whose capabilities are more controlled than those of the standard shell. The actions of *rksh* are identical to those of sh, except that the following are disallowed:

changing directory [see cd(1)],
setting the value of SHELL, ENV, or PATH,
specifying path or command names containing /,
redirecting output (>, >| , <> , and >>).

The restrictions above are enforced after .profile and the ENV files are interpreted.

When a command to be executed is found to be a shell procedure, *rksh* invokes *ksh* to execute it. Thus, it is possible to provide to the end-user shell procedures that have access to the full power of the standard shell, while imposing a limited menu of commands; this scheme assumes that the end-user does not have write and execute permissions in the same directory.

The net effect of these rules is that the writer of the `.profile` has complete control over user actions, by performing guaranteed setup actions and leaving the user in an appropriate directory (probably *not* the login directory).

The system administrator often sets up a directory of commands (i.e., `/usr/rbin`) that can be safely invoked by *rksh*.

EXIT STATUS

Errors detected by the shell, such as syntax errors, cause the shell to return a non-zero exit status. Otherwise, the shell returns the exit status of the last command executed (see also the `exit` command above). If the shell is being used non-interactively then execution of the shell file is abandoned. Run time errors detected by the shell are reported by printing the command or function name and the error condition. If the line number that the error occurred on is greater than one, then the line number is also printed in square brackets (`[]`) after the command or function name.

FILES

/etc/passwd
/etc/profile
/etc/suid_profile
$HOME/.profile
/tmp/sh*
/dev/null

SEE ALSO

`cat`(1), `cd`(1), `chmod`(1), `cut`(1), `echo`(1), `env`(1), `paste`(1), `stty`(1), `test`(1), `umask`(1), and `vi`(1).
`dup`(2), `exec`(2), `fork`(2), `ioctl`(2), `lseek`(2), `pipe`(2), `signal`(2), `umask`(2), `ulimit`(2), `wait`(2), and `rand`(3C) in the *Programmer's Reference Manual.*
`newgrp`(1M), `a.out`(4), `profile`(4), and `environ`(4) in the *System Administrator's Reference Manual.*

Morris I. Bolsky and David G. Korn, *The KornShell Command and Programming Language*, Prentice Hall, 1989.

NOTES

If a command which is a *tracked alias* is executed, and then a command with the same name is installed in a directory in the search path before the directory where the original command was found, the shell will continue to `exec` the original command. Use the `-t` option of the `alias` command to correct this situation.

Some very old shell scripts contain a ^ as a synonym for the pipe character. |.

Using the `fc` built-in command within a compound command will cause the whole command to disappear from the history file.

The built-in command `.` *file* reads the whole file before any commands are executed. Therefore, `alias` and `unalias` commands in the file will not apply to any functions defined in the file.

Traps are not processed while a job is waiting for a foreground process. Thus, a trap on `CHLD` won't be executed until the foreground job terminates.

NAME

`last` – indicate last user or terminal logins

SYNOPSIS

`last` [–n *number* | *–number*] [`-f` *filename*] [*name* | *tty*] ...

DESCRIPTION

The `last` command looks in the **/var/adm/wtmp**, file which records all logins and logouts, for information about a user, a terminal or any group of users and terminals. Arguments specify names of users or terminals of interest. Names of terminals may be given fully or abbreviated. For example `last 10` is the same as `last term/10`. If multiple arguments are given, the information which applies to any of the arguments is printed. For example `last root console` lists all of root's sessions as well as all sessions on the console terminal. `last` displays the sessions of the specified users and terminals, most recent first, indicating the times at which the session began, the duration of the session, and the terminal which the session took place on. If the session is still continuing or was cut short by a reboot, `last` so indicates.

The pseudo-user `reboot` logs in at reboots of the system, thus

```
last reboot
```

will give an indication of mean time between reboot.

`last` with no arguments displays a record of all logins and logouts, in reverse order.

If `last` is interrupted, it indicates how far the search has progressed in `/var/adm/wtmp`. If interrupted with a quit signal (generated by a CTRL-\) `last` indicates how far the search has progressed so far, and the search continues.

The following options are available:

–n *number* | *–number*
: Limit the number of entries displayed to that specified by *number*. These options are identical; the *–number* option is provided as a transition tool only and will be removed in future releases.

`-f` *filename*
: Use *filename* as the name of the accounting file instead of `/var/adm/wtmp`.

FILES

`/var/adm/wtmp` accounting file

SEE ALSO

`utmp`(4) in the *System Administrator's Reference Manual.*

NAME

layers – layer multiplexor for windowing terminals

SYNOPSIS

layers [**-s**] [**-t**] [**-D** [**-m** *max-pkt*] [**-d**] [**-p**] [**-h** *modlist*] [**-f** *file*] [*layersys-prgm*]

DESCRIPTION

layers manages asynchronous windows [see **layers**(5)] on a windowing terminal. Upon invocation, **layers** finds an unused **xt**(7) channel group and associates it with the terminal line on its standard output. It then waits for commands from the terminal.

Command-line options:

-s Report protocol statistics on standard error at the end of the session after you exit from **layers**. The statistics may be printed during a session by invoking the program **xts**(1M).

-t Turn on **xt**(7) driver packet tracing, and produces a trace dump on standard error at the end of the session after you exit from **layers**. The trace dump may be printed during a session by invoking the program **xtt**(1M).

-D Send debugging messages to standard error.

-m *max-pkt*
Set maximum size for the data part of regular **xt** packets sent from the host to the terminal. Legal values are 32 to 252. This option also implies that regular rather than network **xt** protocol should be used. See **xtproto**(5).

-d If a firmware patch has been downloaded, print out the sizes of the text, data, and bss portions of the firmware patch on standard error.

-p If a firmware patch has been downloaded, print the down-loading protocol statistics and a trace on standard error.

-h *modlist*
Push a list of STREAMS modules separated by a comma on a layer.

-f *file* Start **layers** with an initial configuration specified by *file*. Each line of the file represents a layer to be created, and has the following format:

origin_x origin_y corner_x corner_y command_list

The coordinates specify the size and position of the layer on the screen in the terminal's coordinate system. If all four are 0, the user must define the layer interactively. *command_list*, a list of one or more commands, must be provided. It is executed in the new layer using the user's shell (by executing: **$SHELL -i -c** "*command_list*"). This means that the last command should invoke a shell, such as **/usr/bin/sh**. (If the last command is not a shell, then, when the last command has completed, the layer will not be functional.)

layersys-prgm
A file containing a firmware patch that the **layers** command downloads to the terminal before layers are created and *command_list* is executed.

Each layer is in most ways functionally identical to a separate terminal. Characters typed on the keyboard are sent to the standard input of the UNIX system process attached to the current layer (called the host process), and characters written on the standard output by the host process appear in that layer. When a layer is created, a separate shell is established and bound to the layer. If the environment variable SHELL is set, the user gets that shell: otherwise, /usr/bin/sh is used. In order to enable communications with other users via write(1), layers invokes the command relogin(1M) when the first layer is created. relogin(1M) will reassign that layer as the user's logged-in terminal. An alternative layer can be designated by using relogin(1M) directly. layers will restore the original assignment on termination.

Layers are created, deleted, reshaped, and otherwise manipulated in a terminal-dependent manner. For instance, the AT&T 630 MTG terminal provides a mouse-activated pop-up menu of layer operations. The method of ending a layers session is also defined by the terminal.

If a user wishes to take advantage of a terminal-specific application software package, the environment variable DMD should be set to the path name of the directory where the package was installed. Otherwise DMD should not be set.

EXAMPLES

A typical startup command is:

```
layers -f startup
```

where startup contains

```
8 8 700 200 date ; pwd ; exec $SHELL
8 300 780 850 exec $SHELL
```

The command

```
layers -h FILTER,LDTERM
```

pushes the STREAMS modules FILTER and LDTERM on each layer that is opened.

FILES

/dev/xt/??[0-7]
/usr/lib/layersys/lsys.8;7;3
$DMD/lib/layersys/lsys.8;?;?

SEE ALSO

ismpx(1), jterm(1), jwin(1), sh(1), write(1).
relogin(1M), wtinit(1M), xts(1M), xtt(1M), jagent(5), layers(5), xtproto(5), and xt(7).
libwindows(3X) in the *Programmer's Reference Manual*.

NOTES

The xt(7) driver supports an alternate data transmission scheme known as ENCODING MODE. This mode makes layers operation possible even over data links which intercept control characters or do not transmit 8-bit characters. ENCODING MODE is selected either by setting a setup option on your windowing terminal or by setting the environment variable DMDLOAD to the value hex before running layers:

```
DMDLOAD=hex; export DMDLOAD
```

If, after executing `layers -f` *file*, the terminal does not respond in one or more of the layers, often the last command in the *command_list* for that layer did not invoke a shell.

To access this version of `layers`, make sure `/usr/bin` appears before any other directory, such as `$DMD/bin`, you have in your path that contains a layers program. [For information about defining the shell environmental variable `PATH` in your `.profile`, see `profile`(4).] Otherwise, if there is a terminal-dependent version of `layers`, you may get it instead of the correct one.

`layers` sends all debugging and error messages to standard error. Therefore, when invoking `layers` with the `-D`, `-d`, or `-p` option, it is necessary to redirect standard error to a file. For example,

```
layers -D 2>layers.msgs
```

If `layers` encounters an error condition and standard error is not redirected, the last error encountered will be printed when the `layers` commands exits.

When using `layers` the mimimum acceptable baud rate is 1200. Behavior of `layers` is unpredictable when using baud rate below 1200.

When using V7/BSD/Xenix applications (e.g., the `jim` editor) `layers` should be invoked as

```
layers -h ldterm,ttcompat
```

This pushes the `ttcompat` module on each window and converts the BSD interface into the `termio`(7) interface.

NAME

line – read one line

SYNOPSIS

line

DESCRIPTION

line copies one line (up to a new-line) from the standard input and writes it on the standard output. It returns an exit code of 1 on EOF and always prints at least a new-line. It is often used within shell files to read from the user's terminal.

SEE ALSO

sh(1).
read(2) in the *Programmer's Reference Manual.*

NAME

`listusers` – list user login information

SYNOPSIS

`listusers` [`-g` *groups*] [`-l` *logins*]

DESCRIPTION

Executed without any options, this command displays a list of all user logins, sorted by login, and the account field value associated with each login in `/etc/passwd`.

`-g` Lists all user logins belonging to `group`, sorted by login. Multiple groups can be specified as a comma-separated list.

`-l` Lists the user login or logins specified by `logins`, sorted by login. Multiple logins can be specified as a comma-separated list.

NOTES

A user login is one that has a UID of 100 or greater.

The `-l` and `-g` options can be combined. User logins will be listed only once, even if they belong to more than one of the selected groups.

NAME

ln – link files

SYNOPSIS

ln [-f] [-n] [-s] *file1* [*file2*...] *target*

DESCRIPTION

The ln command links *filen* to *target* by creating a directory entry that refers to *target*. By using ln with one or more file names, the user may create one or more links to *target*.

The ln command may be used to create both hard links and symbolic links; by default it creates hard links. A hard link to a file is indistinguishable from the original directory entry. Any changes to a file are effective independent of the name used to reference the file. Hard links may not span file systems and may not refer to directories.

Without the -s option, ln is used to create hard links. *filen* is linked to *target*. If *target* is a directory, another file named *filen* is created in *target* and linked to the original *filen*. If *target* is a file, its contents are overwritten.

If ln determines that the mode of *target* forbids writing, it will print the mode (see chmod(2)), ask for a response, and read the standard input for one line. If the line begins with y, the link occurs, if permissible; otherwise, the command exits.

The following options are recognized:

-f ln will link files without questioning the user, even if the mode of *target* forbids writing. Note that this is the default if the standard input is not a terminal,

-n If the linkname is an existing file, do not overwrite the contents of the file. The -f option overrides this option.

-s ln will create a symbolic link. A symbolic link contains the name of the file to which it is linked. Symbolic links may span file systems and may refer to directories.

If the -s option is used with two arguments, *target* may be an existing directory or a non-existent file. If *target* already exists and is not a directory, an error is returned. *filen* may be any path name and need not exist. If it exists, it may be a file or directory and may reside on a different file system from *target*. If *target* is an existing directory, a file is created in directory *target* whose name is *filen* or the last component of *filen*. This file is a symbolic link that references *filen*. If *target* does not exist, a file with name *target* is created and it is a symbolic link that references *filen*.

If the -s option is used with more than two arguments, *target* must be an existing directory or an error will be returned. For each *filen*, a file is created in *target* whose name is *filen* or its last component; each new *filen* is a symbolic link to the original *filen*. The *files* and *target* may reside on different file systems.

SEE ALSO

`chmod`(1), `cp`(1), `mv`(1), `rm`(1), `link`(2), `readlink`(2), `stat`(2), `symlink`(2).

NOTE

Doing operations that involve ".." (such as "`cd ..`") in a directory that is symbolically linked will reference the original directory not the target.

NAME

`login` – sign on

SYNOPSIS

`login` [`-d` *device*] [*name* [*environ* . . .]]

DESCRIPTION

The `login` command is used at the beginning of each terminal session and allows you to identify yourself to the system. It may be invoked as a command or by the system when a connection is first established. It is invoked by the system when a previous user has terminated the initial shell by typing a `cntrl-d` to indicate an end-of-file.

If `login` is invoked as a command it must replace the initial command interpreter. This is accomplished by typing

```
exec login
```

from the initial shell.

`login` asks for your user name (if it is not supplied as an argument), and if appropriate, your password. Echoing is turned off (where possible) during the typing of your password, so it will not appear on the written record of the session.

If there are no lower-case characters in the first line of input processed, `login` assumes the connecting TTY is an upper-case-only terminal and sets the port's `termio`(7) options to reflect this.

`login` accepts a device option, *device*. *device* is taken to be the path name of the TTY port `login` is to operate on. The use of the device option can be expected to improve `login` performance, since `login` will not need to call `ttyname`(3).

If you make any mistake in the login procedure, the message

```
Login incorrect
```

is printed and a new login prompt will appear. If you make five incorrect login attempts, all five may be logged in `/var/adm/loginlog` (if it exists) and the TTY line will be dropped.

If you do not complete the login successfully within a certain period of time (e.g., one minute), you are likely to be silently disconnected.

After a successful login, accounting files are updated, the `/etc/profile` script is executed, the time you last logged in is printed, `/etc/motd` is printed, the user-ID, group-ID, supplementary group list, working directory, and command interpreter (usually `sh`) are initialized, and the file `.profile` in the working directory is executed, if it exists. The name of the command interpreter is – followed by the last component of the interpreter's path name (e.g., `-sh`). If this field in the password file is empty, then the default command interpreter, `/usr/bin/sh` is used. If this field is *, then the named directory becomes the root directory, the starting point for path searches for path names beginning with a `/`. At that point `login` is re-executed at the new level which must have its own root structure, including `/var/adm/login` and `/etc/passwd`.

The basic *environment* is initialized to:

HOME=*your-login-directory*
LOGNAME=*your-login-name*
PATH=/usr/bin
SHELL=*last-field-of-passwd-entry*
MAIL=/var/mail/*your-login-name*
TZ=*timezone-specification*

The environment may be expanded or modified by supplying additional arguments to login, either at execution time or when login requests your login name. The arguments may take either the form *xxx* or *xxx=yyy*. Arguments without an equal sign are placed in the environment as

L*n*=xxx

where *n* is a number starting at 0 and is incremented each time a new variable name is required. Variables containing an = are placed in the environment without modification. If they already appear in the environment, then they replace the older value. There are two exceptions. The variables PATH and SHELL cannot be changed. This prevents people, logging into restricted shell environments, from spawning secondary shells which are not restricted. login understands simple single-character quoting conventions. Typing a backslash in front of a character quotes it and allows the inclusion of such characters as spaces and tabs.

FILES

/var/adm/utmp	accounting
/var/adm/wtmp	accounting
/var/mail/*your-name*	mailbox for user *your-name*
/var/adm/loginlog	record of failed login attempts
/etc/motd	message-of-the-day
/etc/passwd	password file
/etc/profile	system profile
.profile	user's login profile
/var/adm/lastlog	time of last login

SEE ALSO

mail(1), newgrp(1M), sh(1), su(1M).
loginlog(4), passwd(4), profile(4), environ(5) in the *Programmer's Reference Manual*.

DIAGNOSTICS

login incorrect if the user name or the password cannot be matched.
No shell, cannot open password file, or no directory: consult a system engineer.
No utmp entry. You must exec "login" from the lowest level "sh" if you attempted to execute login as a command without using the shell's exec internal command or from a shell other than the initial shell.

NAME

logname – get login name

SYNOPSIS

logname

DESCRIPTION

logname returns the name of the user running the process.

FILES

/etc/profile

SEE ALSO

env(1), login(1).
cuserid(3C) in the *Programmer's Reference Manual.*
environ(5) in the *System Administrator's Reference Manual.*

NAME

`lp`, `cancel` – send/cancel requests to an LP print service

SYNOPSIS

`lp` [*printing-options*] [*files*]
`lp -i` *request-IDs printing-options*
`cancel` [*request-IDs*] [*printers*]
`cancel -u` *login-ID-list* [*printers*]

DESCRIPTION

The first form of the `lp` command arranges for the named *files* and associated information (collectively called a *request*) to be printed. If no file names are specified on the command line, the standard input is assumed. The standard input may be specified along with named *files* on the command line by listing the file name(s) and specifying – for the standard input. The *files* will be printed in the order in which they appear on the shell command line.

The LP print service associates a unique *request-ID* with each request and displays it on the standard output. This *request-ID* can be used later when canceling or changing a request, or when determining its status. [See the section on `cancel` for details about canceling a request, and `lpstat`(1) for information about checking the status of a print request.]

The second form of `lp` is used to change the options for a request. The print request identified by the *request-ID* is changed according to the printing options specified with this shell command. The printing options available are the same as those with the first form of the `lp` shell command. If the request has finished printing, the change is rejected. If the request is already printing, it will be stopped and restarted from the beginning (unless the `-P` option has been given).

The `cancel` command allows users to cancel print requests previously sent with the `lp` command. The first form of `cancel` permits cancellation of requests based on their *request-ID*. The second form of cancel permits cancellation of requests based on the *login-ID* of their owner.

Sending a Print Request

The first form of the `lp` command is used to send a print request to a particular printer or group of printers.

Options to `lp` must always precede file names, but may be specified in any order. The following options are available for `lp`:

`-c` Make copies of the *files* before printing. Normally, *files* will not be copied, but will be linked whenever possible. If the `-c` option is not given, then the user should be careful not to remove any of the *files* before the request has been printed in its entirety. It should also be noted that if the `-c` option is not specified, any changes made to the named *files* after the request is made but before it is printed will be reflected in the printed output.

`-d` *dest* Choose *dest* as the printer or class of printers that is to do the printing. If *dest* is a printer, then the request will be printed only on that specific printer. If *dest* is a class of printers, then the request will be printed on the first available printer that is a member of the class. If *dest* is any, then the request will be printed on any printer which can handle it. Under certain conditions (unavailability of printers, file space limitations, and so on) requests for specific destinations may not be accepted [see `lpstat(1)`]. By default, *dest* is taken from the environment variable `LPDEST` (if it is set). Otherwise, a default destination (if one exists) for the computer system is used. Destination names vary between systems [see `lpstat(1)`].

`-f` *form-name* [`-d any`]
: Print the request on the form *form-name*. The LP print service ensures that the form is mounted on the printer. If *form-name* is requested with a printer destination that cannot support the form, the request is rejected. If *form-name* has not been defined for the system, or if the user is not allowed to use the form, the request is rejected [see `lpforms(1M)`]. When the `-d any` option is given, the request is printed on any printer that has the requested form mounted and can handle all other needs of the print request.

`-H` *special-handling*
: Print the request according to the value of *special-handling*. Acceptable values for *special-handling* are defined below:

  `hold` Don't print the request until notified. If printing has already begun, stop it. Other print requests will go ahead of a held request until it is resumed.

  `resume` Resume a held request. If it had been printing when held, it will be the next request printed, unless subsequently bumped by an `immediate` request.

  `immediate` (Available only to LP administrators)
  Print the request next. If more than one request is assigned `immediate`, the requests are printed in the reverse order queued. If a request is currently printing on the desired printer, you have to put it on hold to allow the immediate request to print.

`-m` Send mail [see `mail(1)`] after the files have been printed. By default, no mail is sent upon normal completion of the print request.

`-n` *number* Print *number* copies (default is 1) of the output.

`-o` *option* Specify printer-dependent *options*. Several such *options* may be collected by specifying the `-o` keyletter more than once (`-o` $option_1$ `-o` $option_2$ ... `-o` $option_n$), or by specifying a list of options with one `-o` keyletter enclosed in double quotes (that is, `-o` "$option_1$ $option_2$ ... $option_n$"). The standard interface recognizes the following options:

  `nobanner` Do not print a banner page with this request. (The administrator can disallow this option at any time.)

  `nofilebreak`
  Do not insert a form feed between the files given, if submitting a job to print more than one file.

`length`=*scaled-decimal-number*
: Print this request with pages *scaled-decimal-number* lines long. A *scaled-decimal-number* is an optionally scaled decimal number that gives a size in lines, columns, inches, or centimeters, as appropriate. The scale is indicated by appending the letter "i" for inches, or the letter "c" for centimeters. For length or width settings, an unscaled number indicates lines or columns; for line pitch or character pitch settings, an unscaled number indicates lines per inch or characters per inch (the same as a number scaled with "i"). For example, `length=66` indicates a page length of 66 lines, `length=11i` indicates a page length of 11 inches, and `length=27.94c` indicates a page length of 27.94 centimeters.

  This option may not be used with the `-f` option.

`width`=*scaled-decimal-number*
: Print this request with page-width set to *scaled-decimal-number* columns wide. (See the explanation of *scaled-decimal-numbers* in the discussion of `length`, above.) This option may not be used with the `-f` option.

`lpi`=*scaled-decimal-number*
: Print this request with the line pitch set to *scaled-decimal-number* lines per inch. This option may not be used with the `-f` option.

`cpi`=*scaled-decimal-number*
: Print this request with the character pitch set to *scaled-decimal-number* characters per inch. Character pitch can also be set to `pica` (representing 10 characters per inch) or `elite` (representing 12 characters per inch), or it can be `compressed` (representing as many characters as a printer can handle). There is no standard number of characters per inch for all printers; see the Terminfo database [`terminfo`(4)] for the default character pitch for your printer.

  This option may not be used with the `-f` option.

`stty`=*'stty-option-list'*
: A list of options valid for the `stty` command; enclose the list with single quotes if it contains blanks.

`-P` *page-list*
: Print the pages specified in *page-list*. This option can be used only if there is a filter available to handle it; otherwise, the print request will be rejected.

  The *page-list* may consist of range(s) of numbers, single page numbers, or a combination of both. The pages will be printed in ascending order.

-q *priority-level*
: Assign this request *priority-level* in the printing queue. The values of *priority-level* range from 0, the highest priority, to 39, the lowest priority. If a priority is not specified, the default for the print service is used, as assigned by the system administrator. A priority limit may be assigned to individual users by the system administrator.

-s
: Suppress messages from `lp` such as those that begin with `request id is`.

-S *character-set* [-d any]
-S *print-wheel* [-d any]
: Print this request using the specified *character-set* or *print-wheel*. If a form was requested and it requires a character set or print wheel other than the one specified with the -S option, the request is rejected.

For printers that take print wheels: if the print wheel specified is not one listed by the administrator as acceptable for the printer specified in this request, the request is rejected unless the print wheel is already mounted on the printer.

For printers that use selectable or programmable character sets: if the *character-set* specified is not one defined in the Terminfo database for the printer [see `terminfo`(4)], or is not an alias defined by the administrator, the request is rejected.

When the -d any option is used, the request is printed on any printer that has the print wheel mounted or any printer that can select the character set, and that can handle any other needs of the request.

-t *title*
: Print *title* on the banner page of the output. The default is no title. Enclose *title* in quotes if it contains blanks.

-T *content-type* [-r]
: Print the request on a printer that can support the specified *content-type*. If no printer accepts this type directly, a filter will be used to convert the content into an acceptable type. If the -r option is specified, a filter will not be used. If -r is specified, and no printer accepts the *content-type* directly, the request is rejected. If the *content-type* is not acceptable to any printer, either directly or with a filter, the request is rejected.

-w
: Write a message on the user's terminal after the *files* have been printed. If the user is not logged in, then mail will be sent instead.

-y *mode-list*
: Print this request according to the printing modes listed in *mode-list*. The allowed values for *mode-list* are locally defined. This option may be used only if there is a filter available to handle it; otherwise, the print request will be rejected.

Canceling a Print Request

The `cancel` command cancels requests for print jobs made with the `lp` command. The first form allows a user to specify one or more *request-IDs* of print jobs to be canceled. Alternatively, the user can specify one or more *printers*, on which only the currently printing job will be canceled.

The second form of `cancel` permits a user to cancel all of his or her own jobs on all printers. In this form the *printers* option can be used to restrict the printers on which the user's jobs will be canceled. Note that in this form, when the *printers* option is used, all jobs queued for those printers will be canceled. A printer class is not a valid argument.

Users without special privileges can cancel only requests associated with their own login IDs. The system administrator can cancel jobs submitted by any user. The *login-ID-list* must be enclosed in quotes if it contains blanks.

NOTES

Printers for which requests are not being accepted will not be considered when the `lp` command is run and the destination is `any`. (Use the `lpstat -a` command to see which printers are accepting requests.) On the other hand, if (1) a request is destined for a class of printers and (2) the class itself is accepting requests, then *all* printers in the class will be considered, regardless of their acceptance status.

For printers that take mountable print wheels or font cartridges, if you do not specify a particular print wheel or font with the `-S` option, whichever one happens to be mounted at the time your request is printed will be used. Use the `lpstat -p` *printer* `-l` command to see which print wheels are available on a particular printer, or the `lpstat -S -l` command to find out what print wheels are available and on which printers. For printers that have selectable character sets, you will get the standard character set if you don't use the `-S` option.

FILES

`/var/spool/lp/*`

SEE ALSO

`enable`(1), `lpstat`(1), `mail`(1).
`accept`(1M), `lpadmin`(1M), `lpfilter`(1M), `lpforms`(1M), `lpsched`(1M), `lpsystem`(1M), `lpusers`(1M) in the *System Administrator's Reference Manual*.
`terminfo`(4) in the *Programmer's Reference Manual*.

NAME

`lpstat` – print information about the status of the LP print service

SYNOPSIS

`lpstat` [*options*]

DESCRIPTION

The `lpstat` command prints information about the current status of the LP print service.

If no options are given, then `lpstat` prints the status of all the user's print requests made by `lp` [see `lp`(1)]. Any arguments that are not *options* are assumed to be *request-IDs* as returned by `lp`. The `lpstat` command prints the status of such requests. The *options* may appear in any order and may be repeated and intermixed with other arguments. Some of the keyletters below may be followed by an optional *list* that can be in one of two forms: a list of items separated from one another by a comma, or a list of items separated from one another by spaces enclosed in quotes. For example:

```
-u "user1, user2, user3"
```

Specifying `all` after any keyletter that takes *list* as an argument causes all information relevant to the keyletter to be printed. For example, the command

```
lpstat -o all
```

prints the status of all output requests.

The omission of a *list* following such key letters causes all information relevant to the key letter to be prined. For example, the command

```
lpstat -o
```

prints the status of all output requests.

`-a` [*list*] Reports whether print destinations are accepting requests. *list* is a list of intermixed printer names and class names.

`-c` [*list*] Reports name of all classes and their members. *list* is a list of class names.

`-d` Reports the system default destination for output requests.

`-f` [*list*] [`-l`]
Prints a verification that the forms in *list* are recognized by the LP print service. *list* is a list of forms; the default is `all`. The `-l` option will list the form descriptions.

`-o` [*list*] Reports the status of output requests: *list* is a list of intermixed printer names, class names, and *request-IDs*. The keyletter `-o` may be omitted.

`-p` [*list*] [`-D`] [`-l`]
Reports the status of printers. *list* is a list of printer names. If the `-D` option is given, a brief description is printed for each printer in *list*. If the `-l` option is given, and the printer is on the local machine, a full description of each printer's configuration is given, including the form mounted, the acceptable content and printer types, a printer description, the interface used, and so on. If the `-l` option is given and the printer is remote, the only information given is the remote machine and printer

names, and the shell-commands used for file transfer and remote execution.

`-r` Reports whether the LP request scheduler is on or off.

`-R` Reports a number showing the position of the job in the print queue.

`-s` Displays a status summary, including the status of the LP scheduler, the system default destination, a list of class names and their members, a list of printers and their associated devices, a list of the machines sharing print services, a list of all forms currently mounted, and a list of all recognized character sets and print wheels.

`-S` [*list*] [`-l`]
Prints a verification that the character sets or the print wheels specified in *list* are recognized by the LP print service. Items in *list* can be character sets or print wheels; the default for the list is **`all`**. If the `-l` option is given, each line is appended by a list of printers that can handle the print wheel or character set. The list also shows whether the print wheel or character set is mounted or specifies the built-in character set into which it maps.

`-t` Displays all status information: all the information obtained with the `-s` option, plus the acceptance and idle/busy status of all printers.

`-u` [*login-ID-list*]
Displays the status of output requests for users. The *login-ID-list* argument may include any or all of the following constructs:

login-ID	a user on any system
system_name`!`*login-ID*	a user on system *system_name*
system_name`!all`	all users on system *system_name*
`all!`*login-ID*	a user on all systems
`all`	all users on all systems

`-v` [*list*] Reports the names of printers and the pathnames of the devices associated with them or remote system names for network printers: *list* is a list of printer names.

FILES

`/var/spool/lp/*`
`/etc/lp/*`

SEE ALSO

`enable`(1), `lp`(1).

NAME

ls − list contents of directory

SYNOPSIS

ls [-RadLCxmlnogrtucpFbqisf1] [*names*]

DESCRIPTION

For each directory argument, ls lists the contents of the directory; for each file argument, ls repeats its name and any other information requested. The output is sorted alphabetically by default. When no argument is given, the current directory is listed. When several arguments are given, the arguments are first sorted appropriately, but file arguments appear before directories and their contents.

There are three major listing formats. The default format for output directed to a terminal is multi−column with entries sorted down the columns. The −1 option allows single column output and −m enables stream output format. In order to determine output formats for the −C, −x, and −m options, ls uses an environment variable, COLUMNS, to determine the number of character positions available on one output line. If this variable is not set, the terminfo(4) database is used to determine the number of columns, based on the environment variable TERM. If this information cannot be obtained, 80 columns are assumed.

The ls command has the following options:

−R Recursively list subdirectories encountered.

−a List all entries, including those that begin with a dot (.), which are normally not listed.

−d If an argument is a directory, list only its name (not its contents); often used with −l to get the status of a directory.

−L If an argument is a symbolic link, list the file or directory the link references rather than the link itself.

−C Multi-column output with entries sorted down the columns. This is the default output format.

−x Multi-column output with entries sorted across rather than down the page.

−m Stream output format; files are listed across the page, separated by commas.

−l List in long format, giving mode, number of links, owner, group, size in bytes, and time of last modification for each file (see below). If the file is a special file, the size field instead contains the major and minor device numbers rather than a size. If the file is a symbolic link, the filename is printed followed by "−>" and the pathname of the referenced file.

−n The same as −l, except that the owner's UID and group's GID numbers are printed, rather than the associated character strings.

−o The same as −l, except that the group is not printed.

- `-g` The same as `-l`, except that the owner is not printed.
- `-r` Reverse the order of sort to get reverse alphabetic or oldest first as appropriate.
- `-t` Sort by time stamp (latest first) instead of by name. The default is the last modification time. (See -n and -c.)
- `-u` Use time of last access instead of last modification for sorting (with the `-t` option) or printing (with the `-l` option).
- `-c` Use time of last modification of the i-node (file created, mode changed, etc.) for sorting (`-t`) or printing (`-l`).
- `-p` Put a slash (/) after each filename if the file is a directory.
- `-F` Put a slash (/) after each filename if the file is a directory, an asterisk (*) if the file is an executable, and an ampersand (@) if the file is a symbolic link.
- `-b` Force printing of non-printable characters to be in the octal *ddd* notation.
- `-q` Force printing of non-printable characters in file names as the character question mark (?).
- `-i` For each file, print the i-node number in the first column of the report.
- `-s` Give size in blocks, including indirect blocks, for each entry.
- `-f` Force each argument to be interpreted as a directory and list the name found in each slot. This option turns off `-l`, `-t`, `-s`, and `-r`, and turns on `-a`; the order is the order in which entries appear in the directory.
- `-1` Print one entry per line of output.

The mode printed under the `-l` option consists of ten characters. The first character may be one of the following:

- `d` the entry is a directory;
- `l` the entry is a symbolic link;
- `b` the entry is a block special file;
- `c` the entry is a character special file;
- `m` the entry is XENIX shared data (memory) file;
- `p` the entry is a fifo (a.k.a. "named pipe") special file;
- `s` the entry is a XENIX semaphore;
- `-` the entry is an ordinary file.

The next 9 characters are interpreted as three sets of three bits each. The first set refers to the owner's permissions; the next to permissions of others in the user-group of the file; and the last to all others. Within each set, the three characters indicate permission to read, to write, and to execute the file as a program, respectively. For a directory, "execute" permission is interpreted to mean permission to search the directory for a specified file.

`ls -l` (the `long` list) prints its output as follows:

```
-rwxrwxrwx  1 smith  dev    10876  May 16 9:42 part2
```

Reading from right to left, you see that the current directory holds one file, named `part2`. Next, the last time that file's contents were modified was 9:42 A.M. on May 16. The file contains 10,876 characters, or bytes. The owner of the file, or the user, belongs to the group `dev` (perhaps indicating "development"), and his or her login name is `smith`. The number, in this case `1`, indicates the number of links to file `part2`; see `cp`(1). Finally, the dash and letters tell you that user, group, and others have permissions to read, write, and execute `part2`.

The execute (`x`) symbol here occupies the third position of the three-character sequence. A – in the third position would have indicated a denial of execution permissions.

The permissions are indicated as follows:

- `r` the file is readable
- `w` the file is writable
- `x` the file is executable
- `-` the indicated permission is *not* granted
- `l` mandatory locking occurs during access (the set-group-ID bit is on and the group execution bit is off)
- `s` the set-user-ID or set-group-ID bit is on, and the corresponding user or group execution bit is also on
- `S` undefined bit-state (the set-user-ID bit is on and the user execution bit is off)
- `t` the 1000 (octal) bit, or sticky bit, is on [see `chmod`(1)], and execution is on
- `T` the 1000 bit is turned on, and execution is off (undefined bit-state)

For user and group permissions, the third position is sometimes occupied by a character other than `x` or `–`. `s` also may occupy this position, referring to the state of the set-ID bit, whether it be the user's or the group's. The ability to assume the same ID as the user during execution is, for example, used during login when you begin as root but need to assume the identity of the user you login as.

In the case of the sequence of group permissions, `l` may occupy the third position. `l` refers to mandatory file and record `l`ocking. This permission describes a file's ability to allow other files to lock its reading or writing permissions during access.

For others permissions, the third position may be occupied by `t` or `T`. These refer to the state of the sticky bit and execution permissions.

EXAMPLES

An example of a file's permissions is:

```
-rwxr--r--
```

This describes a file that is readable, writable, and executable by the user and readable by the group and others.

Another example of a file's permissions is:

```
-rwsr-xr-x
```

This describes a file that is readable, writable, and executable by the user, readable and executable by the group and others, and allows its user-ID to be assumed, during execution, by the user presently executing it.

Another example of a file's permissions is:

```
-rw-rwl---
```

This describes a file that is readable and writable only by the user and the group and can be locked during access.

An example of a command line:

```
ls -a
```

This command prints the names of all files in the current directory, including those that begin with a dot (`.`), which normally do not print.

Another example of a command line:

```
ls -aisn
```

This command provides information on all files, including those that begin with a dot (a), the i-number—the memory address of the i-node associated with the file—printed in the left-hand column (i); the size (in blocks) of the files, printed in the column to the right of the i-numbers (s); finally, the report is displayed in the numeric version of the long list, printing the UID (instead of user name) and GID (instead of group name) numbers associated with the files.

When the sizes of the files in a directory are listed, a total count of blocks, including indirect blocks, is printed.

FILES

`/etc/passwd`	user IDs for `ls -l` and `ls -o`
`/etc/group`	group IDs for `ls -l` and `ls -g`
`/usr/share/lib/terminfo/?/*`	terminal information database

SEE ALSO

chmod(1), find(1).

NOTES

In a Remote File Sharing environment, you may not have the permissions that the output of the `ls -l` command leads you to believe. For more information see the *Getting Started*.

Unprintable characters in file names may confuse the columnar output options.

The total block count will be incorrect if if there are hard links among the files.

NAME

machid: pdp11, u3b, u3b2, u3b5, u3b15, vax, 386, u370 – get processor type truth value

SYNOPSIS

pdp11

u3b

u3b2

u3b5

u3b15

vax

u370

DESCRIPTION

The following commands will return a true value (exit code of 0) if you are on a processor that the command name indicates.

pdp11	True if you are on a PDP-11/45™ or PDP-11/70™.
u3b	True if you are on a 3B20 computer.
u3b2	True if you are on a 3B2 computer.
u3b5	True if you are on a 3B5 computer.
u3b15	True if you are on a 3B15 computer.
vax	True if you are on a VAX-11/750™ or VAX-11/780™.
u370	True if you are on an IBM® System/370™ computer.

The commands that do not apply will return a false (non-zero) value. These commands are often used within makefiles [see make(1)] and shell procedures [see sh(1)] to increase portability.

SEE ALSO

sh(1), test(1), true(1), uname.
make(1) in the *Programmer's Reference Manual*.

NOTES

This command supercedes the old machid family (pdp11, u3b2, u3b5, u3b15, vax, 386, u370) manual page which is obsolescent.

NAME

mail, rmail – read mail or send mail to users

SYNOPSIS

Sending mail:

mail [-tw] [-m *message_type*] *recipient* . . .

rmail [-tw] [-m *message_type*] *recipient* . . .

Reading mail:

mail [-ehpPqr] [-f *file*]

Forwarding mail:

mail -F *recipient* . . .

Debugging:

mail [-x*debug_level*] [*other_mail_options*] *recipient* . . .

mail -T *mailsurr_file recipient* . . .

DESCRIPTION

A *recipient* is usually a user name recognized by login(1). When *recipients* are named, mail assumes a message is being sent (except in the case of the -F option). It reads from the standard input up to an end-of-file (cntrl-d) or, if reading from a terminal device, until it reads a line consisting of just a period. When either of those indicators is received, mail adds the *letter* to the *mailfile* for each *recipient*.

A *letter* is composed of some *header lines* followed by a blank line followed by the *message content*. The *header lines* section of the letter consists of one or more UNIX postmarks:

From *sender date_and_time* [remote from *remote_system_name*]

followed by one or more standardized message header lines of the form:

keyword-name: [*printable text*]

where *keyword-name* is comprised of any printable, non-whitespace, characters other than colon (':'). A Content-Length: header line, indicating the number of bytes in the *message content* will always be present. A Content-Type: header line that describes the type of the *message content* (such as text, binary, multipart, etc.) will always be present unless the letter consists of only header lines with no message content. Header lines may be contined on the following line if that line starts with white space.

Sending mail:

The following command-line arguments affect SENDING mail:

- -m causes a Message-Type: line to be added to the message header with the value of *message_type*.
- -t causes a To: line to be added to the message header for each of the intended recipients.
- -w causes a letter to be sent to a remote recipient without waiting for the completion of the remote transfer program.

If a letter is found to be undeliverable, it is returned to the sender with diagnostics that indicate the location and nature of the failure. If `mail` is interrupted during input, the message is saved in the file `dead.letter` to allow editing and resending. `dead.letter` is always appended to, thus preserving any previous contents. The initial attempt to append to (or create) `dead.letter` will be in the current directory. If this fails, `dead.letter` will be appended to (or created in) the user's login directory. If the second attempt also fails, no `dead.letter` processing will be done.

`rmail` only permits the sending of mail; uucp(1C) uses `rmail` as a security precaution. Any application programs that generate mail messages should be sure to invoke `rmail` rather than `mail` for message transport and/or delivery.

If the local system has the Basic Networking Utilities installed, mail may be sent to a recipient on a remote system. There are numerous ways to address mail to recipients on remote systems depending on the transport mechanisms available to the local system. The two most prevalent addressing schemes are UUCP-style and Domain-style. With UUCP-style addressing, remote recipients are specified by prefixing the recipient name with the remote system name and an exclamation point (such as sysa!user). A series of system names separated by exclamation points can be used to direct a letter through an extended network (such as `sysa!sysb!sysc!user`). With Domain-style addressing, remote recipients are specified by appending an '@' and domain (and possibly sub-domain) information to the recipient name (such as `user@sf.att.com`). (The local System Administrator should be consulted for details on which addressing conventions are available on the local system.)

Reading Mail:

The following command-line arguments affect READING mail:

- `-e` causes mail not to be printed. An exit value of 0 is returned if the user has mail; otherwise, an exit value of 1 is returned.
- `-h` causes a window of headers to be initially displayed rather than the latest message. The display is followed by the '?' prompt.
- `-p` causes all messages to be printed without prompting for disposition.
- `-P` causes all messages to be printed with *all* header lines displayed, rather than the default selective header line display.
- `-q` causes `mail` to terminate after interrupts. Normally an interrupt causes only the termination of the message being printed.
- `-r` causes messages to be printed in first-in, first-out order.
- **-f** *file* causes `mail` to use *file* (such as `mbox`) instead of the default *mailfile*.

`mail`, unless otherwise influenced by command-line arguments, prints a user's mail messages in last-in, first-out order. The default mode for printing messages is to display only those header lines of immediate interest. These include, but are not limited to, the UNIX `From` and `>From` postmarks, `From:`, `Date:`, `Subject:`, and `Content-Length:` header lines, and any recipient header lines such as `To:`, `Cc:`, `Bcc:`, etc. After the header lines have been displayed, `mail` will display the contents (body) of the message only if it contains no unprintable characters. Otherwise, `mail` will issue a warning statement about the message having binary content and `not` display the content. (This may be overridden via the `p` command. See below.)

For each message, the user is prompted with a ?, and a line is read from the standard input. The following commands are available to determine the disposition of the message:

#	Print the number of the current message.
-	Print previous message.
<new-line>, +, or n	Print the next message.
!*command*	Escape to the shell to do *command*.
a	Print message that arrived during the `mail` session.
d, or dp	Delete the current message and print the next message.
d *n*	Delete message number *n*. Do not go on to next message.
dq	Delete message and quit `mail`.
h	Display a window of headers around current message.
h *n*	Display a window of headers around message number *n*.
h a	Display headers of all messages in the user's *mailfile*.
h d	Display headers of messages scheduled for deletion.
m [*persons*]	Mail (and delete) the current message to the named *person(s)*.
n	Print message number *n*.
p	Print current message again, overriding any indications of binary (that is, unprintable) content.
P	Override default brief mode and print current message again, displaying all header lines.
q, or cntrl-D	Put undeleted mail back in the *mailfile* and quit `mail`.
r [*users*]	Reply to the sender, and other *user(s)*, then delete the message.
s [*files*]	Save message in the named *file*(s) (mbox is default) and delete the message.
u [*n*]	Undelete message number *n* (default is last read).
w [*files*]	Save message contents, without any header lines, in the named *files* (mbox is default) and delete the message.
x	Put all mail back in the *mailfile* unchanged and exit `mail`.
y [*files*]	Same as save.
?	Print a command summary.

When a user logs in, the presence of mail, if any, is usually indicated. Also, notification is made if new mail arrives while using `mail`.

The permissions of *mailfile* may be manipulated using chmod in two ways to alter the function of `mail`. The other permissions of the file may be read-write (0666), read-only (0664), or neither read nor write (0660) to allow different levels of privacy. If changed to other than the default (mode 0660), the file will be preserved even when empty to perpetuate the desired permissions. (The administrator may override this file preservation using the `DEL_EMPTY_MAILFILE` option of `mailcnfg`.)

The group id of the mailfile must be `mail` to allow new messages to be delivered, and the mailfile must be writable by group `mail`.

Forwarding mail:

The following command-line argument affects FORWARDING of mail:

`-F` *recipients*
: Causes all incoming mail to be forwarded to *recipients*. The mailbox must be empty.

The `-F` option causes the *mailfile* to contain a first line of:

`Forward to` *recipient*...

Thereafter, all mail sent to the owner of the *mailfile* will be forwarded to each *recipient*.

An `Auto-Forwarded-From: ...` line will be added to the forwarded message's header. This is especially useful in a multi-machine environment to forward all a person's mail to a single machine, and to keep the recipient informed if the mail has been forwarded.

Installation and removal of forwarding is done with the `-F` invocation option. To forward all your mail to `systema!user` enter:

```
mail -F systema!user
```

To forward to more than one recipient enter:

```
mail -F "user1,user2@att.com,systemc!systemd!user3"
```

Note that when more than one recipient is specified, the entire list should be enclosed in double quotes so that it may all be interpreted as the operand of the `-F` option. The list can be up to 1024 bytes; either commas or white space can be used to separate users.

If the first character of any forwarded-to recipient name is the pipe symbol ('|'), the remainder of the line will be interpreted as a command to pipe the current mail message to. The command, known as a *Personal Surrogate,* will be executed in the environment of the recipient of the message (that is, basename of the *mailfile*). For example, if the mailfile is `/var/mail/foo`, `foo` will be looked up in `/etc/passwd` to determine the correct userID, groupID, and `HOME` directory. The command's environment will be set to contain only `HOME`, `LOGNAME`, `TZ`, `PATH` (= `/usr/usr/bin:`), and `SHELL` (= `/usr/bin/sh`), and the command will execute in the recipient's `HOME` directory. If the message recipient cannot be found in /etc/passwd, the command will not be executed and a non-delivery notification with appropriate diagnostics will be sent to the message's originator.

After the pipe symbol, escaped double quotes should be used to have strings with embedded whitespace be considered as single arguments to the command being executed. No shell syntax or metacharacters may be used unless the command specified is `/usr/bin/sh`. For example,

```
mail -F "|/bin/sh -c \"shell_command_line\""
```

will work, but is not advised since using double quotes and backslashes within the shell_command_line is difficult to do correctly and becomes tedious very quickly.

Certain %keywords are allowed within the piped-to command specification and will be textually substituted for *before* the command line is executed.

`%R`	Return path to the message originator.
`%c`	Value of the `Content-Type:` header line if present.
`%S`	Value of the `Subject:` header line if present.

If the command being piped to exits with any non-zero value, `mail` will assume that message delivery failed and will generate a non-delivery notification to the message's originator. It is allowable to forward mail to other recipients and pipe it to a command, as in

```
mail -F "carol,joe,|myvacationprog %R"
```

Two UNIX System facilities that use the forwarding of messages to commands are `notify`(1), which causes asynchronous notification of new mail, and `vacation`(1), which provides an auto-answer capability for messages when the recipient will be unavailable for an extended period of time.

To remove forwarding enter:

```
mail -F ""
```

The pair of double quotes is mandatory to set a NULL argument for the −F option.

In order for forwarding to work properly the *mailfile* should have `mail` as group ID, and the group permission should be read-write.

`mail` will exit with a return code of 0 if forwarding was successfully installed or removed.

Debugging:

The following command-line arguments cause `mail` to provide DEBUGGING information:

`-T` *mailsurr_file*	causes `mail` to display how it will parse and interpret the `mailsurr` file.
-x*debug_level*	causes `mail` to create a trace file containing debugging information.

The `-T` option requires an argument that will be taken as the pathname of a test `mailsurr` file. If NULL (as in `-T ""`), the system `mailsurr` file will be used. To use, type '`mail -T` *test_file recipient*' and some trivial message (like "testing"), followed by a line with either just a dot ('.') or a cntrl-D. The result of using the `-T` option will be displayed on standard output and show the inputs and resulting transformations as `mailsurr` is processed by the `mail` command for the indicated recipient. Mail messages will never actually be sent or delivered when the `-T` option is used.

The `-x` option causes `mail` to create a file named `/tmp/MLDBG`*process_id* that contains debugging information relating to how `mail` processed the current message. The absolute value of *debug_level* controls the verboseness of the debug information. Zero implies no debugging. If *debug_level* is greater than zero, the debug file will be retained only if `mail` encountered some problem while processing the message. If *debug_level* is less than zero the debug file will always be retained. The *debug_level* specified via `-x` overrides any specification of `DEBUG` in `/etc/mail/mailcnfg`. The information provided by the `-x` option is esoteric and is probably only useful to System Administrators. The output produced by the `-x` option is a superset of that provided by the `-T` option.

Delivery Notification

Several forms of notification are available for mail by including one of the following lines in the message header.

`Transport-Options:` [/*options*]

`Default-Options:` [/*options*]

`>To:` *recipient* [/*options*]

Where the "/*options*" may be one or more of the following:

`/delivery` Inform the sender that the message was successfully delivered to the *recipient*'s mailbox.

`/nodelivery` Do not inform the sender of successful deliveries.

`/ignore` Do not inform the sender of unsuccessful deliveries.

`/return` Inform the sender if mail delivery fails. Return the failed message to the sender.

`/report` Same as `/return` except that the original message is not returned.

The default is `/nodelivery/return`. If contradictory options are used, the first will be recognized and later, conflicting, terms will be ignored.

FILES

`dead.letter`	unmailable text
`/etc/passwd`	to identify sender and locate recipients
`/etc/mail/mailsurr`	routing / name translation information
`/etc/mail/mailcnfg`	initialization information
`$HOME/mbox`	saved mail
`$MAIL`	variable containing path name of *mailfile*
`/tmp/ma*`	temporary file
`/tmp/MLDBG*`	debug trace file
`/var/mail/*.lock`	lock for mail directory
`/var/mail/:saved`	directory for holding temp files to prevent loss of data in the event of a system crash.
`/var/mail/`*user*	incoming mail for *user*; that is, the *mailfile*

SEE ALSO

chmod(1), login(1), mailx(1), notify(1), write(1), vacation(1)

mail_pipe(1M), mailsurr(4), mailcnfg(4) in the *System Administrator's Reference Manual.*

User's Guide.

NOTES

The "Forward to recipient" feature may result in a loop. Local loops (messages sent to usera, which are forwarded to userb, which are forwarded to usera) will be detected immediately. Remote loops (mail sent to sys1!usera1 which is forwarded to sys2!userb, which is forwarded to sys1!usera) will also be detected, but only after the message has exceeded the built-in hop count limit of 20. Both cases of forwarding loops will result in a non-delivery notification being sent to the message originator.

As a security precaution, the equivalent of a chmod s+g is performed on the *mailfile* whenever forwarding is activated via the -F option, and a chmod s-g is done when forwarding is removed via the -F option. If the setGID mode bit is not set when mail attempts to forward an incoming message to a command, the operation will fail and a non-delivery report with appropriate diagnostics will be sent to the message's originator.

The interpretation and resulting action taken because of the header lines described in the Delivery Notifications section above will only occur if this version of mail is installed on the system where the delivery (or failure) happens. Earlier versions of mail may not support any types of delivery notification.

Conditions sometimes result in a failure to remove a lock file.

After an interrupt, the next message may not be printed; printing may be forced by typing a p.

NAME

`mailalias` – translate mail alias names

SYNOPSIS

`mailalias` [`-s`] [`-v`] *name* ...

DESCRIPTION

`mailalias` is called by `mail`. It places on the standard output a list of mail addresses corresponding to *name*. The mail addresses are found by performing the following steps:

1. Look for the file `/var/mail/`*name*. If found, print *name* and exit.
2. Look for a match in the user's local alias file `$HOME/lib/names`. If a line is found beginning with the word *name*, print the rest of the line on standard output and exit.
3. Look for a match in the system-wide alias files, which are listed in the master path file `/etc/mail/namefiles`. If a line is found beginning with the word *name*, print the rest of the line on standard output and exit.

If an alias file is a directory name *dir*, then search the file *dir*/*name*. By default, the file `/etc/mail/namefiles` lists the directory `/etc/mail/lists` and the file `/etc/mail/names`.

4. Otherwise print *name* and exit.

The alias files may contain comments (lines beginning with `#`) and information lines of the form:

name list-of-addresses

Tokens on these lines are separated by white-space. Lines may be continued by placing a backslash (\) at the end of the line.

If the `-s` option is not specified and more than one name is being translated, each line of output will be prefixed with the name being translated.

The `-v` option causes debugging information to be written to standard output.

FILES

`$HOME/lib/names`	private aliases
`/etc/mail/namefiles`	list of files to search
`/etc/mail/names`	standard file to search

SEE ALSO

`uucp`(1), `mail`(1).
`smtp`(1M), `smtpd`(1M), `smtpqer`(1M), `smtpsched`(1M), `tosmtp`(1M) in the *System Administrator's Reference Manual.*

NAME

`mailx` – interactive message processing system

SYNOPSIS

`mailx` [*options*] [*name* ...]

DESCRIPTION

The command `mailx` provides a comfortable, flexible environment for sending and receiving messages electronically. When reading mail, `mailx` provides commands to facilitate saving, deleting, and responding to messages. When sending mail, `mailx` allows editing, reviewing and other modification of the message as it is entered.

Many of the remote features of `mailx` work only if the Basic Networking Utilities are installed on your system.

Incoming mail is stored in a standard file for each user, called the `mailbox` for that user. When `mailx` is called to read messages, the `mailbox` is the default place to find them. As messages are read, they are marked to be moved to a secondary file for storage, unless specific action is taken, so that the messages need not be seen again. This secondary file is called the `mbox` and is normally located in the user's `HOME` directory [see `MBOX` (ENVIRONMENT VARIABLES) for a description of this file]. Messages can be saved in other secondary files named by the user. Messages remain in a secondary file until forcibly removed.

The user can access a secondary file by using the `-f` option of the `mailx` command. Messages in the secondary file can then be read or otherwise processed using the same COMMANDS as in the primary `mailbox`. This gives rise within these pages to the notion of a current `mailbox`.

On the command line, *options* start with a dash (–) and any other arguments are taken to be destinations (recipients). If no recipients are specified, `mailx` attempts to read messages from the `mailbox`. Command-line options are:

`-d` Turn on debugging output.

`-e` Test for presence of mail. `mailx` prints nothing and exits with a successful return code if there is mail to read.

`-f` [*filename*] Read messages from *filename* instead of `mailbox`. If no *filename* is specified, the `mbox` is used.

`-F` Record the message in a file named after the first recipient. Overrides the `record` variable, if set (see ENVIRONMENT VARIABLES).

`-h` *number* The number of network "hops" made so far. This is provided for network software to avoid infinite delivery loops. This option and its argument is passed to the delivery program.

`-H` Print header summary only.

`-i` Ignore interrupts. See also `ignore` (ENVIRONMENT VARIABLES).

`-I`	Include the newsgroup and article-id header lines when printing mail messages. This option requires the `-f` option to be specified.
`-n`	Do not initialize from the system default *mailx.rc* file.
`-N`	Do not print initial header summary.
`-r` *address*	Use *address* as the return address when invoking the delivery program. All tilde commands are disabled. This option and its argument is passed to the delivery program.
`-s` *subject*	Set the Subject header field to *subject*.
`-T` *file*	Message-id and article-id header lines are recorded in *file* after the message is read. This option will also set the `-I` option.
`-u` *user*	Read *user's* `mailbox`. This is only effective if *user's* `mailbox` is not read protected.
`-U`	Convert **uucp** style addresses to internet standards. Overrides the **conv** environment variable.
`-V`	Print the `mailx` version number and exit.

When reading mail, `mailx` is in *command mode.* A header summary of the first several messages is displayed, followed by a prompt indicating `mailx` can accept regular commands (see COMMANDS below). When sending mail, `mailx` is in *input mode.* If no subject is specified on the command line, a prompt for the subject is printed. (A subject longer than 1024 characters causes `mailx` to print the message *mail: ERROR signal 10*; the mail will not be delivered.) As the message is typed, `mailx` reads the message and store it in a temporary file. Commands may be entered by beginning a line with the tilde (~) escape character followed by a single command letter and optional arguments. See TILDE ESCAPES for a summary of these commands.

At any time, the behavior of `mailx` is governed by a set of *environment variables.* These are flags and valued parameters which are set and cleared via the **set** and **unset** commands. See ENVIRONMENT VARIABLES below for a summary of these parameters.

Recipients listed on the command line may be of three types: login names, shell commands, or alias groups. Login names may be any network address, including mixed network addressing. If mail is found to be undeliverable, an attempt is made to return it to the sender's *mailbox.* If the recipient name begins with a pipe symbol (|), the rest of the name is taken to be a shell command to pipe the message through. This provides an automatic interface with any program that reads the standard input, such as `lp(1)` for recording outgoing mail on paper. Alias groups are set by the **alias** command (see COMMANDS below) and are lists of recipients of any type.

Regular commands are of the form

[*command*] [*msglist*] [*arguments*]

If no command is specified in *command mode*, print is assumed. In *input mode*, commands are recognized by the escape character, and lines not treated as commands are taken as input for the message.

Each message is assigned a sequential number, and there is at any time the notion of a current message, marked by a right angle bracket (>) in the header summary. Many commands take an optional list of messages (*msglist*) to operate on. The default for *msglist* is the current message. A *msglist* is a list of message identifiers separated by spaces, which may include:

`n` Message number `n`.

`.` The current message.

`^` The first undeleted message.

`$` The last message.

`*` All messages.

`n-m` An inclusive range of message numbers.

`user` All messages from `user`.

`/string`
: All messages with `string` in the subject line (case ignored).

`:c` All messages of type *c*, where *c* is one of:

- `d` deleted messages
- `n` new messages
- `o` old messages
- `r` read messages
- `u` unread messages

Note that the context of the command determines whether this type of message specification makes sense.

Other arguments are usually arbitrary strings whose usage depends on the command involved. File names, where expected, are expanded via the normal shell conventions [see sh(1)]. Special characters are recognized by certain commands and are documented with the commands below.

At start-up time, `mailx` tries to execute commands from the optional system-wide file (`/etc/mail/mailx.rc`) to initialize certain parameters, then from a private start-up file (`$HOME/.mailrc`) for personalized variables. With the exceptions noted below, regular commands are legal inside start-up files. The most common use of a start-up file is to set up initial display options and alias lists. The following commands are not legal in the start-up file: !, Copy, edit, followup, Followup, hold, mail, preserve, reply, Reply, shell, and visual. An error in the start-up file causes the remaining lines in the file to be ignored. The `.mailrc` file is optional, and must be constructed locally.

COMMANDS

The following is a complete list of `mailx` commands:

! *shell-command*
Escape to the shell. See SHELL (ENVIRONMENT VARIABLES).

comment
Null command (comment). This may be useful in .mailrc files.

= Print the current message number.

? Prints a summary of commands.

alias *alias name ...*
group *alias name ...*
Declare an alias for the given names. The names are substituted when *alias* is used as a recipient. Useful in the .mailrc file.

alternates *name ...*
Declares a list of alternate names for your login. When responding to a message, these names are removed from the list of recipients for the response. With no arguments, alternates prints the current list of alternate names. See also allnet (ENVIRONMENT VARIABLES).

cd [*directory*]
chdir [*directory*]
Change directory. If *directory* is not specified, $HOME is used.

copy [*filename*]
copy [*msglist*] *filename*
Copy messages to the file without marking the messages as saved. Otherwise equivalent to the save command.

Copy [*msglist*]
Save the specified messages in a file whose name is derived from the author of the message to be saved, without marking the messages as saved. Otherwise equivalent to the Save command.

delete [*msglist*]
Delete messages from the mailbox. If autoprint is set, the next message after the last one deleted is printed (see ENVIRONMENT VARIABLES).

discard [*header-field ...*]
ignore [*header-field ...*]
Suppresses printing of the specified header fields when displaying messages on the screen. Examples of header fields to ignore are status and cc. The fields are included when the message is saved. The Print and Type commands override this command. If no header is specified, the current list of header fields being ignored will be printed. See also the undiscard and unignore commands.

dp [*msglist*]
dt [*msglist*]
Delete the specified messages from the mailbox and print the next message after the last one deleted. Roughly equivalent to a delete command followed by a print command.

echo *string* ...
: Echo the given strings [like echo(1)].

edit [*msglist*]
: Edit the given messages. The messages are placed in a temporary file and the EDITOR variable is used to get the name of the editor (see ENVIRONMENT VARIABLES). Default editor is ed(1).

exit
xit
: Exit from mailx, without changing the mailbox. No messages are saved in the mbox (see also quit).

file [*filename*]
folder [*filename*]
: Quit from the current file of messages and read in the specified file. Several special characters are recognized when used as file names, with the following substitutions:

%	the current mailbox.
%*user*	the mailbox for *user*.
#	the previous file.
&	the current mbox.

Default file is the current mailbox.

folders
: Print the names of the files in the directory set by the folder variable (see ENVIRONMENT VARIABLES).

followup [*message*]
: Respond to a message, recording the response in a file whose name is derived from the author of the message. Overrides the record variable, if set. See also the Followup, Save, and Copy commands and outfolder (ENVIRONMENT VARIABLES).

Followup [*msglist*]
: Respond to the first message in the *msglist*, sending the message to the author of each message in the *msglist*. The subject line is taken from the first message and the response is recorded in a file whose name is derived from the author of the first message. See also the followup, Save, and Copy commands and outfolder (ENVIRONMENT VARIABLES).

from [*msglist*]
: Prints the header summary for the specified messages.

group *alias name* ...
alias *alias name* ...
: Declare an alias for the given names. The names are substituted when *alias* is used as a recipient. Useful in the .mailrc file.

headers [*message*]
: Prints the page of headers which includes the message specified. The screen variable sets the number of headers per page (see ENVIRONMENT VARIABLES). See also the z command.

help Prints a summary of commands.

hold [*msglist*]
preserve [*msglist*]
Holds the specified messages in the mailbox.

if s | r
mail-commands
else
mail-commands
endif Conditional execution, where *s* executes following *mail-commands*, up to an else or endif, if the program is in *send* mode, and *r* causes the *mail-commands* to be executed only in *receive* mode. Useful in the .mailrc file.

ignore [*header-field* ...]
discard [*header-field* ...]
Suppresses printing of the specified header fields when displaying messages on the screen. Examples of header fields to ignore are status and cc. All fields are included when the message is saved. The Print and Type commands override this command. If no header is specified, the current list of header fields being ignored will be printed. See also the undiscard and unignore commands.

list Prints all commands available. No explanation is given.

mail *name* ...
Mail a message to the specified users.

Mail *name*
Mail a message to the specified user and record a copy of it in a file named after that user.

mbox [*msglist*]
Arrange for the given messages to end up in the standard mbox save file when mailx terminates normally. See MBOX (ENVIRONMENT VARIABLES) for a description of this file. See also the exit and quit commands.

next [*message*]
Go to next message matching *message*. A *msglist* may be specified, but in this case the first valid message in the list is the only one used. This is useful for jumping to the next message from a specific user, since the name would be taken as a command in the absence of a real command. See the discussion of *msglists* above for a description of possible message specifications.

pipe [*msglist*] [*shell-command*]
| [*msglist*] [*shell-command*]
Pipe the message through the given *shell-command*. The message is treated as if it were read. If no arguments are given, the current message is piped through the command specified by the value of the cmd variable. If the page variable is set, a form feed character is inserted after each message (see ENVIRONMENT VARIABLES).

preserve [*msglist*]
hold [*msglist*]
Preserve the specified messages in the `mailbox`.

Print [*msglist*]
Type [*msglist*]
Print the specified messages on the screen, including all header fields. Overrides suppression of fields by the `ignore` command.

print [*msglist*]
type [*msglist*]
Print the specified messages. If `crt` is set, the messages longer than the number of lines specified by the `crt` variable are paged through the command specified by the `PAGER` variable. The default command is pg(1) (see ENVIRONMENT VARIABLES).

quit Exit from `mailx`, storing messages that were read in `mbox` and unread messages in the `mailbox`. Messages that have been explicitly saved in a file are deleted.

Reply [*msglist*]
Respond [*msglist*]
Send a response to the author of each message in the *msglist*. The subject line is taken from the first message. If `record` is set to a file name, the response is saved at the end of that file (see ENVIRONMENT VARIABLES).

reply [*message*]
respond [*message*]
Reply to the specified message, including all other recipients of the message. If `record` is set to a file name, the response is saved at the end of that file (see ENVIRONMENT VARIABLES).

Save [*msglist*]
Save the specified messages in a file whose name is derived from the author of the first message. The name of the file is taken to be the author's name with all network addressing stripped off. See also the Copy, followup, and Followup commands and `outfolder` (ENVIRONMENT VARIABLES).

save [*filename*]
save [*msglist*] *filename*
Save the specified messages in the given file. The file is created if it does not exist. The file defaults to `mbox`. The message is deleted from the `mailbox` when `mailx` terminates unless `keepsave` is set (see also ENVIRONMENT VARIABLES and the exit and quit commands).

set
set *name*
set *name=string*
set *name=number*
Define a variable called *name*. The variable may be given a null, string, or numeric value. Set by itself prints all defined variables and their values.

See ENVIRONMENT VARIABLES for detailed descriptions of the `mailx` variables.

shell Invoke an interactive shell [see also **SHELL** (ENVIRONMENT VARIABLES)].

`size` [*msglist*]
Print the size in characters of the specified messages.

source *filename*
Read commands from the given file and return to command mode.

`top` [*msglist*]
Print the top few lines of the specified messages. If the **toplines** variable is set, it is taken as the number of lines to print (see ENVIRONMENT VARIABLES). The default is 5.

touch [*msglist*]
Touch the specified messages. If any message in *msglist* is not specifically saved in a file, it is placed in the **mbox**, or the file specified in the **MBOX** environment variable, upon normal termination. See **exit** and **quit**.

Type [*msglist*]
Print [*msglist*]
Print the specified messages on the screen, including all header fields. Overrides suppression of fields by the `ignore` command.

type [*msglist*]
print [*msglist*]
Print the specified messages. If `crt` is set, the messages longer than the number of lines specified by the `crt` variable are paged through the command specified by the **PAGER** variable. The default command is **pg**(1) (see ENVIRONMENT VARIABLES).

undelete [*msglist*]
Restore the specified deleted messages. Will only restore messages deleted in the current mail session. If `autoprint` is set, the last message of those restored is printed (see ENVIRONMENT VARIABLES).

undiscard *header-field ...*
unignore *header-field ...*
Remove the specified header fields from the list being ignored.

unset *name ...*
Causes the specified variables to be erased. If the variable was imported from the execution environment (i.e., a shell variable) then it cannot be erased.

version
Prints the current version.

visual [*msglist*]
Edit the given messages with a screen editor. The messages are placed in

a temporary file and the VISUAL variable is used to get the name of the editor (see ENVIRONMENT VARIABLES).

write [*msglist*] *filename*
: Write the given messages on the specified file, minus the header and trailing blank line. Otherwise equivalent to the save command.

xit
exit
: Exit from mailx, without changing the mailbox. No messages are saved in the mbox (see also quit).

z[+ | -]
: Scroll the header display forward or backward one screen-full. The number of headers displayed is set by the screen variable (see ENVIRONMENT VARIABLES).

TILDE ESCAPES

The following commands may be entered only from *input mode*, by beginning a line with the tilde escape character (~). See **escape** (ENVIRONMENT VARIABLES) for changing this special character.

~! *shell-command*
: Escape to the shell.

~. Simulate end of file (terminate message input).

~: *mail-command*
~_ *mail-command*
: Perform the command-level request. Valid only when sending a message while reading mail.

~? Print a summary of tilde escapes.

~A Insert the autograph string Sign into the message (see ENVIRONMENT VARIABLES).

~a Insert the autograph string sign into the message (see ENVIRONMENT VARIABLES).

~b *names* ...
: Add the *names* to the blind carbon copy (Bcc) list.

~c *names* ...
: Add the *names* to the carbon copy (Cc) list.

~d Read in the dead.letter file. See DEAD (ENVIRONMENT VARIABLES) for a description of this file.

~e Invoke the editor on the partial message. See also EDITOR (ENVIRONMENT VARIABLES).

~f [*msglist*]
: Forward the specified messages. The messages are inserted into the message without alteration.

`~h` Prompt for Subject line and To, Cc, and Bcc lists. If the field is displayed with an initial value, it may be edited as if you had just typed it.

`~i` *string*
: Insert the value of the named variable into the text of the message. For example, `~A` is equivalent to `Environment variables set and exported in the shell are also accessible by ~i.`

`~m` [*msglist*]
: Insert the specified messages into the letter, shifting the new text to the right one tab stop. Valid only when sending a message while reading mail.

`~p` Print the message being entered.

`~q` Quit from input mode by simulating an interrupt. If the body of the message is not null, the partial message is saved in `dead.letter`. See `DEAD` (ENVIRONMENT VARIABLES) for a description of this file.

`~r` *filename*
`~<` *filename*
`~<` !*shell-command*
: Read in the specified file. If the argument begins with an exclamation point (!), the rest of the string is taken as an arbitrary shell command and is executed, with the standard output inserted into the message.

`~s` *string* ...
: Set the subject line to *string*.

`~t` *names* ...
: Add the given *names* to the To list.

`~v` Invoke a preferred screen editor on the partial message. See also `VISUAL` (ENVIRONMENT VARIABLES).

`~w` *filename*
: Write the message into the given file, without the header.

`~x` Exit as with `~q` except the message is not saved in `dead.letter`.

`~|` *shell-command*
: Pipe the body of the message through the given *shell-command*. If the *shell-command* returns a successful exit status, the output of the command replaces the message.

ENVIRONMENT VARIABLES

The following are environment variables taken from the execution environment and are not alterable within `mailx`.

`HOME`=*directory*
: The user's base of operations.

`MAILRC`=*filename*
: The name of the start-up file. Default is `$HOME/.mailrc`.

The following variables are internal **mailx** variables. They may be imported from the execution environment or set via the **set** command at any time. The unset command may be used to erase variables.

allnet
: All network names whose last component (login name) match are treated as identical. This causes the *msglist* message specifications to behave similarly. Default is **noallnet**. See also the **alternates** command and the **metoo** variable.

append
: Upon termination, append messages to the end of the **mbox** file instead of prepending them. Default is **noappend**.

askcc Prompt for the Cc list after the Subject is entered. Default is **noaskcc**.

askbcc
: Prompt for the Bcc list after the Subject is entered. Default is **noaskbcc**.

asksub
: Prompt for subject if it is not specified on the command line with the **-s** option. Enabled by default.

autoprint
: Enable automatic printing of messages after delete and undelete commands. Default is **noautoprint**.

bang Enable the special-casing of exclamation points (!) in shell escape command lines as in **vi**(1). Default is nobang.

cmd=*shell-command*
: Set the default command for the **pipe** command. No default value.

conv=*conversion*
: Convert uucp addresses to the specified address style. The only valid conversion now is **internet**, which uses domain-style addressing. Conversion is disabled by default. See also the **-U** command-line option.

crt=*number*
: Pipe messages having more than *number* lines through the command specified by the value of the **PAGER** variable [pg(1) by default]. Disabled by default.

DEAD=*filename*
: The name of the file in which to save partial letters in case of untimely interrupt. Default is **$HOME/dead.letter**.

debug Enable verbose diagnostics for debugging. Messages are not delivered. Default is **nodebug**.

dot Take a period on a line by itself during input from a terminal as end-of-file. Default is **nodot**.

EDITOR=*shell-command*
: The command to run when the **edit** or **~e** command is used. Default is **ed**(1).

escape=*c*
Substitute *c* for the ~ escape character. Takes effect with next message sent.

folder=*directory*
The directory for saving standard mail files. User-specified file names beginning with a plus (+) are expanded by preceding the file name with this directory name to obtain the real file name. If *directory* does not start with a slash (/), **$HOME** is prepended to it. In order to use the plus (+) construct on a **mailx** command line, **folder** must be an exported **sh** environment variable. There is no default for the **folder** variable. See also **outfolder** below.

header
Enable printing of the header summary when entering **mailx**. Enabled by default.

hold Preserve all messages that are read in the **mailbox** instead of putting them in the standard **mbox** save file. Default is **nohold**.

ignore
Ignore interrupts while entering messages. Handy for noisy dial-up lines. Default is **noignore**.

ignoreeof
Ignore end-of-file during message input. Input must be terminated by a period (.) on a line by itself or by the **~.** command. Default is **noignoreeof**. See also **dot** above.

keep When the **mailbox** is empty, truncate it to zero length instead of removing it. Disabled by default.

keepsave
Keep messages that have been saved in other files in the **mailbox** instead of deleting them. Default is **nokeepsave**.

MBOX=*filename*
The name of the file to save messages which have been read. The **xit** command overrides this function, as does saving the message explicitly in another file. Default is **$HOME/mbox**.

metoo If your login appears as a recipient, do not delete it from the list. Default is **nometoo**.

LISTER=*shell-command*
The command (and options) to use when listing the contents of the **folder** directory. The default is **ls**(1).

onehop
When responding to a message that was originally sent to several recipients, the other recipient addresses are normally forced to be relative to the originating author's machine for the response. This flag disables alteration of the recipients' addresses, improving efficiency in a network where all machines can send directly to all other machines (i.e., one hop away).

`outfolder`
: Causes the files used to record outgoing messages to be located in the directory specified by the `folder` variable unless the path name is absolute. Default is `nooutfolder`. See `folder` above and the `Save`, `Copy`, `followup`, and `Followup` commands.

`page` Used with the `pipe` command to insert a form feed after each message sent through the pipe. Default is `nopage`.

`PAGER`=*shell-command*
: The command to use as a filter for paginating output. This can also be used to specify the options to be used. Default is `pg`(1).

`prompt`=*string*
: Set the *command mode* prompt to *string*. Default is "`? `".

`quiet` Refrain from printing the opening message and version when entering `mailx`. Default is `noquiet`.

`record`=*filename*
: Record all outgoing mail in *filename*. Disabled by default. See also `outfolder` above. If you have the `record` and `outfolder` variables set but the `folder` variable not set, messages are saved in *+filename* instead of *filename*.

`save` Enable saving of messages in `dead.letter` on interrupt or delivery error. See `DEAD` for a description of this file. Enabled by default.

`screen`=*number*
: Sets the number of lines in a screen-full of headers for the `headers` command. It must be a positive number.

`sendmail`=*shell-command*
: Alternate command for delivering messages. Default is `/usr/bin/rmail`.

`sendwait`
: Wait for background mailer to finish before returning. Default is `nosendwait`.

`SHELL`=*shell-command*
: The name of a preferred command interpreter. Default is `sh`(1).

`showto`
: When displaying the header summary and the message is from you, print the recipient's name instead of the author's name.

`sign`=*string*
: The variable inserted into the text of a message when the `~a` (autograph) command is given. No default [see also `~i` (TILDE ESCAPES)].

`Sign`=*string*
: The variable inserted into the text of a message when the `~A` command is given. No default [see also `~i` (TILDE ESCAPES)].

`toplines=`*number*
: The number of lines of header to print with the `top` command. Default is 5.

`VISUAL=`*shell-command*
: The name of a preferred screen editor. Default is `vi`(1).

FILES

`$HOME/.mailrc`	personal start-up file
`$HOME/mbox`	secondary storage file
`/var/mail/*`	post office directory
`/usr/share/lib/mailx/mailx.help*`	help message files
`/etc/mail/mailx.rc`	optional global start-up file
`/tmp/R[emqsx]*`	temporary files

SEE ALSO

`ls`(1), `mail`(1), `pg`(1).

NOTES

The `-h` and `-r` options can be used only if `mailx` is using a delivery program other than `/usr/bin/rmail`.

Where *shell-command* is shown as valid, arguments are not always allowed. Experimentation is recommended.

Internal variables imported from the execution environment cannot be unset.

The full internet addressing is not fully supported by `mailx`. The new standards need some time to settle down.

Attempts to send a message having a line consisting only of a "." are treated as the end of the message by `mail`(1) (the standard mail delivery program).

NAME

`makekey` – generate encryption key

SYNOPSIS

`/usr/lib/makekey`

DESCRIPTION

`makekey` improves the usefulness of encryption schemes depending on a key by increasing the amount of time required to search the key space. It attempts to read 8 bytes for its *key* (the first eight input bytes), then it attempts to read 2 bytes for its *salt* (the last two input bytes). The output depends on the input in a way intended to be difficult to compute (i.e., to require a substantial fraction of a second).

The first eight input bytes (the *input key*) can be arbitrary ASCII characters. The last two (the *salt*) are best chosen from the set of digits, ., /, and upper- and lower-case letters. The salt characters are repeated as the first two characters of the output. The remaining 11 output characters are chosen from the same set as the salt and constitute the *output key*.

The transformation performed is essentially the following: the salt is used to select one of 4,096 cryptographic machines all based on the National Bureau of Standards DES algorithm, but broken in 4,096 different ways. Using the *input key* as key, a constant string is fed into the machine and recirculated a number of times. The 64 bits that come out are distributed into the 66 *output key* bits in the result.

`makekey` is intended for programs that perform encryption. Usually, its input and output will be pipes.

SEE ALSO

`ed`(1), `crypt`(1), `vi`(1).
`passwd`(4) in the *System Administrator's Reference Manual.*

NOTES

`makekey` can produce different results depending upon whether the input is typed at the terminal or redirected from a file.

This command is provided with the Security Administration Utilities, which is only available in the United States.

NAME

mesg – permit or deny messages

SYNOPSIS

mesg [-n] [-y]

DESCRIPTION

mesg with argument -n forbids messages via write(1) by revoking non-user write permission on the user's terminal. mesg with argument -y reinstates permission. All by itself, mesg reports the current state without changing it.

FILES

/dev/tty*

SEE ALSO

write(1).

DIAGNOSTICS

Exit status is 0 if messages are receivable, 1 if not, 2 on error.

NAME

mkdir − make directories

SYNOPSIS

mkdir [−m mode] [−p] dirname ...

DESCRIPTION

mkdir creates the named directories in mode 777 (possibly altered by umask(1)).

Standard entries in a directory (e.g., the files ., for the directory itself, and .., for its parent) are made automatically. mkdir cannot create these entries by name. Creation of a directory requires write permission in the parent directory.

The owner ID and group ID of the new directories are set to the process's real user ID and group ID, respectively.

Two options apply to mkdir:

−m This option allows users to specify the mode to be used for new directories. Choices for modes can be found in chmod(1).

−p With this option, mkdir creates dirname by creating all the non-existing parent directories first.

EXAMPLE

To create the subdirectory structure ltr/jd/jan, type:

```
mkdir -p ltr/jd/jan
```

SEE ALSO

sh(1), rm(1), umask(1).
intro(2), mkdir(2) in the *Programmer's Reference Manual*.

DIAGNOSTICS

mkdir returns exit code 0 if all directories given in the command line were made successfully. Otherwise, it prints a diagnostic and returns non-zero.

NAME

mkmsgs – create message files for use by gettxt

SYNOPSIS

mkmsgs [–o] [–i *locale*] *inputstrings msgfile*

DESCRIPTION

The mkmsgs utility is used to create a file of text strings that can be accessed using the text retrieval tools (see gettxt(1), srchtxt(1), exstr(1), and gettxt(3C)). It will take as input a file of text strings for a particular geographic locale (see setlocale(3C)) and create a file of text strings in a format that can be retrieved by both gettxt(1) and gettxt(3C). By using the –i option, you can install the created file under the /usr/lib/locale/*locale*/LC_MESSAGES directory (*locale* corresponds to the language in which the text strings are written).

inputstrings the name of the file that contains the original text strings.

msgfile the name of the output file where mkmsgs writes the strings in a format that is readable by gettxt(1) and gettxt(3C). The name of *msgfile* can be up to 14 characters in length, but may not contain either \0 (null) or the ASCII code for / (slash) or : (colon).

–i *locale* install *msgfile* in the /usr/lib/locale/*locale*/LC_MESSAGES directory. Only someone who is super-user or a member of group bin can create or overwrite files in this directory. Directories under /usr/lib/locale will be created if they don't exist.

–o overwrite *msgfile*, if it exists.

The input file contains a set of text strings for the particular geographic locale. Text strings are separated by a new-line character. Nongraphic characters must be represented as alphabetic escape sequences. Messages are transformed and copied sequentially from *inputstrings* to *msgfile*. To generate an empty message in *msgfile*, leave an empty line at the correct place in *inputstrings*.

Strings can be changed simply by editing the file *inputstrings*. New strings must be added only at the end of the file; then a new *msgfile* file must be created and installed in the correct place. If this procedure is not followed, the retrieval function will retrieve the wrong string and software compatibility will be broken.

EXAMPLES

The following example shows an input message source file C.str:

```
File %s:\t cannot be opened\n
%s: Bad directory\n
      .
      .
      .
write error\n
      .
      .
```

The following command uses the input strings from C.str to create text strings in the appropriate format in the file UX in the current directory:

```
mkmsgs C.str UX
```

The following command uses the input strings from FR.str to create text strings in the appropriate format in the file UX in the directory /usr/lib/locale/french/LC_MESSAGES/UX.

```
mkmsgs -i french FR.str UX
```

These text strings would be accessed if you had set the environment variable LC_MESSAGES=french and then invoked one of the text retrieval tools listed at the beginning of the DESCRIPTION section.

FILES

/usr/lib/locale/*locale*/LC_MESSAGES/* message files created by mkmsgs(1M)

SEE ALSO

exstr(1), gettxt(1), srchtxt(1).
gettxt(3C), setlocale(3C) in the *Programmer's Reference Manual*.

NAME

more, page – browse or page through a text file

SYNOPSIS

more [-cdflrsuw] [*–lines*] [*+linenumber*] [*+/pattern*] [*filename* ...]
page [-cdflrsuw] [*–lines*] [*+linenumber*] [*+/pattern*] [*filename* ...]

DESCRIPTION

more is a filter that displays the contents of a text file on the terminal, one screenful at a time. It normally pauses after each screenful, and prints --More-- at the bottom of the screen. **more** provides a two-line overlap between screens for continuity. If **more** is reading from a file rather than a pipe, the percentage of characters displayed so far is also shown.

more scrolls up to display one more line in response to a RETURN character; it displays another screenful in response to a SPACE character. Other commands are listed below.

page clears the screen before displaying the next screenful of text; it only provides a one-line overlap between screens.

more sets the terminal to *noecho* mode, so that the output can be continuous. Commands that you type do not normally show up on your terminal, except for the / and ! commands.

If the standard output is not a terminal, **more** acts just like cat(1V), except that a header is printed before each file in a series.

OPTIONS

The following options are available with **more**:

-c Clear before displaying. Redrawing the screen instead of scrolling for faster displays. This option is ignored if the terminal does not have the ability to clear to the end of a line.

-d Display error messages rather than ringing the terminal bell if an unrecognized command is used. This is helpful for inexperienced users.

-f Do not fold long lines. This is useful when lines contain nonprinting characters or escape sequences, such as those generated when nroff(1) output is piped through ul(1).

-l Do not treat FORMFEED characters (CTRL-D) as page breaks. If -l is not used, **more** pauses to accept commands after any line containing a ^L character (CTRL-D). Also, if a file begins with a FORMFEED, the screen is cleared before the file is printed.

-r Normally, **more** ignores control characters that it does not interpret in some way. The -r option causes these to be displayed as ^C where C stands for any such control character.

-s Squeeze. Replace multiple blank lines with a single blank line. This is helpful when viewing nroff(1) output, on the screen.

−u Suppress generation of underlining escape sequences. Normally, `more` handles underlining, such as that produced by `nroff`(1), in a manner appropriate to the terminal. If the terminal can perform underlining or has a stand-out mode, `more` supplies appropriate escape sequences as called for in the text file.

−w Normally, `more` exits when it comes to the end of its input. With `−w` , however, `more` prompts and waits for any key to be struck before exiting.

−*lines* Display the indicated number of *lines* in each screenful, rather than the default (the number of lines in the terminal screen less two).

+*linenumber* Start up at *linenumber*.

+/*pattern* Start up two lines above the line containing the regular expression *pattern*. Note: unlike editors, this construct should *not* end with a '/'. If it does, then the trailing slash is taken as a character in the search pattern.

USAGE

Environment

`more` uses the terminal's `termcap`(5) entry to determine its display characteristics, and looks in the environment variable for any preset options. For instance, to page through files using the `−c` mode by default, set the value of this variable to `−c`. (Normally, the command sequence to set up this environment variable is placed in the `.login` or `.profile` file).

Commands

The commands take effect immediately; it is not necessary to type a carriage return. Up to the time when the command character itself is given, the user may type the line kill character to cancel the numerical argument being formed. In addition, the user may type the erase character to redisplay the '`--More--(`*xx*`%)`' message.

In the following commands, *i* is a numerical argument (`1` by default).

*i*SPACE Display another screenful, or *i* more lines if *i* is specified.

*i*RETURN Display another line, or *i* more lines, if specified.

i`^D` (CTRL−D) Display (scroll down) 11 more lines. If *i* is given, the scroll size is set to *i* .

i`d` Same as `^D`.

i`z` Same as SPACE, except that *i* , if present, becomes the new default number of lines per screenful.

i`s` Skip *i* lines and then print a screenful.

i`f` Skip *i* screenfuls and then print a screenful.

i`^B` (CTRL-B) Skip back *i* screenfuls and then print a screenful.

b Same as `^B` (CTRL-D).

q
Q — Exit from `more`.

= — Display the current line number.

v — Drop into the editor indicated by the `EDITOR` environment variable, at the current line of the current file. The default editor is `ed`(1).

h — Help. Give a description of all the `more` commands.

i/pattern — Search forward for the *i* th occurrence of the regular expression *pattern*. Display the screenful starting two lines before the line that contains the *i* th match for the regular expression *pattern*, or the end of a pipe, whichever comes first. If `more` is displaying a file and there is no such match, its position in the file remains unchanged. Regular expressions can be edited using erase and kill characters. Erasing back past the first column cancels the search command.

in — Search for the *i* th occurrence of the last *pattern* entered.

' — Single quote. Go to the point from which the last search started. If no search has been performed in the current file, go to the beginning of the file.

!*command* — Invoke a shell to execute *command*. The characters `%` and `!`, when used within *command* are replaced with the current filename and the previous shell command, respectively. If there is no current filename, `%` is not expanded. Prepend a backslash to these characters to escape expansion.

i:n — Skip to the *i* th next filename given in the command line, or to the last filename in the list if *i* is out of range.

i:p — Skip to the *i* th previous filename given in the command line, or to the first filename if *i* is out of range. If given while `more` is positioned within a file, go to the beginning of the file. If `more` is reading from a pipe, `more` simply rings the terminal bell.

:f — Display the current filename and line number.

:q
:Q — Exit from `more` (same as `q` or `Q`).

. — Dot. Repeat the previous command.

^\ — Halt a partial display of text. `more` stops sending output, and displays the usual `--More--` prompt. Unfortunately, some output is lost as a result.

FILES

`/usr/share/lib/termcap` — terminal data base

`/usr/lib/more.help` — help file

SEE ALSO

`cat`(1), `csh`(1), `man`(1), `script`(1), `sh`(1)
`environ`(5V), `termcap`(5) in the *System Administrator's Reference Manual.*

NOTES

Skipping backwards is too slow on large files.

NAME

mv – move files

SYNOPSIS

mv [-f] [-i] *file1* [*file2* ...] *target*

DESCRIPTION

The mv command moves *filen* to *target*. *filen* and *target* may not have the same name. (Care must be taken when using sh(1) metacharacters). If *target* is not a directory, only one file may be specified before it; if it is a directory, more than one file may be specified. If *target* does not exist, mv creates a file named *target*. If *target* exists and is not a directory, its contents are overwritten. If *target* is a directory the file(s) are moved to that directory.

If mv determines that the mode of *target* forbids writing, it will print the mode (see chmod(2)), ask for a response, and read the standard input for one line. If the line begins with y, the mv occurs, if permissible; otherwise, the command exits. When the parent directory of *filen* is writable and has the sticky bit set, one or more of the following conditions must be true:

the user must own the file
the user must own the directory
the file must be writable by the user
the user must be a privileged user

The following options are recognized:

-i mv will prompt for confirmation whenever the move would overwrite an existing *target*. A y answer means that the move should proceed. Any other answer prevents mv from overwriting the *target*.

-f mv will move the file(s) without prompting even if it is writing over an existing *target*. This option overrides the -i option. Note that this is the default if the standard input is not a terminal.

If *filen* is a directory, *target* must be a directory in the same physical file system. *target* and *filen* do not have to share the same parent directory.

If *filen* is a file and *target* is a link to another file with links, the other links remain and *target* becomes a new file.

NOTES

If *filen* and *target* are on different file systems, mv copies the file and deletes the original; any links to other files are lost.

A -- permits the user to mark explicitly the end of any command line options, allowing mv to recognize filename arguments that begin with a -. As an aid to BSD migration, mv will accept - as a synonym for --. This migration aid may disappear in a future release. If a -- and a - both appear on the same command line, the second will be interpreted as a filename.

SEE ALSO

chmod(1), cp(1), cpio(1), ln(1), rm(1).

NAME

nawk – pattern scanning and processing language

SYNOPSIS

nawk [**–F** *re*] [**–v** *var=value*] [*'prog'*] [*file...*]
nawk [**–F** *re*] [**–v** *var=value*] [**–f** *progfile*] [*file...*]

DESCRIPTION

nawk scans each input *file* for lines that match any of a set of patterns specified in *prog*. The *prog* string must be enclosed in single quotes (') to protect it from the shell. For each pattern in *prog* there may be an associated action performed when a line of a *file* matches the pattern. The set of pattern-action statements may appear literally as *prog* or in a file specified with the **–f** *progfile* option. Input files are read in order; if there are no files, the standard input is read. The file name – means the standard input.

Each input line is matched against the pattern portion of every pattern-action statement; the associated action is performed for each matched pattern. Any *file* of the form **var**=*value* is treated as an assignment, not a filename, and is executed at the time it would have been opened if it were a filename, and is executed at the time it would have been opened if it were a filename. The option **–v** followed by **var**=*value* is an assignment to be done before *prog* is executed; any number of **–v** options may be present.

An input line is normally made up of fields separated by white space. (This default can be changed by using the **FS** built-in variable or the **–F** *re* option.) The fields are denoted **$1**, **$2**, ...; **$0** refers to the entire line.

A pattern-action statement has the form:

pattern { *action* }

Either pattern or action may be omitted. If there is no action with a pattern, the matching line is printed. If there is no pattern with an action, the action is performed on every input line. Pattern-action statements are separated by newlines or semicolons.

Patterns are arbitrary Boolean combinations (**!**, **||**, **&&**, and parentheses) of relational expressions and regular expressions. A relational expression is one of the following:

expression relop expression
expression matchop regular_expression
expression **in** *array-name*
(*expression*, *expression*, ...) **in** *array-name*

where a *relop* is any of the six relational operators in C, and a *matchop* is either **~** (contains) or **!~** (does not contain). An *expression* is an arithmetic expression, a relational expression, the special expression

var **in** *array*

or a Boolean combination of these.

Regular expressions are as in **egrep**(1). In patterns they must be surrounded by slashes. Isolated regular expressions in a pattern apply to the entire line. Regular expressions may also occur in relational expressions. A pattern may consist of two patterns separated by a comma; in this case, the action is performed for all lines between an occurrence of the first pattern and the next occurrence of the second pattern.

The special patterns `BEGIN` and `END` may be used to capture control before the first input line has been read and after the last input line has been read respectively. These keywords do not combine with any other patterns.

A regular expression may be used to separate fields by using the **-F** *re* option or by assigning the expression to the built-in variable FS. The default is to ignore leading blanks and to separate fields by blanks and/or tab characters. However, if FS is assigned a value, leading blanks are no longer ignored.

Other built-in variables include:

`ARGC`	command line argument count
`ARGV`	command line argument array
`ENVIRON`	array of environment variables; subscripts are names
`FILENAME`	name of the current input file
`FNR`	ordinal number of the current record in the current file
`FS`	input field separator regular expression (default blank and tab)
`NF`	number of fields in the current record
`NR`	ordinal number of the current record
`OFMT`	output format for numbers (default `%.6g`)
`OFS`	output field separator (default blank)
`ORS`	output record separator (default new-line)
`RS`	input record separator (default new-line)
`SUBSEP`	separates multiple subscripts (default is 034)

An action is a sequence of statements. A statement may be one of the following:

```
if ( expression ) statement [ else statement ]
while ( expression ) statement
do statement while ( expression )
for ( expression ; expression ; expression ) statement
for ( var in array ) statement
delete array[subscript] #delete an array element
break
continue
{ [ statement ] ... }
expression     # commonly variable = expression
print [ expression-list ] [ >expression ]
printf format [ , expression-list ] [ >expression ]
next           # skip remaining patterns on this input line
```

```
exit [expr] # skip the rest of the input; exit status is expr
return [expr]
```

Statements are terminated by semicolons, new-lines, or right braces. An empty expression-list stands for the whole input line. Expressions take on string or numeric values as appropriate, and are built using the operators +, −, *, /, %, ^ and concatenation (indicated by a blank). The operators ++ −− += −= *= /= %= ^= > >= < <= == != ?: are also available in expressions. Variables may be scalars, array elements (denoted x[i]), or fields. Variables are initialized to the null string or zero. Array subscripts may be any string, not necessarily numeric; this allows for a form of associative memory. Multiple subscripts such as `[i,j,k]` are permitted; the constituents are concatenated, separated by the value of `SUBSEP`. String constants are quoted (`""`), with the usual C excapes recognized within.

The `print` statement prints its arguments on the standard output, or on a file if >*expression* is present, or on a pipe if | *cmd* is present. The arguments are separated by the current output field separator and terminated by the output record separator. The `printf` statement formats its expression list according to the format [see *printf*(3S) in the *Programmer's Reference Manual*]. The built-in function `close`(*expr*) closes the file or pipe *expr*.

The mathematical functions: `atan2`, `cos`, `exp`, `log`, `sin`, `sqrt`, are built-in.

Other built-in functions include:

`gsub`(*for, repl, in*)
: behaves like `sub` (see below), except that it replaces successive occurrences of the regular expression (like the `ed` global substitute command).

`index(`*s*`,` *t*`)`
: returns the position in string *s* where string *t* first occurs, or 0 if it does not occur at all.

`int`
: truncates to an integer value.

`length(`*s*`)`
: returns the length of its argument taken as a string, or of the whole line if there is no argument.

`match(`*s*`,` *re*`)`
: returns the position in string *s* where the regular expression *re* occurs, or 0 if it does not occur at all. `RSTART` is set to the starting position (which is the same as the returned value), and `RLENGTH` is set to the length of the matched string.

`rand`
: random number on (0, 1).

`split(`*s*`,` *a*`,` *fs*`)`
: splits the string *s* into array elements *a*[*1*], *a*[*2*], *a*[*n*], and returns *n*. The separation is done with the regular expression *fs* or with the field separator `FS` if *fs* is not given.

`srand`
: sets the seed for `rand`

`sprintf(`*fmt*`,` *expr*`,` *expr*`, ...)`
: formats the expressions according to the `printf`(3S) format given by *fmt* and returns the resulting string.

sub(*for, repl, in*) substitutes the string *repl* in place of the first instance of the regular expression *for* in string *in* and returns the number of substitutions. If *in* is omitted, **nawk** substitutes in the current record ($0).

substr(*s, m, n*) returns the *n*-character substring of *s* that begins at position *m*.

The input/output built-in functions are:

close(*filename*) closes the file or pipe named *filename*.

cmd | getline pipes the output of *cmd* into getline; each successive call to *getline* returns the next line of output from *cmd*.

getline sets $0 to the next input record from the current input file.

getline <*file* sets $0 to the next record from *file*.

getline *x* sets variable *x* instead.

getline *x* <*file* sets *x* from the next record of *file*.

system(*cmd*) executes *cmd* and returns its exit status.

All forms of getline return 1 for successful input, 0 for end of file, and −1 for an error.

nawk also provides user-defined functions. Such functions may be defined (in the pattern position of a pattern-action statement) as

```
function name(args,...) { stmts }
```

Function arguments are passed by value if scalar and by reference if array name. Argument names are local to the function; all other variable names are global. Function calls may be nested and functions may be recursive. The return statement may be used to return a value.

EXAMPLES

Print lines longer than 72 characters:

```
length > 72
```

Print first two fields in opposite order:

```
{ print $2, $1 }
```

Same, with input fields separated by comma and/or blanks and tabs:

```
BEGIN { FS = ",[ \t]*|[ \t]+" }
      { print $2, $1 }
```

Add up first column, print sum and average:

```
      { s += $1 }
END   { print "sum is", s, " average is", s/NR }
```

Print fields in reverse order:

```
{ for (i = NF; i > 0; --i) print $i }
```

Print all lines between start/stop pairs:

```
/start/, /stop/
```

Print all lines whose first field is different from previous one:

```
$1 != prev { print; prev = $1 }
```

Simulate echo(1):

```
BEGIN {
      for (i = 1; i < ARGC; i++)
            printf "%s", ARGV[i]
      printf "\n"
      exit
      }
```

Print a file, filling in page numbers starting at 5:

```
/Page/      { $2 = n++; }
      { print }
```

Assuming this program is in a file named prog, the following command line prints the file input numbering its pages starting at 5: `nawk -f prog n=5 input`.

SEE ALSO

egrep(1), grep(1), sed(1).
lex(1), printf(3S) in the *Programmer's Reference Manual.*
The **awk** chapter in the *User's Guide.*
A. V. Aho, B. W. Kerninghan, P. J. Weinberger, *The AWK Programming Language* Addison-Wesley, 1988.

NOTES

nawk is a new version of **awk** that provides capabilities unavailable in previous versions. This version will become the default version of **awk** in the next major UNIX system release.

Input white space is not preserved on output if fields are involved.

There are no explicit conversions between numbers and strings. To force an expression to be treated as a number add 0 to it; to force it to be treated as a string concatenate the null string ("") to it.

NAME

newform – change the format of a text file

SYNOPSIS

newform [-s] [-itabspec] [-otabspec] [-bn] [-en] [-pn] [-an] [-f] [-cchar] [-ln] [files]

DESCRIPTION

newform reads lines from the named *files*, or the standard input if no input file is named, and reproduces the lines on the standard output. Lines are reformatted in accordance with command line options in effect.

Except for -s, command line options may appear in any order, may be repeated, and may be intermingled with the optional *files*. Command line options are processed in the order specified. This means that option sequences like "-e15 -l60" will yield results different from "-l60 -e15". Options are applied to all *files* on the command line.

-s Shears off leading characters on each line up to the first tab and places up to 8 of the sheared characters at the end of the line. If more than 8 characters (not counting the first tab) are sheared, the eighth character is replaced by a * and any characters to the right of it are discarded. The first tab is always discarded.

An error message and program exit will occur if this option is used on a file without a tab on each line. The characters sheared off are saved internally until all other options specified are applied to that line. The characters are then added at the end of the processed line.

For example, to convert a file with leading digits, one or more tabs, and text on each line, to a file beginning with the text, all tabs after the first expanded to spaces, padded with spaces out to column 72 (or truncated to column 72), and the leading digits placed starting at column 73, the command would be:

```
newform -s -i -l -a -e file-name
```

-i*tabspec* Input tab specification: expands tabs to spaces, according to the tab specifications given. *Tabspec* recognizes all tab specification forms described in tabs(1). In addition, *tabspec* may be --, in which newform assumes that the tab specification is to be found in the first line read from the standard input (see fspec(4)). If no *tabspec* is given, *tabspec* defaults to -8. A *tabspec* of -0 expects no tabs; if any are found, they are treated as -1.

-o*tabspec* Output tab specification: replaces spaces by tabs, according to the tab specifications given. The tab specifications are the same as for -i*tabspec*. If no *tabspec* is given, *tabspec* defaults to -8. A *tabspec* of -0 means that no spaces will be converted to tabs on output.

-b*n* Truncate *n* characters from the beginning of the line when the line length is greater than the effective line length (see -l*n*). Default is to truncate the number of characters necessary to obtain the effective line length. The default value is used when -b with no *n* is used. This option can be used to delete the sequence numbers from a COBOL program as follows:

`newform -l1 -b7` *file-name*

-e*n* Same as **-b***n* except that characters are truncated from the end of the line.

-p*n* Prefix *n* characters (see **-c***k*) to the beginning of a line when the line length is less than the effective line length. Default is to prefix the number of characters necessary to obtain the effective line length.

-a*n* Same as **-p***n* except characters are appended to the end of a line.

-f Write the tab specification format line on the standard output before any other lines are output. The tab specification format line which is printed will correspond to the format specified in the *last* **-o** option. If no **-o** option is specified, the line which is printed will contain the default specification of **-8**.

-c*k* Change the prefix/append character to *k*. Default character for *k* is a space.

-l*n* Set the effective line length to *n* characters. If *n* is not entered, **-l** defaults to 72. The default line length without the **-l** option is 80 characters. Note that tabs and backspaces are considered to be one character (use **-i** to expand tabs to spaces).

The **-l1** must be used to set the effective line length shorter than any existing line in the file so that the **-b** option is activated.

DIAGNOSTICS

All diagnostics are fatal.

`usage: ...`	`newform` was called with a bad option.
`"not -s format"`	There was no tab on one line.
`"can't open file"`	Self-explanatory.
`"internal line too long"`	A line exceeds 512 characters after being expanded in the internal work buffer.
`"tabspec in error"`	A tab specification is incorrectly formatted, or specified tab stops are not ascending.
`"tabspec indirection illegal"`	A *tabspec* read from a file (or standard input) may not contain a *tabspec* referencing another file (or standard input).

0 – normal execution
1 – for any error

SEE ALSO

`csplit`(1), `tabs`(1).
`fspec`(4) in the *System Administrator's Reference Manual.*

NOTES

`newform` normally only keeps track of physical characters; however, for the `-i` and -o options, **`newform`** will keep track of backspaces in order to line up tabs in the appropriate logical columns.

`newform` will not prompt the user if a *tabspec* is to be read from the standard input (by use of `-i--` or -o--).

If the `-f` option is used, and the last -o option specified was -o--, and was preceded by either a -o-- or a `-i--`, the tab specification format line will be incorrect.

NAME

newgrp – log in to a new group

SYNOPSIS

newgrp [–] [group]

DESCRIPTION

newgrp changes a user's real and effective group ID. The user remains logged in and the current directory is unchanged. The user is always given a new shell, replacing the current shell, by **newgrp**, regardless of whether it terminated successfully or due to an error condition (i.e., unknown group).

Exported variables retain their values after invoking **newgrp**; however, all unexported variables are either reset to their default value or set to null. System variables (such as PS1, PS2, PATH, MAIL, and HOME), unless exported by the system or explicitly exported by the user, are reset to default values. For example, a user has a primary prompt string (PS1) other than $ (default) and has not exported PS1. After an invocation of **newgrp**, successful or not, the user's PS1 will now be set to the default prompt string $. Note that the shell command **export** [see the **sh**(1) manual page] is the method to export variables so that they retain their assigned value when invoking new shells.

With no arguments, **newgrp** changes the user's group IDs (real and effective) back to the group specified in the user's password file entry. This is a way to exit the effect of an earlier **newgrp** command.

If the first argument to **newgrp** is a –, the environment is changed to what would be expected if the user actually logged in again as a member of the new group.

A password is demanded if the group has a password and the user is not listed in /etc/group as being a member of that group.

FILES

/etc/group	system's group file
/etc/passwd	system's password file

SEE ALSO

login(1), sh(1) in the *User's Reference Manual*.
group(4), passwd(4), environ(5) in the *System Administrator's Reference Manual.*
see intro(2) "Effective User ID and Effective Group ID" in *Programmer's Reference Manual*

NAME

news – print news items

SYNOPSIS

news [-a] [-n] [-s] [*items*]

DESCRIPTION

news is used to keep the user informed of current events. By convention, these events are described by files in the directory **/var/news**.

When invoked without arguments, **news** prints the contents of all current files in **/var/news**, most recent first, with each preceded by an appropriate header. news stores the "currency" time as the modification date of a file named .news_time in the user's home directory (the identity of this directory is determined by the environment variable $HOME); only files more recent than this currency time are considered "current."

-a option causes news to print all items, regardless of currency. In this case, the stored time is not changed.

-n option causes news to report the names of the current items without printing their contents, and without changing the stored time.

-s option causes news to report how many current items exist, without printing their names or contents, and without changing the stored time. It is useful to include such an invocation of news in one's .profile file, or in the system's /etc/profile.

All other arguments are assumed to be specific news items that are to be printed.

If a *delete* is typed during the printing of a news item, printing stops and the next item is started. Another *delete* within one second of the first causes the program to terminate.

FILES

/etc/profile
/var/news/*
$HOME/.news_time

SEE ALSO

profile(4), environ(5) in the *System Administrator's Reference Manual.*

NAME

newvt – opens virtual terminals.

SYNOPSIS

`newvt [-eprog] [-n vt_number]`

DESCRIPTION

Use the **newvt** command to open a new virtual terminal. The newly opened virtual terminal will inherit your environment.

-e Specifies a program (*prog*) to execute in the new virtual terminal. Without the **-e** option, the program pointed to by the **$SHELL** environment variable is started in the new virtual terminal. If **$SHELL** is NULL or points to a nonexecutable program, then /bin/sh is invoked.

-n Specifies a particular virtual terminal (*vt_number*) to open. If the -n option is not specified, then the next available virtual terminal is opened. Close virtual terminals by pressing CTRL-d (control d). Repeat CTRL-d until all open virtual terminals are closed.

DIAGNOSTICS

The **newvt** command will fail under the following conditions:

If an illegal option is specified.
If the device cannot be opened.
If newvt is invoked from a remote terminal.
If no virtual terminals are available (-n option not specified).
If the requested virtual terminal is not available (-n option specified).
If the requested virtual terminal cannot be opened.
If the specified command cannot be executed (-e option specified).
If the $SHELL program cannot be executed ($SHELL set and -e option not specified).
If /dev/vtmon cannot be opened.

SEE ALSO

vtlmgr(1)
vtgetty(1M) in the *System Administrator's Reference Manual.*

NAME

nice – run a command at low priority

SYNOPSIS

nice [*–increment*] *command* [*arguments*]

DESCRIPTION

nice executes *command* with a lower CPU scheduling priority. The priocntl command is a more general interface to scheduler functions.

The invoking process (generally the user's shell) must be in the time-sharing scheduling class. The *command* is executed in the time-sharing class.

If the *increment* argument (in the range 1–19) is given, it is used; if not, an increment of 10 is assumed.

The super-user may run commands with priority higher than normal by using a negative increment, e.g., --10.

SEE ALSO

nohup(1), priocntl(1).
nice(2) in the *Programmer's Reference Manual.*

DIAGNOSTICS

nice returns the exit status of *command*.

NOTES

An *increment* larger than 19 is equivalent to 19.

NAME

nl – line numbering filter

SYNOPSIS

nl [–b*type*] [–f*type*] [–h*type*] [–v*start#*] [–i*incr*] [–p] [–l*num*] [–s*sep*] [–w*width*] [–n*format*] [–d*delim*] [*file*]

DESCRIPTION

nl reads lines from the named *file*, or the standard input if no *file* is named, and reproduces the lines on the standard output. Lines are numbered on the left in accordance with the command options in effect.

nl views the text it reads in terms of logical pages. Line numbering is reset at the start of each logical page. A logical page consists of a header, a body, and a footer section. Empty sections are valid. Different line numbering options are independently available for header, body, and footer. For example, –bt (the default) numbers non-blank lines in the body section and does not number any lines in the header and footer sections.

The start of logical page sections are signaled by input lines containing nothing but the following delimiter character(s):

Line contents	*Start of*
\:\:\:	header
\:\:	body
\:	footer

Unless optioned otherwise, nl assumes the text being read is in a single logical page body.

Command options may appear in any order and may be intermingled with an optional file name. Only one file may be named. The options are:

–b*type* Specifies which logical page body lines are to be numbered. Recognized *types* and their meanings are:

a	number all lines
t	number lines with printable text only
n	no line numbering
p*exp*	number only lines that contain the regular expression specified in *exp* (see ed(1))

Default *type* for logical page body is t (text lines numbered).

–f*type* Same as –b*type* except for footer. Default *type* for logical page footer is n (no lines numbered).

–h*type* Same as –b*type* except for header. Default *type* for logical page header is n (no lines numbered).

–v*start#* *start#* is the initial value used to number logical page lines. Default *start#* is 1.

-i*incr* *incr* is the increment value used to number logical page lines. Default *incr* is 1.

-p Do not restart numbering at logical page delimiters.

-l*num* *num* is the number of blank lines to be considered as one. For example, -l2 results in only the second adjacent blank being numbered (if the appropriate -ha, -ba, and/or -fa option is set). Default *num* is 1.

-s*sep* *sep* is the character(s) used in separating the line number and the corresponding text line. Default *sep* is a tab.

-w*width* *width* is the number of characters to be used for the line number. The default for *width* is 6. The maximum for *width* is 100. If a number greater than the maximum is specified for *width*, the maximum is automatically be used.

-n*format* *format* is the line numbering format. Recognized values are: ln, left justified, leading zeroes suppressed; rn, right justified, leading zeroes suppressed; rz, right justified, leading zeroes kept. Default *format* is rn (right justified).

-d*delim* The two delimiter characters specifying the start of a logical page section may be changed from the default characters (\:) to two user-specified characters. If only one character is entered, the second character remains the default character (:). No space should appear between the -d and the delimiter characters. To enter a backslash, use two backslashes.

EXAMPLE

The command:

```
nl -v10 -i10 -d!+ file1
```

will cause the first line of the page body to be numbered 10, the second line of the page body to be numbered 20, the third 30, and so forth. The logical page delimiters are !+.

SEE ALSO

pr(1), ed(1).

NAME

nohup – run a command immune to hangups and quits

SYNOPSIS

nohup *command* [*arguments*]

DESCRIPTION

nohup executes *command* with hangups and quits ignored. If output is not redirected by the user, both standard output and standard error are sent to nohup.out. If nohup.out is not writable in the current directory, output is redirected to $HOME/nohup.out.

EXAMPLE

It is frequently desirable to apply nohup to pipelines or lists of commands. This can be done only by placing pipelines and command lists in a single file, called a shell procedure. One can then issue:

```
nohup sh file
```

and the nohup applies to everything in *file*. If the shell procedure *file* is to be executed often, then the need to type sh can be eliminated by giving *file* execute permission. Add an ampersand and the contents of *file* are run in the background with interrupts also ignored (see sh(1)):

```
nohup file &
```

An example of what the contents of *file* could be is:

```
sort ofile > nfile
```

SEE ALSO

chmod(1), nice(1), sh(1),
signal(2) in the *Programmer's Reference Manual.*

NOTES

In the case of the following command

```
nohup command1; command2
```

nohup applies only to command1. The command

```
nohup (command1; command2)
```

is syntactically incorrect.

NAME

`notify` – notify user of the arrival of new mail

SYNOPSIS

`notify -y` [`-m` *mailfile*]
`notify` [`-n`]

DESCRIPTION

When a new mail message arrives, the `mail` command first checks if the recipient's mailbox indicates that the message is to be forwarded elsewhere (to some other recipient or as the input to some command). `notify` is used to set up forwarding on the user's mailbox so that the new message is saved into an alternative mailbox and, if the user is currently logged in, he or she is notified immediately of the arrival of new mail.

Command-line options are:

`-m` *mailfile*	File to save mail messages into while automatic notification is activated. If not specified, it defaults to *$HOME/.mailfile*.
`-n`	Remove mail notification facility
`-y`	Install mail notification facility

If invoked with no arguments, `notify` reports whether automatic mail notification is activated or not.

The notification is done by looking in `/var/adm/utmp` to determine if the recipient is currently logged in, and if so, on which terminal device. Then the terminal device is opened for writing and the user is notified about the new message. The notification will indicate who the message is from. If the message contains a `Subject:` header line it will be included. (For security, all unprintable characters within the header will be converted to an exclamation point.)

If the user is logged in multiple times he or she will get multiple notifications, one per terminal. To disable notifications to a particular login session, the `mesg`(1) command can be used to disable writing to that terminal.

If there are multiple machines connected together via RFS or NFS, `notify` will look up the `/var/adm/utmp` files on the other systems as well. To do this, the file `/etc/mail/notify.sys` will be consulted, which will contain two columns, the first being the name of a system and the second being a path to find the root filesystem for that machine.

If `notify` has troubles delivering the mail to the specified mailfile, `notify` will look up the directory of the mailfile in `/etc/mail/notify.fsys`. If the file's directory is found in the first column of the file, the mail will be forwarded to the system listed in the second column instead of being returned to the sender.

FILES

`/tmp/notif*`	temporary file
`/var/mail/*`	users' standard mailboxes
`/usr/lib/mail/notify2`	program that performs the notification

`/etc/mail/notify.fsys`
: list of file systems and home systems

`/etc/mail/notify.sys`
: list of machines and paths to their root filesystems

`/var/adm/utmp` list of users who are logged in

SEE ALSO

`mail`(1), `mesg`(1).
User's Guide.

NOTES

Because `notify` uses the "`Forward to` |*command*" facility of `mail` to implement notifications, `/var/mail/`*username* should not be specified as the place to put newly arrived messages via the `-m` invocation option. The `mail` command uses `/var/mail/`*username* to hold either mail messages, or indications of mail forwarding, but not both simultaneously.

If the user is using `layers`(1), the notification will only appear in the `login` window.

NAME

od – octal dump

SYNOPSIS

od [-bcDdFfOoSsvXx] [*file*] [[+]*offset*[. | b]]

DESCRIPTION

od displays *file* in one or more formats, as selected by the first argument. If the first argument is missing, -o is default. If no *file* is specified, the standard input is used. For the purposes of this description, "word" refers to a 16-bit unit, independent of the word size of the machine; "long word" refers to a 32-bit unit, and "double long word" refers to a 64-bit unit. The meanings of the format options are:

-b Interpret bytes in octal.

-c Interpret bytes as single-byte characters. Certain non-graphic characters appear as C-language escapes: null=\0, backspace=\b, form-feed=\f, newline=\n, return=\r, tab=\t; others appear as 3-digit octal numbers. For example:

```
echo "hello world" | od -c
0000000   h   e   l   l   o       w   o   r   l   d  \n
0000014
```

-D Interpret long words in unsigned decimal.

-d Interpret words in unsigned decimal.

-F Interpret double long words in extended precision.

-f Interpret long words in floating point.

-O Interpret long words in unsigned octal.

-o Interpret words in octal.

-S Interpret long words in signed decimal.

-s Interpret words in signed decimal.

-v Show all data (verbose).

-X Interpret long words in hex.

-x Interpret words in hex.

offset specifies an offset from the beginning of *file* where the display will begin. *offset* is normally interpreted as octal bytes. If . is appended, *offset* is interpreted in decimal. If b is appended, *offset* is interpreted in blocks of 512 bytes. If *file* is omitted, *offset* must be preceded by +.

The display continues until an end-of-file is reached.

NAME

pack, pcat, unpack – compress and expand files

SYNOPSIS

pack [–] [-f] *name* ...

pcat *name* ...

unpack *name* ...

DESCRIPTION

pack attempts to store the specified files in a compressed form. Wherever possible (and useful), each input file *name* is replaced by a packed file *name*.z with the same access modes, access and modified dates, and owner as those of *name*. The -f option will force packing of *name*. This is useful for causing an entire directory to be packed even if some of the files will not benefit. If **pack** is successful, *name* will be removed. Packed files can be restored to their original form using unpack or pcat.

pack uses Huffman (minimum redundancy) codes on a byte-by-byte basis. If the – argument is used, an internal flag is set that causes the number of times each byte is used, its relative frequency, and the code for the byte to be printed on the standard output. Additional occurrences of – in place of *name* will cause the internal flag to be set and reset.

The amount of compression obtained depends on the size of the input file and the character frequency distribution. Because a decoding tree forms the first part of each .z file, it is usually not worthwhile to pack files smaller than three blocks, unless the character frequency distribution is very skewed, which may occur with printer plots or pictures.

Typically, text files are reduced to 60-75% of their original size. Load modules, which use a larger character set and have a more uniform distribution of characters, show little compression, the packed versions being about 90% of the original size.

pack returns a value that is the number of files that it failed to compress.

No packing will occur if:

the file appears to be already packed;
the file name has more than 12 characters;
the file has links;
the file is a directory;
the file cannot be opened;
no disk storage blocks will be saved by packing;
a file called *name*.z already exists;
the .z file cannot be created;
an I/O error occurred during processing.

The last segment of the file name must contain no more than 12 characters to allow space for the appended .z extension. Directories cannot be compressed.

pcat does for packed files what **cat**(1) does for ordinary files, except that **pcat** cannot be used as a filter. The specified files are unpacked and written to the standard output. Thus to view a packed file named **name.z** use:

```
pcat name.z
```

or just:

```
pcat name
```

To make an unpacked copy, say nnn, of a packed file named **name.z** (without destroying **name.z**) use the command:

```
pcat name >nnn
```

pcat returns the number of files it was unable to unpack. Failure may occur if:

the file name (exclusive of the **.z**) has more than 12 characters;
the file cannot be opened;
the file does not appear to be the output of **pack**.

unpack expands files created by **pack**. For each file *name* specified in the command, a search is made for a file called *name*.**z** (or just *name*, if *name* ends in **.z**). If this file appears to be a packed file, it is replaced by its expanded version. The new file has the **.z** suffix stripped from its name, and has the same access modes, access and modification dates, and owner as those of the packed file.

Unpack returns a value that is the number of files it was unable to unpack. Failure may occur for the same reasons that it may in **pcat**, as well as for the following:

a file with the "unpacked" name already exists;
if the unpacked file cannot be created.

SEE ALSO

cat(1), compress(1).

NAME

passwd – change login password and password attributes

SYNOPSIS

passwd [*name*]

passwd [-l | -d] [-f] [-n *min*] [-x *max*] [-w *warn*] *name*

passwd -s [-a]

passwd -s [*name*]

DESCRIPTION

The **passwd** command changes the password or lists password attributes associated with the user's login *name*. Additionally, privileged-users may use **passwd** to install or change passwords and attributes associated with any login *name*.

When used to change a password, **passwd** prompts ordinary users for their old password, if any. It then prompts for the new password twice. When the old password is entered, **passwd** checks to see if it has "aged" sufficiently. If "aging" is insufficient, **passwd** terminates; see **shadow**(4).

If the user's password aging has not neen turned on, then password aging is turned on for the user using the MAXWEEK and MINWEEK parameters in /etc/default/passwd. If password aging is turned on the password aging information in /etc/shadow remains unmodified.

Assuming aging is sufficient, a check is made to ensure that the new password meets construction requirements. When the new password is entered a second time, the two copies of the new password are compared. If the two copies are not identical the cycle of prompting for the new password is repeated for at most two more times.

Passwords must be constructed to meet the following requirements:

> Each password must have at least PASSLENGTH characters as set in /etc/default/passwd. PASSLENGTH must contain a minimum of six characters, but only the first eight characters are significant.
>
> Each password must contain at least two alphabetic characters and at least one numeric or special character. In this case, "alphabetic" refers to all upper or lower case letters.
>
> Each password must differ from the user's login *name* and any reverse or circular shift of that login *name*. For comparison purposes, an upper case letter and its corresponding lower case letter are equivalent.
>
> New passwords must differ from the old by at least three characters. For comparison purposes, an upper case letter and its corresponding lower case letter are equivalent.

Super-users (e.g., real and effective uid equal to zero, see id(1M) and su(1M)) may change any password; hence, **passwd** does not prompt privileged-users for the old password. Privileged-users are not forced to comply with password aging and password construction requirements. A privileged-user can create a null password by entering a carriage return in response to the prompt for a new password. (This differs from passwd -d because the "password" prompt will still be displayed.)

Any user may use the `-s` option to show password attributes for his or her own login *name*.

The format of the display will be:

name status mm/dd/yy min max warn

or, if password aging information is not present,

name status

where

name — The login ID of the user.

status — The password status of *name*: "PS" stands for passworded or locked, "LK" stands for locked, and "NP" stands for no password.

mm/dd/yy — The date password was last changed for *name*. (Note that all password aging dates are determined using Greenwich Mean Time and, therefore, may differ by as much as a day in other time zones.)

min — The minimum number of days required between password changes for *name*. MINWEEKS is found in `/etc/default/passwd` and is set to NULL.

max — The maximum number of days the password is valid for *name*. MAXWEEKS is found in `/etc/default/passwd` and is set to NULL.

warn — The number of days relative to *max* before the password expires that the *name* will be warned.

Only a privileged-user can use the following options:

`-l` — Locks password entry for *name*.

`-d` — Deletes password for *name*. The login *name* will not be prompted for password.

`-n` — Set minimum field for *name*. The *min* field contains the minimum number of days between password changes for *name*. If *min* is greater than *max*, the user may not change the password. Always use this option with the `-x` option, unless *max* is set to −1 (aging turned off). In that case, *min* need not be set.

`-x` — Set maximum field for *name*. The *max* field contains the number of days that the password is valid for *name*. The aging for *name* will be turned off immediately if *max* is set to -1. If it is set to 0, then the user is forced to change the password at the next login session and aging is turned off.

`-w` — Set warn field for *name*. The *warn* field contains the number of days before the password expires that the user will be warned.

`-a` — Show password attributes for all entries. Use only with `-s` option; *name* must not be provided.

`-f` — Force the user to change password at the next login by expiring the password for *name*.

FILES

/etc/shadow, /etc/passwd, /etc/oshadow

SEE ALSO

`login`(1).
`crypt`(3C) in the *Programmer's Reference Manual.*
`useradd`(1M), `usermod`(1M), `userdel`(1M), `id`(1M), `passmgmt`(1M), `pwconv`(1M), `su`(1M), `passwd`(4), `shadow`(4) in the *System Administrator's Reference Manual.*

DIAGNOSTICS

The `passwd` command exits with one of the following values:

0 SUCCESS.

1 Permission denied.

2 Invalid combination of options.

3 Unexpected failure. Password file unchanged.

4 Unexpected failure. Password file(s) missing.

5 Password file(s) busy. Try again later.

6 Invalid argument to option.

WARNING

If root deletes a password for a user with the *passwd -d* command and password aging is in effect for that user, the user will not be allowed to add a new password until the NULL password has been aged. This is true even if the PASSREQ flag in `/etc/login/default` is set to YES. This results in a user without a password. It is recommended that the `-f` option be used whenever the `-d` (delete) option is used. This will force a user to change the password at the next login.

If a user is to be set up without a password, the password entry of the user must be absent from the `/etc/shadow` file. (When a user has no password, `passwd -s` *user* should return NP.)

NAME

paste – merge same lines of several files or subsequent lines of one file

SYNOPSIS

paste *file1 file2 ...*
paste -d*list file1 file2 ...*
paste -s [**-d***list*] *file1 file2 ...*

DESCRIPTION

In the first two forms, **paste** concatenates corresponding lines of the given input files *file1*, *file2*, etc. It treats each file as a column or columns of a table and pastes them together horizontally (parallel merging). If you will, it is the counterpart of **cat**(1) which concatenates vertically, i.e., one file after the other. In the last form above, **paste** replaces the function of an older command with the same name by combining subsequent lines of the input file (serial merging). In all cases, lines are glued together with the *tab* character, or with characters from an optionally specified *list*. Output is to the standard output, so it can be used as the start of a pipe, or as a filter, if – is used in place of a file name.

The meanings of the options are:

-d Without this option, the new-line characters of each but the last file (or last line in case of the **-s** option) are replaced by a *tab* character. This option allows replacing the *tab* character by one or more alternate characters (see below).

list One or more characters immediately following **-d** replace the default *tab* as the line concatenation character. The list is used circularly, i.e., when exhausted, it is reused. In parallel merging (i.e., no **-s** option), the lines from the last file are always terminated with a new-line character, not from the *list*. The list may contain the special escape sequences: \n (newline), \t (tab), \\ (backslash), and \0 (empty string, not a null character). Quoting may be necessary, if characters have special meaning to the shell (e.g., to get one backslash, use *-d* \\\\"").

-s Merge subsequent lines rather than one from each input file. Use *tab* for concatenation, unless a *list* is specified with **-d** option. Regardless of the *list*, the very last character of the file is forced to be a new-line.

– May be used in place of any file name, to read a line from the standard input. (There is no prompting).

EXAMPLES

`ls	paste -d" " -`	list directory in one column
`ls	paste - - - -`	list directory in four columns
`paste -s -d"\t\n" file`	combine pairs of lines into lines

SEE ALSO

cut(1), **grep**(1), **pr**(1).

DIAGNOSTICS

`"line too long"`	Output lines are restricted to 511 characters.
`"too many files"`	Except for **-s** option, no more than 12 input files may be specified.

NAME

pg − file perusal filter for CRTs

SYNOPSIS

pg [−*number*] [−p *string*] [−cefnrs] [+*linenumber*] [+/*pattern*/] [*file* ...]

DESCRIPTION

The pg command is a filter that allows the examination of *files* one screenful at a time on a CRT. (If no *file* is specified or if it encounters the file name −, pg reads from standard input.) Each screenful is followed by a prompt. If the user types a carriage return, another page is displayed; other possibilities are listed below.

This command is different from previous paginators in that it allows you to back up and review something that has already passed. The method for doing this is explained below.

To determine terminal attributes, pg scans the terminfo(4) data base for the terminal type specified by the environment variable TERM. If TERM is not defined, the terminal type dumb is assumed.

The command line options are:

−*number*
: An integer specifying the size (in lines) of the window that pg is to use instead of the default. (On a terminal containing 24 lines, the default window size is 23).

−c
: Home the cursor and clear the screen before displaying each page. This option is ignored if clear_screen is not defined for this terminal type in the terminfo(4) data base.

−e
: Causes pg *not* to pause at the end of each file.

−f
: Normally, pg splits lines longer than the screen width, but some sequences of characters in the text being displayed (e.g., escape sequences for underlining) generate undesirable results. The −f option inhibits pg from splitting lines.

−n
: Normally, commands must be terminated by a <*newline*> character. This option causes an automatic end of command as soon as a command letter is entered.

−p *string*
: Causes pg to use *string* as the prompt. If the prompt string contains a %d, the first occurrence of %d' in the prompt will be replaced by the current page number when the prompt is issued. The default prompt string is ":".

−r
: Restricted mode. The shell escape is disallowed. pg will print an error message but does not exit.

−s
: Causes pg to print all messages and prompts in standout mode (usually inverse video).

+*linenumber*
: Start up at *linenumber*.

+/pattern/
: Start up at the first line containing the regular expression pattern.

The responses that may be typed when pg pauses can be divided into three categories: those causing further perusal, those that search, and those that modify the perusal environment.

Commands that cause further perusal normally take a preceding *address*, an optionally signed number indicating the point from which further text should be displayed. This *address* is interpreted in either pages or lines depending on the command. A signed *address* specifies a point relative to the current page or line, and an unsigned *address* specifies an address relative to the beginning of the file. Each command has a default address that is used if none is provided.

The perusal commands and their defaults are as follows:

(+1)*<newline>* or *<blank>*
: This causes one page to be displayed. The address is specified in pages.

(+1) `l` With a relative address this causes pg to simulate scrolling the screen, forward or backward, the number of lines specified. With an absolute address this command prints a screenful beginning at the specified line.

(+1) `d` or `^D`
: Simulates scrolling half a screen forward or backward.

i`f` Skip *i* screens of text.

i`z` Same as *<newline>* except that *i*, if present, becomes the new default number of lines per screenful.

The following perusal commands take no *address*.

`.` or `^L`
: Typing a single period causes the current page of text to be redisplayed.

`$` Displays the last windowful in the file. Use with caution when the input is a pipe.

The following commands are available for searching for text patterns in the text. The regular expressions described in ed(1) are available. They must always be terminated by a *<newline>*, even if the −*n* option is specified.

i/pattern/
: Search forward for the *i*th (default *i*=1) occurrence of *pattern*. Searching begins immediately after the current page and continues to the end of the current file, without wrap-around.

*i^pattern^*
i?pattern?
: Search backwards for the *i*th (default *i*=1) occurrence of *pattern*. Searching begins immediately before the current page and continues to the beginning of the current file, without wrap-around. The ^ notation is useful for Adds 100 terminals which will not properly handle the ?.

After searching, pg will normally display the line found at the top of the screen. This can be modified by appending m or b to the search command to leave the line found in the middle or at the bottom of the window from now on. The suffix t can be used to restore the original situation.

The user of pg can modify the environment of perusal with the following commands:

*i*n Begin perusing the *i*th next file in the command line. The *i* is an unsigned number, default value is 1.

*i*p Begin perusing the *i*th previous file in the command line. *i* is an unsigned number, default is 1.

*i*w Display another window of text. If *i* is present, set the window size to *i*.

s *filename*
Save the input in the named file. Only the current file being perused is saved. The white space between the s and *filename* is optional. This command must always be terminated by a <*newline*>, even if the $-n$ option is specified.

h Help by displaying an abbreviated summary of available commands.

q or Q Quit pg.

!*command*
Command is passed to the shell, whose name is taken from the SHELL environment variable. If this is not available, the default shell is used. This command must always be terminated by a <*newline*>, even if the $-n$ option is specified.

At any time when output is being sent to the terminal, the user can hit the quit key (normally CTRL-\) or the interrupt (break) key. This causes pg to stop sending output, and display the prompt. The user may then enter one of the above commands in the normal manner. Unfortunately, some output is lost when this is done, because any characters waiting in the terminal's output queue are flushed when the quit signal occurs.

If the standard output is not a terminal, then pg acts just like cat(1), except that a header is printed before each file (if there is more than one).

EXAMPLE

The following command line uses pg to read the system news:

```
news | pg -p "(Page %d):"
```

FILES

/usr/share/lib/terminfo/?/*
terminal information database

/tmp/pg* temporary file when input is from a pipe

SEE ALSO

ed(1), grep(1), more(1)
terminfo(4) in the *System Administrator's Reference Manual*.

NOTES

While waiting for terminal input, pg responds to BREAK, DEL, and CTRL-\ by terminating execution. Between prompts, however, these signals interrupt pg's current task and place the user in prompt mode. These should be used with caution when input is being read from a pipe, since an interrupt is likely to terminate the other commands in the pipeline.

The terminal /, ^, or ? may be omitted from the searching commands.

If terminal tabs are not set every eight positions, undesirable results may occur.

When using pg as a filter with another command that changes the terminal I/O options, terminal settings may not be restored correctly.

NAME

pr – print files

SYNOPSIS

pr [[**–***columns*] [**–w***width*] [**–a**]] [**–e***ck*] [**–i***ck*] [**–drtfp**] [**+page**] [**–n***ck*] [**–o***offset*] [**–l***length*] [**–s***separator*] [**–h***header*] [**–F**] [*file* ...]

pr [[**–m**] [**–w***width*]] [**–e***ck*] [**–i***ck*] [**–drtfp**] [**+page**] [**–n***ck*] [**–o***offset*] [**–l***length*] [**–s***separator*] [**–h***header*] [**–F**] [*file1 file2* ...]

DESCRIPTION

The **pr** command formats and prints the contents of a file. If *file* is –, or if no files are specified, **pr** assumes standard input. **pr** prints the named files on standard output.

By default, the listing is separated into pages, each headed by the page number, the date and time that the file was last modified, and the name of the file. Page length is 66 lines which includes 10 lines of header and trailer output. The header is composed of 2 blank lines, 1 line of text (can be altered with **–h**), and 2 blank lines; the trailer is 5 blank lines. For single column output, line width may not be set and is unlimited. For multicolumn output, line width may be set and the default is 72 columns. Diagnostic reports (failed options) are reported at the end of standard output associated with a terminal, rather than interspersed in the output. Pages are separated by series of line feeds rather than form feed characters.

By default, columns are of equal width, separated by at least one space; lines which do not fit are truncated. If the **–s** option is used, lines are not truncated and columns are separated by the *separator* character.

Either –*columns* or **–m** should be used to produce multi-column output. **–a** should only be used with –*columns* and not **–m**.

Command line options are

+page Begin printing with page numbered *page* (default is 1).

–columns Print *columns* columns of output (default is 1). Output appears as if **–e** and **–i** are on for multi-column output. May not use with **–m**.

–a Print multi-column output across the page one line per column. *columns* must be greater than one. If a line is too long to fit in a column, it is truncated.

–m Merge and print all files simultaneously, one per column. The maximum number of files that may be specified is eight. If a line is too long to fit in a column, it is truncated. May not use with –*column*.

–d Double-space the output. Blank lines that result from double-spacing are dropped when they occur at the top of a page.

–e*ck* Expand input tabs to character positions *k*+1, 2**k*+1, 3**k*+1, etc. If *k* is 0 or is omitted, default tab settings at every eighth position are assumed. Tab characters in the input are expanded into the appropriate number of spaces. If *c* (any non-digit character) is given, it is treated as the input tab character (default for *c* is the tab character).

`-ick` In output, replace white space wherever possible by inserting tabs to character positions *k*+1, 2**k*+1, 3**k*+1, etc. If *k* is 0 or is omitted, default tab settings at every eighth position are assumed. If *c* (any non-digit character) is given, it is treated as the output tab character (default for *c* is the tab character).

`-nck` Provide *k*-digit line numbering (default for *k* is 5). The number occupies the first *k*+1 character positions of each column of single column output or each line of `-m` output. If *c* (any non-digit character) is given, it is appended to the line number to separate it from whatever follows (default for *c* is a tab).

`-wwidth` Set the width of a line to *width* character positions (default is 72). This is effective only for multi-column output (*-column* and `-m`). There is no line limit for single column output.

`-ooffset` Offset each line by *offset* character positions (default is 0). The number of character positions per line is the sum of the width and offset.

`-llength` Set the length of a page to *length* lines (default is 66). A *length* of 0 specifies the default length. By default, output contains 5 lines of header and 5 lines of trailer leaving 56 lines for user-supplied text. When `-l`*length* is used and *length* exceeds 10, then *length*−10 lines are left per page for user supplied text. When *length* is 10 or less, header and trailer output is omitted to make room for user supplied text; see the `-t` option.

`-h` *header* Use *header* as the text line of the header to be printed instead of the file name. `-h` is ignored when `-t` is specified or `-l`*length* is specified and the value of *length* is 10 or less. (`-h` is the only `pr` option requiring space between the option and argument.)

`-p` Pause before beginning each page if the output device is a terminal. `pr` rings the terminal bell and waits for a carriage return.

`-f` Use a single form-feed character for new pages (default is to use a sequence of line feeds). Pause before beginning the first page if the standard output is associated with a terminal.

`-r` Print no diagnostic reports on files that cannot be opened.

`-t` Print neither the five-line identifying header nor the five-line trailer normally supplied for each page. Quit printing after the last line of each file without spacing to the end of the page. Use of `-t` overrides the `-h` option.

`-sseparator`
Separate columns by the single character *separator* instead of by the appropriate number of spaces (default for *separator* is a tab). Prevents truncation of lines on multicolumn output unless `-w` is specified.

`-F` Fold the lines of the input file. When used in multi-column mode (with the `-a` or `-m` options) lines will be folded to fit the current column's width, otherwise they will be folded to fit the current line width (80 columns).

EXAMPLES

Print file1 and file2 as a double-spaced, three-column listing headed by "file list":

```
pr -3dh "file list" file1 file2
```

Copy file1 to file2, expanding tabs to columns 10, 19, 28, 37, ... :

```
pr -e9 -t < file1 > file2
```

Print file1 and file2 simultaneously in a two-column listing with no header or trailer where both columns have line numbers:

```
pr -t -n file1 | pr -t -m -n file2 -
```

FILES

/dev/tty* If standard output is directed to one of the special files /dev/tty*, then other output directed to this terminal is delayed until standard output is completed. This prevents error messages from being interspersed throughout the output.

SEE ALSO

cat(1), fold(1), more(1), pg(1), page(1).

NAME

`printf` – print formatted output

SYNOPSIS

`printf` *format* [*arg* ...]

DESCRIPTION

The `printf` command converts, formats, and prints its *arg*s under control of the *format*. It fully supports conversion specifications for strings (`%s` descriptor); however, the results are undefined for the other conversion specifications supported by `printf`(3S).

format a character string that contains three types of objects: 1) plain characters, which are simply copied to the output stream; 2) conversion specifications, each of which results in fetching zero or more *arg*s; and 3) C-language escape sequences, which are translated into the corresponding characters.

arg string(s) to be printed under the control of *format*. The results are undefined if there are insufficient *arg*s for the format. If the format is exhausted while *arg*s remain, the excess *arg*s are simply ignored.

Each conversion specification is introduced by the character `%`. After the `%`, the following appear in sequence:

An optional field, consisting of a decimal digit string followed by a `$`, specifying the next *arg* to be converted. If this field is not provided, the *arg* following the last *arg* converted is used.

An optional decimal digit string specifying a minimum *field width*. If the converted value has fewer characters than the field width, it is padded on the left (or right, if the left-adjustment flag '–' has been given) to the field width. The padding is with blanks unless the field width digit string starts with a zero, in which case the padding is with zeros.

An optional *precision* that gives the maximum number of characters to be printed from a string in `%s` conversion. The precision takes the form of a period (`.`) followed by a decimal digit string; a null digit string is treated as zero (nothing is printed). Padding specified by the precision overrides the padding specified by the field width. That is, if *precision* is specified, its value is used to control the number of characters printed.

A field width or precision or both may be indicated by an asterisk (`*`) instead of a digit string. In this case, an integer *arg* supplies the field width or precision. The *arg* that is actually converted is not fetched until the conversion letter is seen, so the *arg*s specifying field width or precision must appear *before* the *arg* (if any) to be converted. A negative field width argument is taken as a `'–'` (left-adjustment) flag followed by a positive field width. If the precision argument is negative, it is changed to zero (nothing is printed). In no case does a non-existent or small field width cause truncation of a field; if the result of a conversion is wider than the field width, the field is simply expanded to contain the conversion result.

The conversion characters and their meanings are:

`%s` The *arg* is taken to be a string and characters from the string are printed until a null character (\0) is encountered or the number of characters indicated by the precision specification is reached. If the precision is missing, it is taken to be infinite, so all characters up to the first null character are printed. A null value for *arg* yields undefined results.

`%%` Print a `%`; no argument is converted.

EXAMPLES

The command

```
printf '%s %s %s\n' Good Morning World
```

results in the output:

```
Good Morning World
```

The following command produces the same output.

```
printf '%2$s %s %1$s\n' World Good Morning
```

Here is an example that prints the first 6 characters of **$PATH** left-adjusted in a 10-character field:

```
printf 'First 6 chars of %s are %-10.6s.\n' $PATH $PATH
```

If **$PATH** has the value `/usr/bin:/usr/local/bin`, then the above command would print the following output:

```
First 6 chars of /usr/bin:/usr/local/bin are /usr/b .
```

SEE ALSO

`printf`(3S) in the *Programmer's Reference Manual*.

NAME

`priocntl` – process scheduler control

SYNOPSIS

`priocntl -l`
`priocntl -d` [`-i` *idtype*] [*idlist*]
`priocntl -s` [`-c` *class*] [*class-specific options*] [`-i` *idtype*] [*idlist*]
`priocntl -e` [`-c` *class*] [*class-specific options*] *command* [*argument(s)*]

DESCRIPTION

The `priocntl` command displays or sets scheduling parameters of the specified process(es). It can also be used to display the current configuration information for the system's process scheduler or execute a command with specified scheduling parameters.

Processes fall into distinct classes with a separate scheduling policy applied to each class. The two process classes currently supported are the real-time class and the time-sharing class. The characteristics of these two classes and the class-specific options they accept are described below under the headings REAL-TIME CLASS and TIME-SHARING CLASS. With appropriate permissions, the `priocntl` command can change the class and other scheduling parameters associated with a running process.

In the default configuration, a runnable real-time process runs before any other process. Therefore, inappropriate use of real-time processes can have a dramatic negative impact on system performance.

The command

```
priocntl -l
```

displays a list of classes currently configured in the system along with class-specific information about each class. The format of the class-specific information displayed is described under the appropriate heading below.

The `-d` and `-s` options to `priocntl` allow the user to display or set the scheduling parameters associated with a set of processes. The `-i` option and its associated *idtype* argument, together with the *idlist* arguments to `priocntl` (if any), specify one or more processes to which the `priocntl` command is to apply. The interpretation of *idlist* depends on the value of *idtype*. The valid *idtype* arguments and corresponding interpretations of *idlist* are as follows:

`-i` *pid* *idlist* is a list of process *IDs*. The `priocntl` command applies to the specified processes.

`-i` *ppid*
: *idlist* is a list of parent process *IDs*. The `priocntl` command applies to all processes whose parent process *ID* is in the list.

`-i` *pgid*
: *idlist* is a list of process group *IDs*. The `priocntl` command applies to all processes in the specified process groups.

`-i` *sid* *idlist* is a list of session *IDs*. The `priocntl` command applies to all processes in the specified sessions.

`-i` *class*
idlist consists of a single class name (`RT` for real-time or `TS` for time-sharing). The `priocntl` command applies to all processes in the specified class.

`-i` *uid* *idlist* is a list of user *IDs*. The `priocntl` command applies to all processes with an effective user *ID* equal to an *ID* from the list.

`-i` *gid* *idlist* is a list of group *IDs*. The `priocntl` command applies to all processes with an effective group *ID* equal to an *ID* from the list.

`-i` *all* The `priocntl` command applies to all existing processes. No *idlist* should be specified (if one is it is ignored). The permission restrictions described below still apply.

If the `-i` *idtype* option is omitted when using the `-d` or `-s` options the default *idtype* of *pid* is assumed.

If an *idlist* is present it must appear last on the command line and the elements of the list must be separated by white space. If no *idlist* is present an *idtype* argument of *pid, ppid, pgid, sid, class, uid,* or *gid* specifies the process *ID*, parent process *ID*, process group *ID*, session *ID*, class, user *ID*, or group *ID* respectively of the `priocntl` command itself.

The command

`priocntl -d` [`-i` *idtype*] [*idlist*]

displays the class and class-specific scheduling parameters of the process(es) specified by *idtype* and *idlist.*

The command

`priocntl -s` [`-c` *class*] [*class-specific options*] [`-i` *idtype*] [*idlist*]

sets the class and class-specific parameters of the specified processes to the values given on the command line. The `-c` *class* option specifies the class to be set. (The valid *class* arguments are `RT` for real-time or `TS` for time-sharing). The class-specific parameters to be set are specified by the class-specific options as explained under the appropriate heading below. If the `-c` *class* option is omitted, *idtype* and *idlist* must specify a set of processes which are all in the same class, otherwise an error results. If no class-specific options are specified the process's class-specific parameters are set to the default values for the class specified by `-c` *class* (or to the default parameter values for the process's current class if the `-c` *class* option is also omitted).

In order to change the scheduling parameters of a process using `priocntl` the real or effective user *ID* of the user invoking `priocntl` must match the real or effective user *ID* of the receiving process or the effective user *ID* of the user must be super-user. These are the minimum permission requirements enforced for all classes. An individual class may impose additional permissions requirements when setting processes to that class or when setting class-specific scheduling parameters.

When *idtype* and *idlist* specify a set of processes, `priocntl` acts on the processes in the set in an implementation-specific order. If `priocntl` encounters an error for one or more of the target processes, it may or may not continue through the set of processes, depending on the nature of the error. If the error is related to permissions, `priocntl` prints an error message and then continue through the process set, resetting the parameters for all target processes for which the user has appropriate permissions. If `priocntl` encounters an error other than permissions, it does not continue through the process set but prints an error message and exits immediately.

A special **sys** scheduling class exists for the purpose of scheduling the execution of certain special system processes (such as the swapper process). It is not possible to change the class of any process to **sys**. In addition, any processes in the **sys** class that are included in the set of processes specified by *idtype* and *idlist* are disregarded by `priocntl`. For example, if *idtype* were *uid*, an *idlist* consisting of a zero would specify all processes with a *UID* of zero except processes in the **sys** class and (if changing the parameters using the **-s** option) the `init` process.

The `init` process (process *ID* 1) is a special case. In order for the `priocntl` command to change the class or other scheduling parameters of the `init` process, *idtype* must be *pid* and *idlist* must be consist of only a 1. The `init` process may be assigned to any class configured on the system, but the time-sharing class is almost always the appropriate choice. (Other choices may be highly undesirable; see the *Getting Started* for more information.)

The command

`priocntl` **-e** [**-c** *class*] [*class-specific options*] *command* [*argument(s)*]

executes the specified command with the class and scheduling parameters specified on the command line (*arguments* are the arguments to the command). If the **-c** *class* option is omitted the command is run in the user's current class.

REAL-TIME CLASS

The real-time class provides a fixed priority preemptive scheduling policy for those processes requiring fast and deterministic response and absolute user/application control of scheduling priorities. If the real-time class is configured in the system it should have exclusive control of the highest range of scheduling priorities on the system. This ensures that a runnable real-time process is given CPU service before any process belonging to any other class.

The real-time class has a range of real-time priority (*rtpri*) values that may be assigned to processes within the class. Real-time priorities range from 0 to *x*, where the value of *x* is configurable and can be displayed for a specific installation by using the command

```
priocntl -l
```

The real-time scheduling policy is a fixed priority policy. The scheduling priority of a real-time process never changes except as the result of an explicit request by the user/application to change the *rtpri* value of the process.

For processes in the real-time class, the *rtpri* value is, for all practical purposes, equivalent to the scheduling priority of the process. The *rtpri* value completely determines the scheduling priority of a real-time process relative to other processes within its class. Numerically higher *rtpri* values represent higher priorities. Since the real-time class controls the highest range of scheduling priorities in the system it is guaranteed that the runnable real-time process with the highest *rtpri* value is always selected to run before any other process in the system.

In addition to providing control over priority, `priocntl` provides for control over the length of the time quantum allotted to processes in the real-time class. The time quantum value specifies the maximum amount of time a process may run assuming that it does not complete or enter a resource or event wait state (`sleep`). Note that if another process becomes runnable at a higher priority the currently running process may be preempted before receiving its full time quantum.

The command

`priocntl -d` [`-i` *idtype*] [*idlist*]

displays the real-time priority and time quantum (in millisecond resolution) for each real-time process in the set specified by *idtype* and *idlist*.

The valid class-specific options for setting real-time parameters are:

`-p` *rtpri* Set the real-time priority of the specified process(es) to *rtpri*.

`-t` *tqntm* [`-r` *res*] Set the time quantum of the specified process(es) to *tqntm*. You may optionally specify a resolution as explained below.

Any combination of the `-p` and `-t` options may be used with `priocntl -s` or `priocntl -e` for the real-time class. If an option is omitted and the process is currently real-time the associated parameter is unaffected. If an option is omitted when changing the class of a process to real-time from some other class, the associated parameter is set to a default value. The default value for *rtpri* is 0 and the default for time quantum is dependent on the value of *rtpri* and on the system configuration; see `rt_dptbl`(4).

When using the `-t` *tqntm* option you may optionally specify a resolution using the `-r` *res* option. (If no resolution is specified, millisecond resolution is assumed.) If *res* is specified it must be a positive integer between 1 and 1,000,000,000 inclusive and the resolution used is the reciprocal of *res* in seconds. For example, specifying `-t 10 -r 100` would set the resolution to hundredths of a second and the resulting time quantum length would be 10/100 seconds (one tenth of a second). Although very fine (nanosecond) resolution may be specified, the time quantum length is rounded up by the system to the next integral multiple of the system clock's resolution. For example the finest resolution currently available on the 3B2 is 10 milliseconds (1 "tick"). If the `-t` and `-r` options are used to specify a time quantum of 34 milliseconds, it is rounded up to 4 ticks (40 milliseconds) on the 3B2. Requests for time quantums of zero or quantums greater than the (typically very large) implementation-specific maximum quantum result in an error.

In order to change the class of a process to real-time (from any other class) the user invoking `priocntl` must have super-user privileges. In order to change the *rtpri* value or time quantum of a real-time process the user invoking `priocntl` must either be super-user, or must currently be in the real-time class (shell running as a real-time process) with a real or effective user *ID* matching the real or effective user *ID* of the target process.

The real-time priority and time quantum are inherited across the `fork`(2) and `exec`(2) system calls.

Examples

`priocntl -s -c RT -t 1 -r 10 -i` *idtype idlist*

sets the class of any non-real-time processes selected by *idtype* and *idlist* to real-time and sets their real-time priority to the default value of 0. The real-time priorities of any processes currently in the real-time class are unaffected. The time quantums of all of the specified processes are set to 1/10 seconds.

`priocntl -e -c RT -p 15 -t 20` *command*

executes *command* in the real-time class with a real-time priority of 15 and a time quantum of 20 milliseconds.

TIME-SHARING CLASS

The time-sharing scheduling policy provides for a fair and effective allocation of the CPU resource among processes with varying CPU consumption characteristics. The objectives of the time-sharing policy are to provide good response time to interactive processes and good throughput to CPU-bound jobs while providing a degree of user/application control over scheduling.

The time-sharing class has a range of time-sharing user priority (*tsupri*) values that may be assigned to processes within the class. User priorities range from $-x$ to $+x$, where the value of x is configurable. The range for a specific installation can be displayed by using the command

`priocntl -l`

The purpose of the user priority is to provide some degree of user/application control over the scheduling of processes in the time-sharing class. Raising or lowering the *tsupri* value of a process in the time-sharing class raises or lowers the scheduling priority of the process. It is not guaranteed, however, that a time-sharing process with a higher *tsupri* value will run before one with a lower *tsupri* value. This is because the *tsupri* value is just one factor used to determine the scheduling priority of a time-sharing process. The system may dynamically adjust the internal scheduling priority of a time-sharing process based on other factors such as recent CPU usage.

In addition to the system-wide limits on user priority (displayed with `priocntl -l`), there is a per process user priority limit (*tsuprilim*), which specifies the maximum *tsupri* value that may be set for a given process.

The command

`priocntl -d [-i idtype] [idlist]`

displays the user priority and user priority limit for each time-sharing process in the set specified by *idtype* and *idlist*.

The valid class-specific options for setting time-sharing parameters are:

-m *tsuprilim*	Set the user priority limit of the specified process(es) to *tsuprilim*.
-p *tsupri*	Set the user priority of the specified process(es) to *tsupri*.

Any time-sharing process may lower its own *tsuprilim* (or that of another process with the same user *ID*). Only a time-sharing process with super-user privileges may raise a *tsuprilim*. When changing the class of a process to time-sharing from some other class, super-user privileges are required in order to set the initial *tsuprilim* to a value greater than zero.

Any time-sharing process may set its own *tsupri* (or that of another process with the same user *ID*) to any value less than or equal to the process's *tsuprilim*. Attempts to set the *tsupri* above the *tsuprilim* (and/or set the *tsuprilim* below the *tsupri*) result in the *tsupri* being set equal to the *tsuprilim*.

Any combination of the `-l` and `-p` options may be used with `priocntl -s` or `priocntl -e` for the time-sharing class. If an option is omitted and the process is currently time-sharing the associated parameter is normally unaffected. The exception is when the `-p` option is omitted and `-l` is used to set a *tsuprilim* below the current *tsupri*. In this case the *tsupri* is set equal to the *tsuprilim* which is being set. If an option is omitted when changing the class of a process to time-sharing from some other class, the associated parameter is set to a default value. The default value for *tsuprilim* is 0 and the default for *tsupri* is to set it equal to the *tsuprilim* value which is being set.

The time-sharing user priority and user priority limit are inherited across the `fork`(2) and `exec`(2) system calls.

Examples

`priocntl -s -c TS -i idtype idlist`

sets the class of any non-time-sharing processes selected by *idtype* and *idlist* to time-sharing and sets both their user priority limit and user priority to 0. Processes already in the time-sharing class are unaffected.

`priocntl -e -c TS -l 0 -p -15 command [arguments]`

executes *command* with the arguments *arguments* in the time-sharing class with a user priority limit of 0 and a user priority of −15.

SEE ALSO

`ps`(1), `nice`(1), `priocntl`(2), rt_dptbl(4).

DIAGNOSTICS

`priocntl` prints the following error messages:

`Process(es) not found:` None of the specified processes exists.

`Specified processes from different classes`: The **-s** option is being used to set parameters, the **-c** *class* option is not present, and processes from more than one class are specified.

`Invalid option or argument`: An unrecognized or invalid option or option argument is used.

NAME

ps – report process status

SYNOPSIS

ps [*options*]

DESCRIPTION

ps prints information about active processes. Without *options*, ps prints information about processes associated with the controlling terminal. The output contains only the process ID, terminal identifier, cumulative execution time, and the command name. Otherwise, the information that is displayed is controlled by the *options*.

Some options accept lists as arguments. Items in a list can be either separated by commas or else enclosed in double quotes and separated by commas or spaces. Values for *proclist* and *grplist* must be numeric.

The *options* are:

- `-e` Print information about every process now running.
- `-d` Print information about all processes except session leaders.
- `-a` Print information about all processes most frequently requested: all those except process group leaders and processes not associated with a terminal.
- `-j` Print session ID and process group ID.
- `-f` Generate a `full` listing. (See below for significance of columns in a full listing.)
- `-l` Generate a `long` listing. (See below.)
- `-c` Print information in a format that reflects scheduler properties as described in `priocntl`(1). The `-c` option affects the output of the `-f` and `-l` options, as described below.
- `-t` *termlist* List only process data associated with the terminal given in *termlist*. Terminal identifiers may be specified in one of two forms: the device's file name (e.g., `tty04`) or, if the device's file name starts with `tty`, just the digit identifier (e.g., `04`).
- `-p` *proclist* List only process data whose process ID numbers are given in *proclist*.
- `-u` *uidlist* List only process data whose user ID number or login name is given in *uidlist*. In the listing, the numerical user ID will be printed unless you give the `-f` option, which prints the login name.
- `-g` *grplist* List only process data whose group leader's ID number(s) appears in *grplist*. (A group leader is a process whose process ID number is identical to its process group ID number.
- `-s` *sesslist* List information on all session leaders whose IDs appear in *sesslist*.

Under the `-f` option, ps tries to determine the command name and arguments given when the process was created by examining the user block. Failing this, the command name is printed, as it would have appeared without the `-f` option, in square brackets.

The column headings and the meaning of the columns in a `ps` listing are given below; the letters `f` and `l` indicate the option (`full` or `long`, respectively) that causes the corresponding heading to appear; `all` means that the heading always appears. Note that these two options determine only what information is provided for a process; they do not determine which processes will be listed.

`F` (l) Flags (hexadecimal and additive) associated with the process

00	Process has terminated: process table entry now available.
01	A system process: always in primary memory.
02	Parent is tracing process.
04	Tracing parent's signal has stopped process: parent is waiting [`ptrace`(2)].
08	Process is currently in primary memory.
10	Process currently in primary memory: locked until an event completes.

`S` (l) The state of the process:

O	Process is running on a processor.
S	Sleeping: process is waiting for an event to complete.
R	Runnable: process is on run queue.
I	Idle: process is being created.
Z	Zombie state: process terminated and parent not waiting.
T	Traced: process stopped by a signal because parent is tracing it.
X	SXBRK state: process is waiting for more primary memory.

`UID` (f,l) The user ID number of the process owner (the login name is printed under the `-f` option).

`PID` (all) The process ID of the process (this datum is necessary in order to kill a process).

`PPID` (f,l) The process ID of the parent process.

`C` (f,l) Processor utilization for scheduling. Not printed when the `-c` option is used.

`CLS` (f,l) Scheduling class. Printed only when the `-c` option is used.

`PRI` (l) The priority of the process. Without the `-c` option, higher numbers mean lower priority. With the `-c` option, higher numbers mean higher priority.

`NI` (l) Nice value, used in priority computation. Not printed when the `-c` option is used. Only processes in the time-sharing class have a nice value.

`ADDR` (l) The memory address of the process.

`SZ`	(l)	The size (in pages or clicks) of the swappable process's image in main memory.
`WCHAN`	(l)	The address of an event for which the process is sleeping, or in SXBRK state, (if blank, the process is running).
`STIME`	(f)	The starting time of the process, given in hours, minutes, and seconds. (A process begun more than twenty-four hours before the **ps** inquiry is executed is given in months and days.)
`TTY`	(all)	The controlling terminal for the process (the message, `?`, is printed when there is no controlling terminal).
`TIME`	(all)	The cumulative execution time for the process.
`COMMAND`	(all)	The command name (the full command name and its arguments are printed under the `-f` option).

A process that has exited and has a parent, but has not yet been waited for by the parent, is marked `<defunct>`.

FILES

`/dev`	
`/dev/sxt/*`	
`/dev/tty*`	
`/dev/xt/*`	terminal ("tty") names searcher files
`/dev/kmem`	kernel virtual memory
`/dev/swap`	the default swap device
`/dev/mem`	memory
`/etc/passwd`	UID information supplier
`/etc/ps_data`	internal data structure

SEE ALSO

`kill`(1), `nice`(1), `priocntl`(1).
`getty`(1M) in the *System Administrator's Reference Manual.*

NOTES

Things can change while **ps** is running; the snap-shot it gives is true only for a split-second, and it may not be accurate by the time you see it. Some data printed for defunct processes is irrelevant.

If no *termlist, proclist, uidlist,* or *grplist* is specified, **ps** checks `stdin`, `stdout`, and `stderr` in that order, looking for the controlling terminal and will attempt to report on processes associated with the controlling terminal. In this situation, if `stdin`, `stdout`, and `stderr` are all redirected, **ps** will not find a controlling terminal, so there will be no report.

On a heavily loaded system, **ps** may report an `lseek` error and exit. **ps** may seek to an invalid user area address: having obtained the address of a process' user area, **ps** may not be able to seek to that address before the process exits and the address becomes invalid.

`ps -ef` may not report the actual start of a tty login session, but rather an earlier time, when a getty was last respawned on the tty line.

NAME

pwd – working directory name

SYNOPSIS

pwd

DESCRIPTION

pwd prints the path name of the working (current) directory.

SEE ALSO

cd(1).

DIAGNOSTICS

"Cannot open .." and "Read error in .." indicate possible file system trouble and should be referred to a UNIX system administrator.

NOTES

If you move the current directory or one above it, **pwd** may not give the correct response. Use the cd(1) command with a full path name to correct this situation.

NAME

`rcp` – remote file copy

SYNOPSIS

`rcp` [`-p`] *filename1 filename2*
`rcp` [`-pr`] *filename...directory*

DESCRIPTION

The `rcp` command copies files between machines. Each *filename* or *directory* argument is either a remote file name of the form:

hostname:path

or a local file name (containing no : characters, or a / before any : characters).

If a *filename* is not a full path name, it is interpreted relative to your home directory on *hostname*. A *path* on a remote host may be quoted (using \, ", or ') so that the metacharacters are interpreted remotely.

`rcp` does not prompt for passwords; your current local user name must exist on *hostname* and allow remote command execution by **rsh**(1).

`rcp` handles third party copies, where neither source nor target files are on the current machine. Hostnames may also take the form

username@hostname:filename

to use *username* rather than your current local user name as the user name on the remote host. `rcp` also supports Internet domain addressing of the remote host, so that:

username@host.domain:filename

specifies the username to be used, the hostname, and the domain in which that host resides. Filenames that are not full path names will be interpreted relative to the home directory of the user named *username*, on the remote host.

The destination hostname may also take the form *hostname.username:filename* to support destination machines that are running older versions of `rcp`.

The following options are available:

`-p` Attempt to give each copy the same modification times, access times, and modes as the original file.

`-r` Copy each subtree rooted at *filename*; in this case the destination must be a directory.

FILES

`$HOME/.profile`

SEE ALSO

`ftp`(1), `rlogin`(1), `rsh`(1), `hosts.equiv`(4).

NOTES

`rcp` is meant to copy between different hosts; attempting to `rcp` a file onto itself, as with:

```
rcp tmp/file myhost:/tmp/file
```

results in a severely corrupted file.

`rcp` does not detect all cases where the target of a copy might be a file in cases where only a directory should be legal.

`rcp` can become confused by output generated by commands in a `$HOME/.profile` on the remote host.

`rcp` requires that the source host have permission to execute commands on the remote host when doing third-party copies.

If you forget to quote metacharacters intended for the remote host you get an incomprehensible error message.

NAME

relogin – rename login entry to show current layer

SYNOPSIS

/usr/lib/layersys/relogin [-s] [*line*]

DESCRIPTION

The relogin command changes the terminal *line* field of a user's utmp entry to the name of the windowing terminal layer attached to standard input. write messages sent to this user are directed to this layer. In addition, the who command will show the user associated with this layer. relogin may only be invoked under layers.

relogin is invoked automatically by layers to set the utmp entry to the terminal line of the first layer created upon startup, and to reset the utmp entry to the real line on termination. It may be invoked by a user to designate a different layer to receive write messages.

-s Suppress error messages.

line Specifies which utmp entry to change. The utmp file is searched for an entry with the specified *line* field. That field is changed to the line associated with the standard input. (To learn what lines are associated with a given user, say jdoe, type ps -f -u jdoe and note the values shown in the TTY field [see ps(1)]).

FILES

/var/adm/utmp database of users versus terminals

SEE ALSO

layers(1), mesg(1), ps(1), who(1), write(1), in the *User's Reference Manual*.
utmp(4).

DIAGNOSTICS

Returns 0 upon successful completion, 1 otherwise.

NOTES

relogin will fail, if *line* does not belong to the user issuing the relogin command or standard input is not associated with a terminal.

NAME

`rlogin` – remote login

SYNOPSIS

`rlogin` [`-L`] [`-8`] [`-e` *c*] [`-l` *username*] *hostname*

DESCRIPTION

`rlogin` establishes a remote login session from your terminal to the remote machine named *hostname*.

Hostnames are listed in the *hosts* database, which may be contained in the `/etc/hosts` file, the Internet domain name server, or in both. Each host has one official name (the first name in the database entry), and optionally one or more nicknames. Either official hostnames or nicknames may be specified in *hostname*.

Each remote machine may have a file named `/etc/hosts.equiv` containing a list of trusted hostnames with which it shares usernames. Users with the same username on both the local and remote machine may `rlogin` from the machines listed in the remote machine's `/etc/hosts.equiv` file without supplying a password. Individual users may set up a similar private equivalence list with the file `.rhosts` in their home directories. Each line in this file contains two names: a *hostname* and a *username* separated by a space. An entry in a remote user's `.rhosts` file permits the user named *username* who is logged into *hostname* to log in to the remote machine as the remote user without supplying a password. If the name of the local host is not found in the `/etc/hosts.equiv` file on the remote machine, and the local username and hostname are not found in the remote user's `.rhosts` file, then the remote machine will prompt for a password. Hostnames listed in `/etc/hosts.equiv` and `.rhosts` files must be the official hostnames listed in the hosts database; nicknames may not be used in either of these files.

To counter security problems, the `.rhosts` file must be owned by either the remote user or by root.

The remote terminal type is the same as your local terminal type (as given in your environment TERM variable). The terminal or window size is also copied to the remote system if the server supports the option, and changes in size are reflected as well. All echoing takes place at the remote site, so that (except for delays) the remote login is transparent. Flow control using CTRL–S and CTRL–Q and flushing of input and output on interrupts are handled properly.

The following options are available:

`-L` Allow the `rlogin` session to be run in litout mode.

`-8` Pass eight-bit data across the net instead of seven-bit data.

`-e` *c* Specify a different escape character, *c*, for the line used to disconnect from the remote host.

`-l` *username*
Specify a different *username* for the remote login. If you do not use this option, the remote username used is the same as your local username.

Escape Sequences

Lines that you type which start with the tilde character are escape sequences (the escape character can be changed using the **-e** options):

~. Disconnect from the remote host — this is not the same as a logout, because the local host breaks the connection with no warning to the remote end.

susp Suspend the login session (only if you are using a shell with Job Control). **susp** is your suspend character, usually see **tty**(1).

FILES

/etc/passwd	
/usr/hosts/*	for *hostname* version of the command
/etc/hosts.equiv	list of trusted hostnames with shared usernames
$HOME/.rhosts	private list of trusted hostname/username combinations

SEE ALSO

rsh(1), **stty**(1), **tty**(1), **named**(1M), **hosts**(4), **hosts.equiv**(4).

NOTES

When a system is listed in **hosts.equiv**, its security must be as good as local security. One insecure system listed in **hosts.equiv** can compromise the security of the entire system.

If you use a windowing terminal and you intend to run **layers**(1) on the remote system, then you must invoke **rlogin** with the **-8** option.

This implementation can only use the TCP network service.

NAME

`rm`, `rmdir` – remove files or directories

SYNOPSIS

`rm` [`-f`] [`-i`] *file* ...

`rm -r` [`-f`] [`-i`] `dirname` ... [*file* ...]

`rmdir` [`-p`] [`-s`] `dirname` ...

DESCRIPTION

`rm` removes the entries for one or more files from a directory. If a file has no write permission and the standard input is a terminal, the full set of permissions (in octal) for the file are printed followed by a question mark. This is a prompt for confirmation. If the answer begins with `y` (for yes), the file is deleted, otherwise the file remains.

If *file* is a symbolic link, the link will be removed, but the file or directory to which it refers will not be deleted. A user does not need write permission on a symbolic link to remove it, provided they have write permissions in the directory.

Note that if the standard input is not a terminal, the command will operate as if the `-f` option is in effect.

Three options apply to `rm`:

`-f` This option causes the removal of all files (whether write-protected or not) in a directory without prompting the user. In a write-protected directory, however, files are never removed (whatever their permissions are), but no messages are displayed. If the removal of a write-protected directory is attempted, this option will not suppress an error message.

`-r` This option causes the recursive removal of any directories and subdirectories in the argument list. The directory will be emptied of files and removed. Note that the user is normally prompted for removal of any write-protected files which the directory contains. The write-protected files are removed without prompting, however, if the `-f` option is used, or if the standard input is not a terminal and the `-i` option is not used.

Symbolic links that are encountered with this option will not be traversed.

If the removal of a non-empty, write-protected directory is attempted, the command will always fail (even if the `-f` option is used), resulting in an error message.

`-i` With this option, confirmation of removal of any write-protected file occurs interactively. It overrides the `-f` option and remains in effect even if the standard input is not a terminal.

Two options apply to `rmdir`:

`-p` This option allows users to remove the directory *dirname* and its parent directories which become empty. A message is printed on standard output about whether the whole path is removed or part of the path remains for some reason.

-s This option is used to suppress the message printed on standard error when **-p** is in effect.

DIAGNOSTICS

All messages are generally self-explanatory.

It is forbidden to remove the files "." and ".." in order to avoid the consequences of inadvertently doing something like the following:

```
rm -r .*
```

Both `rm` and `rmdir` return exit codes of 0 if all the specified directories are removed successfully. Otherwise, they return a non-zero exit code.

SEE ALSO

`unlink`(2), `rmdir`(2) in the *Programmer's Reference Manual*.

NOTES

A -- permits the user to mark explicitly the end of any command line options, allowing `rm` to recognize filename arguments that begin with a -. As an aid to BSD migration, `rm` will accept - as a synonym for --. This migration aid may disappear in a future release. If a -- and a - both appear on the same command line, the second will be interpreted as a filename.

NAME

rsh – remote shell

SYNOPSIS

rsh [-n] [-l *username*] *hostname command*

rsh *hostname* [-n] [-l *username*] *command*

hostname [-n] [-l *username*] *command*

DESCRIPTION

rsh connects to the specified *hostname* and executes the specified *command*. rsh copies its standard input to the remote command, the standard output of the remote command to its standard output, and the standard error of the remote command to its standard error. Interrupt, quit and terminate signals are propagated to the remote command; rsh normally terminates when the remote command does.

If you omit *command*, instead of executing a single command, rsh logs you in on the remote host using rlogin(1). Shell metacharacters which are not quoted are interpreted on the local machine, while quoted metacharacters are interpreted on the remote machine. See EXAMPLES.

Hostnames are given in the *hosts* database, which may be contained in the /etc/hosts file, the Internet domain name database, or both. Each host has one official name (the first name in the database entry) and optionally one or more nicknames. Official hostnames or nicknames may be given as *hostname*.

If the name of the file from which rsh is executed is anything other than rsh, rsh takes this name as its *hostname* argument. This allows you to create a symbolic link to rsh in the name of a host which, when executed, will invoke a remote shell on that host. By creating a directory and populating it wih symbolic links in the names of commonly used hosts, then including the directory in your shell's search path, you can run rsh by typing *hostname* to your shell.

Each remote machine may have a file named /etc/hosts.equiv containing a list of trusted hostnames with which it shares usernames. Users with the same username on both the local and remote machine may rsh from the machines listed in the remote machine's /etc/hosts file. Individual users may set up a similar private equivalence list with the file .rhosts in their home directories. Each line in this file contains two names: a *hostname* and a *username* separated by a space. The entry permits the user named *username* who is logged into *hostname* to use rsh to access the remote machine as the remote user. If the name of the local host is not found in the /etc/hosts.equiv file on the remote machine, and the local username and hostname are not found in the remote user's .rhosts file, then the access is denied. The hostnames listed in the /etc/hosts.equiv and .rhosts files must be the official hostnames listed in the hosts database; nicknames may not be used in either of these files.

rsh will not prompt for a password if access is denied on the remote machine unless the *command* argument is omitted.

OPTIONS

`-l` *username*
: Use *username* as the remote username instead of your local username. In the absence of this option, the remote username is the same as your local username.

`-n`
: Redirect the input of `rsh` to `/dev/null`. You sometimes need this option to avoid unfortunate interactions between `rsh` and the shell which invokes it. For example, if you are running `rsh` and invoke a `rsh` in the background without redirecting its input away from the terminal, it will block even if no reads are posted by the remote command. The -n option will prevent this.

The type of remote shell (`sh`, `rsh`, or other) is determined by the user's entry in the file `/etc/passwd` on the remote system.

EXAMPLES

The command:

```
rsh lizard cat lizard.file >> example.file
```

appends the remote file `lizard.file` from the machine called "lizard" to the file called `example.file` on the local machine, while the command:

```
rsh lizard cat lizard.file ">>" lizard.file2
```

appends the file `lizard.file` on the machine called "lizard" to the file `lizard.file2` which also resides on the machine called "lizard."

FILES

`/etc/hosts`
`/etc/passwd`

SEE ALSO

`rlogin`(1), `vi`(1), `named`(1M), `hosts`(4), `hosts.equiv`(4).

NOTES

When a system is listed in `hosts.equiv`, its security must be as good as local security. One insecure system listed in `hosts.equiv` can compromise the security of the entire system.

You cannot run an interactive command [such as `vi`(1)]; use `rlogin` if you wish to do so.

Stop signals stop the local `rsh` process only; this is arguably wrong, but currently hard to fix for reasons too complicated to explain here.

The current local environment is not passed to the remote shell.

Sometimes the `-n` option is needed for reasons that are less than obvious. For example, the command:

```
rsh somehost dd if=/dev/nrmt0 bs=20b | tar xvpBf -
```

will put your shell into a strange state. Evidently, what happens is that the `tar` terminates before the `rsh`. The `rsh` then tries to write into the "broken pipe" and, instead of terminating neatly, proceeds to compete with your shell for its standard input. Invoking `rsh` with the -n option avoids such incidents.

This bug occurs only when `rsh` is at the beginning of a pipeline and is not reading standard input. Do not use the `-n` if `rsh` actually needs to read standard input. For example,

```
tar cf - . | rsh sundial dd of=/dev/rmt0 obs=20b
```

does not produce the bug. If you were to use the `-n` in a case like this, `rsh` would incorrectly read from `/dev/null` instead of from the pipe.

NAME

ruptime – show host status of local machines

SYNOPSIS

ruptime [**-alrtu**]

DESCRIPTION

ruptime gives a status line like **uptime** for each machine on the local network; these are formed from packets broadcast by each host on the network once a minute.

Machines for which no status report has been received for 5 minutes are shown as being down.

Normally, the listing is sorted by host name, but this order can be changed by specifying one of the options listed below.

The following options are available:

- **-a** Count even those users who have been idle for an hour or more.
- **-l** Sort the display by load average.
- **-r** Reverse the sorting order.
- **-t** Sort the display by up time.
- **-u** Sort the display by number of users.

FILES

`/var/spool/rwho/whod.*` data files

SEE ALSO

rwho(1), **rwhod**(1M).

NAME

rwho – who's logged in on local machines

SYNOPSIS

rwho [-a]

DESCRIPTION

The rwho command produces output similar to who(1), but for all machines on your network. If no report has been received from a machine for 5 minutes, rwho assumes the machine is down, and does not report users last known to be logged into that machine.

If a user has not typed to the system for a minute or more, rwho reports this idle time. If a user has not typed to the system for an hour or more, the user is omitted from the output of rwho unless the -a flag is given.

The -a option reports all users whether or not they have typed to the system in the past hour.

FILES

/var/spool/rwho/whod.* information about other machines

SEE ALSO

finger(1), ruptime(1), who(1), rwhod(1M).

NOTES

Does not work through gateways.

This is unwieldy when the number of machines on the local net is large.

The rwho service daemon, rwhod(1M), must be enabled for this command to return useful results.

NAME

sag – system activity graph

SYNOPSIS

sag [options]

DESCRIPTION

sag graphically displays the system activity data stored in a binary data file by a previous **sar**(1) run. Any of the **sar** data items may be plotted singly, or in combination; as cross plots, or versus time. Simple arithmetic combinations of data may be specified. **sag** invokes **sar** and finds the desired data by string-matching the data column header (run **sar** to see what is available). These *options* are passed through to **sar**:

–s *time* Select data later than *time* in the form hh[:mm]. Default is 08:00.

–e *time* Select data up to *time*. Default is 18:00.

–i *sec* Select data at intervals as close as possible to *sec* seconds.

–f *file* Use *file* as the data source for **sar**. Default is the current daily data file **/usr/adm/sa/sa***dd*.

Other *options*:

–T *term* Produce output suitable for terminal *term*. See **tplot**(1G) for known terminals. Default for *term* is **$TERM**.

–x *spec* x axis specification with *spec* in the form:
"name[op name]...[lo hi]"

–y *spec* y axis specification with *spec* in the same form as above.

Name is either a string that will match a column header in the **sar** report, with an optional device name in square brackets, e.g., **r+w/s[dsk-1]**, or an integer value. *Op* is + – * or / surrounded by blanks. Up to five names may be specified. Parentheses are not recognized. Contrary to custom, + and – have precedence over * and /". Evaluation is left to right. Thus A / A + B * 100 is evaluated (A/(A+B))*100, and A + B / C + D is (A+B)/(C+D). *Lo* and *hi* are optional numeric scale limits. If unspecified, they are deduced from the data.

A single *spec* is permitted for the x axis. If unspecified, *time* is used. Up to 5 *spec*'s separated by ; may be given for –**y**. Enclose the –**x** and –**y** arguments in " " if they include whitespace. The –**y** default is:

```
-y "%usr 0 100; %usr + %sys 0 100; %usr + %sys + %wio 0 100"
```

EXAMPLES

To see today's CPU utilization:

```
sag
```

To see activity over 15 minutes of all disk drives:

```
TS=date +%H:%M
sar -o tempfile 60 15
TE=date +%H:%M
sag -f tempfile -s $TS -e $TE -y "r+w/s[dsk]"
```

FILES

`/usr/adm/sa/sa`*dd* daily data file for day *dd*.

SEE ALSO

`sar`(1).

NAME

sar − system activity reporter

SYNOPSIS

sar [−ubdycwaqvmpgrkxDSAC] [−o *file*] *t* [*n*]

sar [−ubdycwaqvmpgrkxDSAC] [−s *time*] [−e *time*] [−i *sec*] [−f *file*]

DESCRIPTION

sar in the first instance, samples cumulative activity counters in the operating system at *n* intervals of *t* seconds, where *t* should be 5 or greater. If *t* is specified with more than one option, all headers are printed together and the output may be difficult to read. (If the sampling interval is less than 5, the activity of sar itself may affect the sample.) If the −o option is specified, it saves the samples in *file* in binary format. The default value of *n* is 1. In the second instance, with no sampling interval specified, **sar** extracts data from a previously recorded *file*, either the one specified by the −f option or, by default, the standard system activity daily data file /var/adm/sa/sa*dd* for the current day *dd*. The starting and ending times of the report can be bounded via the −s and −e *time* arguments of the form *hh*[:*mm*[:*ss*]]. The −i option selects records at *sec* second intervals. Otherwise, all intervals found in the data file are reported.

In either case, subsets of data to be printed are specified by option:

−u Report CPU utilization (the default):
%usr, %sys, %wio, %idle − portion of time running in user mode, running in system mode, idle with some process waiting for block I/O, and otherwise idle. When used with −D, %sys is split into percent of time servicing requests from remote machines (%sys remote) and all other system time (%sys local). If you are using a 3B2 Computer with a co-processor the CPU utilization (default) report will contain the following fields:
%usr, %sys, %idle, scall/s − where scalls/s is the number of system calls, of all types, encountered on the co-processor per second.

−b Report buffer activity:
bread/s, bwrit/s − transfers per second of data between system buffers and disk or other block devices;
lread/s, lwrit/s − accesses of system buffers;
%rcache, %wcache − cache hit ratios, i. e., (1−bread/lread) as a percentage;
pread/s, pwrit/s − transfers via raw (physical) device mechanism. When used with −D, buffer caching is reported for locally-mounted remote resources.

−d Report activity for each block device, e. g., disk or tape drive, with the exception of XDC disks and tape drives. When data is displayed, the device specification *dsk-* is generally used to represent a disk drive. The device specification used to represent a tape drive is machine dependent. The activity data reported is:
%busy, avque − portion of time device was busy servicing a transfer request, average number of requests outstanding during that time;
r+w/s, blks/s − number of data transfers from or to device, number of bytes transferred in 512-byte units;

avwait, avserv – average time in ms. that transfer requests wait idly on queue, and average time to be serviced (which for disks includes seek, rotational latency and data transfer times).

–y Report TTY device activity:
rawch/s, canch/s, outch/s – input character rate, input character rate processed by canon, output character rate;
rcvin/s, xmtin/s, mdmin/s – receive, transmit and modem interrupt rates.

–c Report system calls:
scall/s – system calls of all types;
sread/s, swrit/s, fork/s, exec/s – specific system calls;
rchar/s, wchar/s – characters transferred by read and write system calls. When used with –D, the system calls are split into incoming, outgoing, and strictly local calls. No incoming or outgoing fork and exec calls are reported.

–w Report system swapping and switching activity:
swpin/s, swpot/s, bswin/s, bswot/s – number of transfers and number of 512-byte units transferred for swapins and swapouts (including initial loading of some programs);
pswch/s – process switches.

–a Report use of file access system routines:
iget/s, namei/s, dirblk/s.

–q Report average queue length while occupied, and % of time occupied:
runq-sz, %runocc – run queue of processes in memory and runnable;
swpq-sz, %swpocc – these are no longer reported by sar.

–v Report status of process, i-node, file tables:
proc-sz, inod-sz, file-sz, lock-sz – entries/size for each table, evaluated once at sampling point;
ov – overflows that occur between sampling points for each table.

–m Report message and semaphore activities:
msg/s, sema/s – primitives per second.

–p Report paging activities:
atch/s – page faults per second that are satisfied by reclaiming a page currently in memory (attaches per second);
pgin/s – page-in requests per second;
ppgin/s – pages paged-in per second;
pflt/s – page faults from protection errors per second (illegal access to page) or "copy-on-writes";
vflt/s – address translation page faults per second (valid page not in memory);
slock/s – faults per second caused by software lock requests requiring physical I/O.

–g Report paging activities:
pgout/s – page-out requests per second;
ppgout/s – pages paged-out per second;
pgfree/s – pages per second placed on the free list by the page stealing daemon;

pgscan/s – pages per second scanned by the page stealing daemon.
%s5ipf – the percentage of S5 inodes taken off the freelist by iget which had reusable pages associated with it. These pages are flushed and cannot be reclaimed by processes. Thus this is the percentage of igets with page flushes.

–r Report unused memory pages and disk blocks:
freemem – average pages available to user processes;
freeswap – disk blocks available for page swapping.

–k Report kernel memory allocation (KMA) activities:
sml_mem, alloc, fail – information about the memory pool reserving and allocating space for small requests: the amount of memory in bytes KMA has for the small pool, the number of bytes allocated to satisfy requests for small amounts of memory, and the number of requests for small amounts of memory that were not satisfied (failed);
lg_mem, alloc, fail – information for the large memory pool (analogous to the information for the small memory pool);
ovsz_alloc, fail – the amount of memory allocated for oversize requests and the number of oversize requests which could not be satisfied (because oversized memory is allocated dynamically, there is not a pool).

–x Report remote file sharing (RFS) operations:
open/s, create/s, lookup/s, readdir/s, getpage/s, putpage/s, other/s – The number of open, create, lookup, readdir, getpage, putpage, and other operations made per second by clients (incoming) and by the server (outgoing).

–D Report Remote File Sharing activity:
When used in combination with –u, –b or –c, it causes sar to produce the remote file sharing version of the corresponding report. –Du is assumed when only –D is specified.

–S Report server and request queue status:
serv/lo-hi – average number of Remote File Sharing servers on the system (lo and hi are the minimum and maximum number of servers respectively.)
request %busy – % of time receive descriptors are on the request queue
request avg lgth – average number of receive descriptors waiting for service when queue is occupied
server %avail – % of time there are idle servers
server avg avail – average number of idle servers when idle ones exist

–A Report all data. Equivalent to –udqbwcayvmpgrkxSDC.

–C Report Remote File Sharing data caching overhead:
snd-inv/s – number of invalidation messages per second sent by your machine as a server.
snd-msg/s – total outgoing RFS messages sent per second.
rcv-inv/s – number of invalidation messages received from the remote server.
rcv-msg/s – total number of incoming RFS messages received per second.
dis-bread/s – number of read messages that would be eligible for caching if caching had not been turned off because of an invalidation message. (Indicates the penalty incurred because of the invalidation message.)

blk-inv/s – number of pages removed from the client cache in response to cache invalidation messages.

EXAMPLES

To see today's CPU activity so far:

```
sar
```

To watch CPU activity evolve for 10 minutes and save data:

```
sar -o temp 60 10
```

To later review disk and tape activity from that period:

```
sar -d -f temp
```

FILES

`/var/adm/sa/sa`*dd* daily data file, where *dd* are digits representing the day of the month.

SEE ALSO

sag(1G), sar(1M).

NAME

`script` – make typescript of a terminal session

SYNOPSIS

`script` [**-a**] [*filename*]

DESCRIPTION

`script` makes a typescript of everything printed on your terminal. The typescript is written to *filename*, or appended to *filename* if the **-a** option is given. If no file name is given, the typescript is saved in the file **`typescript`**.

The script ends when the forked shell exits or when ctrl-D is typed.

NOTES

`script` places *everything* that appears on the screen in the log file, including prompts.

NAME

`sdiff` – print file differences side-by-side

SYNOPSIS

`sdiff` [*options*] *file1 file2*

DESCRIPTION

`sdiff` uses the output of the `diff` command to produce a side-by-side listing of two files indicating lines that are different. Lines of the two files are printed with a blank gutter between them if the lines are identical, a < in the gutter if the line appears only in *file1*, a > in the gutter if the line appears only in *file2*, and a | for lines that are different. For example:

```
x   |   y
a       a
b   <
c   <
d       d
    >   c
```

Valid options are:

`-w` *n* Use the argument *n* as the width of the output line. The default line length is 130 characters.

`-l` Print only the left side of any lines that are identical.

`-s` Do not print identical lines.

`-o` *output* Use the argument *output* as the name of a third file that is created as a user-controlled merge of *file1* and *file2*. Identical lines of *file1* and *file2* are copied to *output*. Sets of differences, as produced by `diff`, are printed; where a set of differences share a common gutter character. After printing each set of differences, `sdiff` prompts the user with a `%` and waits for one of the following user-typed commands:

`l` Append the left column to the output file.
`r` Append the right column to the output file.
`s` Turn on silent mode; do not print identical lines.
`v` Turn off silent mode.
`e l` Call the editor with the left column.
`e r` Call the editor with the right column.
`e b` Call the editor with the concatenation of left and right.
`e` Call the editor with a zero length file.
`q` Exit from the program.

On exit from the editor, the resulting file is concatenated to the end of the *output* file.

SEE ALSO

`diff`(1), `ed`(1).

NAME

sed – stream editor

SYNOPSIS

sed [–n] [**–e** *script*] [**–f** *sfile*] [*file* ...]

DESCRIPTION

sed copies the named *file* (standard input default) to the standard output, edited according to a script of commands. The **–f** option causes the script to be taken from file *sfile*; these options accumulate. If there is just one **–e** option and no **–f** options, the flag **–e** may be omitted. The **–n** option suppresses the default output. A script consists of editing commands, one per line, of the following form:

[*address* [, *address*]] *function* [*arguments*]

In normal operation, **sed** cyclically copies a line of input into a *pattern space* (unless there is something left after a D command), applies in sequence all commands whose *addresses* select that pattern space, and at the end of the script copies the pattern space to the standard output (except under –n) and deletes the pattern space.

Some of the commands use a *hold space* to save all or part of the *pattern space* for subsequent retrieval.

An *address* is either a decimal number that counts input lines cumulatively across files, a **$** that addresses the last line of input, or a context address, i.e., a */regular expression/* in the style of ed(1) modified thus:

In a context address, the construction \?*regular expression*?, where ? is any character, is identical to */regular expression/*. Note that in the context address **\xabc\xdefx**, the second **x** stands for itself, so that the regular expression is **abcxdef**.

The escape sequence \n matches a new-line *embedded* in the pattern space.

A period (.) matches any character except the *terminal* new-line of the pattern space.

A command line with no addresses selects every pattern space.

A command line with one address selects each pattern space that matches the address.

A command line with two addresses selects the inclusive range from the first pattern space that matches the first address through the next pattern space that matches the second address. (If the second address is a number less than or equal to the line number selected by the first address, only the line corresponding to the first address is selected.) Thereafter the process is repeated, looking again for the first address.

Editing commands can be applied only to non-selected pattern spaces by use of the negation function ! (below).

In the following list of functions the maximum number of permissible addresses for each function is indicated in parentheses.

The *text* argument consists of one or more lines, all but the last of which end with \ to hide the new-line. Backslashes in text are treated like backslashes in the replacement string of an **s** command, and may be used to protect initial blanks and tabs against the stripping that is done on every script line. The *rfile* or *wfile* argument must terminate the command line and must be preceded by exactly one blank. Each *wfile* is created before processing begins. There can be at most 10 distinct *wfile* arguments.

(1) `a\`
text Append. Place *text* on the output before reading the next input line.

(2) `b` *label* Branch to the : command bearing the *label*. If *label* is empty, branch to the end of the script.

(2) `c\`
text Change. Delete the pattern space. Place *text* on the output. Start the next cycle.

(2) `d` Delete the pattern space. Start the next cycle.

(2) `D` Delete the initial segment of the pattern space through the first new-line. Start the next cycle.

(2) `g` Replace the contents of the pattern space by the contents of the hold space.

(2) `G` Append the contents of the hold space to the pattern space.

(2) `h` Replace the contents of the hold space by the contents of the pattern space.

(2) `H` Append the contents of the pattern space to the hold space.

(1) `i\`
text Insert. Place *text* on the standard output.

(2) `l` List the pattern space on the standard output in an unambiguous form. Non-printable characters are displayed in octal notation and long lines are folded.

(2) `n` Copy the pattern space to the standard output. Replace the pattern space with the next line of input.

(2) `N` Append the next line of input to the pattern space with an embedded new-line. (The current line number changes.)

(2) `p` Print. Copy the pattern space to the standard output.

(2) `P` Copy the initial segment of the pattern space through the first new-line to the standard output.

(1) `q` Quit. Branch to the end of the script. Do not start a new cycle.

(2) `r` *rfile* Read the contents of *rfile*. Place them on the output before reading the next input line.

(2) `s/`*regular expression*`/`*replacement*`/`*flags*
Substitute the *replacement* string for instances of the *regular expression* in the pattern space. Any character may be used instead of /. For a fuller description see ed(1). *flags* is zero or more of:

- *n* — *n*= 1 - 512. Substitute for just the *n*th occurrence of the *regular expression*.
- g — Global. Substitute for all nonoverlapping instances of the *regular expression* rather than just the first one.
- p — Print the pattern space if a replacement was made.
- w *wfile* — Write. Append the pattern space to *wfile* if a replacement was made.

(2) t *label* Test. Branch to the : command bearing the *label* if any substitutions have been made since the most recent reading of an input line or execution of a t. If *label* is empty, branch to the end of the script.

(2) w *wfile* Write. Append the pattern space to *wfile*. The first occurrence of w will cause *wfile* to be cleared. Subsequent invocations of w will append. Each time the sed command is used, *wfile* is overwritten.

(2) x Exchange the contents of the pattern and hold spaces.

(2) y/*string1*/*string2*/
Transform. Replace all occurrences of characters in *string1* with the corresponding characters in *string2*. *string1* and *string2* must have the same number of characters.

(2) ! *function*
Don't. Apply the *function* (or group, if *function* is { }) only to lines *not* selected by the address(es).

(0) : *label* This command does nothing; it bears a *label* for b and t commands to branch to.

(1) = Place the current line number on the standard output as a line.

(2) { Execute the following commands through a matching } only when the pattern space is selected.

(0) An empty command is ignored.

(0) # If a # appears as the first character on a line of a script file, then that entire line is treated as a comment, with one exception: if a # appears on the first line and the character after the # is an n, then the default output will be suppressed. The rest of the line after #n is also ignored. A script file must contain at least one non-comment line.

SEE ALSO

awk(1), ed(1), grep(1).

NAME

sh, jsh, rsh – shell, the standard, job control, and restricted command interpreter

SYNOPSIS

sh [-acefhiknprstuvx] [*args*]
jsh [-acefhiknprstuvx] [*args*]
/usr/lib/rsh [-acefhiknprstuvx] [*args*]

DESCRIPTION

sh is a command programming language that executes commands read from a terminal or a file. The command jsh is an interface to the shell which provides all of the functionality of sh and enables Job Control (see "Job Control," below). /usr/lib/rsh is a restricted version of the standard command interpreter sh; It is used to restrict logins to execution environments whose capabilities are more controlled than those of the standard shell. See "Invocation," below for the meaning of arguments to the shell.

Definitions

A *blank* is a tab or a space. A *name* is a sequence of ASCII letters, digits, or underscores, beginning with a letter or an underscore. A *parameter* is a name, a digit, or any of the characters *, @, #, ?, –, $, and !.

Commands

A *simple-command* is a sequence of non-blank *words* separated by *blanks*. The first *word* specifies the name of the command to be executed. Except as specified below, the remaining *words* are passed as arguments to the invoked command. The command name is passed as argument 0 [see exec(2)]. The *value* of a *simple-command* is its exit status if it terminates normally, or (octal) 200+*status* if it terminates abnormally; see signal(5) for a list of status values.

A *pipeline* is a sequence of one or more *commands* separated by |. The standard output of each *command* but the last is connected by a pipe(2) to the standard input of the next *command*. Each *command* is run as a separate process; the shell waits for the last *command* to terminate. The exit status of a *pipeline* is the exit status of the last command in the *pipeline*.

A *list* is a sequence of one or more *pipelines* separated by ;, &, &&, or ||, and optionally terminated by ; or &. Of these four symbols, ; and & have equal precedence, which is lower than that of && and ||. The symbols && and || also have equal precedence. A semicolon (;) causes sequential execution of the preceding *pipeline* (i.e., the shell waits for the *pipeline* to finish before executing any commands following the semicolon); an ampersand (&) causes asynchronous execution of the preceding pipeline (i.e., the shell does *not* wait for that pipeline to finish). The symbol && (||) causes the *list* following it to be executed only if the preceding pipeline returns a zero (non-zero) exit status. An arbitrary number of new-lines may appear in a *list*, instead of semicolons, to delimit commands.

A *command* is either a *simple-command* or one of the following. Unless otherwise stated, the value returned by a command is that of the last *simple-command* executed in the command.

`for` *name* [`in` *word* ...] do *list* done
: Each time a `for` command is executed, *name* is set to the next *word* taken from the `in` *word* list. If `in` *word* ... is omitted, then the `for` command executes the `do` *list* once for each positional parameter that is set (see "Parameter Substitution," below). Execution ends when there are no more words in the list.

`case` *word* `in` [*pattern* [| *pattern*] ...) *list* ;;] ... **esac**
: A **case** command executes the *list* associated with the first *pattern* that matches *word*. The form of the patterns is the same as that used for file-name generation (see "File Name Generation") except that a slash, a leading dot, or a dot immediately following a slash need not be matched explicitly.

`if` *list* **then** *list* [**elif** *list* **then** *list*] ... [**else** *list*] **fi**
: The *list* following **if** is executed and, if it returns a zero exit status, the *list* following the first **then** is executed. Otherwise, the *list* following **elif** is executed and, if its value is zero, the *list* following the next **then** is executed. Failing that, the **else** *list* is executed. If no **else** *list* or **then** *list* is executed, then the `if` command returns a zero exit status.

while *list* do *list* done
: A **while** command repeatedly executes the **while** *list* and, if the exit status of the last command in the list is zero, executes the do *list*; otherwise the loop terminates. If no commands in the do *list* are executed, then the **while** command returns a zero exit status; `until` may be used in place of **while** to negate the loop termination test.

(*list*)
: Execute *list* in a sub-shell.

{ *list*; }
: *list* is executed in the current (that is, parent) shell. The { must be followed by a space.

name () { *list*; }
: Define a function which is referenced by *name*. The body of the function is the *list* of commands between { and }. The { must be followed by a space. Execution of functions is described below (see "Execution"). The { and } are unnecessary if the body of the function is a *command* as defined above, under "Commands."

The following words are only recognized as the first word of a command and when not quoted:

`if then else elif fi case esac for while until do done { }`

Comments

A word beginning with # causes that word and all the following characters up to a new-line to be ignored.

Command Substitution

The shell reads commands from the string between two grave accents (\` \`) and the standard output from these commands may be used as all or part of a word. Trailing new-lines from the standard output are removed.

No interpretation is done on the string before the string is read, except to remove backslashes (\) used to escape other characters. Backslashes may be used to escape a grave accent (\`) or another backslash (\) and are removed before the command string is read. Escaping grave accents allows nested command substitution. If the command substitution lies within a pair of double quotes (" ...\` ...\` ... "), a backslash used to escape a double quote (\") will be removed; otherwise, it will be left intact.

If a backslash is used to escape a new-line character (\new-line), both the backslash and the new-line are removed (see the later section on "Quoting"). In addition, backslashes used to escape dollar signs (\$) are removed. Since no parameter substitution is done on the command string before it is read, inserting a backslash to escape a dollar sign has no effect. Backslashes that precede characters other than \, \` , ", new-line, and $ are left intact when the command string is read.

Parameter Substitution

The character $ is used to introduce substitutable *parameters*. There are two types of parameters, positional and keyword. If *parameter* is a digit, it is a positional parameter. Positional parameters may be assigned values by set. Keyword parameters (also known as variables) may be assigned values by writing:

name=value [*name=value*] ...

Pattern-matching is not performed on *value*. There cannot be a function and a variable with the same *name*.

${*parameter*}
: The value, if any, of the parameter is substituted. The braces are required only when *parameter* is followed by a letter, digit, or underscore that is not to be interpreted as part of its name. If *parameter* is * or @, all the positional parameters, starting with $1, are substituted (separated by spaces). Parameter $0 is set from argument zero when the shell is invoked.

${*parameter*:-*word*}
: If *parameter* is set and is non-null, substitute its value; otherwise substitute *word*.

${*parameter*:=*word*}
: If *parameter* is not set or is null set it to *word*; the value of the parameter is substituted. Positional parameters may not be assigned in this way.

${*parameter*:?*word*}
: If *parameter* is set and is non-null, substitute its value; otherwise, print *word* and exit from the shell. If *word* is omitted, the message "parameter null or not set" is printed.

${*parameter*:+*word*}
: If *parameter* is set and is non-null, substitute *word*; otherwise substitute nothing.

In the above, *word* is not evaluated unless it is to be used as the substituted string, so that, in the following example, `pwd` is executed only if `d` is not set or is null:

```
echo ${d:-`pwd`}
```

If the colon (:) is omitted from the above expressions, the shell only checks whether *parameter* is set or not.

The following parameters are automatically set by the shell.

- `#` The number of positional parameters in decimal.
- `-` Flags supplied to the shell on invocation or by the `set` command.
- `?` The decimal value returned by the last synchronously executed command.
- `$` The process number of this shell.
- `!` The process number of the last background command invoked.

The following parameters are used by the shell. The parameters in this section are also referred to as environment variables.

HOME
: The default argument (home directory) for the `cd` command, set to the user's login directory by `login`(1) from the password file [see `passwd`(4)].

PATH The search path for commands (see "Execution," below). The user may not change *PATH* if executing under `/usr/lib/rsh`.

CDPATH
: The search path for the `cd` command.

MAIL If this parameter is set to the name of a mail file *and* the *MAILPATH* parameter is not set, the shell informs the user of the arrival of mail in the specified file.

MAILCHECK
: This parameter specifies how often (in seconds) the shell will check for the arrival of mail in the files specified by the *MAILPATH* or *MAIL* parameters. The default value is `600` seconds (10 minutes). If set to `0`, the shell will check before each prompt.

MAILPATH
: A colon (`:`) separated list of file names. If this parameter is set, the shell informs the user of the arrival of mail in any of the specified files. Each file name can be followed by `%` and a message that will be printed when the modification time changes. The default message is `you have mail`.

PS1 Primary prompt string, by default "`$ `".

PS2 Secondary prompt string, by default "`> `".

IFS Internal field separators, normally `space`, `tab`, and `new-line` (see "Blank Interpretation"). The user can modify `IFS` to allow additional field separators, but space, tab and new-line are always included in the list of field separators.

LANG If this parameter is set, the shell will use it to determine the current locale; see `environ`(5), `setlocale`(3C).

SHACCT
If this parameter is set to the name of a file writable by the user, the shell will write an accounting record in the file for each shell procedure executed.

SHELL
When the shell is invoked, it scans the environment (see "Environment," below) for this name. If it is found and `rsh` is the file name part of its value, the shell becomes a restricted shell.

The shell gives default values to *PATH, PS1, PS2, MAILCHECK,* and *IFS*. *HOME* and *MAIL* are set by `login`(1).

Blank Interpretation

After parameter and command substitution, the results of substitution are scanned for internal field separator characters (those found in *IFS*) and split into distinct arguments where such characters are found. Explicit null arguments ("" or ´´) are retained. Implicit null arguments (those resulting from *parameters* that have no values) are removed.

Input/Output

A command's input and output may be redirected using a special notation interpreted by the shell. The following may appear anywhere in a *simple-command* or may precede or follow a *command* and are *not* passed on as arguments to the invoked command. Note that parameter and command substitution occurs before *word* or *digit* is used.

<*word* Use file *word* as standard input (file descriptor 0).

>*word* Use file *word* as standard output (file descriptor 1). If the file does not exist, it is created; otherwise, it is truncated to zero length.

>>*word* Use file *word* as standard output. If the file exists, output is appended to it (by first seeking to the end-of-file); otherwise, the file is created.

<<[–]*word* After parameter and command substitution is done on *word*, the shell input is read up to the first line that literally matches the resulting *word*, or to an end-of-file. If, however, – is appended to <<:

1) leading tabs are stripped from *word* before the shell input is read (but after parameter and command substitution is done on *word*),
2) leading tabs are stripped from the shell input as it is read and before each line is compared with *word*, and
3) shell input is read up to the first line that literally matches the resulting *word*, or to an end-of-file.

If any character of *word* is quoted (see "Quoting," later), no additional processing is done to the shell input. If no characters of *word* are quoted:

1) parameter and command substitution occurs,
2) (escaped) `\new-lines` are removed, and
3) \ must be used to quote the characters \, $, and `.

The resulting document becomes the standard input.

<&*digit* Use the file associated with file descriptor *digit* as standard input. Similarly for the standard output using >&*digit*.

<&− The standard input is closed. Similarly for the standard output using >&−.

If any of the above is preceded by a digit, the file descriptor which will be associated with the file is that specified by the digit (instead of the default 0 or 1). For example:

```
... 2>&1
```

associates file descriptor 2 with the file currently associated with file descriptor 1.

The order in which redirections are specified is significant. The shell evaluates redirections left-to-right. For example:

```
... 1>xxx 2>&1
```

first associates file descriptor 1 with file *xxx*. It associates file descriptor 2 with the file associated with file descriptor 1 (i.e., *xxx*). If the order of redirections were reversed, file descriptor 2 would be associated with the terminal (assuming file descriptor 1 had been) and file descriptor 1 would be associated with file *xxx*.

Using the terminology introduced on the first page, under "Commands," if a *command* is composed of several *simple commands*, redirection will be evaluated for the entire *command* before it is evaluated for each *simple command*. That is, the shell evaluates redirection for the entire *list*, then each *pipeline* within the *list*, then each *command* within each *pipeline*, then each *list* within each *command*.

If a command is followed by & the default standard input for the command is the empty file `/dev/null`. Otherwise, the environment for the execution of a command contains the file descriptors of the invoking shell as modified by input/output specifications.

Redirection of output is not allowed in the restricted shell.

File Name Generation

Before a command is executed, each command *word* is scanned for the characters *, ?, and [. If one of these characters appears the word is regarded as a *pattern*. The word is replaced with alphabetically sorted file names that match the pattern. If no file name is found that matches the pattern, the word is left unchanged. The character . at the start of a file name or immediately following a /, as well as the character / itself, must be matched explicitly.

* Matches any string, including the null string.

? Matches any single character.

[...] Matches any one of the enclosed characters. A pair of characters separated by − matches any character lexically between the pair, inclusive. If the first character following the opening [is a !, any character not enclosed is matched.

Note that all quoted characters (see below) must be matched explicitly in a filename.

Quoting

The following characters have a special meaning to the shell and cause termination of a word unless quoted:

; & ( ) | ^ < > new-line space tab

A character may be *quoted* (i.e., made to stand for itself) by preceding it with a backslash (\) or inserting it between a pair of quote marks (' ' or ""). During processing, the shell may quote certain characters to prevent them from taking on a special meaning. Backslashes used to quote a single character are removed from the word before the command is executed. The pair \new-line is removed from a word before command and parameter substitution.

All characters enclosed between a pair of single quote marks (' '), except a single quote, are quoted by the shell. Backslash has no special meaning inside a pair of single quotes. A single quote may be quoted inside a pair of double quote marks (for example, " ' "), but a single quote can not be quoted inside a pair of single quotes.

Inside a pair of double quote marks (""), parameter and command substitution occurs and the shell quotes the results to avoid blank interpretation and file name generation. If $* is within a pair of double quotes, the positional parameters are substituted and quoted, separated by quoted spaces ("$1 $2 ..."); however, if $@ is within a pair of double quotes, the positional parameters are substituted and quoted, separated by unquoted spaces ("$1" "$2" ...). \ quotes the characters \, ` , ", and $. The pair \new-line is removed before parameter and command substitution. If a backslash precedes characters other than \, ` , ", $, and new-line, then the backslash itself is quoted by the shell.

Prompting

When used interactively, the shell prompts with the value of PS1 before reading a command. If at any time a new-line is typed and further input is needed to complete a command, the secondary prompt (i.e., the value of PS2) is issued.

Environment

The *environment* [see environ(5)] is a list of name-value pairs that is passed to an executed program in the same way as a normal argument list. The shell interacts with the environment in several ways. On invocation, the shell scans the environment and creates a parameter for each name found, giving it the corresponding value. If the user modifies the value of any of these parameters or creates new parameters, none of these affects the environment unless the export command is used to bind the shell's parameter to the environment (see also set -a). A parameter may be removed from the environment with the unset command. The environment seen by any executed command is thus composed of any unmodified name-value pairs originally inherited by the shell, minus any pairs removed by unset, plus any modifications or additions, all of which must be noted in export commands.

The environment for any *simple-command* may be augmented by prefixing it with one or more assignments to parameters. Thus:

```
TERM=450 cmd                              and
(export TERM; TERM=450; cmd)
```

are equivalent as far as the execution of *cmd* is concerned if *cmd* is not a Special Command. If *cmd* is a Special Command, then

```
TERM=450 cmd
```

will modify the TERM variable in the current shell.

If the -k flag is set, *all* keyword arguments are placed in the environment, even if they occur after the command name. The following first prints a=b c and c:

```
echo a=b c
set -k
echo a=b c
```

Signals

The INTERRUPT and QUIT signals for an invoked command are ignored if the command is followed by &; otherwise signals have the values inherited by the shell from its parent, with the exception of signal 11 (but see also the trap command below).

Execution

Each time a command is executed, the command substitution, parameter substitution, blank interpretation, input/output redirection, and filename generation listed above are carried out. If the command name matches the name of a defined function, the function is executed in the shell process (note how this differs from the execution of shell procedures). If the command name does not match the name of a defined function, but matches one of the *Special Commands* listed below, it is executed in the shell process. The positional parameters $1, $2, ... are set to the arguments of the function. If the command name matches neither a *Special Command* nor the name of a defined function, a new process is created and an attempt is made to execute the command via exec(2).

The shell parameter *PATH* defines the search path for the directory containing the command. Alternative directory names are separated by a colon (:). The default path is /usr/bin. The current directory is specified by a null path name, which can appear immediately after the equal sign, between two colon delimiters anywhere in the path list, or at the end of the path list. If the command name contains a / the search path is not used; such commands will not be executed by the restricted shell. Otherwise, each directory in the path is searched for an executable file. If the file has execute permission but is not an a.out file, it is assumed to be a file containing shell commands. A sub-shell is spawned to read it. A parenthesized command is also executed in a sub-shell.

The location in the search path where a command was found is remembered by the shell (to help avoid unnecessary *execs* later). If the command was found in a relative directory, its location must be re-determined whenever the current directory changes. The shell forgets all remembered locations whenever the *PATH* variable is changed or the hash -r command is executed (see below).

Special Commands

Input/output redirection is now permitted for these commands. File descriptor 1 is the default output location. When Job Control is enabled, additional *Special Commands* are added to the shell's environment (see "Job Control").

: No effect; the command does nothing. A zero exit code is returned.

. *file* Read and execute commands from *file* and return. The search path specified by *PATH* is used to find the directory containing *file*.

`break` [*n*]
: Exit from the enclosing `for` or `while` loop, if any. If *n* is specified, break *n* levels.

`continue` [*n*]
: Resume the next iteration of the enclosing `for` or `while` loop. If *n* is specified, resume at the *n*-th enclosing loop.

`cd` [*arg*]
: Change the current directory to *arg*. The shell parameter *HOME* is the default *arg*. The shell parameter *CDPATH* defines the search path for the directory containing *arg*. Alternative directory names are separated by a colon (:). The default path is `<null>` (specifying the current directory). Note that the current directory is specified by a null path name, which can appear immediately after the equal sign or between the colon delimiters anywhere else in the path list. If *arg* begins with a / the search path is not used. Otherwise, each directory in the path is searched for *arg*. The `cd` command may not be executed by `/usr/lib/rsh`.

`echo` [*arg* ...]
: Echo arguments. See echo(1) for usage and description.

`eval` [*arg* ...]
: The arguments are read as input to the shell and the resulting command(s) executed.

`exec` [*arg* ...]
: The command specified by the arguments is executed in place of this shell without creating a new process. Input/output arguments may appear and, if no other arguments are given, cause the shell input/output to be modified.

`exit` [*n*]
: Causes a shell to exit with the exit status specified by *n*. If *n* is omitted the exit status is that of the last command executed (an end-of-file will also cause the shell to exit.)

`export` [*name* ...]
: The given *names* are marked for automatic export to the *environment* of subsequently executed commands. If no arguments are given, variable names that have been marked for export during the current shell's execution are listed. (Variable names exported from a parent shell are listed only if they have been exported again during the current shell's execution.) Function names are *not* exported.

`getopts`
Use in shell scripts to support command syntax standards [see `intro`(1)]; it parses positional parameters and checks for legal options. See `getopts`(1) for usage and description.

`hash` [`-r`] [*name* ...]
For each *name*, the location in the search path of the command specified by *name* is determined and remembered by the shell. The `-r` option causes the shell to forget all remembered locations. If no arguments are given, information about remembered commands is presented. *Hits* is the number of times a command has been invoked by the shell process. *Cost* is a measure of the work required to locate a command in the search path. If a command is found in a "relative" directory in the search path, after changing to that directory, the stored location of that command is recalculated. Commands for which this will be done are indicated by an asterisk (*) adjacent to the *hits* information. *Cost* will be incremented when the recalculation is done.

`newgrp` [*arg*]
Equivalent to `exec newgrp` *arg*. See `newgrp`(1M) for usage and description.

`pwd` Print the current working directory. See `pwd`(1) for usage and description.

`read` *name* ...
One line is read from the standard input and, using the internal field separator, `IFS` (normally space or tab), to delimit word boundaries, the first word is assigned to the first *name*, the second word to the second *name*, etc., with leftover words assigned to the last *name*. Lines can be continued using `\new-line`. Characters other than `new-line` can be quoted by preceding them with a backslash. These backslashes are removed before words are assigned to *names*, and no interpretation is done on the character that follows the backslash. The return code is 0, unless an end-of-file is encountered.

`readonly` [*name* ...]
The given *names* are marked *readonly* and the values of the these *names* may not be changed by subsequent assignment. If no arguments are given, a list of all *readonly* names is printed.

`return` [*n*]
Causes a function to exit with the return value specified by *n*. If *n* is omitted, the return status is that of the last command executed.

`set` [`--aefhkntuvx` [*arg* ...]]

- `-a` Mark variables which are modified or created for export.
- `-e` Exit immediately if a command exits with a non-zero exit status.
- `-f` Disable file name generation
- `-h` Locate and remember function commands as functions are defined (function commands are normally located when the function is executed).

-k All keyword arguments are placed in the environment for a command, not just those that precede the command name.

-n Read commands but do not execute them.

-t Exit after reading and executing one command.

-u Treat unset variables as an error when substituting.

-v Print shell input lines as they are read.

-x Print commands and their arguments as they are executed.

-- Do not change any of the flags; useful in setting `$1` to -.

Using + rather than - causes these flags to be turned off. These flags can also be used upon invocation of the shell. The current set of flags may be found in `$-`. The remaining arguments are positional parameters and are assigned, in order, to `$1`, `$2`, ... If no arguments are given the values of all names are printed.

`shift` [*n*]

The positional parameters from `$`*n*`+1` ... are renamed `$1` .... If *n* is not given, it is assumed to be 1.

`test`

Evaluate conditional expressions. See `test`(1) for usage and description.

`times`

Print the accumulated user and system times for processes run from the shell.

`trap` [*arg*] [*n*] ...

The command *arg* is to be read and executed when the shell receives numeric or symbolic signal(s) (*n*). (Note that *arg* is scanned once when the trap is set and once when the trap is taken.) Trap commands are executed in order of signal number or corresponding symbolic names. Any attempt to set a trap on a signal that was ignored on entry to the current shell is ineffective. An attempt to trap on signal 11 (memory fault) produces an error. If *arg* is absent all trap(s) *n* are reset to their original values. If *arg* is the null string this signal is ignored by the shell and by the commands it invokes. If *n* is 0 the command *arg* is executed on exit from the shell. The `trap` command with no arguments prints a list of commands associated with each signal number.

`type` [*name* ...]

For each *name*, indicate how it would be interpreted if used as a command name.

`ulimit` [-[HS][a | cdfnstv]]

`ulimit` [-[HS][c | d | f | n | s | t | v]] *limit*

`ulimit` prints or sets hard or soft resource limits. These limits are described in `getrlimit`(2).

If *limit* is not present, `ulimit` prints the specified limits. Any number of limits may be printed at one time. The `-a` option prints all limits.

If *limit* is present, `ulimit` sets the specified limit to *limit*. The string `unlimited` requests the largest valid limit. Limits may be set for only one resource at a time. Any user may set a soft limit to any value below the hard limit. Any user may lower a hard limit. Only a super-user may raise a hard limit; see `su`(1).

The `-H` option specifies a hard limit. The `-S` option specifies a soft limit. If neither option is specified, `ulimit` will set both limits and print the soft limit.

The following options specify the resource whose limits are to be printed or set. If no option is specified, the file size limit is printed or set.

- `-c` maximum core file size (in 512-byte blocks)
- `-d` maximum size of data segment or heap (in kbytes)
- `-f` maximum file size (in 512-byte blocks)
- `-n` maximum file descriptor plus 1
- `-s` maximum size of stack segment (in kbytes)
- `-t` maximum CPU time (in seconds)
- `-v` maximum size of virtual memory (in kbytes)

`umask` [*nnn*]
The user file-creation mask is set to *nnn* [see `umask`(1)]. If *nnn* is omitted, the current value of the mask is printed.

`unset` [*name* ...]
For each *name*, remove the corresponding variable or function value. The variables *PATH, PS1, PS2, MAILCHECK,* and *IFS* cannot be unset.

`wait` [*n*]
Wait for your background process whose process id is *n* and report its termination status. If *n* is omitted, all your shell's currently active background processes are waited for and the return code will be zero.

Invocation

If the shell is invoked through `exec`(2) and the first character of argument zero is -, commands are initially read from `/etc/profile` and from `$HOME/.profile`, if such files exist. Thereafter, commands are read as described below, which is also the case when the shell is invoked as `/usr/bin/sh`. The flags below are interpreted by the shell on invocation only. Note that unless the `-c` or `-s` flag is specified, the first argument is assumed to be the name of a file containing commands, and the remaining arguments are passed as positional parameters to that command file:

`-c` *string* If the `-c` flag is present commands are read from *string*.

`-i` If the `-i` flag is present or if the shell input and output are attached to a terminal, this shell is *interactive*. In this case TERMINATE is ignored (so that `kill 0` does not kill an interactive shell) and INTERRUPT is caught and ignored (so that `wait` is interruptible). In all cases, QUIT is ignored by the shell.

- `-p` If the `-p` flag is present, the shell will not set the effective user and group *IDs* to the real user and group *IDs*.
- `-r` If the `-r` flag is present the shell is a restricted shell.
- `-s` If the `-s` flag is present or if no arguments remain, commands are read from the standard input. Any remaining arguments specify the positional parameters. Shell output (except for *Special Commands*) is written to file descriptor 2.

The remaining flags and arguments are described under the `set` command above.

Job Control (jsh)

When the shell is invoked as `jsh`, Job Control is enabled in addition to all of the functionality described previously for `sh`. Typically Job Control is enabled for the interactive shell only. Non-interactive shells typically do not benefit from the added functionality of Job Control.

With Job Control enabled every command or pipeline the user enters at the terminal is called a *job*. All jobs exist in one of the following states: foreground, background or stopped. These terms are defined as follows: 1) a job in the foreground has read and write access to the controlling terminal; 2) a job in the background is denied read access and has conditional write access to the controlling terminal [see `stty`(1)]; 3) a stopped job is a job that has been placed in a suspended state, usually as a result of a `SIGTSTP` signal [see `signal`(5)].

Every job that the shell starts is assigned a positive integer, called a *job number* which is tracked by the shell and will be used as an identifier to indicate a specific job. Additionally the shell keeps track of the *current* and *previous* jobs. The *current job* is the most recent job to be started or restarted. The *previous job* is the first non-current job.

The acceptable syntax for a Job Identifier is of the form:

`%`*jobid*

where, *jobid* may be specified in any of the following formats:

- `%` or `+` for the current job
- `–` for the previous job
- `?`<*string*> specify the job for which the command line uniquely contains *string*.
- *n* for job number *n*, where *n* is a job number
- *pref* where *pref* is a unique prefix of the command name (for example, if the command `ls -l foo` were running in the background, it could be referred to as `%ls`); *pref* cannot contain blanks unless it is quoted.

When Job Control is enabled, the following commands are added to the user's environment to manipulate jobs:

`bg` [`%`*jobid* ...]

Resumes the execution of a stopped job in the background. If `%`*jobid* is omitted the current job is assumed.

`fg` [`%`*jobid* ...]

Resumes the execution of a stopped job in the foreground, also moves an executing background job into the foreground. If `%`*jobid* is omitted the current job is assumed.

`jobs` [`-p`|`-l`] [`%`*jobid* ...]

`jobs -x` *command* [*arguments*]

Reports all jobs that are stopped or executing in the background. If `%`*jobid* is omitted, all jobs that are stopped or running in the background will be reported. The following options will modify/enhance the output of `jobs`:

- `-l` Report the process group *ID* and working directory of the jobs.
- `-p` Report only the process group *ID* of the jobs.
- `-x` Replace any *jobid* found in *command* or *arguments* with the corresponding process group *ID*, and then execute *command* passing it *arguments*.

`kill` [`-signal`] `%`*jobid*

Builtin version of `kill` to provide the functionality of the `kill` command for processes identified with a *jobid*.

`stop %`*jobid* ...

Stops the execution of a background job(s).

`suspend`

Stops the execution of the current shell (but not if it is the login shell).

`wait` [`%`*jobid* ...]

`wait` builtin accepts a job identifier. If `%`*jobid* is omitted `wait` behaves as described above under `Special Commands`.

Restricted Shell (/usr/lib/rsh) Only

`/usr/lib/rsh` is used to set up login names and execution environments whose capabilities are more controlled than those of the standard shell. The actions of `/usr/lib/rsh` are identical to those of sh, except that the following are disallowed:

changing directory [see cd(1)],
setting the value of *$PATH*,
specifying path or command names containing /,
redirecting output (> and >>).

The restrictions above are enforced after `.profile` is interpreted.

A restricted shell can be invoked in one of the following ways: (1) `/usr/lib/rsh` is the last entry in the `/etc/passwd` file [see passwd(4)]; (2) the environment variable `SHELL` exists and `/usr/lib/rsh` is its value; (3) the shell is invoked and `/usr/lib/rsh` is argument 0; (4) the shell is invoke with the `-r` option.

When a command to be executed is found to be a shell procedure, /usr/lib/rsh invokes sh to execute it. Thus, it is possible to provide to the end-user shell procedures that have access to the full power of the standard shell, while imposing a limited menu of commands; this scheme assumes that the end-user does not have write and execute permissions in the same directory.

The net effect of these rules is that the writer of the .profile [see profile(4)] has complete control over user actions by performing guaranteed setup actions and leaving the user in an appropriate directory (probably *not* the login directory).

The system administrator often sets up a directory of commands (i.e., /usr/rbin) that can be safely invoked by a restricted shell. Some systems also provide a restricted editor, red.

EXIT STATUS

Errors detected by the shell, such as syntax errors, cause the shell to return a non-zero exit status. If the shell is being used non-interactively execution of the shell file is abandoned. Otherwise, the shell returns the exit status of the last command executed (see also the exit command above).

jsh Only

If the shell is invoked as jsh and an attempt is made to exit the shell while there are stopped jobs, the shell issues one warning:

```
There are stopped jobs.
```

This is the only message. If another exit attempt is made, and there are still stopped jobs they will be sent a SIGHUP signal from the kernel and the shell is exited.

FILES

/etc/profile
$HOME/.profile
/tmp/sh*
/dev/null

SEE ALSO

cd(1), echo(1), getopts(1), intro(1), login(1), pwd(1), stty(1), test(1), umask(1), wait(1).
dup(2), exec(2), fork(2), getrlimit(2), pipe(2), ulimit(2), setlocale(3C) in the *Programmer's Reference Manual.*
newgrp(1M), profile(4), environ(5), signal(5) in the *System Administrator's Reference Manual.*

NOTES

Words used for filenames in input/output redirection are not interpreted for filename generation (see "File Name Generation," above). For example, cat file1 >a* will create a file named a*.

Because commands in pipelines are run as separate processes, variables set in a pipeline have no effect on the parent shell.

If you get the error message `cannot fork, too many processes` , try using the `wait`(1) command to clean up your background processes. If this doesn't help, the system process table is probably full or you have too many active foreground processes. (There is a limit to the number of process ids associated with your login, and to the number the system can keep track of.)

Only the last process in a pipeline can be waited for.

If a command is executed, and a command with the same name is installed in a directory in the search path before the directory where the original command was found, the shell will continue to **exec** the original command. Use the **hash** command to correct this situation.

NAME

shl – shell layer manager

SYNOPSIS

shl

DESCRIPTION

shl allows a user to interact with more than one shell from a single terminal. The user controls these shells, known as **layers**, using the commands described below.

The *current layer* is the layer which can receive input from the keyboard. Other layers attempting to read from the keyboard are blocked. Output from multiple layers is multiplexed onto the terminal. To have the output of a layer blocked when it is not current, the **stty** option **loblk** may be set within the layer.

The **stty** character **swtch** (set to ^Z if NUL) is used to switch control to **shl** from a layer. **shl** has its own prompt, >>>, to help distinguish it from a layer.

A *layer* is a shell which has been bound to a virtual tty device (/dev/sxt???). The virtual device can be manipulated like a real tty device using stty(1) and ioctl(2). Each layer has its own process group id.

Definitions

A *name* is a sequence of characters delimited by a blank, tab or new-line. Only the first eight characters are significant. The *names* (1) through (7) cannot be used when creating a layer. They are used by **shl** when no name is supplied. They may be abbreviated to just the digit.

Commands

The following commands may be issued from the **shl** prompt level. Any unique prefix is accepted.

create [*name*]
: Create a layer called *name* and make it the current layer. If no argument is given, a layer will be created with a name of the form *(#)* where # is the last digit of the virtual device bound to the layer. The shell prompt variable PS1 is set to the name of the layer followed by a space. A maximum of seven layers can be created.

block *name* [*name* ...]
: For each *name*, block the output of the corresponding layer when it is not the current layer. This is equivalent to setting the **stty** option **-loblk** within the layer.

delete *name* [*name* ...]
: For each *name*, delete the corresponding layer. All processes in the process group of the layer are sent the SIGHUP signal (see signal(2)).

help (or ?)
: Print the syntax of the **shl** commands.

layers [-l] [*name* ...]
: For each *name*, list the layer name and its process group. The -l option produces a ps(1)-like listing. If no arguments are given, information is presented for all existing layers.

`resume` [*name*]
: Make the layer referenced by *name* the current layer. If no argument is given, the last existing current layer will be resumed.

`toggle`
: Resume the layer that was current before the last current layer.

`unblock` *name* [*name* ...]
: For each *name*, do not block the output of the corresponding layer when it is not the current layer. This is equivalent to setting the `stty` option `-loblk` within the layer.

`quit` Exit `shl`. All layers are sent the SIGHUP signal.

name Make the layer referenced by *name* the current layer.

FILES

/dev/sxt???	Virtual tty devices
$SHELL	Variable containing path name of the shell to use (default is /bin/sh).

SEE ALSO

`sh`(1), `stty`(1).
`ioctl`(2), `signal`(2) in the *Programmer's Reference Manual.*
`sxt`(7) in the *System Administrator's Reference Manual.*

WARNING

To avoid disabling the suspend character when in the job control environment, the *swtch* character must be redefined.

NAME

`sleep` – suspend execution for an interval

SYNOPSIS

`sleep` *time*

DESCRIPTION

`sleep` suspends execution for *time* seconds. It is used to execute a command after a certain amount of time, as in:

```
(sleep 105; command)&
```

or to execute a command every so often, as in:

```
while true
do
        command
        sleep 37
done
```

SEE ALSO

`alarm`(2), `sleep`(3C) in the *Programmer's Reference Manual.*

NAME

`sort` – sort and/or merge files

SYNOPSIS

`sort` [`-cmu`] [-o*output*] [-y*kmem*] [-z*recsz*] [`-dfiMnr`] [`-btx`]
[+*pos1* [-*pos2*]] [*files*]

DESCRIPTION

The `sort` command sorts lines of all the named files together and writes the result on the standard output. The standard input is read if – is used as a file name or no input files are named.

Comparisons are based on one or more sort keys extracted from each line of input. By default, there is one sort key, the entire input line, and ordering is lexicographic by bytes in machine collating sequence.

The following options alter the default behavior:

-c Check that the input file is sorted according to the ordering rules; give no output unless the file is out of sort.

-m Merge only, the input files are already sorted.

-u Unique: suppress all but one in each set of lines having equal keys.

-o*output*
The argument given is the name of an output file to use instead of the standard output. This file may be the same as one of the inputs. There may be optional blanks between -o and *output*.

-y*kmem*
The amount of main memory used by `sort` has a large impact on its performance. Sorting a small file in a large amount of memory is a waste. If this option is omitted, `sort` begins using a system default memory size, and continues to use more space as needed. If this option is presented with a value, `kmem`, `sort` will start using that number of kilobytes of memory, unless the administrative minimum or maximum is violated, in which case the corresponding extremum will be used. Thus, -y0 is guaranteed to start with minimum memory. By convention, -y (with no argument) starts with maximum memory.

-z*recsz*
The size of the longest line read is recorded in the sort phase so buffers can be allocated during the merge phase. If the sort phase is omitted via the -c or -m options, a popular system default size will be used. Lines longer than the buffer size will cause `sort` to terminate abnormally. Supplying the actual number of bytes in the longest line to be merged (or some larger value) will prevent abnormal termination.

The following options override the default ordering rules.

-d "Dictionary" order: only letters, digits, and blanks (spaces and tabs) are significant in comparisons.

`-f` Fold lower-case letters into upper case.

`-i` Ignore non-printable characters.

`-M` Compare as months. The first three non-blank characters of the field are folded to upper case and compared. For example, in English the sorting order is "JAN" < "FEB" < ... < "DEC". Invalid fields compare low to "JAN". The `-M` option implies the `-b` option (see below).

`-n` An initial numeric string, consisting of optional blanks, optional minus sign, and zero or more digits with optional decimal point, is sorted by arithmetic value. The `-n` option implies the `-b` option (see below). Note that the `-b` option is only effective when restricted sort key specifications are in effect.

`-r` Reverse the sense of comparisons.

When ordering options appear before restricted sort key specifications, the requested ordering rules are applied globally to all sort keys. When attached to a specific sort key (described below), the specified ordering options override all global ordering options for that key.

The notation *+pos1 −pos2* restricts a sort key to one beginning at *pos1* and ending just before *pos2*. The characters at position *pos1* and just before *pos2* are included in the sort key (provided that *pos2* does not precede *pos1*). A missing *−pos2* means the end of the line.

Specifying *pos1* and *pos2* involves the notion of a field, a minimal sequence of characters followed by a field separator or a new-line. By default, the first blank (space or tab) of a sequence of blanks acts as the field separator. All blanks in a sequence of blanks are considered to be part of the next field; for example, all blanks at the beginning of a line are considered to be part of the first field. The treatment of field separators can be altered using the options:

`-b` Ignore leading blanks when determining the starting and ending positions of a restricted sort key. If the `-b` option is specified before the first *+pos1* argument, it will be applied to all *+pos1* arguments. Otherwise, the `b` flag may be attached independently to each *+pos1* or *−pos2* argument (see below).

`-t`*x* Use *x* as the field separator character; *x* is not considered to be part of a field (although it may be included in a sort key). Each occurrence of *x* is significant (for example, *xx* delimits an empty field).

pos1 and *pos2* each have the form *m*.*n* optionally followed by one or more of the flags `bdfinr`. A starting position specified by +*m*.*n* is interpreted to mean the *n*+1st character in the *m*+1st field. A missing .*n* means .0, indicating the first character of the *m*+1st field. If the `b` flag is in effect *n* is counted from the first non-blank in the *m*+1st field; +*m*.0`b` refers to the first non-blank character in the *m*+1st field.

A last position specified by −*m*.*n* is interpreted to mean the *n*th character (including separators) after the last character of the *m th* field. A missing .*n* means .0, indicating the last character of the *m*th field. If the `b` flag is in effect *n* is counted from the last leading blank in the *m*+1st field; −*m*.1`b` refers to the first non-blank in the *m*+1st field.

When there are multiple sort keys, later keys are compared only after all earlier keys compare equal. Lines that otherwise compare equal are ordered with all bytes significant.

EXAMPLES

Sort the contents of *infile* with the second field as the sort key:

`sort +1 -2` *infile*

Sort, in reverse order, the contents of *infile1* and *infile2*, placing the output in *outfile* and using the first character of the second field as the sort key:

`sort -r -o` *outfile* `+1.0 -1.2` *infile1 infile2*

Sort, in reverse order, the contents of *infile1* and *infile2* using the first non-blank character of the second field as the sort key:

`sort -r +1.0b -1.1b` *infile1 infile2*

Print the password file [**passwd**(4)] sorted by the numeric user ID (the third colon-separated field):

`sort -t: +2n -3 /etc/passwd`

Print the lines of the already sorted file *infile*, suppressing all but the first occurrence of lines having the same third field (the options `-um` with just one input file make the choice of a unique representative from a set of equal lines predictable):

`sort -um +2 -3` *infile*

FILES

`/var/tmp/stm???`

SEE ALSO

`comm`(1), `join`(1), `uniq`(1).

NOTES

Comments and exits with non-zero status for various trouble conditions (for example, when input lines are too long), and for disorder discovered under the `-c` option. When the last line of an input file is missing a `new-line` character, `sort` appends one, prints a warning message, and continues.

`sort` does not guarantee preservation of relative line ordering on equal keys.

NAME

spell, hashmake, spellin, hashcheck – find spelling errors

SYNOPSIS

spell [-v] [-b] [-x] [-l] [+*local_file*] [*files*]

/usr/lib/spell/hashmake

/usr/lib/spell/spellin *n*

/usr/lib/spell/hashcheck *spelling_list*

DESCRIPTION

spell collects words from the named *files* and looks them up in a spelling list. Words that neither occur among nor are derivable (by applying certain inflections, prefixes, and/or suffixes) from words in the spelling list are printed on the standard output. If no *files* are named, words are collected from the standard input.

spell ignores most troff(1), tbl(1), and eqn(1) constructions.

- -v All words not literally in the spelling list are printed, and plausible derivations from the words in the spelling list are indicated.
- -b British spelling is checked. Besides preferring centre, colour, programme, speciality, travelled, etc., this option insists upon *-ise* in words like standardise.
- -x Every plausible stem is displayed, one per line, with = preceding each word.
- -l Follow the chains of *all* included files. By default, spell (like deroff(1)) follows chains of included files (.so and .nx troff(1) requests), *unless* the names of such included files begin with /usr/lib.
- +*local_file* Words found in *local_file* are removed from spell's output. *local_file* is the name of a user-provided file that contains a sorted list of words, one per line. The list must be sorted with the ordering used by sort(1) (e.g. upper case preceding lower case). If this ordering is not followed, some entries in *local_file* may be ignored. With this option, the user can specify a set of words that are correct spellings (in addition to spell's own spelling list) for each job.

The spelling list is based on many sources, and while more haphazard than an ordinary dictionary, is also more effective with respect to proper names and popular technical words. Coverage of the specialized vocabularies of biology, medicine, and chemistry is light.

Alternate auxiliary files (spelling lists, stop list, history file) may be specified on the command line by using environment variables. These variables and their default settings are shown in the FILES section. Copies of all output are accumulated in the *history* file. The *stop list* filters out misspellings (e.g., thier=thy-y+ier) that would otherwise pass.

Three routines help maintain and check the hash lists used by **spell**:

hashmake Reads a list of words from the standard input and writes the corresponding nine-digit hash code on the standard output. This is the first step in creating a new spelling list or adding words to an existing list; it must be used prior to using **spellin**.

spellin Reads *n* hash codes (created by **hashmake**) from the standard input and writes a compressed spelling list on the standard output. Use **spellin** to add words to an existing spelling list or create a new spelling list.

hashcheck Reads a compressed *spelling_list* and recreates the nine-digit hash codes for all the words in it; it writes these codes on the standard output. It takes as input an existing spelling list (**hlista** or **hlistb**) or a list created or modified by **spellin**. By using **hashcheck** on an existing compressed *spelling_list* and **hashmake** on a file of selected words, you can compare the two output files to determine if the selected words are present in the existing *spelling_list*.

FILES

D_SPELL=/usr/share/lib/spell/hlist[ab]	hashed spelling lists, American & British
S_SPELL=/usr/share/lib/spell/hstop	hashed stop list
H_SPELL=/var/adm/spellhist	history file
/usr/lib/spell/spellprog	program

SEE ALSO

deroff(1), **sed**(1), **sort**(1), **tee**(1).
eqn(1), **tbl**(1), **troff**(1) in the *DOCUMENTER'S WORKBENCH Software Technical Discussion and Reference Manual.*

NOTES

The spelling list's coverage is uneven; new installations will probably wish to monitor the output for several months to gather local additions; typically, these are kept in a separate local file that is added to the hashed *spelling_list* via -**spellin**.

NAME

`split` – split a file into pieces

SYNOPSIS

`split` [*–n*] [*file* [*name*]]

DESCRIPTION

`split` reads *file* and writes it in *n*-line pieces (default 1000 lines) onto a set of output files. The name of the first output file is *name* with **aa** appended, and so on lexicographically, up to **zz** (a maximum of 676 files). The maximum length of *name* is 2 characters less than the maximum filename length allowed by the filesystem. See **statvfs**(2). If no output name is given, **x** is default.

If no input file is given, or if – is given in its stead, then the standard input file is used.

SEE ALSO

`bfs`(1), `csplit`(1).

`statvfs`(2) in the *Programmer's Reference Manual.*

NAME

srchtxt – display contents of, or search for a text string in, message data bases

SYNOPSIS

srchtxt [-s] [-l *locale*] [-m *msgfile*, ...] [*text*]

DESCRIPTION

The **srchtxt** utility is used to display all the text strings in message data bases, or to search for a text string in message data bases (see **mkmsgs**(1)). These data bases are files in the directory /usr/lib/locale/*locale*/LC_MESSAGES (see setlocale(3C)), unless a file name given with the -m option contains a /. The directory *locale* can be viewed as the name of the language in which the text strings are written. If the -l option is not specified, the files accessed will be determined by the value of the environment variable LC_MESSAGES. If LC_MESSAGES is not set, the files accessed will be determined by the value of the environment variable **LANG**. If **LANG** is not set, the files accessed will be in the directory /usr/lib/locale/C/LC_MESSAGES, which contains default strings.

If no *text* argument is present, then all the text strings in the files accessed will be displayed.

The meanings of the options are as follows:

- **-s** suppress printing of the message sequence numbers of the messages being displayed
- -l *locale* access files in the directory /usr/lib/locale/*locale*/LC_MESSAGES. If -m *msgfile* is also supplied, *locale* is ignored for *msgfiles* containing a /.
- -m *msgfile* access file(s) specified by one or more *msgfiles*. If *msgfile* contains a / character, then *msgfile is* interpreted as a pathname; otherwise, it will be assumed to be in the directory determined as described above. To specify more than one *msgfile*, separate the file names using commas.
- *text* search for the text string specified by *text* and display each one that matches. *text* can take the form of a regular expression (see ed(1)).

If the **-s** option is not specified, the displayed text is prefixed by message sequence numbers. The message sequence numbers are enclosed in angle brackets: <*msgfile*:*msgnum*>.

- *msgfile* name of the file where the displayed text occurred
- *msgnum* sequence number in *msgfile* where the displayed text occurred

This display is in the format used by gettxt(1) and gettxt(3C).

EXAMPLES

The following examples show uses of srchtxt.

Example 1:

> If message files have been installed in a locale named french by using **mkmsgs**(1), then you could display the entire set of text strings in the french locale (/usr/lib/locale/french/LC_MESSAGES/*) by typing:

```
srchtxt -l french
```

Example 2:

If a set of error messages associated with the UNIX operating system have been installed in the file `UX` in the `french` locale (`/usr/lib/locale/french/LC_MESSAGES/UX`), then, using the value of the `LANG` environment variable to determine the locale to be searched, you could search that file in that locale for all error messages dealing with files by typing:

```
LANG=french; export LANG
srchtxt -m UX "[Ff]ichier"
```

If `/usr/lib/locale/french/LC_MESSAGES/UX` contained the following strings:

```
Erreur E/S\n
Liste d'arguments trop longue\n
Fichier inexistant\n
Argument invalide\n
Trop de fichiers ouverts\n
Fichier trop long\n
Trop de liens\n
Argument hors du domaine\n
Identificateur supprim\n
Etreinte fatale\n
   .
   .
   .
```

then the following strings would be displayed:

```
<UX:3>Fichier inexistant\n
<UX:5>Trop de fichiers ouverts\n
<UX:6>Fichier trop long\n
```

Example 3:

If a set of error messages associated with the UNIX operating system have been installed in the file `UX` and a set of error messages associated with the INGRESS data base product have been installed in the file `ingress`, both in the `german` locale, then you could search for the pattern `[Dd]atei` in both the files `UX` and `ingress` in the `german` locale by typing:

```
srchtxt -l german -m UX,ingress "[Dd]atei"
```

FILES

`/usr/lib/locale/C/LC_MESSAGES/*`	default files created by `mkmsgs(1)`
`/usr/lib/locale/`*locale*`/LC_MESSAGES/*`	message files created by `mkmsgs(1)`

SEE ALSO

`ed(1)`, `exstr(1)`, `gettxt(1)`, `mkmsgs(1)`.
`gettxt(3C)`, `setlocale(3C)` in the *Programmer's Reference Manual*.

DIAGNOSTICS

The error messages produced by `srchtxt` are intended to be self-explanatory. They indicate an error in the command line or errors encountered while searching for a particular locale and/or message file.

NAME

strchg, strconf – change or query stream configuration

SYNOPSIS

```
strchg -h module1 [,module2 ...]
strchg -p [-a | -u module]
strchg -f file
strconf [-t | -m module]
```

DESCRIPTION

These commands are used to alter or query the configuration of the stream associated with the user's standard input. The strchg command pushes modules on and/or pops modules off the stream. The strconf command queries the configuration of the stream. Only the super-user or owner of a STREAMS device may alter the configuration of that stream.

With the -h option, strchg pushes modules onto a stream; it takes as arguments the names of one or more pushable streams modules. These modules are pushed in order; that is, *module1* is pushed first, *module2* is pushed second, etc.

The -p option pops modules off the stream. With the -p option alone, strchg pops the topmost module from the stream. With the -p and -a options, all the modules above the topmost driver are popped. When the -p option is followed by -u *module*, then all modules above but not including *module* are popped off the stream. The -a and -u options are mutually exclusive.

With the -f option, the user can specify a *file* that contains a list of modules representing the desired configuration of the stream. Each module name must appear on a separate line where the first name represents the topmost module and the last name represents the module that should be closest to the driver. The strchg command will determine the current configuration of the stream and pop and push the necessary modules in order to end up with the desired configuration.

The -h, -f and -p options are mutually exclusive.

Invoked without any arguments, strconf prints a list of all the modules in the stream as well as the topmost driver. The list is printed with one name per line where the first name printed is the topmost module on the stream (if one exists) and the last item printed is the name of the driver. With the -t option, only the topmost module (if one exists) is printed. The -m option determines if the named *module* is present on a stream. If it is, strconf prints the message yes and returns zero. If not, strconf prints the message no and returns a non-zero value. The -t and -m options are mutually exclusive.

EXAMPLES

The following command pushes the module ldterm on the stream associated with the user's standard input:

```
strchg -h ldterm
```

The following command pops the topmost module from the stream associated with /dev/term/24. The user must be the owner of this device or the super-user.

```
strchg -p < /dev/term/24
```

If the file `fileconf` contains the following:

```
compat
ldterm
ptem
```

then the command

```
strchg -f fileconf
```

will configure the user's standard input stream so that the module `ptem` is pushed over the driver, followed by `ldterm` and `compat` closest to the stream head.

The `strconf` command with no arguments lists the modules and topmost driver on the stream; for a stream that has only the module `ldterm` pushed above the `ports` driver, it would produce the following output:

```
ldterm
ports
```

The following command asks if `ldterm` is on the stream

```
strconf -m ldterm
```

and produces the following output while returning an exit status of 0:

```
yes
```

SEE ALSO

`streamio`(7) in the *Programmer's Guide: STREAMS.*

DIAGNOSTICS

`strchg` returns zero on success. It prints an error message and returns non-zero status for various error conditions, including usage error, bad module name, too many modules to push, failure of an ioctl on the stream, or failure to open *file* from the `-f` option.

`strconf` returns zero on success (for the `-m` or `-t` option, "success" means the named or topmost module is present). It returns a non-zero status if invoked with the `-m` or `-t` option and the module is not present. It prints an error message and returns non-zero status for various error conditions, including usage error or failure of an `ioctl` on the stream.

NOTES

If the user is neither the owner of the stream nor the super-user, the `strchg` command will fail. If the user does not have read permissions on the stream and is not the super-user, the `strconf` command will fail.

If modules are pushed in the wrong order, one could end up with a stream that does not function as expected. For ttys, if the line discipline module is not pushed in the correct place, one could have a terminal that does not respond to any commands.

NAME

`strings` – find printable strings in an object file or binary

SYNOPSIS

`strings` [-a] [-o] [-n *number* | *–number*] *filename...*

DESCRIPTION

The `strings` command looks for ASCII strings in a binary file. A string is any sequence of 4 or more printing characters ending with a newline or a null character.

`strings` is useful for identifying random object files and many other things.

The following options are available:

-a	Look everywhere in the file for strings. If this flag is omitted, `strings` only looks in the initialized data space of object files.
-o	Precede each string by its offset in the file.
-n *number*	Use *number* as the minimum string length rather than 4.

SEE ALSO

od(1)

NOTES

The algorithm for identifying strings is extremely primitive.

For backwards compatibility, *–number* can be used in place of -n *number*. Similarly, the -a and a – option are interchangeable. The – and the *–number* variations are obsolescent.

NAME

`stty` – set the options for a terminal

SYNOPSIS

`stty [-a] [-g]` [*options*]

DESCRIPTION

`stty` sets certain terminal I/O options for the device that is the current standard input; without arguments, it reports the settings of certain options.

In this report, if a character is preceded by a caret (^), then the value of that option is the corresponding control character (e.g., "^h" is CTRL-h; in this case, recall that CTRL-h is the same as the "back-space" key.) The sequence "^`" means that an option has a null value.

`-a` reports all of the option settings;

`-g` reports current settings in a form that can be used as an argument to another `stty` command.

For detailed information about the modes listed from Control Modes through Local Modes, below, see `termio`(7). For detailed information about the modes listed under Hardware Flow Control Modes and Clock Modes, below, see `termiox`(7). Options described in the Combination Modes section are implemented using options in the earlier sections. Note that many combinations of options make no sense, but no sanity checking is performed. Hardware flow control and clock modes options may not be supported by all hardware interfaces. The options are selected from the following:

Control Modes

`parenb (-parenb)` enable (disable) parity generation and detection.

`parext (-parext)` enable (disable) extended parity generation and detection for mark and space parity.

`parodd (-parodd)` select odd (even) parity, or mark (space) parity if `parext` is enabled.

`cs5 cs6 cs7 cs8` select character size [see `termio`(7)].

`0` hang up line immediately.

`110 300 600 1200 1800 2400 4800 9600 19200 38400`
Set terminal baud rate to the number given, if possible. (All speeds are not supported by all hardware interfaces.)

`ispeed 0 110 300 600 1200 1800 2400 4800 9600 19200 38400`
Set terminal input baud rate to the number given, if possible. (Not all hardware supports split baud rates.) If the input baud rate is set to zero, the input baud rate will be specified by the value of the output baud rate.

`ospeed 0 110 300 600 1200 1800 2400 4800 9600 19200 38400`
Set terminal output baud rate to the number given, if possible. (Not all hardware supports split baud rates.) If the output baud rate is set to zero, the line will be hung up immediately.

`hupcl (-hupcl)`	hang up (do not hang up) connection on last close.
`hup (-hup)`	same as `hupcl (-hupcl)`.
`cstopb (-cstopb)`	use two (one) stop bits per character.
`cread (-cread)`	enable (disable) the receiver.
`clocal (-clocal)`	n assume a line without (with) modem control.
`loblk (-loblk)`	block (do not block) output from a non-current layer.

Input Modes

`ignbrk (-ignbrk)`	ignore (do not ignore) break on input.
`brkint (-brkint)`	signal (do not signal) INTR on break.
`ignpar (-ignpar)`	ignore (do not ignore) parity errors.
`parmrk (-parmrk)`	mark (do not mark) parity errors [see `termio`(7)].
`inpck (-inpck)`	enable (disable) input parity checking.
`istrip (-istrip)`	strip (do not strip) input characters to seven bits.
`inlcr (-inlcr)`	map (do not map) NL to CR on input.
`igncr (-igncr)`	ignore (do not ignore) CR on input.
`icrnl (-icrnl)`	map (do not map) CR to NL on input.
`iuclc (-iuclc)`	map (do not map) upper-case alphabetics to lower case on input.
`ixon (-ixon)`	enable (disable) START/STOP output control. Output is stopped by sending STOP control character and started by sending the START control character.
`ixany (-ixany)`	allow any character (only DC1) to restart output.
`ixoff (-ixoff)`	request that the system send (not send) START/STOP characters when the input queue is nearly empty/full.
`imaxbel (-imaxbel)`	echo (do not echo) BEL when the input line is too long.
`KB_ENABLE`	performs a TIOCKBON which allows extended characters to be transmitted to the user's program. Extended characters are transmitted as a null byte followed by a second byte containing the character's extended code. [see `keyboard`(7)].
`DB_DISABLE`	performs a TIOCKBON which disables the transmission of extended characters. This is the default. [see `keyboard`]

Output Modes

`opost (-opost)`	post-process output (do not post-process output; ignore all other output modes).

`olcuc (-olcuc)`	map (do not map) lower-case alphabetics to upper case on output.
`onlcr (-onlcr)`	map (do not map) NL to CR-NL on output.
`ocrnl (-ocrnl)`	map (do not map) CR to NL on output.
`onocr (-onocr)`	do not (do) output CRs at column zero.
`onlret (-onlret)`	on the terminal NL performs (does not perform) the CR function.
`ofill (-ofill)`	use fill characters (use timing) for delays.
`ofdel (-ofdel)`	fill characters are DELs (NULs).
`cr0 cr1 cr2 cr3`	select style of delay for carriage returns [see `termio`(7)].
`nl0 nl1`	select style of delay for line-feeds [see `termio`(7)].
`tab0 tab1 tab2 tab3`	select style of delay for horizontal tabs [see `termio`(7)].
`bs0 bs1`	select style of delay for backspaces [see `termio`(7)].
`ff0 ff1`	select style of delay for form-feeds [see `termio`(7)].
`vt0 vt1`	select style of delay for vertical tabs [see `termio`(7)].

Local Modes

`isig (-isig)`	enable (disable) the checking of characters against the special control characters INTR, QUIT, and SWTCH.
`icanon (-icanon)`	enable (disable) canonical input (ERASE and KILL processing).
`xcase (-xcase)`	canonical (unprocessed) upper/lower-case presentation.
`echo (-echo)`	echo back (do not echo back) every character typed.
`echoe (-echoe)`	echo (do not echo) ERASE character as a backspace-space-backspace string. Note: this mode will erase the ERASEed character on many CRT terminals; however, it does not keep track of column position and, as a result, may be confusing on escaped characters, tabs, and backspaces.
`echok (-echok)`	echo (do not echo) NL after KILL character.
`lfkc (-lfkc)`	the same as `echok (-echok)`; obsolete.
`echonl (-echonl)`	echo (do not echo) NL.
`noflsh (-noflsh)`	disable (enable) flush after INTR, QUIT, or SWTCH.
`stwrap (-stwrap)`	disable (enable) truncation of lines longer than 79 characters on a synchronous line. (Does not apply to the 3B2.)
`tostop (-tostop)`	send (do not send) SIGTTOU when background processes write to the terminal.

echoctl (-echoctl)
: echo (do not echo) control characters as ^*char*, delete as ^?

echoprt (-echoprt)
: echo (do not echo) erase character as character is "erased".

echoke (-echoke)
: BS-SP-BS erase (do not BS-SP-BS erase) entire line on line kill.

flusho (-flusho)
: output is (is not) being flushed.

pendin (-pendin)
: retype (do not retype) pending input at next read or input character.

iexten (-iexten)
: enable (disable) extended (implementation-defined) functions for input data.

stflush (-stflush)
: enable (disable) flush on a synchronous line after every **write**(2).

stappl (-stappl)
: use application mode (use line mode) on a synchronous line.

Hardware Flow Control Modes

rtsxoff (-rtsxoff)
: enable (disable) RTS hardware flow control on input.

ctsxon (-ctsxon)
: enable (disable) CTS hardware flow control on output.

dtrxoff (-dtrxoff)
: enable (disable) DTR hardware flow control on input.

cdxon (-cdxon)
: enable (disable) CD hardware flow control on output.

isxoff (-isxoff)
: enable (disable) isochronous hardware flow control on input.

Clock Modes

xcibrg
: get transmit clock from internal baud rate generator.

xctset
: get the transmit clock from transmitter signal element timing (DCE source) lead, CCITT V.24 circuit 114, EIA-232-D pin 15.

xcrset
: get transmit clock from receiver signal element timing (DCE source) lead, CCITT V.24 circuit 115, EIA-232-D pin 17.

rcibrg
: get receive clock from internal baud rate generator.

rctset
: get receive clock from transmitter signal element timing (DCE source) lead, CCITT V.24 circuit 114, EIA-232-D pin 15.

rcrset
: get receive clock from receiver signal element timing (DCE source) lead, CCITT V.24 circuit 115, EIA-232-D pin 17.

tsetcoff
: transmitter signal element timing clock not provided.

tsetcrbrg output receive baud rate generator on transmitter signal element timing (DTE source) lead, CCITT V.24 circuit 113, EIA-232-D pin 24.

tsetctbrg output transmit baud rate generator on transmitter signal element timing (DTE source) lead, CCITT V.24 circuit 113, EIA-232-D pin 24.

tsetctset output tranmitter signal element timing (DCE source) on transmitter signal element timing (DTE source) lead, CCITT V.24 circuit 113, EIA-232-D pin 24.

tsetcrset output receiver signal element timing (DCE source) on transmitter signal element timing (DTE source) lead, CCITT V.24 circuit 113, EIA-232-D pin 24.

rsetcoff receiver signal element timing clock not provided.

rsetcrbrg output receive baud rate generator on receiver signal element timing (DTE source) lead, CCITT V.24 circuit 128, no EIA-232-D pin.

rsetctbrg output transmit baud rate generator on receiver signal element timing (DTE source) lead, CCITT V.24 circuit 128, no EIA-232-D pin.

rsetctset output transmitter signal element timing (DCE source) on receiver signal element timing (DTE source) lead, CCITT V.24 circuit 128, no EIA-232-D pin.

rsetcrset output receiver signal element timing (DCE source) on receiver signal element timing (DTE source) lead, CCITT V.24 circuit 128, no EIA-232-D pin.

Control Assignments

control-character c set *control-character* to *c*, where *control-character* is **ctab**, **discard**, **dsusp**, **eof**, **eol**, **eol2**, **erase**, **intr**, **kill**, **lnext**, **quit**, **reprint**, **start**, **stop**, **susp**, **swtch**, or **werase**. [**ctab** is used with **-stappl** [see **termio**(7)]. If *c* is preceded by a caret (^) indicating an escape from the shell, then the value used is the corresponding control character (e.g., "^d" is a CTRL-d). "^?" is interpreted as DEL and "^-" is interpreted as undefined.

min, time number Set the value of *min* or *time* to *number*. *min* and *time* are used in Non-Canonical mode input processing (**-icanon**).

line i set line discipline to *i* (0 < *i* < 127).

Combination Modes

evenp or **parity** enable **parenb** and **cs7**.

oddp	enable **parenb**, **cs7**, and **parodd**.
spacep	enable **parenb**, **cs7**, and **parext**.
markp	enable **parenb**, **cs7**, **parodd**, and **parext**.
-parity, or -evenp	disable **parenb**, and set **cs8**.
-oddp	disable **parenb** and **parodd**, and set **cs8**.
-spacep	disable **parenb** and **parext**, and set **cs8**.
-markp	disable **parenb**, **parodd**, and **parext**, and set **cs8**.
raw (-raw or cooked)	enable (disable) raw input and output (no ERASE, KILL, INTR, QUIT, SWTCH, EOT, or output post processing).
nl (-nl)	unset (set) **icrnl**, **onlcr**. In addition **-nl** unsets **inlcr**, **igncr**, **ocrnl**, and **onlret**.
lcase (-lcase)	set (unset) **xcase**, **iuclc**, and **olcuc**.
LCASE (-LCASE)	same as **lcase** (**-lcase**).
tabs (-tabs or tab3)	preserve (expand to spaces) tabs when printing.
ek	reset ERASE and KILL characters back to normal # and @.
sane	resets all modes to some reasonable values.
term	set all modes suitable for the terminal type *term*, where *term* is one of tty33, tty37, vt05, tn300, ti700, or tek.
async	set normal asynchronous communications where clock settings are xcibrg, rcibrg, tsetcoff and rsetcoff.

Window Size

rows *n*	set window size to *n* rows.
columns *n*	set window size to *n* columns.
ypixels *n*	set vertical window size to *n* pixels.
xpixels *n*	set horizontal window size to *n* pixels.

Control Modes for the Video Monitor

mono	Selects the monochrome display as the output device for the console screen. This mode is valid if a standard monochrome adapter is present or if a standard enhanced graphics adapter (EGA) is present and the EGA is currently in one of the monochrome display modes.
color	Selects a standard regular color display as the output device for the console screen. This mode is valid if a color graphics adapter is present or if a standard EGA is present and is currently in one of the color graphics compatibility modes.

enhanced Selects the enhanced color display as the output device for the console screen. This mode is valid if an EGA is present and is currently in a non-monochrome display mode.

pro Selects the professional graphics adapter as the output device for the system console. This mode is valid if a VGA is present.

Control Modes for the Attached Display Devices

B40x25 Selects 40x25 (40 columns x 25 rows) black and white text display mode.

C40x25 Selects 40x25 color text display mode.

B80x25 Selects 80x25 black and white text display mode.

C80x25 Selects 80x25 color display text mode.

BG320 Selects 320x200 black and white graphics display mode.

CG320 Selects 320x200 color graphics display mode.

BG640 Selects 640x200 black and white graphics display mode.

The keyboard and display control modes above are valid for the following configurations: standard color graphics adapter (CGA) attached to an standard regular color display; standard enhanced graphics adapter (EGA) (modes 0-6) attached to a standard regular color display or standard enhanced color display.

CG320_D
Selects EGA support for 320x200 graphics display mode (EGA mode D).

CG640_E
Selects EGA support for 640x200 graphics display mode (EGA mode E).

The two options above are only valid when an EGA is attached to a standard regular color display or an enhanced color display.

EGAMONO80x25
Selects EGA Mode 7 as the display mode. Emulates the support provided by the standard monochrome display adapter.

EGAMONOAPA
Selects EGA support for 640x350 graphics display mode (EGA mode F).

ENHMONOAPA2
Selects EGA mode F*.

The three options above are only valid when a standard EGA is attached to an IBM monochrome display.

ENH_B40x25
Selects enhanced EGA support for 40x25 black and white text display mode (EGA mode 0*).

ENH_C40x25
Selects enhanced EGA support for 40x25 color text display mode (EGA mode 1*).

ENH_B80x25
Selects enhanced EGA support for 80x25 black and white text display mode (EGA mode 2*).

ENH_C80x25
Selects enhanced EGA support for 80x25 color text display mode (EGA mode 3*).

ENH_B80x43
Selects enhanced EGA support for 80x43 black and white text display mode.

ENH_C80x43
Selects enhanced EGA support for 80x43 color text display mode.

CG640x350
Selects EGA support for 640x350 graphics display mode (EGA mode 10).

ENH_CG640
Selects EGA mode 10*.

The options above are only valid when a standard EGA is attached to a standard enhanced color display.

MCAMODE
Reinitializes the monochrome graphics adapter.

ENH_CGA
Selects CGA hardware emulation, when an AT&T Super-Vu video controller is attached.

SEE ALSO

tabs(1) in the *User's Reference Manual.*
ioctl(2).
termio(7), termiox(7) in the *System Administrator's Reference Manual.*

NAME

su – become super-user or another user

SYNOPSIS

su [–] [*name* [*arg* ...]]

DESCRIPTION

su allows one to become another user without logging off. The default user *name* is `root` (that is, super-user).

To use `su`, the appropriate password must be supplied (unless one is already `root`). If the password is correct, `su` will execute a new shell with the real and effective user and group IDs and supplementary group list set to that of the specified user. The new shell will be the optional program named in the shell field of the specified user's password file entry [see **passwd**(4)] or `/usr/bin/sh` if none is specified [see **sh**(1)]. To restore normal user ID privileges, type an EOF character (CTRL–d) to the new shell.

Any additional arguments given on the command line are passed to the program invoked as the shell. When using programs such as **sh**, an *arg* of the form `-c` *string* executes *string* via the shell and an arg of `-r` gives the user a restricted shell.

The following statements are true only if the optional program named in the shell field of the specified user's password file entry is like `sh`. If the first argument to `su` is a `-`, the environment will be changed to what would be expected if the user actually logged in as the specified user. This is done by invoking the program used as the shell with an *arg0* value whose first character is `-`, thus causing first the system's profile (`/etc/profile`) and then the specified user's profile (`.profile` in the new HOME directory) to be executed. Otherwise, the environment is passed along with the possible exception of `$PATH`, which is set to `/sbin:/usr/sbin:/usr/bin:/etc` for `root`. Note that if the optional program used as the shell is `/usr/bin/sh`, the user's `.profile` can check *arg0* for `-sh` or `-su` to determine if it was invoked by `login` or `su`, respectively. If the user's program is other than `/usr/bin/sh`, then `.profile` is invoked with an *arg0* of *-program* by both `login` and `su`.

All attempts to become another user using `su` are logged in the `log` file `/var/adm/sulog`.

EXAMPLES

To become user `bin` while retaining your previously exported environment, execute:

```
su bin
```

To become user `bin` but change the environment to what would be expected if `bin` had originally logged in, execute:

```
su - bin
```

To execute *command* with the temporary environment and permissions of user `bin`, type:

su - bin -c "*command args*"

FILES

`/etc/passwd`	system's password file
`/etc/profile`	system's profile
`$HOME/.profile`	user's profile
`/var/adm/sulog`	log file
`/etc/default/su`	the default parameters that live here are:

`SULOG:`	If defined, all attempts to `su` to another user are logged in the indicated file.
`CONSOLE:`	If defined, all attempts to `suroot` are logged on the console.
`PATH:`	Default path.
`SUPATH:`	Default path for a user invoking `suroot`.

SEE ALSO

`env`(1), `login`(1), `sh`(1) in the *User's Reference Manual*.
`passwd`(4), `profile`(4), `environ`(5) in the *Programmer's Reference Manual*.

NAME

sum – print checksum and block count of a file

SYNOPSIS

sum [–r] *file*

DESCRIPTION

sum calculates and prints a 16-bit checksum for the named file, and also prints the number of 512 byte blocks in the file. It is typically used to look for bad spots, or to validate a file communicated over some transmission line. The option –r causes an alternate algorithm to be used in computing the checksum.

SEE ALSO

wc(1).

DIAGNOSTICS

"Read error" is indistinguishable from end of file on most devices; check the block count.

NAME

sync – update the super block

SYNOPSIS

sync

DESCRIPTION

sync executes the sync system primitive. If the system is to be stopped, sync must be called to insure file system integrity. It will flush all previously unwritten system buffers out to disk, thus assuring that all file modifications up to that point will be saved. See sync(2) for details.

NOTE

If you have done a write to a file on a remote machine in a Remote File Sharing environment, you cannot use sync to force buffers to be written out to disk on the remote machine. sync will only write local buffers to local disks.

SEE ALSO

sync(2) in the *Programmer's Reference Manual.*

NAME

tabs − set tabs on a terminal

SYNOPSIS

tabs [*tabspec*] [−T*type*] [+m*n*]

DESCRIPTION

tabs sets the tab stops on the user's terminal according to the tab specification *tabspec*, after clearing any previous settings. The user's terminal must have remotely settable hardware tabs.

tabspec Four types of tab specification are accepted for *tabspec*. They are described below: canned (−*code*), repetitive (−*n*), arbitrary (*n1*,*n2*,...), and file (−−*file*). If no *tabspec* is given, the default value is −8, i.e., UNIX system "standard" tabs. The lowest column number is 1. Note that for tabs, column 1 always refers to the leftmost column on a terminal, even one whose column markers begin at 0, e.g., the DASI 300, DASI 300s, and DASI 450.

−code Use one of the codes listed below to select a *canned* set of tabs. The legal codes and their meanings are as follows:

−a 1,10,16,36,72
Assembler, IBM S/370, first format

−a2 1,10,16,40,72
Assembler, IBM S/370, second format

−c 1,8,12,16,20,55
COBOL, normal format

−c2 1,6,10,14,49
COBOL compact format (columns 1-6 omitted). Using this code, the first typed character corresponds to card column 7, one space gets you to column 8, and a tab reaches column 12. Files using this tab setup should include a format specification as follows (see fspec(4)):

```
<:t-c2 m6 s66 d:>
```

−c3 1,6,10,14,18,22,26,30,34,38,42,46,50,54,58,62,67
COBOL compact format (columns 1-6 omitted), with more tabs than −c2. This is the recommended format for COBOL. The appropriate format specification is [see fspec(4)]:

```
<:t-c3 m6 s66 d:>
```

−f 1,7,11,15,19,23
FORTRAN

−p 1,5,9,13,17,21,25,29,33,37,41,45,49,53,57,61
PL/I

−s 1,10,55
SNOBOL

−u 1,12,20,44
UNIVAC 1100 Assembler

−n A *repetitive* specification requests tabs at columns 1+*n*, 1+2**n*, etc. Of particular importance is the value 8: this represents the UNIX system "standard" tab setting, and is the most likely tab setting to be found at a terminal. Another special case is the value 0, implying no tabs at all.

n1,n2,...
The *arbitrary* format permits the user to type any chosen set of numbers, separated by commas, in ascending order. Up to 40 numbers are allowed. If any number (except the first one) is preceded by a plus sign, it is taken as an increment to be added to the previous value. Thus, the formats 1,10,20,30, and 1,10,+10,+10 are considered identical.

−−file If the name of a *file* is given, **tabs** reads the first line of the file, searching for a format specification [see **fspec**(4)]. If it finds one there, it sets the tab stops according to it, otherwise it sets them as **−8**. This type of specification may be used to make sure that a tabbed file is printed with correct tab settings, and would be used with the **pr** command:

tabs −− *file*; **pr** *file*

Any of the following also may be used; if a given flag occurs more than once, the last value given takes effect:

−T*type* **tabs** usually needs to know the type of terminal in order to set tabs and always needs to know the type to set margins. *type* is a name listed in **term**(5). If no **−T** flag is supplied, **tabs** uses the value of the environment variable **TERM**. If **TERM** is not defined in the *environment* [see **environ**(5)], **tabs** tries a sequence that will work for many terminals.

+m*n* The margin argument may be used for some terminals. It causes all tabs to be moved over *n* columns by making column *n+1* the left margin. If +m is given without a value of *n*, the value assumed is 10. For a TermiNet, the first value in the tab list should be 1, or the margin will move even further to the right. The normal (leftmost) margin on most terminals is obtained by **+m0**. The margin for most terminals is reset only when the +m flag is given explicitly.

Tab and margin setting is performed via the standard output.

EXAMPLES

`tabs -a` example using *−code* (*canned* specification) to set tabs to the settings required by the IBM assembler: columns 1, 10, 16, 36, 72.

`tabs -8` example of using *−n* (*repetitive* specification), where *n* is 8, causes tabs to be set every eighth position:
1+(1*8), 1+(2*8), ... which evaluate to columns 9, 17, ...

`tabs 1,8,36` example of using *n1,n2,...* (*arbitrary* specification) to set tabs at columns 1, 8, and 36.

`tabs --$HOME/fspec.list/att4425`
example of using --*file* (*file* specification) to indicate that tabs should be set according to the first line of `$HOME/fspec.list/att4425` [see **fspec**(4)].

DIAGNOSTICS

`illegal tabs` when arbitrary tabs are ordered incorrectly

`illegal increment`
when a zero or missing increment is found in an arbitrary specification

`unknown tab code`
when a *canned* code cannot be found

`can't open` if --*file* option used, and file can't be opened

`file indirection`
if --*file* option used and the specification in that file points to yet another file. Indirection of this form is not permitted

SEE ALSO

`newform`(1), `pr`(1), `tput`(1).
`fspec`(4), `terminfo`(4), `environ`(5), `term`(5) in the *System Administrator's Reference Manual.*

NOTES

There is no consistency among different terminals regarding ways of clearing tabs and setting the left margin.

`tabs` clears only 20 tabs (on terminals requiring a long sequence), but is willing to set 64.

The *tabspec* used with the `tabs` command is different from the one used with the `newform` command. For example, `tabs -8` sets every eighth position; whereas `newform -i-8` indicates that tabs are set every eighth position.

NAME

`tail` – deliver the last part of a file

SYNOPSIS

`tail` [± *number* `lbcr`] [*file*]
`tail` [`-lbcr`] [*file*]
`tail` [± *number* `lbcf`] [*file*]
`tail` [`-lbcf`] [*file*]

DESCRIPTION

`tail` copies the named file to the standard output beginning at a designated place. If no file is named, the standard input is used.

Copying begins at distance *+number* from the beginning, or *–number* from the end of the input (if *number* is null, the value 10 is assumed). *Number* is counted in units of lines, blocks, or characters, according to the appended option `l`, `b`, or `c`. When no units are specified, counting is by lines.

With the `-f` (follow) option, if the input file is not a pipe, the program will not terminate after the line of the input file has been copied, but will enter an endless loop, wherein it sleeps for a second and then attempts to read and copy further records from the input file. Thus it may be used to monitor the growth of a file that is being written by some other process. For example, the command:

```
tail -f fred
```

will print the last ten lines of the file `fred`, followed by any lines that are appended to `fred` between the time `tail` is initiated and killed. As another example, the command:

```
tail -15cf fred
```

will print the last 15 characters of the file `fred`, followed by any lines that are appended to `fred` between the time `tail` is initiated and killed.

The `r` option copies lines from the specified starting point in the file in reverse order. The default for `r` is to print the entire file in reverse order.

The `r` and `f` options are mutually exclusive.

SEE ALSO

`cat`(1), `head`(1), `more`(1), `pg`(1), `tail`(1).
dd(1M) in the *System Administrator's Reference Manual*.

NOTES

Tails relative to the end of the file are stored in a buffer, and thus are limited in length. Various kinds of anomalous behavior may happen with character special files.

The `tail` command will only tail the last 4096 bytes of a file regardless of its line count.

NAME

`talk` – talk to another user

SYNOPSIS

`talk` *username* [*ttyname*]

DESCRIPTION

`talk` is a visual communication program that copies lines from your terminal to that of a user on the same or on another host. *username* is that user's login name.

The program is architecture dependent; it works only between machines of the same architecture.

If you want to talk to a user who is logged in more than once, the *ttyname* argument may be used to indicate the appropriate terminal name.

When first called, `talk` sends the message:

```
Message from TalkDaemon@ her_machine at time ...
talk: connection requested by your_name@your_machine
talk: respond with: talk your_name@your_machine
```

to the user you wish to talk to. At this point, the recipient of the message should reply by typing:

```
talkyour_name@your_machine
```

It does not matter from which machine the recipient replies, as long as the login name is the same. Once communication is established, the two parties may type simultaneously, with their output appearing in separate windows. Typing Ctrl-L redraws the screen, while your erase, kill, and word kill characters will work in `talk` as normal. To exit, just type your interrupt character; `talk` then moves the cursor to the bottom of the screen and restores the terminal.

Permission to talk may be denied or granted by use of the `mesg`(1) command. At the outset talking is allowed. Certain commands, such as `pr`(1), disallow messages in order to prevent messy output.

FILES

`/etc/hosts`	to find the recipient's machine
`/var/adm/utmp`	to find the recipient's tty

SEE ALSO

`mail`(1), `mesg`(1), `pr`(1), `who`(1), `write`(1), `talkd`(1M).

NAME

`tapecntl` – tape control for tape device

SYNOPSIS

`tapecntl` [`-bluetrwv`] [`-f` *arg*] [`-p` *arg*] [`special`]

DESCRIPTION

`tapecntl` will send the optioned commands to the tape device driver sub-device `/dev/rmt/c0s0` for all options except the `-e` option (position), which will use sub-device `/dev/rmt/c0s0n` using the `ioctl` command function. Sub-device `/dev/rmt/c0s0` provides a rewind on close capability, while `/dev/rmt/c0s0n` allows for closing of the device without rewind. Error messages will be written to standard error. `special` is the tape device, and it defaults to `/dev/rmt/c0s0n` if not specified.

Not all options are supported by all tape devices and tape device drivers.

The meaning of the options are:

`-b` block length limits
Reads block length limits from the tape device and displays them.

`-l` load tape
Loads the tape media to the tape device and positions the tape at BOT.

`-u` unload tape
Unloads the tape media from the tape device. Depending on the device, unloading may include ejecting the catridge.

`-e` erase tape
Erasing the tape causes the erase bar to be activated while moving the tape from end to end, causing all data tracks to be erased in a single pass over the tape.

`-t` retension tape
Retensioning the tape causes the tape to be moved from end to end, thereby repacking the tape with the proper tension across its length.

`-r` reset tape device
Reset of the tape device initializes the tape controller registers and positions the tape at the beginning of the tape mark (BOT).

`-w` rewind tape
Rewinding the tape will move the tape to the BOT.

`-v` set variable length block mode
Sets the tape device to read and write variable length blocks.

`-f`[*n*] set fixed length block mode
sets the tape device to read abd write in fixed length blocks of *n* bytes.

-p[*n*] position tape to "end of file" mark – *n*
Positioning the tape command requires an integer argument. Positioning the tape will move the tape forward relative to its current position to the end of the specified file mark. The positioning option used with an argument of zero will be ignored. Illegal or out-of-range value arguments to the positioning command will leave the tape positioned at the end of the last valid file mark.

Options may be used individually or strung together with selected options being executed sequentially from left to right in the command line.

FILES

`/usr/lib/tape/tapecntl`
`/sbin/tapecntl`
`/dev/rmt/c0s0n`
`/dev/rmt/c0s0`

NOTES

Exit codes and their meanings are as follows:

exit (1) device function could not initiate properly due to misconnected cables or poorly inserted tape cartridge.

exit (2) device function failed to complete properly due to unrecoverable error condition, either in the command setup or due to mechanical failure.

exit (3) device function failed due to the cartridge being write protected or to the lack of written data on the tape.

exit (4) device `/dev/rmt/c0s0n` or `/dev/rmt/c0s0` failed to open properly due to already being opened or claimed by another process.

NAME

tar – tape file archiver

SYNOPSIS

/usr/sbin/tar -c[vwfbL[#s]] *device block files ...*
/usr/sbin/tar -r[vwfbL[#s]] *device block files ...*
/usr/sbin/tar -t[vfL[#s] *device [files ...]*
/usr/sbin/tar -u[vwfbL[#s]] *device block files ...*
/usr/sbin/tar -x[lmovwfL[#s]] *device [files ...]*

DESCRIPTION

tar saves and restores files on magnetic tape. Its actions are controlled by the *key* argument. The *key* is a string of characters containing one function letter (c, r, t, u, or x) and possibly followed by one or more function modifiers (v, w, f, b, and #). Other arguments to the command are *files* (or directory names) specifying which files are to be dumped or restored. In all cases, appearance of a directory name refers to the files and (recursively) subdirectories of that directory.

The function portion of the key is specified by one of the following letters:

c	Create a new tape; writing begins at the beginning of the tape, instead of after the last file. This key implies the r key.

r	Replace. The named *files* are written on the end of the tape. The c and u functions imply this function.

t	Table. The names and other information for the specified files are listed each time that they occur on the tape. The listing is similar to the format produced by the ls -l command. If no *files* argument is given, all the names on the tape are listed.

u	Update. The named *files* are added to the tape if they are not already there, or have been modified since last written on that tape. This key implies the r key.

x	Extract. The named *files* are extracted from the tape. If a named file matches a directory whose contents had been written onto the tape, this directory is (recursively) extracted. Use the file or directory's relative path when appropriate, or tar will not find a match. The owner, modification time, and mode are restored (if possible). If no *files* argument is given, the entire content of the tape is extracted. Note that if several files with the same name are on the tape, the last one overwrites all earlier ones.

The characters below may be used in addition to the letter that selects the desired function. Use them in the order shown in the synopsis. Note: the only applicable device information for the 3B2 Computer is as follows:

/dev/mt/ctape [12. . .]

#s	This modifier determines the drive on which the tape is mounted (replace # with the drive number) and the speed of the drive (replace *s* with l, m, or h for low, medium or high). The modifier tells tar to use a drive other than the default drive, or the drive specified with the -f option. For example, with the 5h modifier, tar would use /dev/mt/5h or /dev/mt0 instead of the default drives /dev/mt/0m or /dev/mt0, respectively. However, if for example, -f /dev/rmt0 5h appeared on the command line, `tar` would use /dev/rmt5h or /devmt0. The default entry is 0m.

v Verbose. Normally, `tar` does its work silently. The `v` (verbose) option causes it to type the name of each file it treats, preceded by the function letter. With the `t` function, `v` gives more information about the tape entries than just the name.

w What. This causes `tar` to print the action to be taken, followed by the name of the file, and then wait for the user's confirmation. If a word beginning with `y` is given, the action is performed. Any other input means no. This is not valid with the `t` key.

f File. This causes `tar` to use the *device* argument as the name of the archive instead of /dev/mt/0m or /dev/mt0. If the name of the file is –, `tar` writes to the standard output or reads from the standard input, whichever is appropriate. Thus, `tar` can be used as the head or tail of a pipeline. `tar` can also be used to move hierarchies with the command:

cd *fromdir*; `tar cf - .`(cd *todir*; `tar xf -`)

b Blocking Factor. This causes `tar` to use the *block* argument as the blocking factor for tape records. The default is 1, the maximum is 20. This function should not be supplied when operating on regular archives or block special devices. It is mandatory however, when reading archives on raw magnetic tape archives (see `f` above). The block size is determined automatically when reading tapes created on block special devices (key letters `x` and `t`).

l Link. This tells `tar` to complain if it cannot resolve all of the links to the files being dumped. If `l` is not specified, no error messages are printed.

m Modify. This tells `tar` to not restore the modification times. The modification time of the file will be the time of extraction.

o Ownership. This causes extracted files to take on the user and group identifier of the user running the program, rather than those on tape. This is only valid with the `x` key.

L Follow symbolic links. This causes symbolic links to be followed. By default, symbolic links are not followed.

FILES

/dev/mt/*
/dev/mt*
/dev/mt/ctape
/dev/mt/0m
/dev/rmt/0m
/tmp/tar*

SEE ALSO

`ar`(1), `cpio`(1), `ls`(1).

DIAGNOSTICS

Complaints about bad key characters and tape read/write errors.
Complaints if enough memory is not available to hold the link tables.

NOTES

There is no way to ask for the *n*-th occurrence of a file.

Tape errors are handled ungracefully.

The `u` option can be slow.

The `b` option should not be used with archives that are going to be updated. The current magnetic tape driver cannot backspace raw magnetic tape. If the archive is on a disk file, the `b` option should not be used at all, because updating an archive stored on disk can destroy it.

The current limit on file name length is 100 characters.

`tar` doesn't copy empty directories or special files.

NAME

`tee` – pipe fitting

SYNOPSIS

`tee [-i] [-a]` [*file*] ...

DESCRIPTION

`tee` transcribes the standard input to the standard output and makes copies in the *files*. The

`-i` ignore interrupts;

`-a` causes the output to be appended to the *files* rather than overwriting them.

NAME

`telnet` – user interface to a remote system using the TELNET protocol

SYNOPSIS

`telnet` [*host* [*port*]]

DESCRIPTION

`telnet` communicates with another host using the TELNET protocol. If `telnet` is invoked without arguments, it enters command mode, indicated by its prompt `telnet>`. In this mode, it accepts and executes the commands listed below. If it is invoked with arguments, it performs an open command (see "Telnet Commands" below) with those arguments.

Once a connection has been opened, `telnet` enters input mode. In this mode, text typed is sent to the remote host. The input mode entered will be either character at a time or line by line depending on what the remote system supports.

In character at a time mode, most text typed is immediately sent to the remote host for processing.

In line by line mode, all text is echoed locally, and (normally) only completed lines are sent to the remote host. The local echo character (initially `^E`) may be used to turn off and on the local echo (this would mostly be used to enter passwords without the password being echoed).

In either mode, if the *localchars* toggle is TRUE (the default in line mode; see below), the user's `quit`, `intr`, and `flush` characters are trapped locally, and sent as TELNET protocol sequences to the remote side. There are options (see `toggle`, `autoflush`, and `toggle`, `autosynch`) which cause this action to flush subsequent output to the terminal (until the remote host acknowledges the TELNET sequence) and flush previous terminal input (in the case of `quit` and `intr`).

While connected to a remote host, `telnet` command mode may be entered by typing the `telnet` escape character (initially `^]`). When in command mode, the normal terminal editing conventions are available.

USAGE

Telnet Commands

The following commands are available. Only enough of each command to uniquely identify it need be typed (this is also true for arguments to the `mode`, `set`, `toggle`, and `display` commands).

open *host* [*port*]
: Open a connection to the named host. If no port number is specified, `telnet` will attempt to contact a TELNET server at the default port. The host specification may be either a host name [see `hosts`(4)] or an Internet address specified in the dot notation [see `inet`(7)].

`close` Close any open TELNET session and exit `telnet`. An EOF (in command mode) will also close a session and exit.

`quit` Same as `close`, above.

z
: Suspend **telnet**. This command only works when the user is using a shell that supports job control, such as **sh**(1).

mode *type*
: *type* is either **line** (for line by line mode) or *character* (for character at a time mode). The remote host is asked for permission to go into the requested mode. If the remote host is capable of entering that mode, the requested mode will be entered.

status
: Show the current status of **telnet**. This includes the peer one is connected to, as well as the current mode.

display [*argument...*]
: Display all, or some, of the **set** and **toggle** values (see **toggle**, *arguments*).

? [*command*]
: Get help. With no arguments, **telnet** print a help summary. If a command is specified, **telnet** will print the help information for just that command.

send *arguments*
: Send one or more special character sequences to the remote host. The following are the arguments which may be specified (more than one argument may be specified at a time):

escape
: Send the current **telnet** escape character (initially ^]).

synch
: Send the TELNET **SYNCH** sequence. This sequence discards all previously typed (but not yet read) input on the remote system. This sequence is sent as TCP urgent data (and may not work if the remote system is a 4.2 BSD system — if it does not work, a lower case r may be echoed on the terminal).

brk
: Send the TELNET **BRK** (Break) sequence, which may have significance to the remote system.

ip
: Send the TELNET **IP** (Interrupt Process) sequence, which aborts the currently running process on the remote system.

ao
: Sends the TELNET **AO** (Abort Output) sequence, which flushes all output from the remote system to the user's terminal.

ayt
: Sends the TELNET **AYT** (Are You There) sequence, to which the remote system may or may not choose to respond.

ec
: Sends the TELNET **EC** (Erase Character) sequence, which erases the last character entered.

el
: Sends the TELNET **EL** (Erase Line) sequence, which should cause the remote system to erase the line currently being entered.

ga
: Sends the TELNET **GA** (Go Ahead) sequence, which likely has no significance to the remote system.

nop Sends the TELNET NOP (No Operation) sequence.

? Prints out help information for the **send** command.

set *argument value*

Set any one of a number of telnet variables to a specific value. The special value off turns off the function associated with the variable. The values of variables may be interrogated with the display command. The variables which may be specified are:

echo This is the value (initially ^E) which, when in line by line mode, toggles between doing local echoing of entered characters (for normal processing), and suppressing echoing of entered characters (for example, entering a password).

escape

This is the telnet escape character (initially ^]) which enters telnet command mode (when connected to a remote system).

interrupt

If telnet is in **localchars** mode (see toggle localchars) and the interrupt character is typed, a TELNET IP sequence (see **send** and ip) is sent to the remote host. The initial value for the interrupt character is taken to be the terminal's intr character.

quit If telnet is in **localchars** mode (see toggle localchars) and the quit character is typed, a TELNET BRK sequence (see **send**, **brk**) is sent to the remote host. The initial value for the quit character is taken to be the terminal's quit character.

flushoutput

If telnet is in localchars mode (see toggle localchars) and the flushoutput character is typed, a TELNET AO sequence (see **send**, **ao**) is sent to the remote host. The initial value for the flush character is taken to be the terminal's flush character.

erase If telnet is in localchars mode (see toggle localchars), and if telnet is operating in character at a time mode, then when this character is typed, a TELNET EC sequence (see **send**, **ec**) is sent to the remote system. The initial value for the erase character is taken to be the terminal's erase character.

kill If telnet is in localchars mode (see toggle localchars), and if telnet is operating in character at a time mode, then when this character is typed, a TELNET EL sequence (see **send**, el) is sent to the remote system. The initial value for the kill character is taken to be the terminal's kill character.

eof If telnet is operating in line by line mode, entering this character as the first character on a line sends this character to the remote system. The initial value of the eof character is taken to be the terminal's eof character.

`toggle` *arguments...*

Toggle (between TRUE and FALSE) various flags that control how **telnet** responds to events. More than one argument may be specified. The state of these flags may be interrogated with the **display** command. Valid arguments are:

`autoflush`
: If **autoflush** and **localchars** are both TRUE, then when the **ao**, **intr**, or **quit** characters are recognized (and transformed into TELNET sequences; see **set** for details), **telnet** refuses to display any data on the user's terminal until the remote system acknowledges (using a TELNET **Timing Mark** option) that it has processed those TELNET sequences. The initial value for this toggle is TRUE if the terminal user had not done an stty noflsh, otherwise FALSE [see **stty**(1)].

`autosynch`
: If **autosynch** and **localchars** are both TRUE, then when either the **intr** or *quit* characters are typed (see **set** for descriptions of the **intr** and **quit** characters), the resulting TELNET sequence sent is followed by the TELNET **SYNCH** sequence. This procedure **should** cause the remote system to begin throwing away all previously typed input until both of the TELNET sequences have been read and acted upon. The initial value of this toggle is FALSE.

`crmod` Toggle RETURN mode. When this mode is enabled, most RETURN characters received from the remote host will be mapped into a RETURN followed by a line feed. This mode does not affect those characters typed by the user, only those received from the remote host. This mode is not very useful unless the remote host only sends RETURN, but never LINEFEED. The initial value for this toggle is FALSE.

`debug` Toggle socket level debugging (useful only to the super-user). The initial value for this toggle is FALSE .

`localchars`
: If this is TRUE , then the **flush**, **interrupt**, **quit**, **erase**, and **kill** characters (see **set**) are recognized locally, and transformed into appropriate TELNET control sequences (respectively **ao**, **ip**, **brk**, **ec**, and **el**; see **send**). The initial value for this toggle is TRUE in line by line mode, and FALSE in character at a time mode.

`netdata`
: Toggle the display of all network data (in hexadecimal format). The initial value for this toggle is FALSE.

`options`
: Toggle the display of some internal **telnet** protocol processing

(having to do with TELNET options). The initial value for this toggle is FALSE.

? Display the legal `toggle` commands.

SEE ALSO

`rlogin`(1), `sh`(1), `stty`(1), `hosts`(4), `inet`(7).

NOTES

Do not attempt to run `layers`(1) while using `telnet`.

There is no adequate way for dealing with flow control.

On some remote systems, echo has to be turned off manually when in line by line mode.

There is enough settable state to justify a `.telnetrc` file.

In line by line mode, the terminal's EOF character is only recognized (and sent to the remote system) when it is the first character on a line.

NAME

`test` – condition evaluation command

SYNOPSIS

`test` *expr*
[*expr*]

DESCRIPTION

`test` evaluates the expression *expr* and, if its value is true, sets a zero (true) exit status; otherwise, a non-zero (false) exit status is set; **`test`** also sets a non-zero exit status if there are no arguments. When permissions are tested, the effective user ID of the process is used.

All operators, flags, and brackets (brackets used as shown in the second SYNOPSIS line) must be separate arguments to the `test` command; normally these items are separated by spaces.

The following primitives are used to construct *expr*:

`-r` *file* true if *file* exists and is readable.

`-w` *file* true if *file* exists and is writable.

`-x` *file* true if *file* exists and is executable.

`-f` *file* true if *file* exists and is a regular file. Alternatively, if `/usr/sh` users specify `/usr/ucb` before `/usr/bin` in their PATH environment variable, then **`test`** will return true if *file* exists and is (`not-a-directory`). This is also the default for `/usr/bin/csh` users.

`-d` *file* true if *file* exists and is a directory.

`-h` *file* true if *file* exists and is a symbolic link. With all other primitives (except `-L` *file*), the symbolic links are followed by default.

`-c` *file* true if *file* exists and is a character special file.

`-b` *file* true if *file* exists and is a block special file.

`-p` *file* true if *file* exists and is a named pipe (fifo).

`-u` *file* true if *file* exists and its set-user-ID bit is set.

`-g` *file* true if *file* exists and its set-group-ID bit is set.

`-k` *file* true if *file* exists and its sticky bit is set.

`-s` *file* true if *file* exists and has a size greater than zero.

`-t` [*fildes*] true if the open file whose file descriptor number is *fildes* (1 by default) is associated with a terminal device.

`-z` *s1* true if the length of string *s1* is zero.

`-n` *s1* true if the length of the string *s1* is non-zero.

s1 = *s2* true if strings *s1* and *s2* are identical.

s1 != *s2*	true if strings *s1* and *s2* are *not* identical.
s1	true if *s1* is *not* the null string.
n1 **–eq** *n2*	true if the integers *n1* and *n2* are algebraically equal. Any of the comparisons **–ne**, **–gt**, **–ge**, **–lt**, and **–le** may be used in place of **–eq**.

These primaries may be combined with the following operators:

!	unary negation operator.
–a	binary *and* operator.
–o	binary *or* operator (**–a** has higher precedence than –o).
(*expr*)	parentheses for grouping. Notice also that parentheses are meaningful to the shell and, therefore, must be quoted.

SEE ALSO

find(1), **sh**(1).

NOTES

The **not-a-directory** alternative to the **–f** option is a transition aid for BSD applications and may not be supported in future releases.

The **–L** option is a migration aid for users of other shells which have similar options and may not be supported in future releases.

If you test a file you own (the *-r*, *-w*, or *-x* tests), but the permission tested does not have the *owner* bit set, a non-zero (false) exit status will be returned even though the file may have the **group** or *other* bit set for that permission. The correct exit status will be set if you are super-user.

The = and != operators have a higher precedence than the **–r** through –n operators, and = and != always expect arguments; therefore, = and != cannot be used with the **–r** through –n operators.

If more than one argument follows the **–r** through –n operators, only the first argument is examined; the others are ignored, unless a **–a** or a –o is the second argument.

NAME

`tftp` – trivial file transfer program

SYNOPSIS

`tftp` [*host*]

DESCRIPTION

`tftp` is the user interface to the Internet TFTP (Trivial File Transfer Protocol), which allows users to transfer files to and from a remote machine. The remote *host* may be specified on the command line, in which case `tftp` uses *host* as the default host for future transfers (see the `connect` command below).

USAGE

Commands

Once `tftp` is running, it issues the prompt `tftp>` and recognizes the following commands:

`connect` *host-name* [*port*]
: Set the *host* (and optionally *port*) for transfers. The TFTP protocol, unlike the FTP protocol, does not maintain connections between transfers; thus, the `connect` command does not actually create a connection, but merely remembers what host is to be used for transfers. You do not have to use the `connect` command; the remote host can be specified as part of the `get` or `put` commands.

`mode` *transfer-mode*
: Set the mode for transfers; *transfer-mode* may be one of `ascii` or `binary`. The default is `ascii`.

`put` *filename*
`put` *localfile remotefile*
`put` *filename1 filename2 ... filenameN remote-directory*
: Transfer a file, or a set of files, to the specified remote file or directory. The destination can be in one of two forms: a filename on the remote host if the host has already been specified, or a string of the form

host:*filename*

to specify both a host and filename at the same time. If the latter form is used, the specified host becomes the default for future transfers. If the remote-directory form is used, the remote host is assumed to be running the UNIX system.

`get` *filename*
`get` *remotename localname*
`get` *filename1 filename2 filename3 ... filenameN*
: Get a file or set of files (three or more) from the specified remote *sources*. *source* can be in one of two forms: a filename on the remote host if the host has already been specified, or a string of the form

host:*filename*

to specify both a host and filename at the same time. If the latter form is used, the last host specified becomes the default for future transfers.

`quit` Exit `tftp`. An EOF also exits.

`verbose`
Toggle verbose mode.

`trace` Toggle packet tracing.

`status`
Show current status.

`rexmt` *retransmission-timeout*
Set the per-packet retransmission timeout, in seconds.

`timeout` *total-transmission-timeout*
Set the total transmission timeout, in seconds.

`ascii` Shorthand for `mode ascii`.

`binary`
Shorthand for `mode binary`.

`? [` *command-name* `... ]`
Print help information.

NOTES

Because there is no user-login or validation within the TFTP protocol, many remote sites restrict file access in various ways. Approved methods for file access are specific to each site, and therefore cannot be documented here.

When using the `get` command to transfer multiple files from a remote host, three or more files must be specified. The command returns an error message if only two files are specified.

NAME

`time` – time a command

SYNOPSIS

`time` *command*

DESCRIPTION

The *command* is executed; after it is complete, `time` prints the elapsed time during the command, the time spent in the system, and the time spent in execution of the command. Times are reported in seconds.

The times are printed on standard error.

SEE ALSO

`timex`(1)
`time`(2) in the *Programmer's Reference Manual.*

NAME

`timex` – time a command; report process data and system activity

SYNOPSIS

`timex` [*options*] *command*

DESCRIPTION

The given *command* is executed; the elapsed time, user time and system time spent in execution are reported in seconds. Optionally, process accounting data for the *command* and all its children can be listed or summarized, and total system activity during the execution interval can be reported.

The output of `timex` is written on standard error.

The *options* are:

`-p` List process accounting records for *command* and all its children. This option works only if the process accounting software is installed. Suboptions `f`, `h`, `k`, `m`, `r`, and `t` modify the data items reported. The options are as follows:

- `-f` Print the `fork`(2)/ exec(2) flag and system exit status columns in the output.
- `-h` Instead of mean memory size, show the fraction of total available CPU time consumed by the process during its execution. This "hog factor" is computed as (total CPU time)/(elapsed time).
- `-k` Instead of memory size, show total kcore-minutes.
- `-m` Show mean core size (the default).
- `-r` Show CPU factor (user time/(system-time + user-time).
- `-t` Show separate system and user CPU times. The number of blocks read or written and the number of characters transferred are always reported.

`-o` Report the total number of blocks read or written and total characters transferred by *command* and all its children. This option works only if the process accounting software is installed.

`-s` Report total system activity (not just that due to *command*) that occurred during the execution interval of *command*. All the data items listed in `sar`(1) are reported.

SEE ALSO

`time`(1), `sar`(1).
`times`(2) in the *Programmer's Reference Manual*.

NOTES

Process records associated with *command* are selected from the accounting file `/var/adm/pacct` by inference, since process genealogy is not available. Background processes having the same user ID, terminal ID, and execution time window will be spuriously included.

EXAMPLES

A simple example:

```
timex -ops sleep 60
```

A terminal session of arbitrary complexity can be measured by timing a sub-shell:

```
timex -opskmt sh
        session commands
EOT
```

NAME

touch – update access and modification times of a file

SYNOPSIS

touch [-amc] [*mmddhhmm*[*yy*]] *files*

DESCRIPTION

touch causes the access and modification times of each argument to be updated. The file name is created if it does not exist. If no time is specified [see date(1)] the current time is used. The -a and -m options cause touch to update only the access or modification times respectively (default is -am). The -c option silently prevents touch from creating the file if it did not previously exist.

The return code from touch is the number of files for which the times could not be successfully modified (including files that did not exist and were not created).

SEE ALSO

date(1).
utime(2) in the *Programmer's Reference Manual.*

NOTES

Users familiar with the BSD environment will find that the -f option is accepted, but ignored. The -f option is unnecessary since touch will succeed for all files owned by the user regardless of the permissions on the files.

NAME

tput – initialize a terminal or query terminfo database

SYNOPSIS

tput [–T*type*] *capname* [*parms* ...]

tput [–T*type*] **init**

tput [–T*type*] **reset**

tput [–T*type*] **longname**

tput–S <<

DESCRIPTION

tput uses the **terminfo** database to make the values of terminal-dependent capabilities and information available to the shell (see **sh**(1)), to initialize or reset the terminal, or return the long name of the requested terminal type. **tput** outputs a string if the attribute (*cap*ability *name*) is of type string, or an integer if the attribute is of type integer. If the attribute is of type boolean, **tput** simply sets the exit code (0 for TRUE if the terminal has the capability, 1 for FALSE if it does not), and produces no output. Before using a value returned on standard output, the user should test the exit code [**$?**, see **sh**(1)] to be sure it is 0. (See the EXIT CODES and DIAGNOSTICS sections.) For a complete list of capabilities and the *capname* associated with each, see **terminfo**(4).

–T*type* indicates the *type* of terminal. Normally this option is unnecessary, because the default is taken from the environment variable **TERM**. If **–T** is specified, then the shell variables **LINES** and **COLUMNS** and the layer size [see **layers**(1)] will not be referenced.

capname indicates the attribute from the **terminfo** database.

parms If the attribute is a string that takes parameters, the arguments *parms* will be instantiated into the string. An all numeric argument will be passed to the attribute as a number.

–S allows more than one capability per invocation of **tput**. The capabilities must be passed to **tput** from the standard input instead of from the command line (see example). Only one *capname* is allowed per line. The **–S** option changes the meaning of the 0 and 1 boolean and string exit codes (see the EXIT CODES section).

init If the **terminfo** database is present and an entry for the user's terminal exists (see **–T***type*, above), the following will occur: (1) if present, the terminal's initialization strings will be output (**is1**, **is2**, **is3**, **if**, **iprog**), (2) any delays (e.g., newline) specified in the entry will be set in the tty driver, (3) tabs expansion will be turned on or off according to the specification in the entry, and (4) if tabs are not expanded, standard tabs will be set (every 8 spaces). If an entry does not contain the information needed for any of the four above activities, that activity will silently be skipped.

`reset` Instead of putting out initialization strings, the terminal's reset strings will be output if present (**rs1**, **rs2**, **rs3**, **rf**). If the reset strings are not present, but initialization strings are, the initialization strings will be output. Otherwise, **reset** acts identically to **init**.

`longname` If the **terminfo** database is present and an entry for the user's terminal exists (see −T*type* above), then the long name of the terminal will be put out. The long name is the last name in the first line of the terminal's description in the **terminfo** database [see **term**(5)].

EXAMPLES

`tput init` Initialize the terminal according to the type of terminal in the environmental variable **TERM**. This command should be included in everyone's .profile after the environmental variable **TERM** has been exported, as illustrated on the `profile`(4) manual page.

`tput -T5620 reset`
Reset an AT&T 5620 terminal, overriding the type of terminal in the environmental variable **TERM**.

`tput cup 0 0` Send the sequence to move the cursor to row 0, column 0 (the upper left corner of the screen, usually known as the "home" cursor position).

`tput clear` Echo the clear-screen sequence for the current terminal.

`tput cols` Print the number of columns for the current terminal.

`tput -T450 cols` Print the number of columns for the 450 terminal.

`bold='tput smso'`

`offbold='tput rmso'`
Set the shell variables **bold**, to begin stand-out mode sequence, and **offbold**, to end standout mode sequence, for the current terminal. This might be followed by a prompt: `echo "${bold}Please type in your name: ${offbold}\c"`

`tput hc` Set exit code to indicate if the current terminal is a hardcopy terminal.

`tput cup 23 4` Send the sequence to move the cursor to row 23, column 4.

`tput longname` Print the long name from the **terminfo** database for the type of terminal specified in the environmental variable **TERM**.

```
tput -S <<!
> clear
> cup 10 10
> bold
> !
```

This example shows tput processing several capabilities in one invocation. This example clears the screen, moves the cursor to position 10, 10 and turns on bold (extra bright) mode. The list is terminated by an exclamation mark (!) on a line by itself.

FILES

`/usr/share/lib/terminfo/?/*`	compiled terminal description database
`/usr/include/curses.h`	`curses`(3X) header file
`/usr/include/term.h`	`terminfo` header file
`/usr/lib/tabset/*`	tab settings for some terminals, in a format appropriate to be output to the terminal (escape sequences that set margins and tabs); for more information, see the "Tabs and Initialization" section of `terminfo`(4)

SEE ALSO

`clear`(1), `stty`(1), `tabs`(1).
`profile`(4), `terminfo`(4) in the *System Administrator's Reference Manual.*
Chapter 10 of the *Programmer's Guide.*

EXIT CODES

If *capname* is of type boolean, a value of `0` is set for TRUE and `1` for FALSE unless the `-s` option is used.

If *capname* is of type string, a value of `0` is set if the *capname* is defined for this terminal *type* (the value of *capname* is returned on standard output); a value of `1` is set if *capname* is not defined for this terminal *type* (a null value is returned on standard output).

If *capname* is of type boolean or string and the `-s` option is used, a value of `0` is returned to indicate that all lines were successful. No indication of which line failed can be given so exit code `1` will never appear. Exit codes `2`, `3`, and `4` retain their usual interpretation.

If *capname* is of type integer, a value of `0` is always set, whether or not *capname* is defined for this terminal *type*. To determine if *capname* is defined for this terminal *type*, the user must test the value of standard output. A value of `-1` means that *capname* is not defined for this terminal *type*.

Any other exit code indicates an error; see the DIAGNOSTICS section.

DIAGNOSTICS

`tput` prints the following error messages and sets the corresponding exit codes.

exit code	error message
0	`-1` (*capname* is a numeric variable that is not specified in the `terminfo`(4) database for this terminal type, e.g. `tput -T450 lines` and `tput -T2621 xmc`)
1	no error message is printed, see the **EXIT CODES** section.
2	usage error
3	unknown terminal *type* or no `terminfo` database
4	unknown `terminfo` capability *capname*

NAME

tr – translate characters

SYNOPSIS

tr [-cds] [*string1* [*string2*]]

DESCRIPTION

tr copies the standard input to the standard output with substitution or deletion of selected characters. Input characters found in *string1* are mapped into the corresponding characters of *string2*. Any combination of the options -cds may be used:

-c Complements the set of characters in *string1* with respect to the universe of characters whose ASCII codes are 001 through 377 octal.

-d Deletes all input characters in *string1*.

-s Squeezes all strings of repeated output characters that are in *string2* to single characters.

The following abbreviation conventions may be used to introduce ranges of characters or repeated characters into the strings:

[a-z] Stands for the string of characters whose ASCII codes run from character a to character z, inclusive.

[a*n] Stands for *n* repetitions of a. If the first digit of *n* is 0, *n* is considered octal; otherwise, *n* is taken to be decimal. A zero or missing *n* is taken to be huge; this facility is useful for padding *string2*.

The escape character \ may be used as in the shell to remove special meaning from any character in a string. In addition, \ followed by 1, 2, or 3 octal digits stands for the character whose ASCII code is given by those digits.

EXAMPLE

The following example creates a list of all the words in *file1* one per line in *file2*, where a word is taken to be a maximal string of alphabetics. The strings are quoted to protect the special characters from interpretation by the shell; 012 is the ASCII code for newline.

```
tr -cs "[A-Z][a-z]" "[\012*]" <file1>file2
```

SEE ALSO

ed(1), sh(1).

ascii(5) in the *System Administrator's Reference Manual*.

NOTES

Will not handle ASCII NUL in *string1* or *string2*; always deletes NUL from input.

NAME

`true`, `false` – provide truth values

SYNOPSIS

`true`

`false`

DESCRIPTION

`true` does nothing, successfully. `false` does nothing, unsuccessfully. They are typically used in input to `sh` such as:

```
while true
do
        command
done
```

SEE ALSO

sh(1).

DIAGNOSTICS

`true` has exit status zero, `false`, and nonzero.

NAME

truss – trace system calls and signals

SYNOPSIS

truss [-p] [-f] [-c] [-a] [-e] [-i] [-[tvx] [!] *syscall*...] [-s [!] *signal*...] [-m [!] *fault*...] [-[rw] [!] *fd*...] [-o *outfile*] *command*

DESCRIPTION

truss executes the specified command and produces a trace of the system calls it performs, the signals it receives, and the machine faults it incurs. Each line of the trace output reports either the fault or signal name or the system call name with its arguments and return value(s). System call arguments are displayed symbolically when possible using defines from relevant system header files; for any path-name pointer argument, the pointed-to string is displayed. Error returns are reported using the error code names described in intro(2).

The following options are recognized. For those options which take a list argument, the name all can be used as a shorthand to specify all possible members of the list. If the list begins with a !, the meaning of the option is negated (e.g., exclude rather than trace). Multiple occurrences of the same option may be specified. For the same name in a list, subsequent options (those to the right) override previous ones (those to the left).

-p Interpret the arguments to truss as a list of process-ids for existing processes (see ps(1)) rather than as a command to be executed. truss takes control of each process and begins tracing it provided that the userid and groupid of the process match those of the user or that the user is a privileged user. Processes may also be specified by their names in the /proc directory, e.g., /proc/1234; this works for remotely-mounted /proc directories as well.

-f Follow all children created by fork() and include their signals, faults, and system calls in the trace output. Normally, only the first-level command or process is traced. When -f is specified, the process-id is included with each line of trace output to indicate which process executed the system call or received the signal.

-c Count traced system calls, faults, and signals rather than displaying the trace line-by-line. A summary report is produced after the traced command terminates or when truss is interrupted. If -f is also specified, the counts include all traced system calls, faults, and signals for child processes.

-a Show the argument strings which are passed in each exec() system call.

-e Show the environment strings which are passed in each exec() system call.

-i Don't display interruptible sleeping system calls. Certain system calls, such as open() and read() on terminal devices or pipes can sleep for indefinite periods and are interruptible. Normally, truss reports such sleeping system calls if they remain asleep for more than one second. The system call is reported again a second time when it completes. The `-i` option causes such system calls to be reported only once, when they complete.

`-t` [`!`] *syscall,...*
: System calls to trace or exclude. Those system calls specified in the comma-separated list are traced. If the list begins with a '!', the specified system calls are excluded from the trace output. Default is **`-tall`**.

`-v` [`!`] *syscall,...*
: Verbose. Display the contents of any structures passed by address to the specified system calls (if traced). Input values as well as values returned by the operating system are shown. For any field used as both input and output, only the output value is shown. Default is **`-v!all`**.

`-x` [`!`] *syscall,...*
: Display the arguments to the specified system calls (if traced) in raw form, usually hexadecimal, rather than symbolically. This is for unredeemed hackers who must see the raw bits to be happy. Default is **`-x!all`**.

`-s` [`!`] *signal,...* Signals to trace or exclude. Those signals specified in the comma-separated list are traced. The trace output reports the receipt of each specified signal, even if the signal is being ignored (not blocked) by the process. (Blocked signals are not received until the process releases them.) Signals may be specified by name or number (see **`<sys/signal.h>`**). If the list begins with a '!', the specified signals are excluded from the trace output. Default is **`-sall`**.

`-m` [`!`] *fault,...* Machine faults to trace or exclude. Those machine faults specified in the comma-separated list are traced. Faults may be specified by name or number (see **`<sys/fault.h>`**). If the list begins with a '!', the specified faults are excluded from the trace output. Default is **`-mall -m!fltpage`**.

`-r` [`!`] *fd,...* Show the full contents of the I/O buffer for each **`read()`** on any of the specified file descriptors. The output is formatted 32 bytes per line and shows each byte as an ascii character (preceded by one blank) or as a 2-character C language escape sequence for control characters such as horizontal tab (\t) and newline (\n). If ascii interpretation is not possible, the byte is shown in 2-character hexadecimal representation. (The first 16 bytes of the I/O buffer for each traced **`read()`** are shown even in the absence of `-r`.) Default is **`-r!all`**.

`-w` [`!`] *fd,...* Show the contents of the I/O buffer for each **`write()`** on any of the specified file descriptors (see `-r`). Default is **`-w!all`**.

`-o` *outfile* File to be used for the trace output. By default, the output goes to standard error.

See Section 2 of the *Programmer's Reference Manual* for **syscall** names accepted by the **-t**, **-v**, and **-x** options. System call numbers are also accepted.

If **truss** is used to initiate and trace a specified command and if the **-o** option is used or if standard error is redirected to a non-terminal file, then **truss** runs with hangup, interrupt, and quit signals ignored. This facilitates tracing of interactive programs which catch interrupt and quit signals from the terminal.

If the trace output remains directed to the terminal, or if existing processes are traced (the **-p** option), then **truss** responds to hangup, interrupt, and quit signals by releasing all traced processes and exiting. This enables the user to terminate excessive trace output and to release previously-existing processes. Released processes continue normally, as though they had never been touched.

EXAMPLES

This example produces a trace of the **find**(1) command on the terminal:

```
truss find . -print >find.out
```

Or, to see only a trace of the open, close, read, and write system calls:

```
truss -t open,close,read,write find . -print >find.out
```

This produces a trace of the **spell**(1) command on the file truss.out:

```
truss -f -o truss.out spell document
```

spell is a shell script, so the **-f** flag is needed to trace not only the shell but also the processes created by the shell. (The spell script runs a pipeline of eight concurrent processes.)

A particularly boring example is:

```
truss nroff -mm document >nroff.out
```

because 97% of the output reports **lseek**(), **read**(), and **write**() system calls. To abbreviate it:

```
truss -t !lseek,read,write nroff -mm document >nroff.out
```

This example verbosely traces the activity of process #1, **init**(1M) (provided you are a privileged user):

```
truss -p -v all 1
```

Interrupting **truss** returns **init** to normal operation.

FILES

/proc/*nnnnn*   process files

NOTES

Some of the system calls described in Section 2 of the *Programmer's Reference Manual* differ from the actual operating system interfaces. Do not be surprised by minor deviations of the trace output from the descriptions in Section 2.

Every machine fault (except a page fault) results in the posting of a signal to the process which incurred the fault. A report of a received signal will immediately follow each report of a machine fault (except a page fault) unless that signal is being blocked by the process.

The operating system enforces certain security restrictions on the tracing of processes. In particular, any command whose object file (`a.out`) cannot be read by a user cannot be traced by that user; set-uid and set-gid commands can be traced only by a privileged user. Unless it is run by a privileged user, **truss** loses control of any process which performs an **exec**(2) of a set-id or unreadable object file; such processes continue normally, though independently of **truss**, from the point of the **exec**().

To avoid collisions with other controlling processes, **truss** will not trace a process which it detects is being controlled by another process via the `/proc` interface. This allows **truss** to be applied to *proc*(4)-based debuggers as well as to another instance of itself.

The trace output contains tab characters under the assumption that standard tab stops are set (every eight positions).

The trace output for multiple processes is not produced in strict time order. For example, a **read**() on a pipe may be reported before the corresponding **write**(). For any one process, the output is strictly time-ordered.

The system may run out of per-user process slots when tracing of children is requested. When tracing more than one process, **truss** runs as one controlling process for each process being traced. For the example of the **spell** command shown above, **spell** itself uses 9 process slots, one for the shell and 8 for the 8-member pipeline, while **truss** adds another 9 processes, for a total of 18. This is perilously close to the usual system-imposed limit of 25 processes per user.

truss uses shared memory and semaphores when dealing with more than one process (**-f** option or **-p** with more than one **pid**). It issues a warning message and proceeds when these are needed but not configured in the system. However, the trace output may become garbled in this case and the output of the **-c** option reports only the top-level command or first **pid** and no children are counted.

Not all possible structures passed in all possible system calls are displayed under the **-v** option.

SEE ALSO

`intro`(2), `proc`(4)

NAME

`tty` – get the name of the terminal

SYNOPSIS

`tty` [`-l`] [`-s`]

DESCRIPTION

`tty` prints the path name of the user's terminal.

`-l` prints the synchronous line number to which the user's terminal is connected, if it is on an active synchronous line.

`-s` inhibits printing of the terminal path name, allowing one to test just the exit code.

EXIT CODES

2 if invalid options were specified,
0 if standard input is a terminal,
1 otherwise.

DIAGNOSTICS

''`not on an active synchronous line`'' if the standard input is not a synchronous terminal and `-l` is specified.
''`not a tty`'' if the standard input is not a terminal and `-s` is not specified.

NAME

umask – set file-creation mode mask

SYNOPSIS

umask [*ooo*]

DESCRIPTION

The user file-creation mode mask is set to *ooo*. The three octal digits refer to read/write/execute permissions for *owner*, group, and *others*, respectively (see chmod(2) and umask(2)). The value of each specified digit is subtracted from the corresponding "digit" specified by the system for the creation of a file (see creat(2)). For example, umask 022 removes group and *others* write permission (files normally created with mode 777 become mode 755; files created with mode 666 become mode 644).

If *ooo* is omitted, the current value of the mask is printed.

umask is recognized and executed by the shell.

umask can be included in the user's .profile (see profile(4)) and invoked at login to automatically set the user's permissions on files or directories created.

SEE ALSO

chmod(1), sh(1).
chmod(2), creat(2), umask(2) in the *Programmer's Reference Manual.*
profile(4) in the *System Administrator's Reference Manual.*

NAME

uname – print name of current UNIX system

SYNOPSIS

uname [**-amnprsv**]
uname [-S *system_name*]

DESCRIPTION

uname prints the current system name of the UNIX system to standard output. It is mainly useful to determine which system one is using. The options cause selected information returned by **uname**(2) and/or **sysinfo**(2) to be printed:

- **-a** Print all information.
- **-m** Print the machine hardware name.
- **-n** Print the nodename (the nodename is the name by which the system is known to a communications network). This is the default.
- **-p** Print the current host's processor type.
- **-r** Print the operating system release.
- **-s** Print the name of the operating system (e.g. UNIX System V).
- **-v** Print the operating system version.

On your 3B2 computer, the nodename may be changed by specifying a system name argument to the -S option. The system name argument is restricted to SYS_NMLN characters. SYS_NMLN is an implementation specific value defined in <**sys/utsname.h**>. Only the super-user is allowed this capability.

SEE ALSO

sysinfo(2), **uname**(2) in the *Programmer's Reference Manual*.

NAME

uniq – report repeated lines in a file

SYNOPSIS

uniq [-udc [+n] [-n]] [*input* [*output*]]

DESCRIPTION

uniq reads the input file comparing adjacent lines. In the normal case, the second and succeeding copies of repeated lines are removed; the remainder is written on the output file. *Input* and *output* should always be different. Note that repeated lines must be adjacent in order to be found; see sort(1). If the –u flag is used, just the lines that are not repeated in the original file are output. The –d option specifies that one copy of just the repeated lines is to be written. The normal mode output is the union of the –u and –d mode outputs.

The –c option supersedes –u and –d and generates an output report in default style but with each line preceded by a count of the number of times it occurred.

The *n* arguments specify skipping an initial portion of each line in the comparison:

–*n* The first *n* fields together with any blanks before each are ignored. A field is defined as a string of non-space, non-tab characters separated by tabs and spaces from its neighbors.

+*n* The first *n* characters are ignored. Fields are skipped before characters.

SEE ALSO

comm(1), sort(1).

NAME

`units` – conversion program

SYNOPSIS

`units`

DESCRIPTION

`units` converts quantities expressed in various standard scales to their equivalents in other scales. It works interactively in this fashion:

```
You have: inch
You want: cm
                * 2.540000e+00
                / 3.937008e-01
```

A quantity is specified as a multiplicative combination of units optionally preceded by a numeric multiplier. Powers are indicated by suffixed positive integers, division by the usual sign:

```
You have: 15 lbs force/in2
You want: atm
                * 1.020689e+00
                / 9.797299e-01
```

`units` only does multiplicative scale changes; thus it can convert Kelvin to Rankine, but not Celsius to Fahrenheit. Most familiar units, abbreviations, and metric prefixes are recognized, together with a generous leavening of exotica and a few constants of nature including:

`pi`	ratio of circumference to diameter,
`c`	speed of light,
`e`	charge on an electron,
`g`	acceleration of gravity,
`force`	same as `g`,
`mole`	Avogadro's number,
`water`	pressure head per unit height of water,
`au`	astronomical unit.

`Pound` is not recognized as a unit of mass; `lb` is. Compound names are run together, (e.g., `lightyear`). British units that differ from their U.S. counterparts are prefixed thus: `brgallon`. For a complete list of units, type:

```
cat /usr/lib/unittab
```

FILES

`/usr/lib/unittab`

NAME

uucp, uulog, uuname – UNIX-to-UNIX system copy

SYNOPSIS

uucp [*options*] **source-files destination-file**
uulog [*options*] **system**
uuname [*options*]

DESCRIPTION

uucp

uucp copies files named by the *source-file* arguments to the *destination-file* argument. A source file name may be a patname on your machine, or, may have the form:

system-name!*pathname*

where *system-name* is taken from a list of system names that uucp knows about. The destination *system-name* may also include a list of system names such as

system-name!*system-name*! . . . !*system-name*!*pathname*

In this case, an attempt is made to send the file, via the specified route, to the destination. Care should be taken to ensure that intermediate nodes in the route are willing to forward information (see NOTES below for restrictions).

The shell metacharacters ?, * and [. . .] appearing in *pathname* will be expanded on the appropriate system.

Path names may be one of:

(1) a full pathname;

(2) a pathname preceded by ~*user* where *user* is a login name on the specified system and is replaced by that user's login directory;

(3) a pathname preceded by ~/*destination* where *destination* is appended to /var/spool/uucppublic; (NOTE: This destination will be treated as a file name unless more than one file is being transferred by this request or the destination is already a directory. To ensure that it is a directory, follow the destination with a '/'. For example ~/*dan*/ as the destination will make the directory /var/spool/uucppublic/dan if it does not exist and put the requested file(s) in that directory).

(4) anything else is prefixed by the current directory.

If the result is an erroneous pathname for the remote system, the copy will fail. If the *destination-file* is a directory, the last part of the *source-file* name is used.

uucp removes execute permissions across the transmission and gives 0666 read and write permissions (see chmod(2)).

The following options are interpreted by uucp:

–c Do not copy local file to the spool directory for transfer to the remote machine (default).

- `-C` Force the copy of local files to the spool directory for transfer.
- `-d` Make all necessary directories for the file copy (default).
- `-f` Do not make intermediate directories for the file copy.
- `-g`*grade* *grade* can be either a single letter/number or a string of alphanumeric characters defining a service grade. The `uuglist` command can determine whether it is appropriate to use the single letter/number or a string of alphanumeric characters as a service grade. The output from the uuglist command will be a list of service grades that are available or a message that says to use a single letter/number as a grade of service.
- `-j` Output the `uucp` job identification string on the standard output. This job identification can be used by `uustat` to obtain the status of a `uucp` job or to terminate a `uucp` job. It is valid as long as the job remains queued on the local system.
- `-m` Send mail to the requester when the copy is completed.
- `-n`*user* Notify *user* on the remote system that a file was sent.
- `-r` Do not start the file transfer, just queue the job.
- `-s`*file* Report status of the transfer to *file*. This option overrides the `-m` option.
- `-x`*debug_level*
  Produce debugging output on standard output. *debug_level* is a number between 0 and 9; as it increases to 9, more detailed debugging information is given. This option may not be available on all systems.

uulog

`uulog` queries a log file of `uucp` or `uuxqt` transactions in file `/var/uucp/.Log/uucico/system` or `/var/uucp/.Log/uuxqt/`*system.*

These options cause `uulog` to print logging information:

- `-s`*sys* Print information about file transfer work involving system *sys*.
- `-fsystem` Does a "`tail -f`" of the file transfer log for `system`. (You must hit BREAK to exit this function.)

Other options used in conjunction with the above options are:

- `-x` Look in the `uuxqt` log file for the given system.
- `-`*number* Indicates that a "tail" command of *number* lines should be executed.

uuname

`uuname` lists the names of systems known to uucp. `uuname` recognizes the following options:

- `-c` Returns the names of systems known to `cu`. (The two lists are the same, unless your machine is using different *Systems* files for `cu` and uucp. See the *Sysfiles* file.)

`-l` Return the local system name.

FILES

/var/spool/uucp	spool directories
/var/spool/uucppublic/*	public directory for receiving and sending
/usr/lib/uucp/*	other program files
/etc/uucp/*	other data files

SEE ALSO

mail(1), uuglist(1C), uustat(1C), uux(1C), uuxqt(1M).
chmod(2) in the *Programmer's Reference Manual.*

NOTES

For security reasons, the domain of remotely accessible files may be severely restricted. You will very likely not be able to access files by pathname; ask a responsible person on the remote system to send them to you. For the same reasons you will probably not be able to send files to arbitrary pathnames. As distributed, the remotely accessible files are those whose names begin /var/spool/uucppublic (equivalent to ~/).

All files received by uucp will be owned by uucp.

The -m option will only work sending files or receiving a single file. Receiving multiple files specified by special shell characters ? * [. . .] will not activate the -m option.

The forwarding of files through other systems may not be compatible with the previous version of uucp. If forwarding is used, all systems in the route must have compatible versions of uucp.

NOTES

Protected files and files that are in protected directories that are owned by the requester can be sent by uucp. However, if the requester is root, and the directory is not searchable by "other" or the file is not readable by "other", the request will fail.

NAME

uuencode, uudecode – encode a binary file, or decode its ASCII representation

SYNOPSIS

uuencode [*source-file*] *file-label*

uudecode [*encoded-file*]

DESCRIPTION

uuencode converts a binary file into an ASCII-encoded representation that can be sent using `mail(1)`. It encodes the contents of *source-file*, or the standard input if no *source-file* argument is given. The *file-label* argument is required. It is included in the encoded file's header as the name of the file into which **uudecode** is to place the binary (decoded) data. **uuencode** also includes the ownership and permission modes of *source-file*, so that *file-label* is recreated with those same ownership and permission modes.

uudecode reads an *encoded-file*, strips off any leading and trailing lines added by mailer programs, and recreates the original binary data with the filename and the mode and owner specified in the header.

The encoded file is an ordinary ASCII text file; it can be edited by any text editor. But it is best only to change the mode or file-label in the header to avoid corrupting the decoded binary.

SEE ALSO

`mail(1)`, `uucp(1C)`, `uux(1C)`.

uuencode(5) in the *System Administrator's Reference Manual*.

NOTES

The encoded file's size is expanded by 35% (3 bytes become 4, plus control information), causing it to take longer to transmit than the equivalent binary.

The user on the remote system who is invoking **uudecode** (typically uucp) must have write permission on the file specified in the *file-label*.

Since both **uuencode** and **uudecode** run with user ID set to uucp, uudecode can fail with permission denied when attempted in a directory that does not have write permission allowed for other.

NAME

uuglist − print the list of service grades that are available on this UNIX system

SYNOPSIS

uuglist [−u]

DESCRIPTION

uuglist prints the list of service grades that are available on the system to use with the −g option of uucp(1C) and uux(1C). The −u option lists the names of the service grades that the user is allowed to use with the −g option of the uucp and uux commands.

FILES

/usr/lib/uucp/Grades contains the list of service grades

SEE ALSO

uucp(1C), uux(1C).

NAME

uustat – uucp status inquiry and job control

SYNOPSIS

uustat [-q] or [-m] or [-k*jobid* [-n]] or [-r*jobid* [-n]] or [-p]
uustat [-a] [-s*system* [-j]] [-u*user*] [-S*qric*]
uustat -t*system* [-d*number*] [-c]

DESCRIPTION

uustat functions in the following three areas: displays the general status of, or cancels, previously specified uucp commands; provides remote system performance information, in terms of average transfer rates or average queue times; provides general remote system-specific and user-specific status of uucp connections to other systems.

Here are the options that obtain general status of, or cancel, previously specified uucp commands; uustat allows only one of these options to appear on each uustat command line execution:

-a List all jobs in queue.

-j List the total number of jobs displayed. The -j option must be used in conjunction with the -a or the -s option.

-k*jobid* Kill the uucp request whose job identification is *jobid*. The killed uucp request must belong to the person issuing the uustat command unless one is the super-user or uucp administrator. If the job is killed by the super-user or uucp administrator, electronic mail is sent to the user.

-m Report the status of accessibility of all machines.

-n Suppress all standard out output, but not standard error. The -n option is used in conjunction with the -k and -r options.

-p Execute the command ps -flp for all the process-ids that are in the lock files.

-q List the jobs queued for each machine. If a status file exists for the machine, its date, time and status information are reported. In addition, if a number appears in parentheses next to the number of C or X files, it is the age in days of the oldest C./X. file for that system. The Retry field represents the number of hours until the next possible call. The Count is the number of failure attempts. NOTE: for systems with a moderate number of outstanding jobs, this could take 30 seconds or more of real-time to execute. Here is an example of the output produced by the -q option:

```
eagle     3C    04/07-11:07    NO DEVICES AVAILABLE
mh3bs3    2C    07/07-10:42    SUCCESSFUL
```

The above output tells how many command files are waiting for each system. Each command file may have zero or more files to be sent (zero means to call the system and see if work is to be done). The date and time refer to the previous interaction with the system followed by the status of the interaction.

-r*jobid* Rejuvenate *jobid*. The files associated with *jobid* are touched so that their modification time is set to the current time. This prevents the cleanup daemon from deleting the job until the jobs' modification time reaches the limit imposed by the daemon.

Here are the options that provide remote system performance information, in terms of average transfer rates or average queue times; the -c and -d options can only be used in conjunction with the -t option:

-t*system* Report the average transfer rate or average queue time for the past 60 minutes for the remote *system*. The following parameters can only be used with this option:

-d*number* *number* is specified in minutes. Used to override the 60 minute default used for calculations. These calculations are based on information contained in the optional performance log and therefore may not be available. Calculations can only be made from the time that the performance log was last cleaned up.

-c Average queue time is calculated when the -c parameter is specified and average transfer rate when -c is not specified. For example, the command

```
uustat -teagle -d50 -c
```

produces output in the following format:

```
average queue time to eagle for last 50 minutes: 5 seconds
```

The same command without the -c parameter produces output in the following format:

```
average transfer rate with eagle for last 50 minutes: 2000.88
bytes/sec
```

Here are the options that provide general remote system-specific and user-specific status of uucp connections to other systems. Either or both of the following options can be specified with *uustat*. The -j option can be used in conjunction with the -s option to list the total number of jobs displayed:

-s*system* Report the status of all uucp requests for remote system *system*.

-u*user* Report the status of all uucp requests issued by *user*.

Output for both the -s and -u options has the following format:

```
eagleN1bd7  4/07-11:07  S  eagle  dan  522    /home/dan/A
eagleC1bd8  4/07-11:07  S  eagle  dan   59    D.3b2al2ce4924
            4/07-11:07  S  eagle  dan  rmail  mike
```

With the above two options, the first field is the *jobid* of the job. This is followed by the date/time. The next field is an S if the job is sending a file or an R if the job is requesting a file. The next field is the machine where the file is to be transferred. This is followed by the user-id of the user who queued the job. The next field contains the size of the file, or in the case of a remote execution (rmail is the command used for remote mail), the name of the command. When the size appears in this field, the file name is also given. This can either be the name given by the user or an internal name (e.g., D.3b2alce4924) that is created for data files associated with remote executions (`rmail` in this example).

-Sqric Report the job state: `q` for queued jobs, `r` for running jobs, `i` for interrupted jobs, and `c` for completed jobs.

A job is queued if the transfer has not started. A job is running when the transfer has begun. A job is interrupted if the transfer began but was terminated before the file was completely transferred. A completed job, of course, is a job that successfully transferred. The completed state information is maintained in the accounting log, which is optional and therefore may be unavailable. The parameters can be used in any combination, but at least one parameter must be specified. The `-S` option can also be used with `-s` and `-u` options. The output for this option is exactly like the output for `-s` and `-u` except that the job states are appended as the last output word. Output for a completed job has the following format:

```
eagleC1bd3 completed
```

When no options are given, **uustat** outputs the status of all **uucp** requests issued by the current user.

FILES

`/var/spool/uucp/*`	spool directories
`/var/uucp/.Admin/account`	accounting log
`/var/uucp/.Admin/perflog`	performance log

SEE ALSO

uucp(1C).

DIAGNOSTICS

The `-t` option produces no message when the data needed for the calculations is not being recorded.

NOTES

After the user has issued the uucp request, if the file to be transferred is moved or deleted or was not copied to the spool directory with the `-C` option when the uucp request was made ,`uustat` reports a file size of −99999. This job will eventually fail because the file(s) to be transferred can not be found.

NAME

uuto, **uupick** – public UNIX-to-UNIX system file copy

SYNOPSIS

uuto [*options*] **source-files destination**
uupick [**-s** *system*]

DESCRIPTION

uuto sends *source-files* to *destination*. **uuto** uses the **uucp**(1C) facility to send files, while it allows the local system to control the file access. A source-file name is a path name on your machine. Destination has the form:

system[*!system*] ... *!user*

where **system** is taken from a list of system names that **uucp** knows about (see uuname(1C)). *User* is the login name of someone on the specified system.

Two options are available:

-p Copy the source file into the spool directory before transmission.
-m Send mail to the sender when the copy is complete.

The files (or sub-trees if directories are specified) are sent to *PUBDIR* on **system**, where *PUBDIR* is a public directory defined in the **uucp** source. By default, this directory is **/var/spool/uucppublic**. Specifically the files are sent to

PUBDIR/receive/*user*/*mysystem*/files.

The destined recipient is notified by **mail**(1) of the arrival of files.

uupick accepts or rejects the files transmitted to the user. Specifically, **uupick** searches *PUBDIR* for files destined for the user. For each entry (file or directory) found, the following message is printed on the standard output:

from system *sysname* : [file *file-name*] [dir *dirname*] ?

uupick then reads a line from the standard input to determine the disposition of the file:

<new-line>	Go on to next entry.
d	Delete the entry.
m [*dir*]	Move the entry to named directory *dir*. If *dir* is not specified as a complete path name (in which *$HOME* is legitimate), a destination relative to the current directory is assumed. If no destination is given, the default is the current directory.
a [*dir*]	Same as **m** except moving all the files sent from **system**.
p	Print the content of the file.
q	Stop.
EOT (control-d)	Same as **q**.

!*command*	Escape to the shell to do *command*.
*	Print a command summary.

uupick invoked with the -s system option will only search the *PUBDIR* for files sent from **system**.

FILES

PUBDIR /var/spool/uucppublic public directory

SEE ALSO

mail(1), uucp(1C), uustat(1C), uux(1C).
uucleanup(1M) in the *System Administrator's Reference Manual.*

NOTES

In order to send files that begin with a dot (e.g., .profile), the files must be qualified with a dot. For example, the following files are correct:

.profile .prof* .profil?

The following files are incorrect:

prof ?profile

NAME

uux – UNIX-to-UNIX system command execution

SYNOPSIS

uux [*options*] `command-string`

DESCRIPTION

uux will gather zero or more files from various systems, execute a command on a specified system and then send standard output to a file on a specified system.

NOTE: For security reasons, most installations limit the list of commands executable on behalf of an incoming request from uux, permitting only the receipt of mail (see `mail`(1)). (Remote execution permissions are defined in `/etc/uucp/Permissions`.)

The *command-string* is made up of one or more arguments that look like a shell command line, except that the command and file names may be prefixed by *system-name*`!`. A null *system-name* is interpreted as the local system.

File names may be one of:

(1) a full pathname;

(2) a pathname preceded by ~*xxx*, where *xxx* is a login name on the specified system and is replaced by that user's login directory;

(3) anything else is prefixed by the current directory.

As an example, the command

```
uux "!diff sys1!/home/dan/file1 sys2!/a4/dan/file2 >
!~/dan/file.diff"
```

will get the *file1* and *file2* files from the "sys1" and "sys2" machines, execute a `diff`(1) command and put the results in *file.diff* in the local *PUBDIR*/dan/ directory. *PUBDIR* is a public directory defined in the uucp source. By default, this directory is `/var/spool/uucppublic`

Any special shell characters such as <, >, ;, | should be quoted either by quoting the entire *command-string*, or quoting the special characters as individual arguments.

uux will attempt to get all appropriate files to the specified system where they will be processed. For files that are output files, the file name must be escaped using parentheses. For example, the command:

```
uux "a!cut -f1 b!/usr/file > c!/usr/file"
```

gets "/usr/file" from system "b" and sends it to system "a", performs a `cut` command on that file and sends the result of the `cut` command to system "c".

uux will notify you if the requested command on the remote system was disallowed. This notification can be turned off by the –n option. The response comes by remote mail from the remote machine.

The following *options* are interpreted by uux:

- `-` The standard input to uux is made the standard input to the *command-string*.
- `-a`*name* Use *name* as the user job identification replacing the initiator user-id. (Notification will be returned to user-id *name*.)
- `-b` Return whatever standard input was provided to the uux command if the exit status is non-zero.
- `-c` Do not copy local file to the spool directory for transfer to the remote machine (default).
- `-C` Force the copy of local files to the spool directory for transfer.
- `-g`*grade* *grade* can be either a single letter, number, or a string of alphanumeric characters defining a service grade. The *uuglist*(1C) command determines whether it is appropriate to use the single letter, number, or a string of alphanumeric characters as a service grade. The output from the *uuglist* command will be a list of service grades that are available or a message that says to use a single letter or number as a grade of service.
- `-j` Output the jobid string on the standard output which is the job identification. This job identification can be used by uustat(1C) to obtain the status or terminate a job.
- `-n` Do not notify the user if the command fails.
- `-p` Same as –: The standard input to uux is made the standard input to the *command-string*.
- `-r` Do not start the file transfer, just queue the job.
- `-s`*file* Report status of the transfer in *file*.
- `-x`*debug_level*
  Produce debugging output on the standard output. *debug_level* is a number between 0 and 9; as it increases to 9, more detailed debugging information is given.
- `-z` Send success notification to the user.

FILES

/var/spool/uucp	spool directories
/etc/uucp/Permissions	remote execution permissions
/usr/lib/uucp/*	other programs
/etc/uucp/*	other data and programs

NOTES

Only the first command of a shell pipeline may have a *system-name*!. All other commands are executed on the system of the first command.
The use of the shell metacharacter * will probably not do what you want it to do. The shell tokens << and >> are not implemented.

The execution of commands on remote systems takes place in an execution directory known to the uucp system. All files required for the execution will be put into this directory unless they already reside on that machine. Therefore, the simple file name (without path or machine reference) must be unique within the uux request. The following command will NOT work:

uux "a!diff b!/home/dan/xyz c!/home/dan/xyz > !xyz.diff"

but the command

uux "a!diff a!/home/dan/xyz c!/home/dan/xyz > !xyz.diff"

will work. (If `diff` is a permitted command.)

Protected files and files that are in protected directories that are owned by the requester can be sent in commands using uux. However, if the requester is root, and the directory is not searchable by "other", the request will fail.

SEE ALSO

`cut`(1), `mail`(1), `uuglist`(1C), uucp(1C), `uustat`(1C).

NAME

vacation – automatically respond to incoming mail messages

SYNOPSIS

vacation [-l *logfile*] [-m *mailfile*] [-M *canned_msg_file*] [-F *failsafe*]

DESCRIPTION

When a new mail message arrives, the **mail** command first checks if the recipient's mailbox indicates that the message is to be forwarded elsewhere (to some other recipient or as the input to some command). **vacation** is used to set up forwarding on the user's mailbox so that the new message is saved into an alternative mailbox and a canned response is sent to the message's originator.

Command-line options are:

-l *logfile* File to keep track of which originators have already seen the canned response. If not specified, it defaults to **$HOME/.maillog**.

-m *mailfile* Alternate mailbox to save new messages into. If not specified, it defaults to **$HOME/.mailfile**.

-M *canned_msg_file*
File to send back as the canned response. If *canned_msg_file* is not specified, it defaults to /usr/lib/mail/std_vac_msg, which contains:

```
Subject: AUTOANSWERED!!!

I am on vacation. I will read (and answer if necessary)
your e-mail message when I return.

This message was generated automatically and you will
receive it only once, although all messages you send
me while I am away WILL be saved.
```

-F *failsafe* If mail has troubles delivering to the mailfile specified, it may optionally be forwarded to another login id (*failsafe*) instead of being returned to the sender.

-d The log file will have the day's date appended.

To remove the vacation functionality, use

```
mail -F ""
```

FILES

/tmp/notif*	temporary file
/usr/share/lib/mail/std_vac_msg	default canned response
/var/mail/*	users' standard mailboxes
/usr/lib/mail/vacation2	program that actually sends back the canned response

SEE ALSO

mail(1)
User's Guide.

NOTES

Because `vacation` uses the "`Forward to` |*command*" facility of `mail` to implement notifications, `/var/mail/`*username* should not be specified as the place to put newly arrived messages via the `-m` invocation option. The `mail` command uses `/var/mail/`*username* to hold either mail messages, or indications of mail forwarding, but not both simultaneously.

NAME

vi – screen-oriented (visual) display editor based on ex

SYNOPSIS

vi [-t *tag*] [-r *file*] [-l] [-L] [-w*n*] [-R] [-x] [-C] [-c *command*] *file*...
view [-t *tag*] [-r *file*] [-l] [-L] [-w*n*] [-R] [-x] [-C] [-c *command*] *file*...
vedit [-t *tag*] [-r *file*] [-l] [-L] [-w*n*] [-R] [-x] [-C] [-c *command*] *file*...

DESCRIPTION

vi (visual) is a display-oriented text editor based on an underlying line editor **ex**. It is possible to use the command mode of **ex** from within vi and vice-versa. The visual commands are described on this manual page; how to set options (like automatically numbering lines and automatically starting a new output line when you type carriage return) and all **ex** line editor commands are described on the **ex**(1) manual page.

When using vi, changes you make to the file are reflected in what you see on your terminal screen. The position of the cursor on the screen indicates the position within the file.

Invocation Options

The following invocation options are interpreted by vi (previously documented options are discussed in the NOTES section of this manual page):

-t *tag* Edit the file containing the *tag* and position the editor at its definition.

-r *file* Edit *file* after an editor or system crash. (Recovers the version of *file* that was in the buffer when the crash occurred.)

-l Set up for editing LISP programs.

-L List the name of all files saved as the result of an editor or system crash.

-w*n* Set the default window size to *n*. This is useful when using the editor over a slow speed line.

-R Readonly mode; the readonly flag is set, preventing accidental overwriting of the file.

-x Encryption option; when used, vi simulates the X command of **ex** and prompts the user for a key. This key is used to encrypt and decrypt text using the algorithm of the crypt command. The X command makes an educated guess to determine whether text read in is encrypted or not. The temporary buffer file is encrypted also, using a transformed version of the key typed in for the -x option. See crypt(1). Also, see the WARNING section at the end of this manual page.

-C Encryption option; same as the -x option, except that vi simulates the C command of **ex**. The C command is like the X command of **ex**, except that all text read in is assumed to have been encrypted.

`-c` *command*	Begin editing by executing the specified editor *command* (usually a search or positioning command).

The *file* argument indicates one or more files to be edited.

The *view* invocation is the same as `vi` except that the **`readonly`** flag is set.

The *vedit* invocation is intended for beginners. It is the same as `vi` except that the `report` flag is set to 1, the **`showmode`** and **`novice`** flags are set, and **`magic`** is turned off. These defaults make it easier to learn how to use `vi`.

vi Modes

Command	Normal and initial mode. Other modes return to command mode upon completion. **ESC** (escape) is used to cancel a partial command.
Input	Entered by setting any of the following options: **`a A i I o O c C s S R .`** Arbitrary text may then be entered. Input mode is normally terminated with **ESC** character, or, abnormally, with an interrupt.
Last line	Reading input for `: / ?` or `!`; terminate by typing a carriage return; an interrupt cancels termination.

COMMAND SUMMARY

In the descriptions, CR stands for carriage return and ESC stands for the escape key.

Sample commands

← ↓ ↑ →	arrow keys move the cursor
`h j k l`	same as arrow keys
`i`*text*ESC	insert *text*
`cw`*new*ESC	change word to *new*
`eas`ESC	pluralize word (end of word; append `s`; escape from input state)
`x`	delete a character
`dw`	delete a word
`dd`	delete a line
`3dd`	delete 3 lines
`u`	undo previous change
`ZZ`	exit `vi`, saving changes
`:q!`CR	quit, discarding changes
`/`*text*CR	search for *text*
`^U ^D`	scroll up or down
`:`*cmd*CR	any **ex** or **ed** command

Counts before vi commands

Numbers may be typed as a prefix to some commands. They are interpreted in one of these ways.

line/column number	z G |
scroll amount	^D ^U
repeat effect	most of the rest

Interrupting, canceling

ESC	end insert or incomplete cmd
DEL	(delete or rubout) interrupts

File manipulation

ZZ	if file modified, write and exit; otherwise, exit
:wCR	write back changes
:w!CR	forced write, if permission originally not valid
:qCR	quit
:q!CR	quit, discard changes
:e *name*CR	edit file *name*
:e!CR	reedit, discard changes
:e + *name*CR	edit, starting at end
:e +*n*CR	edit starting at line *n*
:e #CR	edit alternate file
:e! #CR	edit alternate file, discard changes
:w *name*CR	write file *name*
:w! *name*CR	overwrite file *name*
:shCR	run shell, then return
:!*cmd*CR	run *cmd*, then return
:nCR	edit next file in arglist
:n *args*CR	specify new arglist
^G	show current file and line
:ta *tag*CR	position cursor to *tag*

In general, any **ex** or **ed** command (such as *substitute* or *global*) may be typed, preceded by a colon and followed by a carriage return.

Positioning within file

^F	forward screen
^B	backward screen
^D	scroll down half screen
^U	scroll up half screen
*n*G	go to the beginning of the specified line (end default), where *n* is a line number
/*pat*	next line matching *pat*
?*pat*	previous line matching *pat*
n	repeat last / or ? command
N	reverse last / or ? command
/*pat*/+*n*	nth line after *pat*
?*pat*?−*n*	nth line before *pat*
]]	next section/function
[[	previous section/function
(	beginning of sentence
)	end of sentence

{	beginning of paragraph
}	end of paragraph
%	find matching ( ) { or }

Adjusting the screen

^L	clear and redraw window
^R	clear and redraw window if ^L is → key
zCR	redraw screen with current line at top of window
z-CR	redraw screen with current line at bottom of window
z.CR	redraw screen with current line at center of window
/*pat*/z-CR	move *pat* line to bottom of window
z*n*.CR	use *n*-line window
^E	scroll window down 1 line
^Y	scroll window up 1 line

Marking and returning

``	move cursor to previous context
''	move cursor to first non-white space in line
m*x*	mark current position with the ASCII lower-case letter *x*
`*x*	move cursor to mark *x*
'*x*	move cursor to first non-white space in line marked by *x*

Line positioning

H	top line on screen
L	last line on screen
M	middle line on screen
+	next line, at first non-white
–	previous line, at first non-white
CR	return, same as +
↓ or j	next line, same column
↑ or k	previous line, same column

Character positioning

^	first non white-space character
0	beginning of line
$	end of line
h or →	forward
l or ←	backward
^H	same as ← (backspace)
space	same as → (space bar)
f*x*	find next *x*
F*x*	find previous x
t*x*	move to character prior to next *x*
T*x*	move to character following previous *x*
;	repeat last f F t or T
,	repeat inverse of last f F t or T
n|	move to column *n*
%	find matching ({) or }

Words, sentences, paragraphs

`w`	forward a word
`b`	back a word
`e`	end of word
`)`	to next sentence
`}`	to next paragraph
`(`	back a sentence
`{`	back a paragraph
`W`	forward a blank-delimited word
`B`	back a blank-delimited word
`E`	end of a blank-delimited word

Corrections during insert

`^H`	erase last character (backspace)
`^W`	erase last word
erase	your erase character, same as `^H` (backspace)
kill	your kill character, erase this line of input
\	quotes your erase and kill characters
`ESC`	ends insertion, back to command mode
`DEL`	interrupt, terminates insert mode
`^D`	backtab one character; reset left margin of *autoindent*
`^^D`	caret (^) followed by control-d (^D); backtab to beginning of line; do not reset left margin of *autoindent*
`0^D`	backtab to beginning of line; reset left margin of *autoindent*
`^V`	quote non-printable character

Insert and replace

`a`	append after cursor
`A`	append at end of line
`i`	insert before cursor
`I`	insert before first non-blank
`o`	open line below
`O`	open above
`r`*x*	replace single char with *x*
R*text*ESC	replace characters

Operators

Operators are followed by a cursor motion, and affect all text that would have been moved over. For example, since **w** moves over a word, **dw** deletes the word that would be moved over. Double the operator, e.g., dd to affect whole lines.

d	delete
c	change
y	yank lines to buffer
<	left shift
>	right shift
!	filter through command

Miscellaneous Operations

C	change rest of line (c$)
D	delete rest of line (d$)
s	substitute chars (cl)
S	substitute lines (cc)
J	join lines
x	delete characters (dl)
X	delete characters before cursor (dh)
Y	yank lines (yy)

Yank and Put

Put inserts the text most recently deleted or yanked; however, if a buffer is named (using the ASCII lower-case letters a - z), the text in that buffer is put instead.

3yy	yank 3 lines
3yl	yank 3 characters
p	put back text after cursor
P	put back text before cursor
"*x*p	put from buffer *x*
"*x*y	yank to buffer *x*
"*x*d	delete into buffer *x*

Undo, Redo, Retrieve

u	undo last change
U	restore current line
.	repeat last change
"*d*p	retrieve *d*'th last delete

AUTHOR

vi and ex were developed by The University of California, Berkeley California, Computer Science Division, Department of Electrical Engineering and Computer Science.

FILES

/tmp	default directory where temporary work files are placed; it can be changed using the directory option [see the ex(1) set command]
/usr/share/lib/terminfo/?/*	compiled terminal description database
/usr/lib/.COREterm/?/*	subset of compiled terminal description database

NOTES

Two options, although they continue to be supported, have been replaced in the documentation by options that follow the Command Syntax Standard [see intro(1)]. A -r option that is not followed with an option-argument has been replaced by -L and *+command* has been replaced by -c *command*.

The encryption options are provided with the Security Administration Utilities package, which is available only in the United States.

Tampering with entries in /usr/share/lib/terminfo/?/* or /usr/share/lib/terminfo/?/* (for example, changing or removing an entry) can affect programs such as vi that expect the entry to be present and correct. In particular, removing the "dumb" terminal may cause unexpected problems.

Software tabs using ^T work only immediately after the *autoindent*.

Left and right shifts on intelligent terminals do not make use of insert and delete character operations in the terminal.

SEE ALSO

ed(1), edit(1), ex(1).
User's Guide.
Editing Guide.
curses/terminfo chapter of the *Programmer's Guide*.

NAME

vtlmgr – monitors and opens virtual terminals.

SYNOPSIS

vtlmgr [-k]

DESCRIPTION

When you invoke the vtlmgr command (usually from within your .profile), it places itself in the background and monitors /dev/vtmon for signals from the keyboard/display driver to open new virtual terminals.

Option:

-k The -k option sends a SIGHUP signal to all open virtual terminals when you log off (by entering CTRL-d from your home virtual terminal). This automatically closes, if possible, existing virtual terminals. For virtual terminals that cannot be automatically closed, you are asked if you want to close them manually.

After running vtlmgr, you open new virtual terminals and then switch between them by entering a hot-key sequence, specifically:

ALT - SYS-REQ *key*

where *key* is either a function key whose number corresponds to the number of the virtual terminal to switch to, for example, pressing F1 switches you to /dev/vt01 (virtual terminal 01), pressing F2 switches you to /dev/vt02 (virtual terminal 02), and so forth, or one of the letters in the following table:

key	Interpretation
h	home virtual terminal (/dev/vt00)
n	next virtual terminal
p	previous virtual terminal
f	force a switch to a virtual terminal

Use the f key only when the current virtual terminal is essentially locked up or stuck in graphics mode. This will cause the virtual terminal to be reset to a sane text state and all processes associated with the virtual terminal will be killed.

When the hot-key sequence is entered, the executable program pointed to by the $SHELL variable is executed in the new virtual terminal. If $SHELL is NULL or pointing to a program which is not executable, /bin/sh is executed. The newly opened virtual terminal inherits the environment in effect when the vtlmgr command is invoked.

You may perform setup on each new virtual terminal as it is created by vtlmgr through the .vtlrc file. This file should be in your home directory. Its contents are a shell script that will be run by /bin/sh before the shell prompt is displayed. In this way it is similar to your .profile file. However, you may not set and export environment variables to the shell for the virtual terminal because a different shell runs the .vtlrc shell script.

The system administrator can control how many virtual terminals are available by setting a parameter in the file /etc/default/workstations. Virtual terminals 0 - 8 are configured by default and the default keyboard map makes up to 13 virtual terminals available (i.e., an additional 4 virtual terminals can readily be defined within the default settings). The default virtual terminals are the home terminal and one corresponding to each function key. An application can make two more available to the end-user (by reprogramming the keyboard map), or can reserve the last two for programmatic use only, making 15 virtual terminals available in all.

Note that processes that are no longer visible may still be continuing. Standard output is directed to the current virtual terminal's screen. For example, you can issue a `cat` command on one virtual terminal, switch to another virtual terminal to start an application, and then switch to another to do an edit. The `cat` output will be lost if the virtual terminal scrolls the data off the screen unless you initially redirect the output to a file.

DIAGNOSTICS

The `vtlmgr` command will fail under the following conditions:

If an illegal option is specified.
If the device cannot be opened.
If the command is invoked from a remote terminal.
If `/dev/vtmon` cannot be opened.
If `$SHELL` is set and is not executable.
If `$SHELL` is not set and `/bin/sh` cannot be invoked.

SEE ALSO

`newvt(1M)`
`vtgetty`(1M), `keyboard`(7) in the *System Administrator's Reference Manual*

NAME

`wait` – await completion of process

SYNOPSIS

`wait` [*n*]

DESCRIPTION

Wait for your background process whose process id is *n* and report its termination status. If *n* is omitted, all your shell's currently active background processes are waited for and the return code will be zero.

The shell itself executes **`wait`**, without creating a new process.

SEE ALSO

sh(1).

NOTES

If you get the error message **`cannot fork, too many processes`**, try using the `wait` command to clean up your background processes. If this doesn't help, the system process table is probably full or you have too many active foreground processes. (There is a limit to the number of process ids associated with your login, and to the number the system can keep track of.)

Not all the processes of a 3- or more-stage pipeline are children of the shell, and thus cannot be waited for.

If *n* is not an active process id, all your shell's currently active background processes are waited for and the return code will be zero.

NAME

wc – word count

SYNOPSIS

wc [−lwc] [*filenames*]

DESCRIPTION

wc counts lines, words, and characters in the named files, or in the standard input if no *filenames* appear. It also keeps a total count for all named files. A word is a maximal string of characters delimited by spaces, tabs, or new-lines.

The options l, w, and c may be used in any combination to specify that a subset of lines, words, and characters are to be reported. The default is −lwc.

When *filenames* are specified on the command line, they will be printed along with the counts.

NAME

who – who is on the system

SYNOPSIS

who [-uTlHqpdbrtas] [*file*]

who -qn *x* [*file*]

who am i

who am I

DESCRIPTION

who can list the user's name, terminal line, login time, elapsed time since activity occurred on the line, and the process-ID of the command interpreter (shell) for each current UNIX system user. It examines the /var/adm/utmp file to obtain its information. If *file* is given, that file (which must be in utmp[4] format) is examined. Usually, *file* will be /var/adm/wtmp, which contains a history of all the logins since the file was last created.

who with the am i or am I option identifies the invoking user.

The general format for output is:

name [*state*] *line* *time* [*idle*] [*pid*] [*comment*] [*exit*]

The *name, line,* and *time* information is produced by all options except -q; the *state* information is produced only by -T; the *idle* and *pid* information is produced only by -u and -l; and the *comment* and exit information is produced only by -a. The information produced for -p, -d, and -r is explained during the discussion of each option, below.

With options, who can list logins, logoffs, reboots, and changes to the system clock, as well as other processes spawned by the init process. These options are:

-u This option lists only those users who are currently logged in. The *name* is the user's login name. The *line* is the name of the line as found in the directory /dev. The *time* is the time that the user logged in. The *idle* column contains the number of hours and minutes since activity last occurred on that particular line. A dot (.) indicates that the terminal has seen activity in the last minute and is therefore "current". If more than twenty-four hours have elapsed or the line has not been used since boot time, the entry is marked old. This field is useful when trying to determine whether a person is working at the terminal or not. The *pid* is the process-ID of the user's shell. The *comment* is the comment field associated with this line as found in /sbin/inittab [see inittab(4)]. This can contain information about where the terminal is located, the telephone number of the dataset, type of terminal if hard-wired, etc.

-T This option is the same as the -s option, except that the *state* of the terminal line is printed. The *state* describes whether someone else can write to that terminal. A + appears if the terminal is writable by anyone; a – appears if it is not. root can write to all lines having a + or a – in the *state* field. If a bad line is encountered, a ? is printed.

- **-l** This option lists only those lines on which the system is waiting for someone to login. The *name* field is LOGIN in such cases. Other fields are the same as for user entries except that the *state* field does not exist.
- **-H** This option will print column headings above the regular output.
- **-q** This is a quick **who**, displaying only the names and the number of users currently logged on. When this option is used, all other options are ignored.
- **-p** This option lists any other process which is currently active and has been previously spawned by init. The *name* field is the name of the program executed by init as found in /sbin/inittab. The *state*, line, and *idle* fields have no meaning. The *comment* field shows the id field of the line from /sbin/inittab that spawned this process. See inittab(4).
- **-d** This option displays all processes that have expired and not been respawned by init. The exit field appears for dead processes and contains the termination and exit values [as returned by wait(2)], of the dead process. This can be useful in determining why a process terminated.
- **-b** This option indicates the time and date of the last reboot.
- **-r** This option indicates the current *run-level* of the init process. In addition, it produces the process termination status, process id, and process exit status [see utmp(4)] under the *idle*, *pid*, and *comment* headings, respectively.
- **-t** This option indicates the last change to the system clock (via the date command) by root. See su(1M).
- **-a** This option processes /var/adm/utmp or the named *file* with all options turned on.
- **-s** This option is the default and lists only the *name*, line, and *time* fields.
- **-n** *x* This option takes a numeric argument, *x*, which specifies the number of users to display per line. *x* must be at least 1. The −n option must be used with −q.

Note to the super-user: after a shutdown to the single-user state, who returns a prompt; the reason is that since /var/adm/utmp is updated at login time and there is no login in single-user state, who cannot report accurately on this state. who am i, however, returns the correct information.

FILES

/var/adm/utmp
/var/adm/wtmp
/sbin/inittab

SEE ALSO

date(1), login(1), mesg(1), su(1M).
init(1M), inittab(4), utmp(4) in the *System Administrator's Reference Manual*.
wait(2) in the *Programmer's Reference Manual*.

NAME

`whois` – Internet user name directory service

SYNOPSIS

`whois` [`-h` *host*] *identifier*

DESCRIPTION

`whois` searches for an Internet directory entry for an *identifier* which is either a name (such as "Smith") or a handle (such as "SRI-NIC"). To force a name-only search, precede the name with a period; to force a handle-only search, precede the handle with an exclamation point.

To search for a group or organization entry, precede the argument with `*` (an asterisk). The entire membership list of the group will be displayed with the record.

You may of course use an exclamation point and asterisk, or a period and asterisk together.

EXAMPLES

The command

```
whois Smith
```

looks for the name or handle SMITH.

The command

```
whois !SRI-NIC
```

looks for the handle SRI-NIC only.

The command

```
whois .Smith, John
```

looks for the name JOHN SMITH only.

Adding `...` to the name or handle argument will match anything from that point; that is, `ZU ...` will match ZUL, ZUM, and so on.

NAME

`write` – write to another user

SYNOPSIS

`write` *user* [*line*]

DESCRIPTION

`write` copies lines from your terminal to that of another user. When first called, it sends the message:

`Message from` *yourname* `(tty??)` [*date*]. . .

to the person you want to talk to. When it has successfully completed the connection, it also sends two bells to your own terminal to indicate that what you are typing is being sent.

The recipient of the message should write back at this point. Communication continues until an end of file is read from the terminal, an interrupt is sent, or the recipient has executed "mesg n". At that point `write` writes `EOT` on the other terminal and exits.

If you want to write to a user who is logged in more than once, the `line` argument may be used to indicate which line or terminal to send to (e.g., `term/12`); otherwise, the first writable instance of the user found in `/var/adm/utmp` is assumed and the following message posted:

`user is logged on more than one place.`
`You are connected to "`*terminal*`".`
`Other locations are:`
terminal

Permission to write may be denied or granted by use of the `mesg` command. Writing to others is normally allowed by default. Certain commands, such as the pr command, disallow messages in order to prevent interference with their output. However, if the user has super-user permissions, messages can be forced onto a write-inhibited terminal.

If the character `!` is found at the beginning of a line, `write` calls the shell to execute the rest of the line as a command.

`write` runs `setgid()` [see `setuid`(2)] to the group ID `tty`, in order to have write permissions on other user's terminals.

`write` will detect non-printable characters before sending them to the user's terminal. Control characters will appear as a '^' followed by the appropriate ASCII character; characters with the high-order bit set will appear in meta notation. For example, '\003' is displayed as '`^C`' and '\372' as '`M-z`'.

The following protocol is suggested for using `write`: when you first `write` to another user, wait for them to `write` back before starting to send. Each person should end a message with a distinctive signal (i.e., `(o)` for "over") so that the other person knows when to reply. The signal `(oo)` (for "over and out") is suggested when conversation is to be terminated.

FILES

`/var/adm/utmp`
to find user

`/usr/bin/sh`
to execute !

SEE ALSO

mail(1), mesg(1), pr(1), sh(1), who(1), setuid(2).

DIAGNOSTICS

`user is not logged on`	if the person you are trying to **write** to is not logged on.
`Permission denied`	if the person you are trying to **write** to denies that permission (with **mesg**).
`Warning: cannot respond, set mesg -y`	if your terminal is set to **mesg n** and the recipient cannot respond to you.
`Can no longer write to user`	if the recipient has denied permission (**mesg n**) after you had started writing.

NAME

xargs – construct argument list(s) and execute command

SYNOPSIS

xargs [*flags*] [*command* [*initial-arguments*]]

DESCRIPTION

xargs combines the fixed *initial-arguments* with arguments read from standard input to execute the specified *command* one or more times. The number of arguments read for each *command* invocation and the manner in which they are combined are determined by the flags specified.

command, which may be a shell file, is searched for, using one's $PATH. If *command* is omitted, /usr/bin/echo is used.

Arguments read in from standard input are defined to be contiguous strings of characters delimited by one or more blanks, tabs, or new-lines; empty lines are always discarded. Blanks and tabs may be embedded as part of an argument if escaped or quoted. Characters enclosed in quotes (single or double) are taken literally, and the delimiting quotes are removed. Outside of quoted strings a backslash (\) escapes the next character.

Each argument list is constructed starting with the *initial-arguments*, followed by some number of arguments read from standard input (Exception: see -i flag). Flags -i, -l, and -n determine how arguments are selected for each command invocation. When none of these flags are coded, the *initial-arguments* are followed by arguments read continuously from standard input until an internal buffer is full, and then *command* is executed with the accumulated args. This process is repeated until there are no more args. When there are flag conflicts (e.g., -l vs. -n), the last flag has precedence. Valid *flags* are:

-l*number* — *command* is executed for each non-empty *number* lines of arguments from standard input. The last invocation of *command* will be with fewer lines of arguments if fewer than *number* remain. A line is considered to end with the first new-line *unless* the last character of the line is a blank or a tab; a trailing blank/tab signals continuation through the next non-empty line. If *number* is omitted, 1 is assumed. Option -x is forced.

-i*replstr* — Insert mode: *command* is executed for each line from standard input, taking the entire line as a single arg, inserting it in *initial-arguments* for each occurrence of *replstr*. A maximum of 5 arguments in *initial-arguments* may each contain one or more instances of *replstr*. Blanks and tabs at the beginning of each line are thrown away. Constructed arguments may not grow larger than 255 characters, and option -x is also forced. { } is assumed for *replstr* if not specified.

-n*number* — Execute *command* using as many standard input arguments as possible, up to *number* arguments maximum. Fewer arguments are used if their total size is greater than *size* characters, and for the last invocation if there are fewer than *number* arguments remaining. If option -x is also coded, each *number* arguments must fit in the *size* limitation, else xargs terminates execution.

`-t` Trace mode: The *command* and each constructed argument list are echoed to file descriptor 2 just prior to their execution.

`-p` Prompt mode: The user is asked whether to execute *command* each invocation. Trace mode (`-t`) is turned on to print the command instance to be executed, followed by a ?... prompt. A reply of `y` (optionally followed by anything) executes the command; anything else, including just a carriage return, skips that particular invocation of *command*.

`-x` Causes `xargs` to terminate if any argument list would be greater than *size* characters; `-x` is forced by the options `-i` and `-l`. When neither of the options `-i`, `-l`, or `-n` are coded, the total length of all arguments must be within the *size* limit.

`-s`*size* The maximum total size of each argument list is set to *size* characters; *size* must be a positive integer less than or equal to 470. If `-s` is not coded, 470 is taken as the default. Note that the character count for *size* includes one extra character for each argument and the count of characters in the command name.

`-e`*eofstr* *eofstr* is taken as the logical end-of-file string. Underbar (_) is assumed for the logical EOF string if `-e` is not coded. The value `-e` with no *eofstr* coded turns off the logical EOF string capability (underbar is taken literally). `xargs` reads standard input until either end-of-file or the logical EOF string is encountered.

`xargs` terminates if either it receives a return code of `-1` from, or if it cannot execute, *command*. When *command* is a shell program, it should explicitly `exit` (see sh(1)) with an appropriate value to avoid accidentally returning with `-1`.

EXAMPLES

The following examples moves all files from directory $1 to directory $2, and echo each move command just before doing it:

```
ls $1 | xargs -i -t mv $1/{ } $2/{ }
```

The following example combines the output of the parenthesized commands onto one line, which is then echoed to the end of file `log`:

```
(logname; date; echo $0 $*) | xargs >>log
```

The user is asked which files in the current directory are to be archived and archives them into `arch` (1.) one at a time, or (2.) many at a time.

```
1.  ls | xargs -p -l ar r arch
2.  ls | xargs -p -l | xargs ar r arch
```

The following example executes `diff`"(1)" with successive pairs of arguments originally typed as shell arguments:

```
echo $* | xargs -n2 diff
```

SEE ALSO

sh(1).